Trends in International Business:
Critical Perspectives

Edited by
MICHAEL R. CZINKOTA
Georgetown University
and
MASAAKI KOTABE
The University of Texas at Austin

Michael R. Czinkota is Consulting Editor, North America, Blackwell Series in Business

First published 1998

Blackwell Publishers Inc
350 Main Street
Malden, Massachusetts 02148
USA

Blackwell Publishers Ltd
108 Cowley Road
Oxford OX4 IJF
UK

Library of Congress Cataloging-in-Publication Data

Trends in international business : critical perspectives / edited by
   Michael R. Czinkota and Masaaki Kotabe.
       p.   cm.
   Includes bibliographical references and indexes.
   ISBN 0-631-20799-6. — ISBN 1-57718-127-1
   1. International business enterprises.   2. Joint ventures.
   3. International trade.   I. Czinkota, Michael R.   II. Kotabe,
   Masaaki.
   HD2755.5.T73   1998
   338.8'8—DC21   97-29587
                                                                   CIP
ISBN 0-631-20799-6 (hbk)
ISBN 1-577-18127-1 (pbk)

British Library Cataloguing in Publication Data

A CIP catalogue record for this book is available from the British Library

Typeset in 10 on 12 pt Book Antiqua
by Ace Filmsetting Ltd, Frome, Somerset
Printed in Great Britain by T.J. International, Padstow, Cornwall

This book is printed on acid-free paper

To Ilona
MRC

To Kay
MK

Contents

IV MARKETING DIMENSIONS
151

V FINANCIAL AND ACCOUNTING DIMENSIONS
185

VI IMPLEMENTING GLOBAL STRATEGY
223

Preface

There was a time when international business was the realm of a few specialists and multinational corporations. Today, the world has changed, and the international business environment profoundly influences firms, governments, and individuals on a daily basis. Corporations increasingly find their largest growth opportunities to be in distant markets. They learn about new suppliers abroad, which provide for better and less expensive products. They implement global expansion strategies in which components are produced in one country, assembled in another, and sold in yet other nations around the world. Firms are increasingly linked to each other through global supply arrangements and joint undertakings in research and development. Managers experience that competition is no longer just local, and that they better be ready to face the world, even if their firms stay at home. They recognize the need to obtain the production economies of scale, and are beginning to understand how learning in the international arena contributes to innovation and cost benefits that are crucial to survival.

Governments discover that their sovereignty is no longer complete. In many countries, trade in goods and services comprises more than one third of gross national product. Foreign direct investments can make or break local or even national economies. Policy makers are learning that policies which are contrary to market expectations or directions can result in drastic countermoves by global market forces. Global financial flows, measured in trillions of dollars per day can easily wreak havoc with any country's fiscal and monetary policies, and substantially affect trade and investment flows. For example, indirect financial flows, such as domestic bond purchases by foreign institutions, can materially affect government and corporate budgets. At the same time, the traditional and expected effects of exchange rate changes on trade are increasingly difficult to discern or significantly delayed. Governments nonetheless desire to continue to assert their sovereign power over the inflow and outflow of trade. In spite of the existence of harmonized international trade rules, they persevere in their influence on imports through the creative application of these rules, the provision of administrative shelter to their industries, and through other non-tariff barriers. On the export side, foreign policy goals are supported by the ongoing redevelopment of export controls. Governments also begin to recognize that in today's interdependent world some problems are simply too large to be handled by any one country alone. For example, pollution or high acid production in one country may well result in contamination in another. As a result, there is an increasing drive towards global harmonization, but there are also growing areas of conflict between sovereign nations.

Individuals are affected by international business more than ever. Its employment effects provide for rapid growth in some areas, and for major dislocations in others. Employees are facing the disturbing reality that workers throughout the world desire their jobs and are wondering how to stay competitive. International trade and investment brings consumers major benefits in terms of higher quality, lower prices, and an increased variety of choice, but occasionally, also deprives them of products which do not attract sufficient interest. A lack of interest in international business does not prevent individuals from being affected by its activities. For example, young families are exposed to the global influences on the level of mortgage rates; retirees are affected by the international yields of mutual funds.

This book is designed to cover the broad scope of international business and its effects by presenting leading edge analyses of its various components. The reader obtains in-depth exposure to the macro shifts which are redefining the parameters of business, as well as insights into the strategic options which firms can choose to respond to these changes. The book also presents a rich array of implementation examples which demonstrate the capability of firms to stay ahead of the game. One key unique aspect of this book is the fact that it presents concerns and issues in the international business field from a global perspective, including the vantage points of policy makers, business executives, and researchers from the United States, Asia, and Europe. In selecting the articles presented here, we have kept our objective firmly in mind: to offer guide posts for the understanding of change and to increase the capacity of our audience to respond to and use the change in order to be more successful in international business. We aim to delight by improving your accomplishments!

I

THE GLOBAL ENVIRONMENT

The global business environment has undergone profound changes within the past decade. The formation of the World Trade Organization has redefined the structure of the international trade framework. The demise of the Iron Curtain has eliminated key barriers to corporate activity. The resulting new opportunities have restructured relations between nations. Technology is another major factor affecting the competitiveness of countries and companies.

This first section analyzes these shifts and trends in the global business environment. The first chapter outlines how the formation of the World Trade Organization (WTO) affects both countries and corporate activity. It discusses the positive streamlining effects of WTO rulings, but also cautions against the desire of some governments to overload the WTO with social issues and causes not germane to trade and investment. The second chapter focuses on the building of a new world trade order responsive to new conditions and relations between nations. Based on the example of the U.S.–Japanese trade relationship, the authors highlight the importance of the microeconomic efforts of firms in shaping trade relations. They suggest that the principal focus of governmental trade policy needs to be domestically oriented, providing for teamwork between business and government to improve the competitiveness of firms. Chapter 3 highlights how the demise of the political East/West divide has also resulted in a new fragility of trade relations. It is suggested that the major trading nations need to find a new commonality of purpose. Helping the formerly centrally planned economies in their transition to a market-based economy could be a key dimension leading to a new era of global cooperation. Chapter 4 focuses on the importance of a nation's innovative ability as a foundation for future competitiveness in international trade. A comparative analysis of patent applications and grants in the United States, Germany, Japan, and Britain is presented. The findings suggest not only a decline in the U.S. competitive position but also an apparent technological life cycle as well.

1

The World Trade Organization: Perspectives and Prospects

MICHAEL R. CZINKOTA

GEORGETOWN UNIVERSITY

In 1948, after years of negotiations, more than 50 nations signed the Havana Charter to create the ITO, the International Trade Organization. Several major principles were to govern world trade from then on. One of the principles was the non-discriminatory treatment of parties, and a commitment to reduce tariffs and other trade barriers and eliminate quotas. Services were to be covered just as well as products, owners of patents, and intangible assets were to be protected. Foreign direct investment was to receive fair treatment and domestic-content requirements and public subsidies were to be regulated. But in the 1950s, President Truman decided not to re-submit the ITO charter to Congress for ratification due to perceived threats to national sovereignty and the danger of too much ITO intervention in markets (*Guide* 1994).

In 1994, the focus was on a totally new organization which the Uruguay Round negotiations agreed on – the World Trade Organization (WTO). And this WTO, as if by magic, has a lot of components which sound remarkably similar to the provisions of the ITO.

But the world has changed since then. In 1948, total world trade was valued at just above $58 billion, with the United States accounting for 34 percent of free world trade flows (*Yearbook* 1956). Japan's imports exceeded her exports by 160 percent. Today, world trade exceeds $4 trillion, the United States has a share of 12 percent, and Japan has a history of major trade surpluses. But one needs to look beyond the numbers to understand some of the macroeconomics changes that have occurred.

The traditional participants in trade, the Western, industrialized nations have been joined by new players – the dragons or tigers of Asia – Hong Kong, Singapore, Taiwan and South Korea, who are now industrialized nations in their own right. Other countries have been industrializing (for example Indonesia, Malaysia, Thailand, Argentina, Chile) while still others such as China are preparing to become important trade players. In addition, the entire region, which used to be known as the Eastern Bloc, has been converted into emerging market economies, eager and sometimes even ready to enter the world trade field.

Collaborative blocs are emerging among these participants. They range from loose agreements for general collaboration to well-defined economic arrangements such as NAFTA and include intricate political formations such as the European Union. These blocs change the way nations deal with each other; for example, negotiators now often talk to bloc representatives rather than to individual countries.

Simultaneously, blocs have also disappeared – particularly the Communist one. This disappearance has opened up trade and business relations in areas that were off limits only a few years ago. The framework and the way we look at Third World countries and our decisions about whether and how to support them also have been affected. For example, the cold war threat by governments of "changing sides," which often triggered gushers of aid payments, has become meaningless today.

Exchange rates are another area where there has been major change. Currency values used to be fixed; later they started to float. But a key component of exchange rate theory was always that they were the result of international currency demand and supply, which in turn was triggered largely by trade flows and interest rates. Today, financial flows exceed trade flows by vast multiples. For example, the total value of U.S. merchandise exports is about $550 billion per year. In contrast, the value of world-wide currency trades exceeds $1.5 trillion per day. Therefore, currency prices are no longer mainly the result of financial flows that have been caused by trade. Rather, the financial flows around the world set currency values and often impose the level of interest rates. Financial flows can now determine trade flows, since higher currency values mean higher prices for exports and lower ones for imports. Concurrently, a new phenomenon called "sticky prices" manifests itself when trade volumes do not behave the way they should in response to changes in the values of currencies. This occurs, for example, when the Japanese yen shifts from a level of 250 to the U.S. dollar, to less than 100 to the dollar, and the wave of imports still keeps on coming.

There are also major changes in trade and investment orientation. Investments used to be the culmination of a long trade relationship and, due to their distance and riskiness, were infrequent and long term in nature. Today, the rate of global investment growth far exceeds the growth of trade. Such investments have thoroughly affected trade flows both on the export and the import side (Okamatsu 1994). The transplant effect in the automotive sector serves as example for increases in exports and market penetration. The effects of investments on the import side can be seen when scrutinizing out-sourcing investments which are designed to create captive sources of supply. In addition, investments today are often of a short-term nature, moving from country to country in order to benefit from resource and wage advantages.

Major shifts in orientation are also in evidence with regard to trade. Historically, for example, the United States has been "Europe oriented" in its trade outlook. This is easily seen in the number of staffers in government departments who deal with Europe. However, since 1978 U.S./Asia merchandise trade has exceeded U.S./European trade, and the excess is growing rapidly. At the same time, this change is dynamic and has shifted the trade orientation of other nations as well. For example, the United States has already declined dramatically as an export destination for Asia's exports. From a high of 38 percent the U.S. market now accounts for only 28 percent of Japanese exports. The United States is the recipient of only 23 percent of South Korea's exports, rather than the 36 percent it was in the past. Overall, in spite of the mutual feeling of beleaguerment, the exports of Asian countries to the United States average only about 23 percent of their total exports.

The new orientation in trade is accompanied by trade imbalances at unprecedented levels. Today, the United States is running an annual merchandise trade deficit of about $120 billion, with Japan accumulating a global surplus of about the same size. It is hard to remember that in 1972 President Nixon abandoned the gold standard because of a trade deficit of $2.5 billion.

Finally, there is a global recognition of new issues that are too large to be addressed success-fully by any one country, yet too important to be ignored. Society is increasingly preoccupied by the concerns such as air and water pollution, global warming, ecosystem maintenance, and new diseases. Patterns of long-term structural unemployment, systemic weaknesses in educational approaches, and growing safety and health care concerns are just a few other issues which are not local, but global in nature. Governments that attempt to address these issues find out quickly that for reasons of resource constraints or global linkages, their powers are limited, and the effectiveness of their actions is often only minor.

In sum, on a macro level, there are seas of change. These include changing blocs, changing relations, changing flows of funds, changing flows of trade, and a decreasing ability by governments to affect these changes.

The Corporate Perspective

Change is not confined to governments alone. At the global corporate level, many parameters which were believed to be fixed have become fluid. Competition has increased drastically from expected and unexpected quarters. Not meeting the competition no longer results in slight decreases in market share, but in a threat of corporate extinction. At the same time, the capability to stay ahead is getting to be more expensive, with costs of research and development rising exponentially. The speed and ease of technology transfer causes innovations to be diffused very quickly. Today, competitors can copy or improve innovative products rapidly, providing the creator often with only limited opportunity to recoup the investment made. An example illus-trates the type of technological progress achieved. The 1994 innovation period of computer chips was only 18 months. More than 70 percent of the sales of the data processing industry were the result of the sale of devices that did not exist only two years earlier. Experts estimated that this percentage would rise to 80 percent the following year (U.S. Senate Committee 1994).

Advances in information and communications technology have transformed the ability of firms to select their inputs and their locations. These advances allow the separation between the origination and delivery of a product or service, thus offering firms new options for sourcing and foreign direct investment. While the traditional battle in the international market has been one for the right of establishment, the delocalization made possible by telecommunication advances may soon require a striving for the right to operations without establishment. These advances also enable firms to carry out product adaptations and market targeting with surgical precision. However, the competition and consumer expectations often require such changes, whether they be cost effective or not.

Today, firms also have many more options for their organizational structure across borders. Joint ventures, value adding partnerships, strategic coalitions, strategic alliances, cooperative agreements, and industry consortia are only some examples of organizations that allow firms to avoid getting bigger (Naisbitt 1994), yet enable them to exercise their marketing muscle and maximize their production capabilities across national boundaries. Overall, on the micro level, firms see more change, an increase in the speed of change, increasing risk, more capabilities, but also more demands.

The Context of a New Global Trade Framework

What are the governmental goals in the context of world-wide competition? They are threefold and linked to each other: ensuring success for its firms, both at home and abroad; creating employment; and increasing the standard of living. Governments attempt to achieve these goals through both inward and outward oriented activities by focusing on market access, stable rules, and market skills. Pressure for action is exerted within the country through domestic constituents such as voters and special interest groups. From outside the country pressure is exercised by trading partners, trade and investment agreements, and multilateral institutions. As a result of these pressures, all government activities are affected by domestic and international influences. Yet, in the international trade and investment setting, preponderant orientations can be discovered. When governments need to ensure market access for firms, this task requires mainly an outward orientation directed at other countries. Assuring the stability of rules is, again, mainly an outward-oriented activity. The assurance of market skills for firms in terms of product development, process capabilities, and innovation is mainly an inward-looking, domestic activity.

From a long-term perspective, a major shift in priorities can be discovered for these activities. In 1948, during ITO days, the United States was an economically overwhelming global power. When it came to market access, the only issue of consequence was the access to the U.S. market. The stability of rules essentially depended simply on the desire for stability on the part of the United States. Market skills were highly concentrated in U.S. firms. Therefore, within a 20- to 25-years time frame, the ITO and its new rules were offering gains for everyone except the United States. It is no wonder that there was no desire to give up any sovereignty.

But today, things are different. The U.S. government is discovering the limits of policy implementation due to the actions of its trading partners. The importance of market access now is increasingly critical for U.S. firms if they are to be successful. There are now changes in rules and definitions that do not emanate from the United States and are not necessarily in its favor.

The new medium-term perspective, looking forward to the next 20–25 years, shows us that there is major world growth taking place. Access to these growing markets will be crucial for the success of global firms. This growth occurs in Asia, Latin America, and perhaps in the former Eastern Europe. One result of this growth is a new assertiveness by countries around the globe now that the strong bonds forged by the cold war threat have disappeared (Czinkota 1994). One might speculate, for example, that the caning in Singapore was not just a woodshed, but perhaps a watershed of a newly defined U.S. relationship with Asia.

Today, there are key benefits to be gained for the United States by entering into trade agreements. NAFTA, for example, provides U.S. firms with access to a market located next door. It is hard to overestimate just how crucial such access is. Research has shown, for example, that firms decide to go international based on a phenomenon called "psychic distance," which is a variable composed of geographic distance, cultural similarity and market access (Wiedersheim-Paul 1978). More than 60 percent of U.S. firms start to export to markets that are psychically close. NAFTA has brought Mexico psychically much closer and therefore affords new opportunities for U.S. companies to get started in international business and grow into multinational corporations. On a global level, the WTO can now assist countries in achieving the important goals of market access and rules stability, which they might not be able to secure anymore by themselves.

But the WTO will not fix all trade ills. The key third dimension of success – superior market skills – represents mainly a domestic issue in spite of the importance of sharing managerial insights beyond national borders. For the United States, export trade is only one, albeit important, component of the economy. In light of 120 million employed in the United States, and the fact that about 20,000 jobs are associated with a $1 billion increase in U.S. exports (Davis 1992), even a major trade liberalization with $10 billion in new U.S. exports will only create 200,000 jobs. Of much greater importance is a nation's ability to maintain its global competitiveness on a relative basis. GATT economists predict that by the year 2002 annual increases in global exports will be in excess of $755 billion (*Focus* 1994). To persevere against this wave of trade flows, the key to economic progress has been, and continues to be, the fostering of market skills for firms and employees. Encouraging those skills will require stimulating and implementing reforms in the educational system, retraining the labor force, and promoting scientific awareness and progress (Simai 1994). Such an educational push must consist of a two-pronged approach: It needs to include major efforts to get people ready for economic processes, *and* it must redefine the processes to get them ready for the workforce. An example of the latter approach can be found in the computer industry. Its success in penetrating markets is not the result of a major increase in the programming skills of the population at large, but rather of the growing user-friendliness of the machines and software.

The Future of the World Trade Organization

It is meaningful and of value for the United States to be part of the WTO. Congressional ratification was the right step. But the WTO must have the opportunity to become a successful organization. As to the prospects for such success, one must reflect on all the "social causes" that are now being introduced into trade decisions. It is debated whether the WTO should also deal with issues such as labor laws, competition, and emigration freedoms. Clearly, there are many important issues other than trade, in addition to the social issues mentioned above. Religion, health care, the safety of animals, the pursuit of happiness, all of these are worthwhile concerns and desires. There is something of an irony if one considers that all these issues might have been easily included by the United States in the ITO back in 1948.

Today, however, the genie is out of the bottle. There are now 125 governments that participated in the Uruguay Round. They have diverse perspectives, histories, relations, economies, and ambitions. Many of them fear that social causes can be used to devise new rules of protectionism against their exports. There is the question as to how much companies – which, after all, are the ones doing the trading and investing – should be burdened with concerns not germane to their activities. There is today no single country with sufficient global market importance to unilaterally impose its will.

To be successful, the WTO needs to be able to focus on its core mission, which deals with international trade and investment. The piling on of social causes may appear politically expedient, but will be a key cause for divisiveness and dissent within the WTO and thus inhibit progress on further liberalization of trade and investment. Failure to achieve such progress would leave the WTO without teeth and would negate much of the progress achieved in the Uruguay Round negotiations.

There are other organizations that can take on social causes, for example the International Labor Organization, for labor issues. Such groups can and should study ways of further improving the well-being of human kind.

What the WTO can help with is the implementation of activities that work in support of social causes. For example, the International Trade Centre, cosponsored by UNCTAD/GATT, could provide training on how to utilize rain forests or how to improve labor conditions. The core contribution of the WTO, however, will be in the fact that the flag follows trade and investment. Over time, increased economic ties will cross-pollinate cultures, values, and ethics between economic partners and, together with the income effects on individuals and countries, cause changes in the social arena.

Together with the other pillars of the global economy – the World Bank for development and the International Monetary Fund for finance – the WTO can form the underpinnings for a world economic platform. After that platform is secured, further societal dimensions can be built on top of it.

References

Czinkota, Michael R. (1994) "Global Neighbors, Poor Relations." *Marketing Management* **2** (4), 46–52. (see chapter 3.)

Davis, Lester A. (1992) *Contribution of Exports to U.S. Employment*. Washington, D.C: U.S. Department of Commerce.

Focus: GATT Newsletter. "Uruguay Round results to expand trade by $755 billion." May 1994, 6.

Guide to GATT Law and Practice (6th edn). Geneva: General Agreement on Tariffs and Trade, 1994, 5–6

Naisbitt, John (1994) *Global Paradox*. New York: Morrow.

Okamatsu, Sozaburo (1994) "Japan in the World Economy," speech of the Vice Minister of MITI before the Chicago Council of Foreign Relations, 11 May.

Simai, Mihaly (1994) *The Future of Global Governance*. Washington, D.C.: United States Institute of Peace Press.

U.S. Senate Committee on Banking. Housing, and Urban Affairs. Subcommittee on International Finance and Monetary Policy (1994) *Renewal of the Export Administration Act*. 103rd Cong. 2nd sess., 3 February, 2 (testimony of Paul Freedenberg).

Wiedersheim-Paul, Finn, H.C. Olson, and L.S. Welch (1978) "Pre-export Activity: The First Step in the Internationalization," *Journal of International Business Studies*, **9** (Spring/Summer): 47–58.

Yearbook of International Trade Statistics (1956). New York: United Nations.

2

America's New World Trade Order

MICHAEL R. CZINKOTA

GEORGETOWN UNIVERSITY

AND

MASAAKI KOTABE

THE UNIVERSITY OF TEXAS AT AUSTIN

For more than a decade, Japan's economic relations with its major trading partners have become increasingly acrimonious. Its critics decry economic dangers Japan poses to world trade and accuse it of striving for world dominance. Highly public accusations ricochet across the Pacific, many going far beyond economic analysis, pandering to fear.

In the late 1980s, American opinion polls found that more than two-thirds of the public regarded Japan as more threatening than the former Soviet Union. About two-thirds of surveyed consumers said they were willing to boycott Japanese goods if Japan did not abandon its "unfair" trade practices.

By 1992, that intention turned to action, with 63 percent of U.S. consumers telling a *Washington Post*/ABC News poll they make a conscious effort to avoid buying Japanese products. Cities have canceled contracts with Japanese firms, baseball fans vehemently protested Nintendo buying the Seattle Mariners, and companies have publicly offered preferential treatment for buyers of U.S. automobiles. The level of public animosity and its effect on marketing keeps rising.

Meanwhile, pressure from U.S. corporate executives helps to maintain the high visibility of the "Japanese market access" issue; they rightfully recognize that they cannot afford to ignore the second largest market in the world. Many agree with industrialist Peter Grace's forceful statement: "If we can compete with Japanese companies in Japan, we can compete with them around the world."

To some, that means Japan must cease selfish ways, throw open its markets, and provide a "level playing field" for American marketers. But more thoughtful strategists leaven those demands by recognizing the corrections the United States must make in its own public- and private-sector policies.

The authors thank the American Marketing Association and the University of Hawaii for support, and Johnny Johansson for comments on early drafts.

"American's New World Trade Order." by Michael R. Czinkota and Masaaki Kotabe, *Marketing Management,* vol. I, No. 3, pp. 49–56. Used by permission of American Marketing Association.

U.S. policy must move beyond the traditional approach to trade negotiations and the threat of protectionism hanging over such talks. American government and industry together must concentrate on being more competitive, using pooled resources and skills to compete in Japan according to Japanese ways of doing business, with products and services too good for Japanese buyers to ignore.

Election year and its promise of a fresh mandate for whichever party won the White House provided an outstanding opportunity for writing a new chapter in U.S. trade relations. Just as our international politics now address a "new world order," so must our international trade.

U.S. policy must pursue at least four key objectives to succeed in the new global environment. The nation must improve the quality and amount of information government and business share, to facilitate competitiveness. Policy must encourage collaboration among companies in such areas as product and process technologies. Collectively, American industry must overcome its export reluctance and its short-term financial orientation. And, finally, America must invest in its people, providing education and training suited to the challenges of the next century.

Inexorable growth of the global trade community forces America to recast its world economic strategies. In short, domestic policy must become more international in vision, and foreign trade policy must become more domestic.

The evidence indicates that there is no other way to solve the U.S.–Japanese trade predicament.

INTRACTABLE PROBLEMS?

A sagging economy at home, a seemingly unshrinkable $43-billion U.S. trade deficit with Japan, and the legacies of election-year politics help to explain Japan-bashing in the United States. The public debate is tainted by the underlying menace of protectionism. If the trend continues, the problems which have characterized economic relations between Japan and the world in general, and between Japan and the United States specifically, may eventually become intractable. Political expediency may demand a major cleansing event such as a U.S. embargo on Japanese automobile imports.

Japan's government is fully aware of the explosive nature of its trading partner trade imbalances, and has initiated import promotion measures with a genuine desire to correct them. Japan has dispatched special import experts to foreign countries, opened import promotion missions and foreign access zones, and created special tax breaks and low-interest-loans for import expansion.

But those steps haven't mollified the U.S. business community and Congress, whose growing list of complaints demands ever harsher international negotiations and actions. Their public objective is greater penetration of the Japanese market by U.S. products and services. But politics ultimately is local. What policy makers really seek is at home: more jobs and a better trade deficit "scorecard" for the government.

Despite so much effort, the lack of results is painfully apparent. It fuels the mistaken notion that if market forces are incapable of reaching these goals, legislative fiat will have to substitute, particularly because Japanese market impediments cause disequilibrium.

POTENT IMPEDIMENTS

Japanese tariff barriers don't appear to have been a major cause of U.S. trade deficit with Japan over the past 10 years. Data from agencies such as the General Agreement on Tariffs and

Trade and other sources strongly suggest that Japan actually imposes lower tariff barriers than many other major trading nations. Therefore, much of the focus has shifted to non-tariff barriers, which are now considered to be the major source of U.S. industry's lack of success in Japanese markets.

The structure of Japanese channels of distribution is one oft-cited non-tariff impediment. A 1990 report by the U.S. government's International Trade Commission concluded that "the end result of the close, sometimes overlapping relations and practices in Japan's distribution chains is that it may be unusually difficult and expensive for foreigners, including U.S. exporters, to break into the system."

Japan's *keiretsu* are a second, related barrier. Alignments or groupings of companies that do business with one another on a regular and often intimate basis, *keiretsu* stand accused of restricting the opportunities of outsiders wishing to sell to *keiretsu* members. They dominate certain markets, and have been labeled as one of the most important obstacles to foreign companies trying to penetrate the Japanese market.

A third major problem for foreign traders in Japan is the high level of quality expected by Japanese consumers and business buyers, who themselves constantly strive for perfection.

Finally, traders report ongoing problems with testing, product standards, and intellectual property protection practices that discriminate against foreign firms. For example, we have found that Japanese patent practices seem to discriminate against foreign applicants through longer pendency periods than for domestic applicants. That leaves the foreigner's proprietary knowledge vulnerable to competitors. At the same time, U.S., German, and British patent procedures appear to discriminate against foreign applications through lower patent grant ratios than for domestic applicants.

Plenty of talk

To remedy these problems, policy-level discussions have cycled from general talks, to market-oriented sector specific (MOSS) negotiations, only to rise to the macroeconomics heights of the Strategic Impediments Initiative (SII). For almost a year beginning in September 1989, American and Japanese negotiators held intensive discussions to identify and solve structural trade impediments in both countries. The SII exercise, being the most ambitious talks ever between trading partners, strove for wholesale changes in the structure of both the Japanese and U.S. economies.

Some American commitments addressed important areas such as the federal budget deficit, and improvements in U.S. competitiveness, education, and training. As the world community saw it, however, the key changes were to occur in Japan. They included shifting Japanese savings and investment patterns (making the Japanese a bit more like the Americans), altering land use, revamping the distribution system, eliminating exclusionary business practices, loosening *keiretsu* relationships, and facilitating foreign direct investment in Japan.

Despite what critics call a dubious grand design behind such lofty negotiations, it is important to maintain the momentum of the talks. The degree to which perceived or real change will come to relations between the world's two economic superpowers will play a major role in shaping the future world order. As Japan's new ambassador to the United States, Takakazu Kuriyama, stated, both countries are teetering at "a rather crucial period of mutual adjustment."

Expert Predictions

Under the sponsorship of the Global Division of the American Marketing Association, we organized an ambitious international meeting of experts. We intended to focus, in a dispassionate manner, on the rapidly changing trade relations between Japan and other major trading nations. The core emphasis of the meeting was to be the distribution system in Japan, together with the important macroeconomics and policy issues which shape trade relations in general.

STUDY METHOD

In order to maintain a broad perspective, we solicited participation from representatives of the three pillars of the international trade community: business executives, policy makers, and researchers – from Japan, the United States and Europe. Participation by current and former high-level policy makers, representatives of major corporations, and leading academics ensured weighty thinking on the subjects at hand. Eventually, 96 participants with a high level of expertise and interest came together for three days of meetings and discussions on the complexity of distribution and trade practices, impending changes, and future opportunities.

We distributed a questionnaire at the end of the meeting, asking participants to impart their views. The conference being an unusual gathering of experts in terms of knowledge, diversity, and orientation, we expected questionnaire results would shed light on the road to change.

The findings are based on a total of 60 completed responses. Two-thirds of the survey respondents were from the United States, 25 percent from Japan, and 7 percent from Western Europe and elsewhere. Academic researchers comprised 68 percent of the respondents, while 25 percent were business practitioners and the remaining 7 percent were government officials.

Statistically, neither the respondents' occupation nor their nationality had any particular bearing on their response pattern. Such consistency suggests that conference participants generally had a common understanding of the issues, and appeared to be unaffected by politically charged sentiments. Because the conference was designed to analyze trade with detachment if not disinterest, our goal seemed to have been achieved. Here, we report the aggregate findings.

PROBLEMS IDENTIFIED

Initially, the experts identified 16 problem areas for foreign firms doing business in and with Japan. We asked them to rate the importance of the problems and the likelihood that they would change over the next five years. Because we searched for the main impediments, we looked for consistency, depth, and consensus in the responses.

Factor analysis revealed four major types of impediments cited by our respondents:

- Bureaucratic practices
- Very demanding customers
- Government trade barriers
- Distribution and cultural impediments.

Table 2.1 Japanese trade barriers and their likely change for foreign firms

	Level of importance (not at all important = 1; very important = 5)	Likelihood of change (not at all likely = 1; very likely = 5
Bureaucratic practices • Lack of antimonopoly enforcement • Delay in processing patent applications • Delay in processing trademark applications	3.36*	2.87
Very demanding customers • Demanding Japanese consumers • Unwillingness to purchase foreign products • Excessive quality expectations • Unreasonable product standards	3.46*	2.56*
Government trade barriers • Government barriers • High tariffs	3.43*	3.11
Distribution and cultural impediments • Existing close business linkages • High entry cost	4.12*	2.65*

Note: neutral response = 3
*= significantly different from neutral rating

Five other problem areas (cultural barriers, high retail prices, lack of economies of scale, inadequate import infrastructure, and gray market shipments) were not cited consistently in the results.

Table 2.1 reports the summary findings. The first three variables were considered to be moderately important problems, while the close business relations forged by the *keiretsu* and the resultant high cost of market entry were perceived to constitute the important impediment to trade. However, all four of these problem areas were not seen as very likely to change, said the experts, perhaps because all of them are deeply rooted in the political, social, and economic institutions of Japan.

Actually, the most problematic areas, distribution systems and *keiretsu*, appear to be among the least likely to change. There is some expectation of rectification only for the problem of government restrictions. These less-than-optimistic perceptions by the conference participants seem to reflect the recalcitrant nature of Japanese market impediments, their resistance to entry by foreign companies, and the inadequate attention to cultural differences paid by foreign marketers, particularly U.S. firms.

SOLUTIONS WEIGHED

Overall, respondents expressed the rather pessimistic views that none of these impediments to entry is likely to swiftly crumble in the foreseeable future. How, then, should foreign companies and policy makers improve their ability to penetrate the Japanese market? If the market does not change, is there perhaps some area where outside firms and governments can become active to

Table 2.2 Methods of improving foreign firms' ability to penetrate the Japanese market

	Likelihood of improvement (very low = 1; very high = 5)
Trade negotiations	3.33*
Business strategy	4.27*
• Market research	
• Product adaptation	
• Service orientation	
• Collaborative	
• Long-term orientation	

Note: neutral response = 3
*= significantly different from neutral rating

succeed better in Japan? We asked the respondents six questions on that score.

Factor analysis of the response found two principal ways to enhance the ability of foreign firms to enter the Japanese market: trade negotiations and improved business strategy (see table 2.2). While respondents acknowledge that trade negotiations with the Japanese government may be of some help, they see the use of seasoned business practices as the key element which makes market penetration possible. Among those recommended practices: thorough market research and product adaptation, a service orientation, a willingness to collaborate on ventures, and an ability to adopt a long-term perspective. Those are, in fact, practices at which the Japanese themselves have been adept world-wide.

LIKELY STRUCTURAL CHANGES

We also asked our experts to what extent they expect structural changes to occur in Japan in coming years (see table 2.3). Respondents agreed strongly that Japan is the leader of a Pacific trading bloc, within which Japanese-type practices are likely to emerge as more countries emulate Japan's success. Therefore, learning to cope with the Japanese approach becomes even more important for outsiders. Meanwhile, the experts predicted, reduced complexity in Japanese home market distribution systems appears unlikely.

Our panelists expected an increase in Japanese imports, largely through industrial and agricultural purchases. Concurrently, foreign firms will improve their foothold in the Japanese market mainly through the direct investment, rather than through exports, respondents predicted. Strong direct investment signals reliability, a long-term outlook, and corporate commitment, while an export-only strategy may be construed as the opposite.

On balance, the experts' predictions of a continuing high Japanese trade surplus over the next five years, combined with their expectations for more direct investment and greater importing activity, forecasts continued growth in Japanese exports this decade.

Table 2.3 Structural changes in Japan

	Level of agreement (strongly disagree = 1; strongly agree = 5)
Japan will become the leader of a Pacific bloc	4.09*
Japanese firms will increase imports	3.86*
Agricultural imports will increase	3.39*
Foreign direct investment will improve market penetration	3.32*
More exports to Japan will improve market penetration	2.91
The complexity of the Japanese distribution chancel will be reduced	2.85
Japan's trade surplus will decline	2.59*
Japanese competitiveness will decrease	2.27*

Note: neutral response = 3
*= significantly different from neutral rating

The Implications

The most important of the several obstacles plaguing U.S. trade in Japan is not in the government area as many assume, but rather in the field of business culture and close business linkages such as the *keiretsu*. In fact, governmental barriers seem to be the ones most likely to change in the future. As our research found, the main road to success appears to be in the U.S. business approach to Japanese buyers. That insight has major implications for U.S. policy makers and business executives.

NEGOTIATION SHORTCOMINGS

First, the impact of trade trade negotiations must be reexamined. Traditional trade negotiations might lead to some success in the future, particularly if they concentrate on trade restrictions directly controlled by the government. In doing so, however, they focus mainly on issues which, although highly visible and of key concern to particular industries, have only marginal importance to the realignment of trade relations with Japan.

That is not to say that traditional, item- or sector-specific trade negotiations lack value, but rather that they are unlikely to fulfill to any great degree the expectations placed on them by government and the public. Those expectations are wrong on two counts. They are based on the assumption that one can address the trade component of economic activity in isolation. But, trade by its very nature is linked to the world and hardly exists separately from global economies. Also, the public mistakenly expects successful negotiations to affect the domestic economy in a major way, even though the issue addressed or resolved is only of minor economic impact. The fact that specific negotiations might well convey material benefits to narrow industry segments, makes the continuation of them quite desirable for some industries, however.

Malodorous colonialism

An alternative is to make negotiations less traditional by elevating their aim, to areas which have historically not been considered part of trade policy: distribution systems, close business linkages, persistently high Japanese savings rates, and perhaps even Japanese customers' demanding quality expectations. The negotiation goal would be to create environmental conditions abroad which are more palatable for U.S. firms, more like the markets at home. The Strategic Impediments Initiative marked the beginning of such a strategy. The recent consideration the U.S. attorney general gave to the notion of applying U.S. antitrust law to Japanese *keiretsu* might be a portent of more such approaches.

Such a move would attack the problem, but at a visible cost to global harmony. Some might detect the stench of malodorous colonialism in an era where partnership appears to be the coming trend. A number of nations might protest an American extraterritorial reach, putting them in the position of defending the very practices which also hurt their trade.

Even if tried, the success of such action probably would be limited to cosmetic gains, trying as it does to change deeply entrenched cultural values in Japan. And it could backfire, as Akio Morita and Shintaro Ishihara speculated in their realpolitik-minded book *The Japan That Can Say No*. Triggering anti-U.S. sentiment in Japan would imperil existing U.S. sales to Japan, and perhaps even motivate some Japanese firms to limit shipments of crucial components to the United States.

Passivity is another alternative – doing little and waiting for Japanese actions to take care of the problem. With sufficient sensitivity on the part of the Japanese government and Japanese corporations, it would appear that over time, they are likely to engage in more efforts to increase imports from the United States. But a passive strategy is unlikely to be acceptable to U.S. policy makers or executives.It would rely too heavily on Japanese initiative, and it would allow Japanese companies to strengthen their competitiveness while U.S. marketing capabilities weaken.

Seeking Easy Solutions

The most productive American strategy for solving the U.S.–Japan trade imbalance consists of reorienting trade policy, in effect making it more domestic. Such an approach will reduce the pressure on government to pry open foreign markets through politics, and instead concentrate effort on providing firms with the strategic skills and environment to be competitive. This alternative, in essence, would require those selling to Japan to become more Japanese, in both their orientation and location. It would make foreign firms in the Japanese market compete the Japanese way.

It is the essence of the marketing discipline: adapting one's practices to the Japanese environment. If those methods happen also to be crucial in competing with the rest of the world, so much the better. Focusing government concern on a reorientation of business strategy toward market research, product adaptation, service orientation, collaborative ventures, and a long-range vision will not only serve firms well in the Japanese market, but will also have a major impact in domestic and third-country markets. They might actually bear their greatest fruit by allowing U.S. firms to recapture domestic market share thought to be lost to foreign competitors.

GOVERNMENT–BUSINESS PARTNERSHIP

Japan has already taken the lead with such progressive thinking. Historically, its government has helped develop the competitiveness of Japanese firms. More recently, Japan, has taken the next step by sending its trade advisers to U.S. firms in order to improve their competitiveness, and, they hope, enable more successful exports to Japan.

Much decried as "industrial policy led by bureaucrats," the notion of government involvement remains in disrepute in the United States, but the opposition's strength is waning. In part, it is a cyclical phenomenon; historically, the U.S. government has had few qualms taking policy steps that facilitated and triggered private sector action. Development of the land grant college and railroad systems provides a still-current example. Now, emerging market gaps should also propel government policy in a similar direction. Even if the private sector knows that a lighthouse is needed, it still may be hard, time-consuming, and maybe even impossible to build one with private funds alone.

U.S. economic performance has its shortfalls. Some are a function of our domestic economic behavior, others the result of changing global realities. The bottom line is that we cannot afford to continue an exclusive reliance on rugged individualism. The nation must pursue opportunities for collaborative action between industry and government.

We propose four arenas for immediate policy-maker attention:

1. *Information*: In spite of the widespread existence of information, its accessibility, manipulability, and subsequent usage is weak in the United States compared to Japan. Currently, for example, government action tends to concentrate on assisting or bailing out failing industries rather than providing an early warning system alerting business of the potential for failure. Such a system would need to go beyond tracking domestic performance, to evaluating competitive developments world-wide and making the information easily available to U.S. industry.

2. *Collaboration*: Currently, policy makers ponder the relaxation of antitrust law. Government action should go beyond that, however, and actively encourage collaboration among companies, particularly in areas of rapid technological change, substantial social need, and intense international competition. The electric battery consortium is one such important effort, but it needs to be followed by other efforts in areas such as environmental safety, health care, new materials development, and other leading-edge technologies. Collaboration should focus on both product and process technologies. For example, the issue of quality performance can well become the focus of a cooperative effort throughout an entire industry, its suppliers and customers alike.

3. *Export promotion*: Despite a relatively cheaper dollar, the U.S. economy still underexports. Many firms do not participate in the international market because they must act rationally, according to domestic economic realities. For example, the short-term, start-up cost and the higher transaction cost might make it uneconomical for a firm to go international when investors unceasingly demand quarterly performance gains. While it will be important to work on changing the short-term orientation of capital markets through fiscal policies which enhance the capacity of U.S. firms to invest, there is also a need to overcome the short-term gap by providing export assistance to firms just starting up.

4. *Human capital*: There is a clear need to find, develop, and disseminate the best resources this

country has to offer the educational arena. Containing educational talent locally is a luxury America can no longer afford. Technology now allows America's best educational talent to be available nationally. Again, there is a gap to bridge, fostering excellence at the national level through information systems. Electronic instruction and video systems, enabling access to the best teaching methods available nationally, must be regular parts of primary, secondary, and trade education. Just as agricultural universities were the point of advancement in the 1800s, so can high-technology education become the rail switch to the right track of the next century.

ESSENTIAL POLICIES

Whether one calls them "technology initiatives" or "strategic partnerships" is of little concern. What's crucial is government leadership that follows the needs of the market, reaching down into those areas which affect the competitiveness of firms. While private sector strategy advisers such as McKinsey & Company or Boston Consulting Group certainly will continue to provide competitiveness insights at the firm-specific level, government action should focus on the broad national gaps in the fields of research, technology, and information. Success with such measures should make our products and performance so desirable that they can overcome even entrenched cultural impediments such as the Japanese distribution system. It simply must become highly undesirable *not* to deal with U.S. firms.

The development of a global community forces us to recast our approach. Domestic policy needs to become more international, while foreign trade policy needs to become more domestic. Accomplishing that requires three major changes in current thinking: It shifts the direction of trade policy action from abroad to home; it alters the emphasis from a macro to a micro orientation on corporate competitiveness; and it envisions change mainly through the strengthening of private action and capability rather than through international politics and government-to-government negotiation.

While the election year's frenzy heightened the temptation to search for the foreign, non-voting culprit, realism, must have us looking in the mirror at ourselves. The very Yankee spirit which has made the U.S. trader so successful asks us to take the steps that will work.

Additional Reading

Bergsten, C. Fred and William R. Cline (1985) *The United States–Japan Economics Problem*. Institute for International Economics, October.

Czinkota, Michael R, and Masaaki Kotabe (1990) "Product Development the Japanese Way," *Journal of Business Strategy*, 11 (November-December), pp. 31–6.

—— and Jon Woronoff (1991) *Unlocking Japan's Markets*. Chicago: Probus Publishing.

Ministry of International Trade and Industry (1992) *Japan's Import Promotion Measures*, NR–396 (92–4), Tokyo, January.

Kotabe, Masaaki (1992) "A Comparative Study of U.S. and Japanese Patent Systems," *Journal of International Business Studies*, 23 (First Quarter), pp. 147–68.

Lazer, William and Midori Yamanouchi Rynn (1991) "The Japan That Can Say 'No' Revisited," *International Marketing Review*, 8 (5).

March, Robert M (1991) *Honoring the Customer*. New York: John Wiley & Sons.
Morita, Akio, and Shintaro Ishihara (1989) *"No" to Ieru Nippon* [Japan That Can Say No]. Tokyo: Kobunsha.
U.S. International Trade Commission (1990) *Japan's Distribution System and Options for Improving U.S. Access.* Washington D.C., June, p. 2.

3

Global Neighbors: Poor Relations

MICHAEL R. CZINKOTA
SCHOOL OF BUSINESS, GEORGETOWN UNIVERSITY

We are witnessing historic changes in global relations in the '90s. The new greeting in Washington is Shalom-Salaam, the North American Free Trade Accord is becoming a reality, and the disparate nations of Europe are uniting more strongly than under Charlemagne's reign.

However, as the rest of the world leans toward peace, cooperation, and market expansion, friction increasingly mars U.S.–Japanese relations. Critics wallow in the alleged economic dangers that Japan poses to world trade and accuse it of striving for world dominance. Highly public accusations ricochet across the Pacific, many going beyond economic analysis and pandering to fear.

In opinion polls, more than two-thirds of Americans say that they regard Japan as more threatening than the former Soviet Union. *The Washington Post* reports that 63 percent of U.S. consumers claim they make an effort to avoid buying Japanese products. Cities have canceled contracts with Japanese firms, and baseball fans vehemently protested Nintendo's purchase of the Seattle Mariners.

This divisiveness cannot continue. Society is preoccupied with issues such as air and water pollution, global warming, ecosystem maintenance, new diseases, major local conflicts, increases in world armament, and sudden shifts in the world's energy supply. Even industrialized nations face problems such as stagnant demand and rising unemployment. We are coming to recognize that no country can successfully address and resolve these issues alone. We must, therefore, find ways to collaborate.

Improving the U.S.–Japanese trade relationship is key to fostering such collaboration. As U.S. Ambassador to Japan Walter Mondale stated during his confirmation hearings, "Constant trade friction weakens public support in both the United States and Japan for our alliance, and it threatens our ability to cooperate on a broader agenda."

With the demise of the Soviet empire, Japan and the United States have lost much of their former commonality of purpose. The dramatic changes sweeping through Eastern Europe and the former Soviet Union since 1988 have vanquished a major threat that previously tied the two countries closely together. Now that Japan and the United States aren't seeing red anymore, both are trying to decide how much or whether they still need each other.

Close-up inspection without a mutual bond can be detrimental; it lets us discover the warts and the flab without having the relationship. It's important that we find another common purpose that

"Global Neighbors: Poor Relations," by Michael R, Czinkota, *Marketing Management*, Vol. 2, No. 4, pp. 46–52. Used by permission of American Marketing Association.

will build and develop the relationship on an elevated plane. And the former Soviet empire still can be the catalyst that moves us in that direction.

Bilateral Focus

Some of the friction between the United States and Japan stems from the trade negotiations framing the U.S.–Japanese relationship to date. Traditionally, negotiations have focused on foreign access to markets in Japan, a country which historically has tried to insulate itself from imports. Early on, the focus of General Agreement on Tariffs and Trade (GATT) negotiations was on lowering tariffs and reducing entry restrictions.

Although they were onerous and protracted, these negotiations did move a higher volume of imports into Japan. Because of simultaneous large increases in Japanese exports, however, trade imbalances have grown. As a result of the ever-widening U.S. trade deficit with Japan, negotiations have gradually taken on a bilateral focus.

Sector-specific deals, self-imposed quotas, voluntary import expansions, and government-mandated imbalance adjustments now are emerging in these negotiations. Although some U.S. companies and even some industries are boosting their exports to Japan, trade imbalances persist, and no matter what Japan-bashers say, even the most successful negotiations will not affect the domestic economy in any major way.

For example, the U.S. government links $1 billion of U.S. exports to about 19,000 jobs. The harshest among the realistic critics accuse Japan of "rejecting" $10 billion of U.S. trade annually. Therefore, even if the United States immediately increased exports to Japan by this unlikely amount, 190,000 jobs would be created at best. In the context of 8.8 million unemployed, the economic impact of such a trade shift on the United States would not be radical.

However, misleading demagoguery that continuously raises and shatters expectations produces broad-based resentment among the public that eventually may take on a political expression. The level of political discontent is rising in both nations, and the original road toward more liberalized trade may yet turn into a slippery slope leading toward managed trade.

A new, less traditional approach to trade negotiations seeks outcome-based changes in areas that historically have not been considered part of trade policy, such as distribution systems, business linkages, and savings rates. The key idea seems to be to make the market abroad more like the market at home. Even though Japan has asked for some changes in the U.S. economy, these negotiations primarily smooth the way for U.S. firms trying to do business in Japan. The Strategic Impediments Initiative, as put forth during the Bush administration, marked the beginning of such a direction; the current discussion of "Structural Convergence Talks" may be even more wide-ranging.

Because of changes in Japan's domestic business environment and micro-managed, sector-specific trade performance criteria, policy makers expect to correct the trade imbalance at last. But, realistically, such an approach is likely to be limited to cosmetic gains, trying as it does to change deeply entrenched cultural values in Japan. A solution will continue to be elusive and the relationship will only become more troubled. And the approach could backfire if it triggers anti-U.S. sentiment in Japan. This could imperil existing U.S. sales to Japan and perhaps even motivate some Japanese firms to limit shipments of crucial components to the United States, thus leading to a direct confrontation.

Real Alternatives

Some alternatives can lead to real improvement in U.S.–Japanese trade relations. First, U.S. measures should focus on information, collaboration, and human capital. For example, Americans do very little to learn about Japan and absorb widely available information. In 1991, only 1,180 U.S. students attended school in Japan, whereas more than 30,000 Japanese students came to the United States. Unless we learn to observe and absorb Japanese knowledge and know-how to a greater extent, we will continue to be surprised by "new" developments because we weren't paying attention.

In light of the knowledge explosion, the rising cost of research, and the increasing risk of investment, the need for corporate collaboration has never been greater. Contrary to current antitrust legislation, such collaboration should be encouraged, particularly in areas of rapid technological change and substantial social need such as environmental safety, health care new materials development, and biotechnology.

Companies should collaborate on both products and processes. For example, quality performance can become the focus of a cooperative effort throughout an entire industry and include manufacturers, suppliers, and customers at home and abroad.

U.S. firms are trimming down, primarily by shedding personnel. But in many instances, this trend toward leanness means customers receive less and less service. With the demise of mass production and mass consumption, augmented service becomes imperative for global success. We need to instill a service ethic into our work force and managements that not only demands service, but also is prepared to provide it.

JAPAN'S ROLE

Members of the upper echelons of Japan's policy community recognize the need to increase Japan's involvement in world issues and in world imports. However, in shaping new trade relations. Japan's public sector can and must do more. As we have seen, rules and regulations that appeared to be immutable can change. As the vilification of the close business relations of the Japanese *keiretsu* gradually gives way to "relationship marketing" in the United States, Japan is lifting the large-store law restrictions, agreeing to import large quantities of rice, and accepting the practice of discounting.

However, many obstacles to Japanese importation persist, such as closed supplier relationships, secret market sharing arrangements, and collusive bidding practices. It is incumbent on the government of Japan to address and resolve the inequities created by such practices aggressively. But reforms cannot be confined to the public sector, Japanese firms also need to overhaul their thinking.

For example, in Japan, it's considered a good thing for the individual firm to maximize its exports. Yet, when the context is broadened to include political acceptability, repercussions by trading partners, and threats to international market access, such a narrow view of trade participation may be inappropriate. And the public as well as the private sector in Japan must understand that it is rationally and economically necessary to increase the inflow of products and services.

Some experts claim that "endaka," the rising value of the yen, will resolve import problems in Japan by making exports dear and imports cheap. However, because intra-firm and intra-industry trade are rapidly becoming decisive determinants of trade flows, trade follows investment. U.S.

foreign direct investment in Japan amounts to roughly $23 billion. At the same time, Japanese cumulative investment in the United States is more than $87 billion. Unless direct foreign investment in Japan increases dramatically, trade frictions will continue. Making foreign investment growth possible must become a major priority for the Japanese government. It can provide information on and access to investment opportunities and offer an attractive financial and investment environment.

The Big Picture

The best way to resolve the conflicts between the United States and Japan is to emphasize multilateral trade relations within a new context. Take the science of astronomy as an analogy. More than two thousand years ago, Pythagoras and Aristotle, using the best available knowledge, came up with a geocentric view of our universe, where everything circled around the earth. It took until the 16th century before Copernicus and Galileo understood additional factors better and taught (with much inhibition) a heliocentric view, which recognized that the earth revolved around the sun. And only early in this century did Harlow Shapley again broaden our view by discovering that we are only one solar system rotating at the periphery of the Milky Way.

Today we are in a similar situation in our trade relations. During the 1950s, our economic view was strictly domestic-based. By the late 1970s, this perspective expanded to include a few key players one had to take into account. This view prevails today, most likely because the United States and Japan together account for nearly 40% of the world's GNP. But it's time to broaden this perspective. Companies and nations that adopt a "galax-centric" view recognize that many other new, and not so new, players exist out there. And, like it or not, these players must be incorporated into our actions and considerations.

The Russian Connection

The entry of Eastern and Central Europe and the former Soviet Union into our world trade picture offers a new arena for U.S.–Japanese collaboration – as a precursor to global improvement. The member countries of the former Soviet empire together have a GNP of about $3 trillion. Their traditional trade dependence was about $450 billion, with 60–80% of trade carried out within the bloc. Today, trade within the bloc has shrunk to one-fifth of its former value.

Germany is a good benchmark for the region because its economic and political conditions provide the best possible scenario for adjustment. In 1992, capital transfers to the former East Germany amounted to $90 billion; in 1993, the amount transferred rose to $100 billion. Hans Tietmeyer, the president of the Bundesbank, predicts transfers will amount to $1 trillion by the end of this decade.

Projecting these annual transfers of $6,000 per capita into the rest of Eastern Europe comes to $600 billion. For the former Soviet Union, the equivalent transfer amount would be $1.8 trillion per year. These numbers contrast sharply with actual government transfers which, on a world-wide basis, are less than $10 billion, and it's unlikely that public funds will ever exceed a very small percentage of the total funds required. The impetus will have to come from private investment and the retention of current funds (which, according to Yegor Gaidar, one of the economic architects of the new Russia, currently flow out from the former Soviet Union at a rate of about $20 billion a year).

Private investors, however, will be interested only if they can expect an attractive return. The potential is there, but it can only be fulfilled through local production and trade. Given traditional trade dependence estimates, these new participants in world trade can unleash competition to the tune of $270 billion, or 5% of world trade. Although that may not seem like much, such competition is likely to be concentrated in the fields of light manufacturing, steel, agriculture, and textiles because of the competitive structure of the newly liberated economies. And these industries, of course, are the very ones already under heavy competitive pressure; they are the traditional sacred cows of industrial countries and developing nations alike.

Uninhibited trade flow of this magnitude with such a narrow concentration will bring about world production loss and unemployment that far exceeds anything considered in the current U.S.–Japanese trade negotiations. It will have a major impact on employment and economic growth performance, particularly in light of the existing weaknesses in the global economy. But it is also here that major sources of future growth and market expansion lie.

Given these major inflows, nations will display their inherent tendency to erect barriers to these new trade streams. Yet, doing so will jeopardize world stability, because economic barriers are just as painful and divisive as political ones. Even if only a few countries erected barriers to free trade, the onslaught of imports would force other countries to follow suit.

Collaboration and Competition

Multilateral collaboration can avert or at least reduce the threat of such market calamities. Such negotiations offer hope for new market opportunities and contribute to a better and more secure environment around the globe. Yet, collaboration is only part of the answer. Market access is a necessary but insufficient condition for competitive success. As Japan's Ambassador Kuriyama said recently in Washington, it is critical to combine collaboration with competition; after all, lack of competition brought about the collapse of the socialist system. But in order to pass on the competitive spirit, one first must foster competitive capability.

Both Japanese and U.S. firms can make a difference in this area. Collaborative marketing is essential to build markets abroad and develop viable supply sources. The current political shifts in former Eastern Bloc countries signal the *beginning* of a process. The intent to change does not automatically result in change itself. Abolishing a centrally planned economy, for example, does not create a market economy; legislating to permit private sector entrepreneurship does not create entrepreneurship; lifting price controls does not immediately make goods available or affordable.

Deeply ingrained systemic differences between these restructuring economies and market values continue. Highly prized, fully accepted fundamentals of a market economy – such as the reliance on competition, support of the profit motive, and the willingness to live with risk on a corporate and personal level – are not yet accepted in these fledgling democracies. Managerial decision making is new and complicated, and because of the total lack of prior market orientation, even simple reforms require an almost unimaginable array of decisions about licenses, rules, and standards. Because knowledge of pricing, advertising, and research also is lacking, corporate responsiveness to demand is difficult.

Continuing pent-up demand, accompanied by lack of capital, means that product availability and financing matter much more in these countries than does product sophistication. Even buyers need education because they have never been exposed to the problem of decision making and their preferences are vague and undefined.

Filling Gaps

All of these marketing shortcomings must be addressed, especially the gaps in logistics and distribution, which are key to successful competition. Both U.S. and Japanese marketers excel in these areas, and their collaboration in transferring these capabilities to the new players can from the basis for a revised mutual relationship.

The total cost of distribution in both the United States and Japan is running close to 11% of GNP. By 1995, experts predict 40% of shipments in U.S. companies to be under a just-in time/quick response regime. In contrast, Eastern Europe and the former Soviet Union are just beginning to learn about the rhythm of demand and the need to bring supply in line with it.

These countries are battling space constraints, poor supply lines, nonexistent distribution and service centers, limited rolling stock, and insufficient transportation systems. Producers know nothing about benchmarking, inventory carrying cost, store assortment efficiencies, and replenishment techniques. Only poorly understood are the need for information development and exchange systems, for integrated supplier-distributor alliances, and for efficient communication systems such as electronic data interchange. Distribution costs in Eastern Europe and Russia are well above 30% of GNP, and it will take a long time to develop responsive, consumer-driven systems. The United States and Japan can take several steps immediately to assist in overcoming these weaknesses.

INFORMATION ASSISTANCE

Japan and the United States should form a council for distribution and logistics assistance that includes members from the public and private sector. On the public sector side, the council could benefit from the rich resources of military logistics. On the private side, membership should be drawn from architects, transportation planners, warehousing experts, logisticians, and distribution channel authorities.

This council can present proposals for stream-lining and setting priorities for the distribution of existing products and services, as well as assist in establishing requirements for the emerging, market-oriented output. Concurrently, existing programs that fund visiting professors, lecturers, student exchanges, and expert programs, should focus on the distribution and logistics theme. Furthermore, foreign commercial service staff members should be trained in the field so they can recognize and report on situations where assistance would be useful.

IMPLEMENTATION SUPPORT

Portions of existing funding programs should be dedicated to distribution and logistics. This includes funding through development organizations and international institutions as well as commercial transactions. For example, it is of only limited use to allocate funds to provide grain unless the grain gets distributed efficiently. Those who make large investments in telecommunications need to consider the communication/distribution linkages and incorporate specific ties between suppliers and customers at home and abroad.

In general, investment in services designed to improve the logistics infrastructure should receive at least as much encouragement and support as does investment in production facilities. An improved retail structure is just as important as a new bottling plant.

We all must recognize that unless the new players of the former Soviet bloc are empowered by integrating these distribution and logistics dimensions into their market orientation, they will not become part of the competitive market-place of the West. Without such integration, economic friction will soon lead to political heat and destruction that will affect us all.

Inseparable Destinies

Trade negotiations that stress competition and collaboration – with a focus on Eastern Europe and the former Soviet Union – will help create a new paradigm for U.S.–Japanese trade relations. The current narrow view of our relationship must be broadened quickly to achieve positive results. The existing friction can be overcome more easily if we recognize how much more is at stake, living as we do in an era when major fissures are appearing in the parchment of the future writers of history.

The United States and Japan must work together as partners, acknowledging and respecting our differences and striving for global improvement. This must become a decade of collaboration and competition, the era of a galax-centric perspective which provides us again with a commonality of purpose. We need to begin talking with, not at, each other in order to achieve that elusive new world order in a way that is acceptable, tolerable, and beneficial to all participants.

As President Clinton has stated, "There is no more important bilateral relationship in the world than that which exists between the United States and Japan. Our two nations now share a fundamental interdependence, and our destinies have become inseparable." This inseparability is the trigger that will propel us beyond our narrow confines to joint action and elevate any measure of success to a new plateau.

Bridging the geographic and economic distance between Japan and the United States will converge our interests, bring us closer together, and give marketers in both nations the opportunity to perform in their areas of greatest strength, serving as agents of change, fulfilling needs, improving the standard of living, and enhancing the quality of life.

Additional Reading

Bowersox, Donald J., Patricia J. Daugherty, Cornelia L. Droege, Richard N. Germain and Dale S. Rogers (1992) *Logistical Excellence*. Burlington, Mass: Digital Press.

Czinkota, Michael R. and Masaaki Kotabe (eds) (1993) *The Japanese Distribution System* Chicago: Probus Publishers.

Krugman, Paul (ed.) (1991) *Trade With Japan: Has the Door Opened Wider?* Chicago: University of Chicago Press.

Report on Unfair Trade Policies by Major Trading Partners (1993) Subcommittee on Unfair Trade Policies and
Measures, Industrial Structure Council, Ministry of International Trade and Industry, Tokyo, May 11.
Tyson, Laura D. (1992) *Who's Bashing Whom? Trade Conflict in High-Technology Industries*. Washington, D.C.:
Institute for International Economics.
United States International Trade Commission (1990) *Japan's Distribution System and Options for Improving U.S.
Access*. Washington, D.C.: U.S. ITC.

4

Assessment of Shifting Global Competitiveness: Patent Applications and Grants in Four Major Trading Countries

MASAAKI KOTABE

THE UNIVERSITY OF TEXAS AT AUSTIN

AND

ELI P. COX, III

THE UNIVERSITY OF TEXAS AT AUSTIN

Record U.S. trade deficits during the 1980s have directed increasing research attention to national competitiveness. U.S. trade deficits have been equated with the deteriorating competitiveness of U.S. firms in the world market. However, the recent dollar depreciation has allowed U.S. trade deficits to decline, particularly with Western Europe, while the deficits still remain a relatively sticky problem with Japan. In the political arena, foreign trade barriers (particularly in Japan, China, and other Asian Countries) often have been blamed for mounting U.S. trade deficits. However, data from GATT and other sources suggest that in addition to competitive weaknesses in U.S. industry, the United States has a comparably high level of tariff and non-tariff barriers to Western Europe and Japan.

The President's Commission on Industrial Competitiveness (1985) defines U.S. competitiveness as the degree to which the United States can, under free and fair market conditions, produce goods and services that meet the test of international markets while simultaneously maintaining or expanding the real income of its citizens. At a quantitative level, no single indicator accurately measures all aspects of U.S. competitiveness. The trade balance is a partial reflection of a nation's competitiveness, but it also reflects exchange rate fluctuations and trade barriers.

Variants of trade balance, such as a nation's share of world exports and its import penetration, also are frequently used measures of competitiveness. These measures, similar to the trade deficit, reflect past performance and are less indicative of a nation's current and future competitiveness. Numerous studies have shown the importance of a nation's innovative ability as a

Reprinted from *Business Horizons*, January–February 1993. Copyright 1993 by the Foundation for the School of Business at Indiana University. Used with permission.

foundation for future competitiveness in international trade. A nation's product and process innovations have become increasingly critical prerequisites for the success of its firms in global competition.

Patent data also cast some concern over future U.S. competitiveness. About 45 percent of new U.S. patents currently are being granted to foreigners, indicating deep patent penetration by foreign firms. About 20 percent of all U.S. patents granted in 1991 were awarded to the Japanese. In fact, the top four companies receiving U.S. patents in 1991 were all Japanese firms: Toshiba, Hitachi, Canon, and Mitsubishi Electric. On the other hand, only 14 percent of Japanese patents were held by foreigners and only 7 percent of all Japanese patents granted in 1989 were awarded to U.S. companies.

In this article, patent applications and patent grants will be used as measures of innovative ability and subsequent global competitiveness. Counts of patent applications and patent grants probably are the most direct indicators of industrial innovative activity available. To understand the standing of U.S. innovativeness relative to that of its major competitor nations, patent applications filed by and grants made to both residents and nonresidents in the United States, Japan, Germany, and Britain will be compared and contrasted. Patent applications and grants of residents indicate a nation's competitiveness. In contrast, patent applications and grants to non-residents indicate the competitive position being staked out by foreign countries.

Differences Among Patent Systems of Industrialized Countries

The differences among patent systems around the world must be understood before we attempt to compare patent statistics across the four nations being studied. This section reviews the basic dimensions of patent systems to put the patent application and patent grant statistics into proper perspective.

A patent is a legal document issued by a governmental agency that establishes ownership of a piece of "intellectual property" for a specified period. Patent systems have two principal purposes: to protect the property rights of the inventor of a novel and useful product or process; and to encourage a society's inventiveness and technical progress. Most of the important differences in the patent systems of industrialized countries discussed below can be explained by a varying emphasis of these potentially conflicting purposes. The American and Japanese systems will be emphasized in this discussion because they tend to represent the ends of the continuum, with the United States placing the greatest emphasis on the rights of the inventor and Japan emphasizing the societal benefits of an invention.

ORDER OF PRIORITY OF APPLICATIONS RECEIVED

The "first-to-file" principle is employed by a majority of countries in the world except the United States and the Philippines. According to this principle, a patent will be granted to the first person filling an application for it. In contrast, in the United States, where the "first-to-invent" principle is employed, a patent is granted to the person who first develops an invention. Therefore, some patents granted by the U.S. Patent Office are revoked and reassigned to the "real" inventor.

Such a system protects the small inventor who may not have the sophistication or resources needed to file for a patent quickly.

The first-to-file principle has an advantage over the first-to-invent principle. It avoids many potentially expensive lawsuits by legally declaring the first filer to be the owner of a patent. Additionally, the first-to-file system encourages individuals to file for patents quickly as a means of staking out territory where much technological development is taking place. In Japan, for example, it is common for a firm to file preemptive patents to lay claim to an emerging technology even before it can show that the invention has been reduced to practice.

Clearly, the first-to-file/first-to-invent distinction is the most important distinction between the patent systems of the world. However, there are other distinctions that must be kept in mind when examining patent applications and grants as a measure of international competition.

SECRECY

During the examination period, the patent application is maintained in secrecy by the United States Patent and Trademark Office, and no information is released without the consent of the applicant. In this respect, American patent law differs from that of most of the other industrialized countries, where it is the practice to lay open or publish patent applications for inspection or opposition 18 months after the priority application has been filed. Laying open the application allows competitors to use the protected information in their own R&D efforts. If a competitor in Japan uses a core patent to obtain a patent for an improvement, the company earns a right for a license to the core patent for a reasonable fee.

PRE- AND POST-GRANT OPPOSITION

Japan has a system of both pre- and post-grant opposition. Post-grant opposition is an element of the European Patent Office (EPO) practice and is similar to the American reexamination procedure. Since pre-grant opposition is unique to Japan, it will be highlighted here.

Japan's pre-grant procedures are skillfully used by Japanese industry to slow down the issuance of competitors' patents. Virtually any person can file an opposition. The applicant has the duty to respond to each of these oppositions in writing. All firms applying for patents in Japan experience this burden, but foreign applicants, who find it troublesome, view it as a basis for discrimination.

DISCLOSURE OF PRIOR ART

With the first-to-invent principle in the United States, applicants are required to disclose to the Patent Office all information on prior art of which they are aware. Applicants who knowingly fail to disclose such information will lose their patent right and may be subject to criminal penalties or antitrust liabilities. In most of the rest of the world, however, there is no obligation to disclose prior art. The first-to-file system relies on outside parties to bring prior art to the attention of the patent examiner through the opposition process.

SINGLE CLAIM VS. MULTIPLE CLAIM APPLICATIONS

European countries and the United States accept patent applications with multiple claims. Before 1988, the Japanese Patent office required that patent applications be limited to a single claim. This encouraged Japanese firms to file many narrow applications rather than a few broad ones, as is common in the United States and Europe. Such a practice was further encouraged by the prestige attached by the Japanese to receiving a patent. This practice has resulted in a larger number of patent applications relative to the amount of technological development involved as compared to the United States and Europe. It also increased the workload of Japan's patent office, resulting in longer examination periods. Additionally, foreign firms have complained that Japanese firms encircled their core patents with numerous patents representing incremental improvements that would not be patentable abroad.

In 1988, Japanese patent law was amended to conform to the American and European multiclaim systems. While the change has not been in effect long enough to evaluate its impact, it appears that Japanese patent officers still seem to favor very narrow applications.

Patent Activity in Japan, The U.S., Germany, and Great Britain

Statistics have been gathered from World Intellectual Property Organization concerning the rate of patent applications and grants by domestic and foreign firms in Japan, the United States, Germany, and Great Britain from 1963–88. Data have been classified by nationality of grant recipient since 1963 (except Britain, since 1969).

APPLICATIONS AND GRANTS OF JAPANESE PATENTS

Figure 4.1 presents the patent applications and grants in Japan for domestic and foreign firms from 1963 to 1989. Total annual patent applications in Japan have increased greatly over the period. The 357, 464 applications in 1988 was 398 percent greater than the level for 1963.

The total number of patents granted also increased, but at a much slower rate. In 1963 there were 23,303 grants made, while in 1989 there were 63,331. This represents an increase of 172 percent. Thus, while there was one patent granted for every 3.08 applications in 1963, only one patent was granted for every 5.64 applications in 1989.

The increase in patent applications is attributable to the increase in submissions by both domestic and foreign firms. Although foreign submissions increased by 122 percent from 1963 to 1989, Japanese submissions increased by 490 percent over the same period. Thus, the Japanese share of applications grew from 75 percent in 1963 to 89 percent in 1989.

The increase in patents granted by the Japanese government is attributable mainly to increases received by Japanese firms. Japanese grants increased by 266 percent from 1963 to 1989. In contrast, grants to foreign firms increased by a meager 3 percent for the period. Thus, the Japanese share of patents awarded in Japan rose from 64 percent in 1963 to 86 percent in 1989.

Over the 26-year period, the ratio of applications to grants was 4.41 applications for every grant

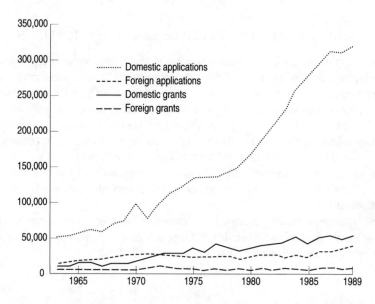

Figure 4.1 Japanese patent applications and grants: 1963–1989

for domestic firms and 2.89 for foreign firms. (A ratio of 1 indicates that a grant was received for every application submitted, while a ratio of 5 indicates that a grant is received for every five applications.) The ratio increased from 3.61 in 1963 to 5.80 in 1989 for domestic firms, while it increased from 2.14 to 4.64 for foreign firms between the same period.

In summary: 1) total patent applications have increased dramatically over the 26-year period examined due primarily to submissions by Japanese firms; 2) the Japanese share of applications in Japan increased by 14 percentage points; 3) patents granted also grew but much more slowly with grants to Japanese firms accounting for all the growth; 4) the Japanese share of patents awarded in Japan increased by 22 percentage points; 5) the number of applications relative to the number of grants grew for both foreign and domestic firms; and 6) foreign applicants have a more favorable application-to-grant ratio than Japanese firms.

APPLICATIONS AND GRANTS OF U.S. PATENTS

As figure 4.2 indicates, the total annual patent applications in the United States have increased modestly for the period from 1963 to 1989. The number of total applications of 161, 660 in 1989 was 88 percent greater than the level for 1963; most of this increase has taken place since 1983.

The increase in patent applications is attributable to a slight increase in submissions by domestic firms. For the 26-year period, applications increased by 21 percent for domestic firms and 311 accounted for 78 percent of all the patent applications in the United States in 1963 but only 51 percent in 1989.

The total number of patents granted increased by 88 percent, while the number of applications increased by 109 percent. Although the number of patents granted to American firms increased absolutely by 35 percent, grants to foreign firms increased by 433 percent. Thus, the U.S. share of

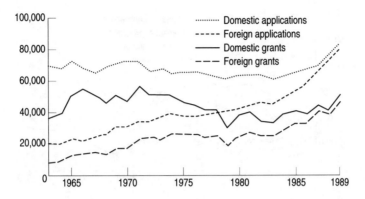

Figure 4.2 U.S. Patent applications and grants: 1963–1989

the patents granted in the United States declined from 81 percent in 1963 to 53 percent in 1989.

Over the 26-year period, the ratio of applications to grants was 1.5 for domestic firms and 1.71 for foreign firms. The ratio declined for foreign firms: the ratio was 2.25 in 1963, but it decreased to 1.74 in 1989. While the ratio for domestic firms also declined slightly from 1.84 to 1.65 during the same period, the figure declined to a low of 1.3 in 1972 but increased from that time on.

In summary: 1) total patent applications have increased modestly over the 26-year period, with foreign firms accounting for almost all the growth; 2) the U.S. share of patent applications made by U.S. firms declined by 27 percentage points over the period; 3) total grants increased at a rate slightly less than applications; 4) the U.S. share of patents granted to American firms declined by 28 percentage points over the period; and 5) while the ratio of applications to grants remained about the same for domestic firms, it declined for foreign applicants.

APPLICATIONS AND GRANTS OF GERMAN PATENTS

Total annual patent applications in Germany increased moderately from 1963 to 1989 (see figure 4.3). The total number of applications (102, 427) for 1989 was 101 percent greater than the level in 1963. However, the year-to-year changes were not at all uniform. Total applications declined from a high of 67,495 in 1967 to a low of 45, 209 in 1984, and then rose to 83,103 in 1985, which represents a one-year increase of 83.8 percent.

The total number of patents granted increased at a much faster rate than applications. In 1963 there were 15,542 grants made; in 1989 there were 42,233. This represents an increase of 172 percent.

The increase in patent applications is attributable primarily to the increased submissions by foreign firms. While applications by domestic firms increased only 14 percent for the 26-year period, foreign applications increased by 137 percent. In fact, foreign applications have exceeded domestic applications since 1985; the difference was of a magnitude of 37 percent in 1989. Although German applications have increased steadily since 1980, foreign applications have increased dramatically since 1984 after a decline since 1973. In 1963, German firms accounted for 60 percent of the applications in Germany, while in 1989 they accounted for 42 percent of the applications.

The increase in patents granted by the German government is attributable to increases received by foreign firms. German grants increased by 73 percent from 1963 to 1989. In contrast, foreign

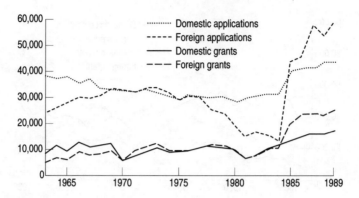

Figure 4.3 German patent applications and grants: 1963–1989

grants increased by 339 percent. It should also be noted that there has been a dramatic increase in patent grants received by foreign firms since 1984.

Over the 26-year period, the ratio of applications to grants was 3.13 for domestic firms and 2.68 for foreign firms. However, the ratio declined for both domestic and foreign firms. In 1963 the ratio was 3.90 for German firms and 4.32 for foreign firms, while the figures in 1989 fell to 2.56 and 2.34, respectively.

In summary: 1) total patent applications increased modestly over the 26-year period because of a relatively large increase by foreign firms and a very modest increase by German firms; 2) the German share of German patent applications declined by 18 percentage points over the period; 3) patent grants grew much more rapidly than applications, reflecting decreasing application-to-patent ratios for both domestic and foreign firms; 4) the increase in grants was accounted for largely by foreign firms; 5) the number of grants to foreign firms has exceeded the number to domestic firms since 1984; and 6) the German share of German patent grants declined by 23 percentage points.

APPLICATIONS AND GRANTS OF BRITISH PATENTS

Total annual patent applications in Britain experienced a moderate increase from 1963 to 1989 (see figure 4.4). The total number of applications in 1989 (90,234) was 75 percent greater than the level in 1963.

The total number of patents granted increased for the period by 2 percent. Thus, while there was one patent granted for every 1.71 applications in 1963, only one patent was granted for every 2.92 applications in 1989.

The increase in patent applications is attributable exclusively to the increased submissions by foreign firms, which increased by 144 percent from 1963 to 1989; domestic submissions declined by 269 applications or about 1 percent of the 1963 total. Accordingly, the British share of the British patent applications declined from 47 percent in 1963 to 27 percent in 1989.

However, the rate of foreign patent applications was not stable over the period: foreign patent applications declined from a high of 37,840 in 1973 to a low of 13,735 in 1984. From 1984 to 1989, they experienced and increase of 382 percent.

British patent grants were not classified in the data based by nationality of the applicant until 1969. From 1969 to 1989, the decline in patents granted was experienced by both domestic and

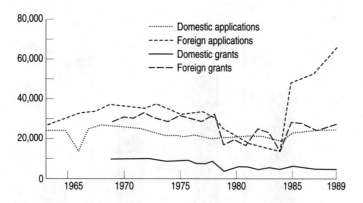

Figure 4.4 British patent applications and grants: 1963–1989

foreign firms, with domestic grants declining by 57 percent and foreign grants declining by 8 percent. Grants to foreign applicants fluctuated considerably over the period, as the figure reveals. The British share of patents granted in Britain declined from 25 percent in 1969 to 14 percent in 1989.

Over the 20-year period, the ratio of grants to applications was 3.97 for domestic firms and 1.61 for foreign firms. However, the ratio has increased for both domestic and foreign firms. In 1969, the ratio was 2.64 for British firms and 1.30 for foreign firms, while the figures rose to 5.68 and 2.48, respectively, in 1989.

In summary: 1) there was a modest increase in patent applications over the 26-year period examined; 2) the increase that took place was solely attributable to foreign firms, particularly since 1984; 3) the British share of applications for patents in Britain declined 20 percentage points for the period; 4) the number of grants to foreign firms have exceeded those to domestic firms over the 20-year-period for which data are available; 5) grants experienced a decline over the 20-year period, particularly for British firms; 6) the British share of patents granted in Britain declined by 11 percentage points during the most recent 20 years; and 7) whereas the ratio of applications to grants was higher for domestic firms than for foreign firms, it has almost doubled for both groups since 1969.

COMPARISONS AMONG THE FOUR COUNTRIES

While the number of patent applications in the United States, Germany, and Britain grew moderately, it increased dramatically in Japan. The number of patent applications in Japan (357, 464) was greater than the combined total for the other three countries (354,321) in 1989. The exceptionally large number of patent applications in Japan is chiefly attributable to a single-claim requirement that was unique to Japan (until 1988). According to one estimate (Quigg 1988), about 25 percent of patent applications in Japan have actually been examined for patentability. In other words, 25 percent of the 357,464 applications, or 89,336 applications, filed in 1989 are expected to be examined eventually by the Japanese Patent Office for patentability. This expected number is about 55 percent of the total number of American applications and is in line with Japan's GNP being a little more than half that of the United States.

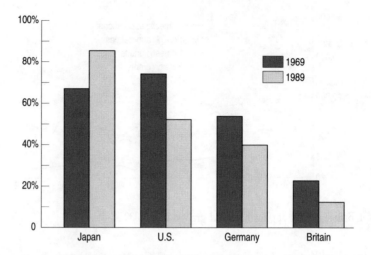

Figure 4.5 Share of grants received by domestic firms

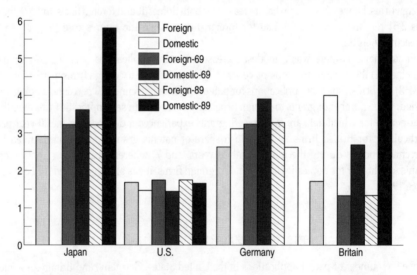

Figure 4.6 Patent Applications to grants ratio for the four countries

While there was a sizable increase in foreign applications in Japan, the greatest increase came from Japanese firms. In sharp contrast, the greatest increases by far came from foreign appplictions in the United States and Germany, and foreign applications offset a decline in the number of domestic applications in Britain. It is also noteworthy that since 1984 there has been a dramatic increase in the number of foreign applications in Germany (347 percent) and Britain (382 percent).

Germany experienced the greatest increase in patent grants, followed closely by Japan. The

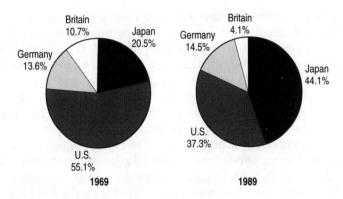

Figure 4.7 Share of domestic grants awarded

United States experienced an increase of slightly more than half that of Japan, and Britain actually experienced a decline over the 26-year period. Foreign firms received a declining share of the growing number of patent grants in Japan. In Britain, foreign firms received an increased share of patent grants despite a decline in the absolute number of grants received because a greater decline was experienced by British firms. In the United States and Germany, foreign firms increased their share of a growing number of patent grants.

Figure 4.5 presents the domestic share of patents granted in 1969 and 1989. Although the United States had the highest share in 1969, this figure declined in 1989, as it did for Germany and Britain. In sharp contrast, the domestic share in Japan increased to 34 percentage points higher than its nearest rival, the United States. In 1989, only 14 percent of the patents granted in Britain were received by British firms.

Figure 4.6 presents the relative ease with which foreign and domestic firms can receive patents in the four countries. The first two bars in each set represent the average applications-to-grants ratios for Japan, the United States, Germany, and Great Britain. The next two represent the applications-to-grants ratios for 1989, and the last two represent the ratios for 1969 in the four countries. The higher the bar, the greater the number of applications for each grant received.

As the figure indicates, the grant yield has been greater for foreign firms than domestic firms in Japan and Great Britain for the three periods examined. The yield in the United States has been remarkably uniform for domestic and foreign firms for the three time periods. In Germany, the yield has been greater for domestic than foreign firms for the period, but there has been a slight shift from a greater yield for foreign firms in 1969 to a greater yield for domestic firms in 1989.

In 1989, Japan, which experienced the lowest grant yield, required 5.64 applications for every grant received. Japan was followed by Britain with a 2.92 ratio. Germany and the United States experienced even higher yields, with figures of 2.43 and 1.69, respectively. However, if the grant yield were corrected for Japan (as only one-fourth of the applications will eventually be examined for patentability), it would be 1.41 applications for every grant and would differ little from that of the United States.

Figure 4.7 presents the domestic grants received by each of the four countries in 1969 and 1989 as a rough measure of innovative activity. From 1969 to 1989, Japan's share more than doubled and Germany's share increased modestly. The U.S. share declined to less than half of the total, and that of Britain is about half of what it was in 1969.

One must be cautious about making direct translations from the number of patents granted into the absolute amount of inventive effort taking place. First, the large number of patent applications in Japan relative to the other three countries is probably attributable in part to the practice in Japan of filing preemptive and single-claim applications (until 1988). In some cases the applicant may have no plans to see the application through to the actual award of a patent.

Second, the actual level of patent-granting activity in Japan may also be inflated by the fact that Japan did not allow multiple claims until 1988. The extent to which this change in law will produce a change in the number of patents granted in Japan remains to be seen.

Third, grants to American firms in the United States have declined from an all-time high in the early 1930s, and the number of patents granted have failed to keep pace with increases in industrial R&D. This fact does not lead to the obvious conclusion that the inventive output of the United States has declined. In fact, the declining rate of patents granted has been associated with an increase in the average "value" of patents. Applications for patents of marginal value are less likely to be submitted as the cost of applying for and receiving a patent increases.

Fourth, many of the fluctuations in patents granted may well be because of bureaucratic factors. For example, short-run fluctuations in patents granted in the United States are much more closely associated with the number of examiners than with the inflow of patent applications. Moreover, there was a sharp drop in patent grants in 1979 because of an inadequate budget for printing the approved patents.

Whereas these four factors indicated why caution is necessary in associating aggregate changes in patents granted in a single country or in making comparisons across countries, they tend to describe environmental factors that seem to apply equally to domestic and foreign applicants within a single patent system. The analysis from this perspective suggests that foreign firms are making significant inroads in the United States, Britain, and Germany. In contrast, foreign firms are losing ground in Japan.

The statistics presented here also provide managerial implications for American firms. Clearly, Japan has become a major source of increasing numbers of emerging technologies; U.S. firms should seriously examine Japan's patent system. For more than 40 years, foreign firms, particularly Japanese firms, have studied U.S. patent laws and learned how to apply them to their advantage. However, in the United States, there has been limited knowledge about the Japanese patent system, which is more similar to European systems than to the American system.

One positive development in the United States is observed in an increasing number of translation businesses catering to American firms that have obtained access to Japanese patent applications published within 18 months of filing. Such access to Japanese patent applications permits American firms to keep abreast of innovations originating from Japan. As a result, American firms can practice the "patent flooding" in Japan by filing many improvements around the original Japanese inventions. After all, this is what Japanese firms have been doing to gain advantage *vis-à-vis* other Japanese competitors for years. American firms can use the Japanese patent system effectively if they are willing to function in that system by filing many patent applications promptly and as narrowly as is permitted under the Japanese patent laws.

With the increasing realization of global markets, firms will need aggressive patent strategies to protect their emerging technologies both domestically and abroad. It is because most industrialized countries have "first-to-file" systems that American firms will have to move decisively. If not, these firms could find themselves restricted to selling products only in the United States or running the risk of violating patents for which they could have filed, but failed to do so.

Suggested Reading

Fred C. Bergsten and William R. Cline (1985) *The United States–Japan Economic Problem*. Washington, D.C.: Institute for International Economics, October.

Zvi Griliches (1990) "Patent Statistics as Economic Indicators: A Survey," *Journal of Economic Literature*, December, pp. 1,661–707.

Gary Hufbauer (1970) "The Impact of National Characteristics and Technology on the Commodity Composition of Trade in Manufactured Goods." In Raymond Vernon, (ed.) *The Technology Factor in International Trade*. New York: Columbia University Press, pp. 145–231.

Chalmers Johnson (1982) *MITI and the Japanese Miracle*. Stanford, CA: Stanford University Press.

Masaaki Kotabe (1990) "Corporate Product Policy and Innovative Behavior of European and Japanese Multinationals: An Empirical Investigation," *Journal of Marketing*, April, pp. 19–33.

Ariel Pakes and Zvi Griliches (1980) "Patents and R&D at the Firm Level: A First Report," *Economics Letters*, 5, 377–81.

Michael E. Porter (1990) *The Comparative Advantage of Nations*. New York: The Free Press.

President's Commission on Industrial Competitiveness (1985) *Global Competition: The New Reality, Vols 1 and 2*. Washington, D.C.: U.S. Government Printing Office.

Donald J. Quigg, Assistant Secretary and Commissioner of Patents and Trademarks before the Committee on Commerce, Science, and Transportation of the United States Senate, Hearing of June 24, 1988.

Donald M. Spero (1990) "Patent Protection or Piracy – A CEO Views Japan," *Harvard Business Review*, September – October, pp. 58–67.

Hilary Stout (1990) "In a Major Turnaround, U.S. is Posting Surplus in Trade with Europe," *Wall Street Journal*, July 10, pp. A1, A4.

U.S. Department of Commerce (1987) *Survey of Current Business*, March.

James M. Utterback (1987) "Innovation and Industrial Evolution in Manufacturing Industries." In Bruce R. Guile and Harvey Brooks, (eds) *Technology and Global Industry*. Washington, D.C.: National Academy Press, pp. 16–48.

Arthur Wineberg (1988) "The Japanese Patent System: A Non-tariff Barrier to Foreign Businesses?" *Journal of World Trade*, February, pp. 11–22.

World Intellectual Property Organization, *Industrial Property Statistics, Part 1: Patents*, for 1986 (published in 1989), 1987 (published in 1989), and 1988 (published in 1990). Geneva: WIPO.

World Intellectual Property Organization (1983) *100 Years of Industrial Property Statistics: Synoptic Tables on Patents, Trademarks, Designs, Utility Models*. Geneva: WIPO.

Stephen K. Yoder (1988) "U.S. Firm Takes On Japan Patent Issue," *Wall Street Journal*, October 13, p. B4.

II

THE ROLE AND INFLUENCE OF GOVERNMENT

The effects of closer global linkages on the economies of countries have been dramatic. Policy makers have increasingly come to the realization that it is very difficult to isolate domestic economic activity from international market events. They find themselves with increasing responsibilities yet with fewer and less effective tools to fulfill these responsibilities. As more parts of a domestic economy are exposed to international shifts and changes, these parts are simultaneously becoming less controllable. The same interdependence that has made countries more affluent has also left them more vulnerable.

Chapter 5 discusses the use of export controls as an economic and foreign policy tool. While the years of the cold war provided for cohesiveness among Western trading partners in the export controls field, the demise of the Communist bloc, the increased foreign availability of high-technology products, and the rapid dissemination of information and innovation have resulted in a decrease in support for such controls. The foundation of a new, multilateral export control regime is presented, together with a discussion of the effect of export controls on the competitiveness of firms. Chapter 6 focuses on the use of antidumping measures by governments. Using the example of the U.S. International Trade Commission (ITC), the danger of a new culture of competition via administrative shelter is explained. An analysis of ITC actions over a 12-year period highlights the complexity of the antidumping tool and suggests corporate strategies to deal with such government actions. Chapter 7 analyzes the purpose and focus of export assistance by the federal government. It explores the dimensions which make exports different from other economic activities and suggests that clarity of purpose, tightness of focus, coordination of approaches, and emphasis on existing exporters' strengths are the key dimensions necessary in formulating export assistance efforts which work. Chapter 8 analyzes export promotion by state governments and its linkage to corporate activities. It explains how firms undergo gradual stages of export involvement, and links these stages with changing needs and concerns of companies. An analysis of the internationalization efforts of manufacturing firms demonstrates the existence of a market gap which retards the international success of firms, and highlights the need for outside export development efforts to be responsive to the stage-specific assistance requirements of corporations.

5

Export Controls: Providing Security in a Volatile Environment

MICHAEL R. CZINKOTA

GEORGETOWN UNIVERSITY

AND

ERWIN DICHTL

UNIVERSITÄT MANNHEIM

Since the 1950s, businesses have been able to rely on the advocacy of free trade by the United States and her Western European allies. This support was instrumental in building strong trade linkages and improving the level of economic welfare in the Western world. In spite of this emphasis on a reduction of governmental interference with trade, however, there also emerged a consistent and growing need to control exports. Driven by its political and economic leadership role, the United States recognized the vital juncture between commercial relations, foreign policy, and security concerns. In the bipolar world created after World War II, it became an important policy goal to limit or delay the export of items that were deemed useful to adversaries. In particular, key attention rested with the prevention of exports of nuclear weapons and conventional armaments, and of facilities, instruments, and knowledge that would enable their production, because such exports could affect the strategic balance of power.

As a result, Western firms' exports were subject to a very broad, sophisticated, and complicated control regime. Even though these export controls were also exercised for reasons of short supply, and to protect national cultural assets and endangered species, the key traditional focus of export controls rested on the principal purposes of the Export Control Act of 1949. This act empowered the U.S. president to control the export of "any articles, materials, or supplies, including technical data" in an effort to deny militarily useful exports to the Soviet Union and its allies (Czinkota 1984).

This research was supported by a grant from the Georgetown Center for International Business Education and Research (CIBER). The authors thank Lew Cramer, Paul Freedenberg, George Shambaugh, and Leslie Stroh for helpful comments and suggestions. Assistance from the CiMar research group is also gratefully acknowledged.

Driven by the recognition that export controls are likely to remain ineffective if not harmonized across nations, the NATO allies, joined by Japan, founded the Coordinating Committee for Multilateral Export Controls (COCOM) in 1949. This multilateral organization held the ultimate authority over the decision of what could and could not be exported by the major Western nations. While most of the COCOM members held exports to be a right if not an imperative for economic progress, U.S. export control policy consistently viewed exporting as being a privilege and not a right (Office 1979). This policy stamped the U.S. export of "goods and technology with a political price tag as well as an economic one" (Nixon 1983). In consequence, COCOM members did not always share the same perspective as to the implementation of specific export controls. Disagreements existed particularly as far as dual use goods, that is, products useful for both military and civilization purposes, were concerned. An example is the export of a supercomputer that can be used both to improve the accuracy of weather predictions and for the calculations in a nuclear weapons program. In spite of such disagreements, however, there was an overall jointness of vision. Export controls were seen as an important element in the armamentarium of national policy, because they permitted strategic action without the deployment of weapons or military force and there was an agreed upon need to contain the expansion of communism.

As a result, a reasonably cohesive export control regime existed within the Western world for decades. From a corporate perspective, the regime produced predictable results, and, quite importantly, produced individual government controls that mostly were sufficiently similar in nature to contain the impact of national export controls on international competitiveness. Over time, however, various developments have caused this cohesion to become severely frayed and have even led to the dissolution of the multilateral mechanism of COCOM in the spring of 1994. This article briefly outlines the changes that have contributed to the current disharmony and the resulting uncertainties encountered by international corporations, highlights the status quo of export controls today, and delineates possible alternatives for the formulation of a realigned and realistic export control regime.

A Changed Environment for Export Controls

Seven major changes have occurred that have fundamentally altered the parameters of the traditional export control regime. The most important of these was the collapse of the Iron Curtain and the subsequent disappearance of the Soviet Union and the "Eastern Bloc." As a result, both the focus and principal objective of export controls have been altered. It makes little sense today to still speak of "Soviet adversaries," nor is the singular objective of maintaining the "strategic balance of power" still valid.

A second change that has taken place derives directly from the first. Nowadays the principal focus of export controls rests on the Third World. Quite a number of countries from this region desire chemical and nuclear weapons and the technology to make use of them. For example, a country like Libya can do little with its poison gas shells without a suitable delivery system (Dichtl 1994). As a result, export controls have moved from a "strategic balance" approach to a "tactical balance" approach. Nevertheless, even though the political hotspots addressed may be less broad in terms of their geographic expanse, the peril emanating from regional disintegration and local conflict may be just as dangerous to the world community as strategic concerns with the Soviet Union, China, or North Korea (Krass 1994).

A third major change consists of the loosening of mutual bonds between allied nations (Czinkota 1994). In spite of the occasional major policy disagreement, it used to be that the United States, Western Europe, and Japan together with emerging industrialized nations, held a generally similar strategic outlook. This outlook was driven by the common desire to reduce, or to at least contain, the influence of communism. With the disappearance of the Soviet Union, however, individual national interests that had been subsumed under the overall strategic objective now gain in importance. As German Defense Minister Ruehe so aptly stated: "Today, the transatlantic partnership is no longer based on our common opposition to an antagonistic bloc. The transatlantic relationship has reached a decisive turning point" (Ruehe 1994). In consequence, differences in perspectives, attitudes, and outlooks can now lead to ever-growing conflicts between the major players in the trade field. The current situation in Bosnia may serve as an example.

Major change has also resulted from the increased availability of high-technology products outside of the COCOM area. In the past two decades, the number of participants in the international trade field has grown rapidly. Earlier, industrializing countries mainly participated in world trade with wage-based offerings. Today they increasingly focus on technology-based competition. As a result, high-technology products are available world-wide from many sources. As a consequence of this broad foreign availability, any denial of such products becomes more difficult to enforce. If a nation does restrict the exports of widely available products, it imposes a major competitive burden on its firms.

The speed of change and the rapid dissemination of information and innovation around the world has also altered the export control picture. An example illustrates the type of technological progress achieved world-wide. The current product life cycle of computer chips is only 18 months. More than 70 percent of the sales of the data processing industry was the result of the sale of devices that did not exist only 2 years ago. Experts estimate that this percentage will rise to 80 percent in 1995 (Freedenberg 1994). This enormous technical progress is accompanied by a radical change in computer technology. For improved performance, one used to replace a PC or a work station with a new computer. Today, it is possible to simply exchange micro-processors or replace mother boards with new ones. Because today's machines can be connected to more than one microprocessor, a user can customize and update configurations almost at will. As a result, export controls based on capacity criteria have become almost irrelevant today, when users simply acquire additional chips and use expansion slots to enhance the capacity of a computer.

In this context one must also question the degree to which the latest technology is required in order for a country to engage in "dangerous" activity. For example, nuclear weapons and sophisticated delivery systems were developed by the United States and the Soviet Union well before supercomputers became available. Therefore, it is reasonable to assert that researchers in countries working with equipment that is less than state of the art or even obsolete may well be able to achieve a threat capability that can result in major destruction and affect the world order.

From a control perspective, there is also the issue of technology size and type to consider. Due to their size, supercomputers and high-technology items used to be fairly difficult to hide. Any movement of such products was easily detectable. Over time, state-of-the-art technology has been miniaturized. Much leading-edge equipment is so small that it can fit into a briefcase. Even major equipment is no larger than the luggage compartment of a car. Given these circumstances, it has become difficult, if not impossible to closely supervise the transfer of such equipment. Of at least equal importance is the type of critical technology. Often it is the software that is even more critical than the hardware. For international transfer purposes software can be placed on disks or, easier yet, simply sent abroad via computer networks.

Finally, there is the key issue of diminishing support for export controls by the policy and business communities and by individual citizens. In light of the decrease in strategic threat, the global availability of products, the growing trade dependence of firms, and the very real possibility of losing business to competitors that are subject to less stringent export controls, the willingness of these communities to support the cost of export controls is decreasing rapidly. Taken together with the increased trade dependence of nations and stagnating domestic economies, such unwillingness can well lead to the undermining of a "voluntary" export control regime.

All these changes have a major impact on the continued existence and enforcement of export controls. They have already given rise to conflicts between nations, agencies, and companies. In essence, they have led to a current situation in which businesses are faced with the major threat of export control regimes diverging across nations and becoming a key determinant of global competitiveness. The following section will briefly review the status quo of export control regimes, and highlight the existing conflicts and problems. Subsequently, recommendations of major steps that need to be undertaken to achieve a functioning export control regime equitable to firms will be made.

Problems and Conflicts in the Current Export Control Regime

While the post-World War II days saw collaborative activities in the export control field in order to make the net that caught the unauthorized exports impermeable, or at least dense, over time the loopholes have been widening rapidly. Old conflicts have become sharper and more acerbic. The dissolution of COCOM threatens the very foundation and purpose of export control enforcement. There are five key problem areas. First is the continuing debate that is now often bilateral rather than multilateral, about what constitutes military use products, civilian use products, and dual use products and the achievement of agreement on such classification. Increasingly, goods are of a dual use nature. The classic example is a pesticide factory that some years later is revealed to be a poison gas factory (Hucko 1993). It is difficult enough to clearly define weapons. It is even more problematic to achieve consensus among nations regarding dual use goods. For example, should one differentiate between screws if they are to be installed in rockets that can either lift a telecommunications satellite or a sophisticated military payload? The problem becomes even greater when one attempts to classify and list subcomponents and regulate their exportation. Individual country lists will lead to a distortion of competition if they deviate markedly from each other. Also, the very task of drawing up any list itself is fraught with difficulty when it comes to components that are assembled. For example, the Patriot missile, which was deployed in the Gulf War, consists, according to German law, only of simple parts whose individual export is permissible. Without the extensive consultation mechanism of COCOM, a harmonized list becomes difficult to draw up.

Even if governments were to be able to agree on lists and continuously update them, the implementation of the resulting control aspects would be fraught with difficulty. To subject only the export of physical goods to surveillance is insufficient. The transfer of knowledge and technology is of equal if not greater importance. Weapons-relevant information can easily be exported via books, periodicals, and disks. Therefore, their content would have to be controlled as well. One would also have to prevent foreigners from gaining access to such sources during visits or from making use of data networks across borders. Effective controls would mean the regulation of attendance at conferences and symposia both by non-citizens in the United States and by U.S. citizens abroad. An attempt to do so in the 1980s was met with such widespread hostility by the business and academic communities that it eventually was abandoned. Today's increase of global linkages through the information superhighway makes the task even more formidable. Controls would mean controlling the flow of data across national borders and continuously scrutinizing communication systems and linkages such as the Internet. Even though there is an ongoing debate about the need to exert greater governmental influence over national and international data transmissions, short of reversing the tidal wave of information flow, such efforts are likely to be unsuccessful.

Then there are the growing differences in country perspectives, based on political and economic relations. For example, concepts such as "peace" and "breach of peace" may be subject to different interpretations. Due to industrial structures, economic interests may vary across nations. In addition, there are geographic and historic ties to consider that shape the trade relations of nations and affect the impact of export controls. While these differences already gave rise to disagreement in the past (Doxey 1980), they can be expected to grow in the face of gradually shifting alliances and the emergence of new relationships.

In light of slow economic growth and persistent structural unemployment, the reluctance of governments to lose jobs due to unilateral export control measures is increasing. For example, over the decades, many nations have built up huge armament industries. With millions of jobs at stake, these industries are now gradually being reduced in size. In spite of multiple defense conversion projects, for many firms the road to immediate survival consists of an increase in exports. A conflict between national control regimes can lead to major inequities in export competitiveness. Given the heightened need of governments to create jobs, there is an innate tendency to look towards the loosening of trade restrictions as one answer to such policy demands. The significance of such an answer can be major. For example, in the United States, a simplification of the licensing procedures and an elimination of controls for products for which there is unrestrained foreign availability, would increase annual exports by up to $20 billion (Richardson 1993). With each $1 billion of exports contributing, on average, to the creation of more than 20,000 jobs, such a change could materially affect domestic economic growth (Davis 1993).

A final source of problems and conflicts emanates from the changing structure of multinational corporations. As firms grow more footloose with hundreds of establishments operating around the globe, they are increasingly less likely to be fazed by prohibitive export control laws that are only imposed by individual countries. Most of the time the larger firms are able to sidestep the unfavorable controls and the resulting damage to their activities. Many firms are doing so already today in order to avoid other restrictions on corporate activities such as genetic research or tax rates. Similarly, overly stringent local export impediments can simply be overcome by transferring activities to a country that offers a comparatively more advantageous export platform. In the European Union (EU), for example, exporters know that it is comparatively easy to deal with the export control regimes of Greece or Portugal (*Frankfurter* 1993). Many firms appreciate the speed and lack of complexity of the export procedures offered by these countries. As long as the pertinent regulations are not harmonized in the EU, every person who wants to can, by founding a separate legal entity, shift export activities into a more desirable country.

All these problems and conflicts will likely produce growing dissent and disagreement between nations in the export control field and lead to greater uncertainties for firms. The question then becomes are export controls still needed, is technology still important in terms of strategic or tactical advantage, and can the tool of export controls still make a difference in a new world order?

As long as technology and knowledge can still confer benefits and can represent power and influence, and as long as nations will have to seek alternatives between acquiescence to disconcerting foreign conduct and going to war, the answer to these questions is likely to be a resounding "yes." However, there remains the major issue of implementation. If we are to continue with an export control regime, how can it be structured in a way that it is equitable to firms and effective?

A Call for a New Approach

It is no longer possible today to fully control all exports with conventional means. The undertaking proves to be simply too costly and too complicated. The criteria applied up to now to the licensing process are no longer based on reality. The potential for slipping through the meshes of the law is enormous. The solution of the problem cannot be the development of a still-higher degree of legal precision.

Governments have already made progress in reducing the burden export controls impose on businesses. In the United States, for example, the strategy of building higher fences around fewer products resulted in a drop of license applications from 125,000 in 1988 to 25,000 5 years later (Czinkota, Ronkainen, and Moffett 1996). Improved coordination between government agencies, the automation of license issuance, and the streamlining of license processing have reduced waiting times substantially. However, the danger of disparate export controls between nations raises the specter of a renewed growth in the control burden on corporations.

There must be a common foundation for export controls subscribed to by the key trading nations in order to galvanize support for such controls. This foundation must rest on three pillars. The first one is the acknowledgement of the fact that exports are useful and are to be encouraged. They contribute to economic welfare and enable companies to compete successfully. They offer choices to the world marketplace and important cost spreading opportunities to producers. It is through the existence of exports that the development of some products and technologies becomes possible at all. For example, many high-technology products and even weapons systems could not be developed and produced were it not for the burden sharing and fixed costs allocation effects achieved through exports. In today's competitive climate, companies must be able to recoup their investment in research and development quickly. Aggressive participation in the global market therefore becomes a requirement for survival. In consequence, exports, particularly from the United States, should no longer be considered a privilege, but a right of companies. There should be, in principle, no more need for export approval, but only for export encouragement.

The second major pillar is the recognition that government interference in trade through exports controls should be minimized. If one considers that 15 nations have joined together to form the EU in order to achieve reductions in transaction costs and that the United States has joined with Canada and Mexico to accomplish the same, it would seem unwise and counterproductive to simultaneously attempt the development of individual government regulatory systems that substantially increase these transaction costs. Any licensing system should therefore be unobtrusive, concentrated in its focus, and exert a low burden on business transactions. This conclusion is reinforced by the fact that the gigantic export control machinery put in place by governments only rejects a minuscule amount of license applications. In Germany, for example, during 1993 only 369 of more than 42,000 applications were rejected, a paltry 0.9 percent (Dichtl

1994). In the United States in 1993, of a total of about 25,000 applications only 498 or less than 2 percent were rejected by the 380-person strong Bureau of Export Administration (Bureau 1994). These low numbers appear to indicate that industry is well in tune with export regulations and self-policing in its license applications.

The third pillar of an export control regime must be the achievement of reasonable *equality in competition*. Unless governments, companies, and also the targets of export controls know that the implementation of export control regimes will not materially affect the competitive position of companies, there will be strong temptation to circumvent export controls. Understanding this need for equality in competition must also lead to a clear understanding that export controls are not an inexpensive means of political action. Export controls may not be on budget, but they are not cost free. They impose a significant national security or foreign policy tax on a narrow sector of the economy. Therefore, in using this tool, policy makers must carefully weigh and balance governmental objectives and economic repercussions. Such balancing would be greatly assisted by a requirement that any export controls be accompanied by burden sharing actions on the part of government. Examples are compensation payments or increased export promotion efforts to permissible destinations.

Based on the foundation erected by these three pillars, a new export control regime can then emerge. In spite of the desire by some to eliminate the distinction between national security and foreign policy controls (Administration 1994), the differentiation needs to be maintained. National security controls should be confined to nuclear weapons and highest technology. Such national security controls will only concern a few products, producers, and destinations. For those products and technology, high fences will have to be built and continuously monitored. Given the very limited number of players to be considered, and the importance of the issue, the high-performance maintenance of such a system is imperative.

The use of foreign policy controls must shift from a strategic to a tactical level. No longer will they necessarily be the outgrowth of large-scale and long-range planning to ensure global security. Rather, these controls will need to mainly focus on regional security issues that may change significantly in relatively short periods of time. Therefore, these types of export controls will be, with increasing frequency, subject to crisis management. Doing so requires the ability of governments to rapidly recast the definition of dual use products. It also requires swift and sudden implementation. As has been shown, "economic coercion" works best if applied with surgical authority and speed (Hufbauer and Schott 1983). To cause major disruption, damage, or delay, such export controls will need to be executed decisively and communicated to the business community speedily. Such controls should also be accompanied by as much additional economic muscle as the controlling country can muster. For example, it should not be unreasonable to consider whether tough export controls should be accompanied by simultaneous domestic market access restrictions through import controls. Furthermore, such controls could well be reinforced by going beyond the traditional confines of trade and including also the financial dimensions of business linkages. Such linkages should not only include the domestic financial community but also international ones such as the International Monetary Fund, the World Bank, or the interregional banks. Such an imposition of controls with lightening speed would create disruptions and the occasional hardship for business. However, the trade-off benefit for firms would be the improved predictability and stability of business relationships in general and the reduction in the regulatory burden due to licensing simplification.

For the export of services, the approach to controls must be reconsidered. First, the value of services transfers must be captured better. For example, in the case of software exports, the value should not be determined by the cost of the disk and the manual, but rather by the content of the disk. Second, for services, controls cannot be exercised at the point of international transfer but need to concentrate on the knowledge source. It is here where an evaluation of the importance of the export and the occasional restriction will be most effective.

On the domestic side, whenever export controls are required, their implementation must be effective. Such effectiveness requires screening and, when necessary, punishment. Any screening mechanism must be encompassing. Typically, the large-scale shippers of products know the regulations and abide by them. While there is a need for information, the risk to national policy posed by these firms is relatively low. The circumvention danger emanates to a much greater degree from the occasional, opportunistic exporter. An analogy might be the air space of Washington, DC. The large jets that file a flight plan for the National Airport need to be monitored. But it is the Cessna without a flight plan and with the noisy engine turned off that crash lands on White House grounds!

Mandatory electronic filing of shipper's export declarations could well make a key difference here. It would allow the comprehensive screening of source, product, and destination information without undue bureaucratic delays. It would permit such screening in a timely manner, before the product has left the country. And it would overcome some of the problems posed by low value shipments. Clearly an exporter determined to violate the law would not list "medium range ballistic missiles to Iraq" on a declaration. However, a comprehensive screening system could discover unusual patterns and shipments more easily than the current process, laying the groundwork for further follow-up investigations.

The punishment aspects of a system that respects the right to export must be severe. Once governmental intervention is triggered by suspicious facts, and purposeful violations are verified, punishment needs to be draconian. Accompanied by major rewards for whistle-blowers, it would have a major dampening effect on the desire to circumvent the rare implementation of export controls.

On the international side, effectiveness requires multilateral collaboration. While such collaboration is essential for national security control issues, it also greatly enhances the effectiveness of foreign policy controls. In consequence, there is a renewed need for multilateral deliberations on a case-by-case basis when the invocation of export controls is necessary. The fact that different nations may have different interests may temper the raising of issues, but certainly does not ameliorate the need for a consensus building new forum. In building such a new organization, the shifts in international economic activity that have taken place since the 1950s need to be understood, accepted, and taken advantage of by policy makers. Hegemonic dominance must be replaced by collaborative partnership. The development of a more broadly based COCOM successor organization must become an international priority.

On the part of the United States, the approach to such a new organization must be driven by a new outlook. During COCOM days, industry was chiefly seen as an adversary, and rarely, if ever consulted. At the same time, other governments virtually included their firms in the discussions at the conference table. It should be recognized that industry has enough at stake to be asked to actively participate in formulating the structure, goals, and processes of a new multilateral organization. If policy makers are not sufficiently enlightened to reach out, firms with international interests must take the first step in advocating the formation of a multilateral body and in demanding continuous corporate involvement.

At the same time, however, multilateral consensus should not be the only criterion for judging the necessity for export controls. The United States should hold itself to highest ethical standards rather than to the lowest common denominator. This means that on occasion, export controls will be implemented in a less than multilateral fashion. It also means that export controls will have to be expanded and inward oriented. For example, domestic export controls should also be designed to keep others abroad secure from items such as dangerous waste, dangerous products, or insufficiently researched chemicals or pharmaceuticals.

Overall, some of the obituaries written about export controls have been premature. These controls are here to stay. They represent an important arrow in the quiver of national instruments to protect national and global security. As such, export controls represent an acceptable deviation from the otherwise strong encouragement of free trade. However, the controls themselves must be equitable, purposeful, and effective, and they must become the exception to the rule. A new export control regime should reduce the burden on business while at the same time ensuring that the world will become better and safer for all of us.

References

Bureau of Export Administration (1994) US Department of Commerce, "Administration Releases Export Administration Proposal," February 24, 1.

Bureau of Export Administration, US Department of Commerce (1994) Oral Communication, September 12.

Czinkota, M.R (1984) "International Economic Sanctions and Trade Controls: A Taxonomic Analysis." In *Export Controls: Building Reasonable Commercial Ties with Political Adversaries*, New York: Praeger, 3–17.

Czinkota, M.R (1994) "Global Neighbors: Poor Relations," *Marketing Management*, **2**, 46–52. (See chapter 3.)

Czinkota, M.R., Ronkainen, I., and Moffett, M., (1996) *International Business*, 4th edn. Fort Worth: Dryden Press.

Davis, L (1993) *Contribution of Exports to U.S. Employment, 1987–1991*, US Department of Commerce, Washington, DC: Government Printing Office.

Dichtl, E (1994) "Defacto Limits of Export Controls: The Need for International Harmonization," Paper presented at the 2nd Annual CiMar Conference, Rio de Janeiro, August.

Doxey, M.P (1980) *Economic Sanctions and International Enforcement*, New York: Oxford University Press, 10.

Frankfurter Allgemeine Zeitung (1993) "Exporteure Ueber Wettbewerbsbedingungen Besorgt," September 8, 17.

Freedenberg, P (1994) Testimony before the Subcommittee on International Finance and Monetary Policy of the Committee on Banking, Housing, and Urban Affairs, United States Senate, Washington, DC., February 3, 2.

Hucko, E.M (1993) *Aussenwirtschaftsrech–Kriegswaffenkontrollrecht, Textsammlung mit Einfuehrung*, 4th edn. Cologne: Bundesanzeiger.

Hufbauer, G.C. and Schott, J.J (1983) *Economic Sanctions in Support of Foreign Policy Goals*, Washington, D.C.: Institute for International Economics.

Krass, A.S (1994) "The Second Nuclear Era: Nuclear Weapons in a Transformed World." In M. Klare and D. Thomas (eds), *World Security: Challenges for a New Century*, 2nd edn. New York: St. Martin's Press, 85–105.

Nixon, R.M., quoted by L.J. Brady (1983) "Trade Policy," *Business Week*, November 21, 23.

Office of Technology Assessment (1979) *Technology and East–West Trade*, Washington, D.C.: U.S. Government Printing Office, 112.

Richardson, D.J (1993) *Sizing Up U.S. Export Disincentives*. Washington, DC.: Institute for International Economics.

Ruehe, V (1994) "U.S. and German Security Partnership of the Future." Speech at the U.S. Military Academy at West Point, May 4, New York, American Council on Germany.

6

A Marketing Perspective of the U.S. International Trade Commission's Antidumping Actions: An Empirical Inquiry

MICHAEL R. CZINKOTA
GEORGETOWN UNIVERSITY

AND

MASAAKI KOTABE
THE UNIVERSITY OF TEXAS AT AUSTIN

Antidumping laws can have a profound effect on both domestic and international firms. These laws were designed to help domestic industries which are injured by unfair competition from abroad due to products being dumped on them. Such dumping refers to the selling of goods overseas at prices lower than those prevailing in the exporter's home market or at a price below the cost of production, or both (Czinkota and Ronkainen 1995). The dumping phenomenon and the concern about it are not new. Already early in this century, the United States and Canada enacted laws to cope with this practice. The Antidumping Duty Act of 1921 and Title VII of the Tariff Act of 1930 form the basis of U.S. antidumping laws. These laws provide for relief to threatened industries in the form of special additional duties that are intended to offset margins of dumping.

   In the United States, antidumping duties are imposed when the U.S. Department of Commerce has determined that imports are being, or are likely to be, sold at less than fair value (LTFV) in the United States and when the U.S. International Trade Commission (ITC) has found that a United States industry is materially injured or threatened with material injury or that the establishment of an industry in the United States is materially retarded by reason of such imports (U.S. International Trade Commission 1994). The Commerce Department and the ITC each conduct separate investigations in making their determinations. Only if both agencies arrive at affirmative findings, can an antidumping action take place.

"A Marketing Perspective of the U.S. International Trade Commission's Antidumping Actions – An Empirical Inquiry," by Michael R. Czinkota and Masaaki Kotabe, *Journal of World Business*, Summer 1997. Reprinted by permission of Jai Press Inc.

The process leading to antidumping duties consists therefore of two stages. The first, directed by the Commerce Department, is designed to investigate costs, market value and unfair discrepancies. The second, conducted by the ITC turns strictly on the injury issue and the relief necessary to remedy the injury. Both stages are narrowly focused on their objectives, and, according to their legislative mandate, preclude even the consideration of broader concepts or concerns such as "comparative advantage" or "consumer impact" (U.S. International Trade Commission 1985).

This article concentrates on the actions undertaken by the U.S. International Trade Commission. It analyzes the activities of the Commission based on the decision outcomes of the cases considered. Areas addressed are the injury concept, the effects of industry structure and type, and the degree to which Commission decisions are proactive or reactive. In addition, the effect of the import source country are investigated, together with the existence of trigger levels of imports.

Firms Affected by Antidumping Actions

Various types of firms are affected by antidumping actions. One group consists of the importing firms that order merchandise from abroad for firm-internal use. Increased intra-firm trade and foreign direct investment may even make some importers synonymous with the foreign producers. A second group of international firms are the domestic distributors of imports. These typically are channel members such as wholesalers and distributors. A third group then consists of domestic producers and marketers of goods which are in competition with the imported merchandise considered to be dumped. A fourth group is constituted by firms abroad which are exporting from their country into the United States. All four of these groups are affected by ITC actions and are often involved in its proceedings.

Antidumping actions by governments are measures which directly affect the pricing strategies of firms and their boundaries. Since antidumping decisions taken by governments can materially change the competitive position of the firm, a better understanding of the decision process of an entity which is a key player in the determination of injury is beneficial for the international firm.

The complexity of the price dimension expands dramatically in the international realm. Several reasons account for that fact. Firms produce and sell in their home market under domestic conditions. International pricing, however, is subject to the volatility of exchange rates. The simple fact that time elapses between the signing of the contract and the delivery of products abroad, may already present a "dumping" risk if exchange rates adjust during that time. While the issue might have been a minor one in times of only small and gradual exchange rate variations, it looms large in an era when, for example, the Mexican Peso can lose 40 percent of its value in a matter of days. Directly affected by such changes are the positioning tactics developed by international marketers, particularly when long-term sourcing contracts have been agreed to. Unless a firm has an understanding of the implications of such fluctuations and is prepared to take appropriate countermeasures or develop contingency plans, carefully planned price-based market entry and penetration measures can go awry.

Irrespective of exchange rate volatility, antidumping actions also affect the pricing options which the international firm can consider. Firms often engage in price discrimination; they charge different prices to different customers for the same product. Private universities charge brilliant students less than average students by providing scholarships (Hunt 1983, p. 135). Special "sale prices" differentiate between times of year or reflect the stock levels of producers. Acceptable and even desirable as such price discrimination has become in a domestic setting, the same discrimination in the international realm meets with government scrutiny. Governments and domestic firms are highly sensitive to international price discrimination, even though buyers may benefit from such actions.

Equally affected may be the entire competitive strategy of the firm. In an era in which the retention and increase of market share plays a major role in the long-term outlook of international corporations, antidumping measures can negate a chosen path. As a result, not only will the activities in the market where such measures have been imposed be affected, but the entire world-wide expansion plan can also be threatened.

Of major concern to international firms is also the growing importance of the so-called "technical track" of trade policy (Finger 1993). It increasingly appears that many companies no longer seek competitive victory in the fields of commerce and trade but in the halls of justice and regulators. They are assisted by governments which are exhibiting extraordinary ingenuity in devising new restrictions to buffer vulnerable industries against competition (Vernon 1992). Antidumping actions are seen as a prime approach used by firms and governments to provide for a competitive advantage which could not be achieved with commercial strategy. For a review perspective of the issue, readers can refer to Baldwin (1985) and Finger (1993).

Some have charged that U.S. antidumping laws have helped in developing a system of "administered protection" which has become a new avenue of industry protection (Cumby and Moran 1994b; Rugman and Anderson 1987). It has been posited that "the most insidious forms of trade protection no longer take the form of raising tariffs. They take the form of trade quotas or trade prohibitions that come at the end of administrative reviews. The largest and most rapidly growing form of administrative review protectionism is antidumping" (Cumby and Moran 1994a, p. 3). Such a strategic use of antidumping provisions for purposes of competitive advantage must be of key interest to the international firm.

The increasing spread of antidumping activities by governments around the world enhances the importance of the issue. For decades, only a few OECD member countries developed and made use of antidumping provisions. Between 1980 and 1989, Australia, the United States, Canada and the European Community initiated 95 percent of the 1,456 antidumping cases reported (U.S. General Accounting Office 1990a, p. 3). More recently, however, a growing number of countries are getting ready to implement antidumping actions. In 1980, ten countries had antidumping laws on the books; by 1994 the number was at 40 and growing (Ritt and Berry 1994). In early 1997 China announced the formulation of antidumping regulations to protect its domestic industries from injury. During 1992 and 1993 alone, more than 70 antidumping cases were filed by developing nations – compared to zero prior to 1988 (*The Economist* 1994).

Furthermore, the passage of the Final Act of the Uruguay Round and the 1995 formation of the Word Trade Organization (WTO) have codified and made available new antidumping regulations to all 125 signatory organizations and governments. Even though this codification provides for some greater degree of transparency, the agreed upon Dispute Settlement Understanding makes it very difficult for the WTO to overturn any dumping decisions by a government. The organization's dispute settlement board can only determine whether a country's authorities have properly established the facts and whether the evaluation of the facts was unbiased and objective. If that is the case, the board cannot overturn a decision even if it would have reached a different conclusion (U.S. International Trade Commission 1995). Given such ongoing latitude for governments to make antidumping determinations, international firms are at greater risk of being caught in the web of this governmental regulation than ever before (Schott 1994).

Research Issues

Despite the statutory role of the ITC as an enforcer of fair market competition, its antidumping actions could be motivated by more political factors as well. Accurate knowledge of the factors determining ITC antidumping actions could not only help U.S. firms materially affected by foreign competition determine when and how to seek protection, it would also give international firms some managerial guidance as to the "political" constraints on viable pricing options for market share objectives and geographic (country-based) price discrimination.

Based on the existing literature on antidumping actions in the United States, the following five issues are raised. Hypotheses are developed and subjected to empirical investigation.

ITC FILINGS AND DECISIONS: STRATEGIC ACTIONS OR SALVAGE OPERATIONS?

It is the mission of the ITC to remedy injury to U.S. industries. This mission has three different components to it as defined by law. First, assistance is to be accorded to an industry that is materially injured. Second, industries which are faced by the threat of material injury are to be protected. Third, non-existing domestic industries are to be given a chance for establishment if their formation is materially retarded by dumped imports. While the last situation is very difficult to ascertain and measure, the first two can be observed and investigated.

Current material injury is most clearly seen when the domestic market share of an industry and the domestic market size itself are declining. For example, in the late 1980s Cementos Mexicanos, S.A. (CEMEX) of Monterrey, Mexico, embarked on a new strategic direction by entering the U.S. market. This largest cement producer in North America established distribution facilities in the Southern United States, extending from Florida to California. Its strategy was successful, and Cemex exports to the United States increased substantially at a time when the U.S. economy, and the construction industry in particular, were experiencing a downturn. To meet the competitive inroad, eight large U.S. cement producers filed an antidumping petition alleging injury by Mexican imports. The ITC ruling that Mexican imports had materially injured the U.S. industry resulted in a 58 percent duty on Cemex' imports (Baron 1995).

In contrast, the threat of injury may well exist even when both market size and the domestic industry's market share are still growing. For example, Wyatt Technology is a firm that sought help from the ITC. The firm produces laser light-scatter instruments. The total U.S. demand for such instruments is estimated at less than 50 units per year, but is increasing rapidly. Wyatt could not afford to get into a head-to-head price war with Japan's larger Otsuka Electronics Co., especially if Otsuka was willing to sell products for less than what it actually cost to make them (Lytle 1990). ITC actions taken in the first instance would merely be reactive, while actions responding to the existence of a future threat would be proactive in nature.

While legislation mandates the ITC to investigate injury in both instances, it would appear possible that due to the greater ease of evaluation, most ITC cases in which positive findings of injury are made focus on those industries in a shrinking domestic market and those losing their market share to imports. If that is the case, the ITC mainly plays the role of a salvage operation. However, if the ITC produces affirmative findings in many instances where the threat is only perceived, i.e. where the industry's market is still stable or growing as is the industry's market share, then the institution takes on more of a strategic, industrial policy role, responsive to firms which cry wolf to keep the foreign competition at bay.

Operationally, the current level of market penetration by imports and the pace at which imports have increased over time are considered two important measures of the competitive strengths of imports over domestic products. For example, the escape clause Article XIX of the General Agreement on Tariffs and Trade specifically refers to "increased quantities" of imports as a trigger factor for countries to suspend GATT obligations (GATT 1947). In GATT practice, an increase in either the absolute volume or the market share of imports serves as an important indicator for the invocations of the escape clause (Sykes 1990). Without an indisputable means of determining whether injury to domestic industry has occurred as a result of dumping, the ITC is likely to use import penetration ratio and import growth rate as surrogate measures of possible injury. Therefore, we present three hypotheses:

Hypothesis 1: Dumping cases will be filed with the ITC not only by industries with declining markets but also by industries with stable or growing markets.

Hypothesis 2: The ITC is more likely to issue positive findings of injury, the higher the import penetration ratio is.

Hypothesis 3: The ITC is more likely to issue positive findings of injury, the faster the import growth rate is.

ITC BENEFICIARIES: CORPORATE BULLIES OR COMPETITIVE UNDERDOGS?

Closely linked to the issue of injury is the question as to who is likely to achieve beneficial ITC decisions. Is it the small, helpless firm under siege, or the industry-leading corporate giant in search of another competitive edge?

Some powerful arguments speak in favor of the large firms with substantial influence in their industry, such as the eight large U.S. cement producers cited earlier. Large firms tend to emphasize the use of non-price strategies and have the wherewithal and the corporate vision to exploit government regulation for their own competitive advantage (White 1983). Even though government is open to all, the interventionist power of oligopolistic firms can successfully induce government to limit imports by introducing quotas, tariffs or trigger prices, irrespective of industry market conditions (Etzioni 1985). Firms that do have special access will have an incentive to exploit it. Developing an antidumping action is also very resource intensive. Within a corporation, accountants and sales personnel need to spend time to gather information of product cost and import activities, while management focuses on developing and guiding the petition. In addition, external resources are required in the form of economic consultants and legal fees, easily requiring the expenditure of $500,000 and above. Therefore, one can argue that only large firms in a leading industry position may be able to muster the wherewithal to file an antidumping action and the clout to see it through successfully.

Alternatively, the argument can also be made that large firms have the resources to focus on a competitive, market-based response. Smaller domestic firms, particularly in atomistic industries may effectively be frozen out from this option and can therefore only seek administrative protection as an effective means of counterattack (Salorio 1993). In conducting an antidumping investigation, the ITC assigns a team of five staff members (the case investigator, an economist, a financial analyst, an industry analyst and an attorney) to work on each case full-time for approximately 20–25 working days. In addition, questionnaires are sent to U.S. producers, importers and sometimes also to purchasers. The Commission also makes field trips, and invites firms to meet with staff. These actions can be seen as important investigative support for a petition. This level of support can encourage small firms in atomistic industries to file for antidumping protection. Even though they may possess little economic power, they can generate interventionist power by forming groups (Etzioni 1985). These groups will then be assisted by a government in favor of the underdog. An example is provided by the filing of the U.S. beekeepers. The members of this industry – many of whom are part-time hobbyists – filed a market disruption case against imports of honey from China, alleging that these imports were increasing rapidly and disrupting the U.S. industry by suppressing prices in the U.S. honey market. After a stinging loss in their administrative filing – the case was rejected due to a huge gap between U.S. production of approximately 200 million pounds and consumption of around 300 million pounds – the beekeepers filed an antidumping petition against Chinese imports with the ITC (Griffith and Phipps 1996). The "small firm" argument is supported by research which was unable to establish that concentrated industries are more likely to gain favorable decisions from the ITC (Finger, Hall, and Nelson 1982; Rehbein and Lenway 1993). To investigate these alternatives, we formulate:

Hypothesis 4a: The ITC is more likely to issue positive findings of injury for industries which are dominated by a few firms, irrespective of market growth rate.

Hypothesis 4b: The ITC is more likely to issue positive findings of injury for atomistic industries if their markets are declining.

DOES THE TYPE OF FILING INFLUENCE THE ITC OUTCOME?

ITC actions are to be based on findings of injury. In this context the question arises whether the overall industry behavior and attitudes have an influence on the outcome of the ITC's decisions. For example, one could surmise that if only one or two firms in an atomistic industry file for antidumping protection, the ITC might not find an assertion of injury to the industry as credible.

If, on the other extreme, all firms of an industry join in such a petition, prima facie evidence would indicate that the industry is suffering. Alternatively, a filing by industry groups or trade associations would also indicate that the pain of injury is widespread. It has been suggested that larger coalitions in antidumping investigations may be interpreted by the ITC commissioners as a signal that greater material injury has taken place (Herander and Pupp 1991).

There is also the question of opposition to a filing. Any antidumping measure will impose a cost on the beneficiary (i.e. customers) of the dumped product, and increase the price of merchandise. As a result, it can be expected that some parties will be opposed to the imposition of surcharges (i.e. penalty duties to be added to the current level of import tariffs on the dumped product upon positive finding by the ITC). Such opposition will be stronger, the higher the existing level of import tariffs. If surcharges are imposed, customers will be penalized doubly by high tariff rates and an additional punitive dumping surcharge. Therefore, if the current import tariff rates are high, the ITC may be reluctant to side with the petitioner.

The next question is how effective such opposition will be. This issue can be analyzed best by differentiating ITC filings into consumer and industrial products. When prices of industrial products are threatened to be increased, opposition is likely to be organized and resourceful, since it benefits from the support of interested firms. However, when consumer product prices are increased, opposition is likely to be much less vocal and strong, due to the mostly widely scattered effects of such increases on the individual, and the resulting decrease in likelihood of organized opposition. The appropriate hypotheses for this investigation are therefore:

Hypothesis 5: Filings by large numbers of firms are more likely to result in positive ITC decisions.

Hypothesis 6: The higher the current import tariff rates, the less likely the ITC is to make positive antidumping decisions.

Hypothesis 7: Consumer goods filings are more likely than industrial product filings to receive positive ITC decisions.

DOES THE COUNTRY OF ORIGIN OF COMPETITION MATTER?

A favorable dumping finding can be driven both by economic and political reasons. Both of these reasons can emerge on a country- or region-specific basis due, for example, to a country's political orientation or economic system. It has been shown that of the European Community's total of 229 antidumping cases for the period 1981–5, 108 or 47 percent focused on centrally planned economies (Hirsch 1988). Other researchers claim that the increased emergence of antidumping cases in Europe which oppose producers in the Far East should be viewed as the latest attempt by the Europeans to solve what is perceived as "The Japan Problem" (Norall 1986), since many of the claims made do not have demonstrable validity (Hindley 1988).

In the ITC, a similar bias might be at work. On the political front, Japan has had increasingly acrimonious relations with the United States since the 1970s and 80s. Critics have decried the economic dangers that Japan poses to world trade and have accused her of striving for world dominance. Highly public accusations ricochet across the Pacific, many going far beyond economic analysis, pandering to fear (Czinkota and Kotabe 1992). It could be possible that this political perception of danger and injury influences ITC decisions.

On the economic side, Japan could be a preferred target as well. Real dumping is closely interconnected with a lack of access to the market of the "dumper". Dumping may only become possible, if a sheltered domestic market allows the firm to charge high prices at home in order to provide it sufficient subsidy for low prices abroad. Without a protected domestic market, a dumping firm will find its home market invaded by lower priced foreign products. As Japan has been accused of maintaining highly restricted market access at home, again the prima facie evidence of unfair pricing may be easier to rationalize. Since Japanese firms have invested widely across Asia, such rationalization can also be expanded to other Asian nations as well. To test for such bias, the following hypothesis is formulated:

Hypothesis 8: The ITC is more likely to issue positive findings of injury for industries where Japan and/or Asian Tigers are accused of dumping than otherwise.

DOES THE PRE-PETITION PROCESS AFFECT TRADE FLOWS?

It could be argued that ITC actions will always be too late, since trade flows will have already adjusted by the time the decision is made. It has been postulated that the mere filing of a petition can be beneficial for the petitioner. Exporters may price more cautiously or otherwise be less aggressive, uncertainty may be created in the minds of domestic users of imports, and prices may even register a small but perceptible uptick (Salorio 1993).

Perhaps the same could be said for the pre-petition filing stage. Typically, antidumping petitions do not happen overnight. Allies are sought, alternatives are explored, and documentation must be collected before such a filing takes place. Many trading partners already know the heavy burden that investigations can place on respondents. Antidumping investigations commonly involve requests that foreign exporters and domestic importers fill out detailed questionnaires, which can be as long as 200 pages. Questionnaires must be completed, translated as necessary, and returned to the investigation authority within about 35 days (U.S. General Accounting Office 1990b, p. 16). For example, the recent steel cases against Japan are said to have cost Japanese steelmakers more than 120 million dollars in personnel expenses and attorneys' fees (Matsumoto 1993). These requirements are likely to be a key deterrent for firms which contemplate dumping. Therefore, a long pre-petition process may discourage foreign exporters and domestic importers from continuing their dumping practices. As a result, the ITC eventually may not need to issue positive injury findings.

To investigate whether such a pre-filing effect exists, the following hypothesis is developed:

Hypothesis 9: A longer pre-petition process is likely to result in negative ITC decisions.

Data

The data for this study were gathered through a systematic and comprehensive review of the original ITC case and investigation ledgers (U.S. ITC Collection 1980–1992). The time period covered was from January 1980 through March 1992. For this period, every final antidumping case decided by the ITC was scrutinized.

Several reasons accounted for this choice of time frame. First was the restructuring of the anti-dumping process in the United States. In late 1979, the U.S. began to adapt the new GATT Antidumping Code which had been enshrined in the Trade Agreements Act of 1979. Concurrently, the investigation activity regarding the less than fair value determination had shifted from the U.S. Treasury to the U.S. Department of Commerce. In addition, the 12 year period captured the holding of office by a Republican Administration. Since political orientation may affect the administration of trade remedy laws, the time period chosen provides for relative stability on this dimension.

Only those cases which underwent a full ITC review were included. As a result, all the cases which were withdrawn before an investigation was initiated and those where the investigation was suspended were not included in this analysis. During the period we investigated, 22 percent of cases were terminated or suspended (U.S. International Trade Commission 1995). Reasons for such actions are negligible imports (where imports from the country subject to investigation account for less than 3 percent of the volume of all such merchandise imported into the United States in the most recent 12 month period preceding the filing of the petition); insufficient information provided by the petitioner; agreement between the U.S. and a foreign government. The rationale for this decision lay in the fact that for all of these cases no information beyond the ITC case number was available.

Table 6.1 Variables

Variable	Operational definition	Statistics	
		Mean	Std. dev.
ITC decision	Positive (1), Negative (0)	63.3% of the cases for positive findings	
Market growth rate[a]	Declining (1), Stable (2), Growing (3)	1.83	0.71
Import penetration ratio	Import value/U.S. consumption value (%)	21.1	16.2
Import growth rate	(Import penetration ratio$_t$ − import penetration ratio$_{t-1}$) /Import penetration ratio$_{t-1}$, where t = current year (%)	39.9	188.0
Industry concentration	Monopolistic (1), Oligopolistic (2), Atomistic (3)	2.43	0.57
Number of petitioners	Actual number	2.94	2.67
Import tariff rate	Actual rate in fraction (%)	5.72	4.27
Type of product	Consumer goods (1), Industrial goods (0)	89.4% consumer goods	
Target country	Japan or Asian Tigers (1), Other (0)	32.3% Japan or Tigers	
Pre-petition process	Number of days from filing a petition to an ITC action	283.2	125.8

Note: The International Trade Commission collects antidumping data based on the above operational definition of the variables, except for type of product and target country which were aggregated by the authors from more detailed information.
[a] Market growth rate was measured based on the change in U.S. apparent consumption (total domestic shipments − exports + imports) over the past 5 year period.

Apart from these deletions, all ITC antidumping decisions during this time period were analyzed. The analysis included all cases which dealt with the same industry or even product, but which the commission had separated by country. The data were collected from the investigative reports compiled by ITC staff contained in the original ITC reports as published. With help of these reports, the following information (by volume and value) was either found or calculated for the 5 years preceding the case: Import quantity, U.S. apparent consumption, and import penetration. In addition, information was gathered on the industry, the overall market, the competition, and the ITC process and decision.

As with any empirical data set, not all values were easily ascertainable. Some data had been suppressed in order to protect proprietary information, other data had not been collected for every case, and some data apparently were simply not available to ITC staff during the time available for research. In such instances, additional efforts were made to locate the information from outside sources, such as governmental economic data or other investigative proceedings.

Overall, 310 cases were analyzed. Yet, due to missing values which could not be obtained, 32 cases were deleted from further analysis. Therefore, our analyses were based on a sample size of 278 cases. The variables used for this study, their operationalization and their summary statistics are presented in table 6.1.

Table 6.2 Domestic market size and antidumping filings

	Domestic market size			
	Declining	Stable	Growing	Total
No. of ITC filings	97 (34.9%)	123 (44.2%)	58(20.9%)	278

Note: For H_0:p (declining) = 1, Z = 12.2, p < 0.0001.

Table 6.3 Logit model for ITC antidumping action

Variable	Estimate	Standard error	χ^2	p value
Intercept	−2.84	1.45	3.59	0.06
Import penetration ratio	1.52	0.80	3.59	0.06
Import growth rate	0.002	0.001	1.57	0.21
Industry concentration	1.16	0.60	3.72	0.05
Market growth rate	1.51	0.78	3.74	0.05
Industry concentration × Market growth rate	−0.63	0.31	4.01	0.04
Number of petitioners	−0.05	0.06	0.67	0.41
Import tariff rate	−1.23	3.57	0.12	0.73
Type of product (consumer = 1, industrial = 0)	−1.05	0.54	3.75	0.05
Target country (Japan or Asian Tigers = 1, others = 0)	−0.66	0.30	5.03	0.02
Pre-petition process	−0.001	0.001	1.17	0.28

χ^2 likelihood ratio = 329.35, d.f. = 233, p < 0.0000
$R = \chi^2/(n + \chi^2)$ = 54.2%

Note: For H4a and H4b, to show how industry concentration ratio (IC) and market growth rate (MG) jointly affect the ITC decision ($D = \log_e [p/(1-p)]$), partial derivatives of the logit equation are taken with respect to IC and MG respectively.

$\delta D/\delta MG = 1.51 - 0.63*IC > 0$ if $IC < 2.4$
$\delta D/\delta IC = 1.16 - 0.63*MG > 0$ if $MG < 1.8$

In other words, the first derivative implies that the impact of market growth rate on the ITC decision is boosted proportionately more, the more concentrated the industry is. If the industry is atomistic ($IC = 3$), the impact of market growth rate on the probability of ITC decision in favor of industry becomes negative (i.e. the ITC is less likely to decide in favor of dumping injury).

Similarly, the second derivative indicates that the impact of industry concentration (IC) on the probability of ITC decision in favor of industry increases proportionately more if the market growth is rated either stable or declining (MG = 2). In other words, if the market is stable or in a decline stage and the industry is of atomistic nature, the ITC tends to decide in favor of dumping injury.

Analysis and Results

The first hypothesis was examined by testing the proportional distribution of cases. For the rest of the hypotheses (2–9), a logit model (SAS package on the mainframe computer) was employed to account for the likelihood of the ITC issuing positive findings of dumping injury. The results of these analyses are presented in tables 6.2 and 6.3, respectively. In order to check for longitudinal variations, we conducted a split half analysis of the data and compared the time periods 1980–6 and 1986–92. All the signs remained the same and no observable differences emerged. For the sake of parsimoniousness, we therefore combined the data over the entire time period.

HYPOTHESIS 1

This hypothesis addressed whether or not the ITC plays a dual role both as a defender of declining industries against the dumping of foreign marketers and as a protector of firms in stable and/or growth industries that are beginning to feel a threat from foreign competition due to dumping. Table 6.2 shows that in only 97 cases, or some 35 percent, of the 278 antidumping cases decided by the ITC, were firms in declining industries which experienced a loss in domestic sales. A proportion test with $H_0:p$(declining) = 1 (i.e. 100 percent) yielded a Z score of 12.2, with $p < 0.0001$. Thus H_0 is rejected since, obviously, dumping cases are filed with the ITC not only by industries in declining markets but also by those in stable or growing markets. Therefore, this hypothesis is supported.

HYPOTHESES 2–9

Our interest lies in assessing the impact of the predictor variables on the likelihood (probability) that the ITC will decide in favor of dumping injury findings. Thus, in our logit model, the criterion variable is the logarithm of the odds for positive findings by the ITC. The predictor variables are import penetration ratio, import growth rate, industry concentration ratio, market growth rate, an interaction term between market growth rate and industry concentration, number of petitioners, import tariff rate, type of product, target country, and pre-petition process.

Initially, there was some concern about multicollinearity between industry concentration and number of petitioners. In general, the more concentrated the industry, the smaller the number of companies in the industry. However, there is no *a priori* reason that more companies will file an antidumping charge with the ITC, the more atomistic industry it is. As suspected, these two predictor variables are somewhat correlated ($r = 0.33, p < 0.05$). Therefore, a preliminary logit model was run both with and without the number of petitioners. The results were essentially identical in both model specifications. Therefore, the full logit model is presented in table 6.3. The model is highly significant ($p < 0.0001$) and accounts for 54.2 percent of the variation in the probability of the ITC finding dumping injury in an industry's favor.

Hypothesis 2 and Hypothesis 3

These hypotheses examine whether or not the import penetration ratio and import growth rate are used by the ITC as two major operational indicators of the severity of dumping. As shown in table 6.3, as expected, both coefficients have a positive sign. However, while the import penetration ratio is found to have a modest level of positive impact on the likelihood of ITC finding dumping injury ($p < 0.10$), import growth rate does not appear to have any significant impact. Obviously, a condition of high import penetration ratio, rather than its rate of change over time, is a better predictor of favorable ITC actions. Therefore, the findings give modest support to hypothesis 2, but reject Hypothesis 3.

Hypothesis 4a and Hypothesis 4b

These hypotheses addressed the political issue of whether firms could influence the ITC decision-making process. Dominant firms in oligopolistic or monopolistic industry are expected to intervene in and influence the ITC process to increase the odds of obtaining a dumping injury decision in the industry's favor. Industry concentration, market growth rate, and their interaction term are all found to be significant ($p < 0.05$). As shown in the footnote to table 6.3, the findings indicate that the impact of the market growth rate on the probability of an ITC decision in favor of dumping injury is higher, the more concentrated the industry is. This means that in antidumping investigations conducted under conditions of growing markets, positive findings mainly occur if the complaining industry is concentrated in the hands of a few large firms. The findings also support the classic role of the ITC in that if the market is in a decline stage and the industry is atomistic in nature, the ITC tends to decide in favor of dumping injury. Therefore, both hypotheses 4a and 4b are supported.

Hypotheses 5-7

These three hypotheses dealt with the impact that the number of companies filing a dumping charge, the current import tariff rates, and the type of product have on the ITC decision outcome. The number of petitioners was expected to have a positive impact on the ITC's injury finding as it represents political clout that may encourage the ITC to make a decision in favor of the industry. However, insignificant results (with an opposite coefficient sign than expected; $p > 0.40$) fail to support hypothesis 5. Similarly, while the import tariff rate has a negative sign as expected, it is not at all significant ($p > 0.70$), therefore rejecting hypothesis 6.

With regards to the type of product in hypothesis 7, consumer products were expected to be more likely to receive a favorable ITC decision than industrial products. However, contrary to our expectation, results show that industrial products are significantly more likely to receive a favorable ITC decision than consumer products ($p < 0.05$). Therefore, no support is found for hypothesis 7.

Hypothesis 8

Here, we expected that Japan and the Asian Tigers were more likely to be the target of U.S. dumping charges. However, the results are surprisingly the opposite of the hypothesis. That is, the ITC was statistically more likely to decide in favor of the petitioners' dumping charges ($p < 0.05$) when countries other than Japan and the Asian Tigers were under dumping investigation

Hypothesis 9

This hypothesis addressed the salutary effect that a lengthy and burdensome pre-petition process may have on dumping in the United States. The lengthier the process is, the more costly it is to international marketers and the more likely it deters their future engagement in dumping. Therefore, our expectation was that once an ITC petition was envisioned, international marketers would correct their dumping behavior, thus requiring fewer ITC dumping injury decisions. However, the results fail to support hypothesis 9 ($p > 0.20$).

Conclusions and Implications

ITC decisions on antidumping charges seem to be systematically affected by a few key situational variables. The most salient industry factors are industry concentration ratio and market growth rate. The findings unequivocally suggest that the ITC tends to support with an antidumping charge not only those atomistic (fragmented) industries with a declining market but also more concentrated industries with a stable or even growing market. Irrespective of the number of petitioners, firms from oligopolistic industries appear to have enough market power to exploit government regulations by mustering ITC support for their dumping accusation against international marketers even if domestic markets are growing. This finding is consistent with White's (1983) market power thesis and indicates that for large U.S. firms antidumping regulations may be useful as a strategic competitive tool. If commercial adversaries are very successful and come from abroad, the seeking of firm-external strategic shelter through administrative action may well represent an alternative to the development of a firm-internal response.

Smaller firms in more atomistic industries are much less likely to be successful with such a strategy, except in instances when markets are already shrinking. The ITC therefore appears to fulfill a dual role: 1) for large firms it may be the source of an arrow in the quiver of the tools of competition; 2) for smaller firms it is mainly the provider of shelter. In order to make better use of ITC actions, both types of firms will need to concentrate increased resources in the market research area both at home and abroad, in order to learn early on about actual and even potential import penetration and to prepare for precautionary analytical activities.

From the international firm's point of view, the ITC's dual role raises a cause for concern about the "politicization" of international competition. Many international firms are attracted to growth markets in the United States. However, if these growth markets are dominated by a few large companies, successful international firms are likely to be threatened by potential dumping charges that may not only tarnish their corporate reputation in the U.S. market, but may also prove to be costly to the firms and their customers, as a positive ITC finding and a subsequently imposed dumping surcharge drives up prices. In consequence, international firms that are entering such growth markets in concentrated industries need to be especially careful in designing their pricing and market penetration strategies. The issue will be of particular importance in growth markets characterized by high technology and high levels of research and development expenditures. In light of the growing need of industries which develop new products faced with uncertain demand to employ forward pricing methods, disputes about cost allocation and market penetration strategies are likely to be increasingly affected by the specter of antidumping proceedings.

Import penetration ratio, which measures the current market share held by imports, also appears to affect ITC decisions modestly. As in traditional antitrust litigation, the market share held by imports is obviously an easy and ready-to-use quantitative measure available to determine the vulnerability of domestic industry to imports. Neither import growth rate nor import tariff rate seems to have any measurable value as the ITC's decision criteria. In other words, it is the level of current import penetration ratio, rather than its change over time or the current tariff protection, that has some bearing on ITC decisions. However, in light of the ITC's definition of negligible imports as 3 percent or below in a 12 month period, firms importing from abroad may be able to use this limitation to carry out selective and limited market tests, without running the risk of incurring the wrath of the ITC.

An empirical question remains as to the levels of import penetration ratio at which the ITC tends to be called to action and to issue positive dumping findings. It is a futile attempt to simply pinpoint a "trigger" level of import penetration ratio, since other factors are additional or even dominant causes. It suffices to report that the mean import penetration ratio for cases investigated by the ITC was 14 percent. For those cases in which the ITC issued positive findings, the import penetration ratio exceeded 20 percent. At least, international firms have to be aware of the possibility of governmental administrative action and subsequent market disruption at these levels of import penetration. Both firms abroad and the domestic firms sourcing imports, should be cognizant of the potential impact of an import penetration threshold, and should therefore see their activities not just in the isolation of their transactions, but within the context of total industry trade sensitivity.

Contrary to our expectation, the ITC has a higher probability of issuing positive findings for industrial goods cases than for consumer goods cases. We initially speculated that when prices of industrial products were threatened to be increased, opposition would be more likely to be organized by the industry being affected than by consumers facing higher prices. Obviously, different forces seem to be at work.

Two plausible alternative explanations can be offered. First, the ITC may recognize that industrial products being affected by dumping, both actual and forecasted, may have a broader impact on U.S. industry than their industry category suggests, particularly when those products are used by a number of different industries. This is primarily the case because technology is blurring the boundaries between industries previously considered unrelated (Dussauge, Hart, and Ramanantsoa 1992; Ela and Irwin 1983). This technological convergence leads to previously unrelated industries finding themselves equally affected by ITC decisions (Capon and Glazer 1987; Kodama 1992). For example, measures taken against copper imports may quickly affect the automotive industry. Second, it could be that consumer welfare considerations do play a role after all. Dumping essentially lowers prices to the consumer. While dumping may affect the domestic industry negatively, it remains beneficial to consumers as long as international firms accused of dumping would not charge monopoly prices once domestic competition is driven out (Kreinin 1987). In spite of their mandate, ITC commissioners may be somewhat reluctant to issue positive findings in support of an industry due to implicit consideration of consumer welfare. Overall, the ITC appears to support industrial goods industries with antidumping findings more than consumer goods industries.

Another unexpected finding is that Japan and the Asian Tigers are not necessarily the targets of U.S. protectionistic sentiment expressed through the ITC. First, only about a third of the dumping filings with the ITC are targeted at Japan and/or the Asian Tigers. Second, the ITC is less likely to issue positive findings against imports from these Asian countries than from other countries (most of which are European). Conceivably, it is because of the very protectionistic sentiment widely recognized throughout the world that the ITC takes a cautious approach to examining dumping charges against the Asian countries and may even be somewhat reluctant to press dumping charges against them unless the preponderance of evidence of dumping injury to domestic industry is ascertained. Other than has been claimed to take place in Europe, the U.S. administrative antidumping decision process for cases involving Japan and the Asian Tigers appears to be quite fair and non-prejudicial judging by the activities of the ITC. This finding should give heart to marketers abroad and may even lead to their preference of the U.S. market over other – particularly European – market opportunities.

Despite the expectation that the onerousness of the pre-petition process required of international firms accused of dumping could both deter them from engaging in dumping and discourage them from continuing their dumping practices in case they are currently dumping, such an effect does not seem to be present. Importing firms seem to continue their pricing behavior in spite of the initiation of an antidumping petition. The clear implication of that fact is that the threat value of the invocation of antidumping procedures seems to be limited. Any company or industry which intends to go that route must be aware of the need to see the process through to the end if relief is to be accomplished.

In sum, all of our hypotheses were derived from common perceptions widely discussed in the literature. While we did not necessarily fully subscribe to all the statements made in the literature, we used this existing and reported stock of knowledge to generate our hypotheses. Since our study rigorously tested the empirical outcome of ITC antidumping actions, a substantial number of surprises and deviations from commonly held perceptions could be expected and, indeed, resulted here.

Some Closing Comments

This research investigated the links between the ITC decision process and outcome with market and industry factors, and has drawn several important conclusions for international marketers. However, the results must be viewed with proper caution. The data set analyzed here has only dealt with ITC decisions which have actually run their full course. It may well be worth investigating those cases which have been abandoned, withdrawn or terminated. Though there are not too many data for these cases, even anecdotal research focusing on these issues could yield interesting findings.

This research was confined to industries which are actually in existence in the United States. If one were able to develop some useful measurement criteria, it might be interesting to investigate how the ITC encourages the establishment of future industries – which, after all, is part of its congressionally defined mission.

This research has covered a 12 year time period and therefore provides a reasonably longitudinal perspective of the ITC decision process. Nevertheless, it must be kept in mind that the process can change over time. Changes in Administration can result in new perspectives regarding international trade. A change in commissioners can gradually introduce new interpretations of evidence and therefore result in new voting patterns. Alterations in the overall U.S. trade position or concern about specific trade relations, e.g. persistent Japanese trade surpluses with the United States, may, over time, affect the ITC process and decisions.

One could also investigate the decision process which leads up to an industry's decision to file an antidumping complaint. It may well be that firm-internal strategic considerations influence this process substantially. For example, established supplier relationships or planned market entry abroad may well sway a firm's participation in a petition. Understanding these linkages is important if one is to have a comprehensive picture of the administrative and corporate strategic process.

Additional research can sharpen the insights presented here. However this work has established that the ITC decision process has two major implications for international firms. For those firms exposed to competition from abroad, it has been clarified how the use of the International Trade Commission can and cannot help them with their domestic market position. For those firms exercising the competition, this clarification has shed light on an important dimension of their marketing strategy. In consequence, both types of firms have been strengthened in their capability for international competitiveness.

References

Baldwin, Robert E (1985) "The Political Economy of Protectionism," *The Political Economy of U.S. Import Policy*, Cambridge, MA: MIT Press

Baron, David P. (1995) "Integrated Strategy: Market and Nonmarket Components," *California Management Review*, **37** (January), 47–65.

Capon, Noel and Rashi Glazer (1987) "Marketing and Technology: A Strategic Coalignment," *Journal of Marketing*, **51** (July), 1–14.

Cumby, Robert E. and Theodore H. Moran (1994a) "Testing Models of the Trade Policy Process: The Case of Anti-dumping in the Uruguay Round," mimeo, Washington, D.C., Georgetown University School of Foreign Service, (Fall).

Cumby, Robert E. and Theodore H. Moran (1994b) "Antidumping as a Current Policy Issue," *World Business Policy Brief*, Washington DC., Georgetown University Center for International Business Education and Research, (December).

Czinkota, Michael R. and Ilkka Ronkainen (1995) *International Marketing*, 4th ed., Fort Worth, TX: Dryden Press, 309.

Czinkota, Michael R. and Masaaki Kotabe (1992), "America's New World Trade Order," *Marketing Management*, **1** (3), 49–56. (See chapter 2.)

Dussauge, Pierre, Stuart Hart, and Bernard Ramanantsoa (1992) *Strategic Technology Management*. John Wiley & Sons.

The Economist (1994) "A Borderline Case," December 17, 73.

Ela, John D. and Manley R. Irwin (1983) "Technology Changes Market Boundaries," *Industrial Marketing Management*, **12** (July), 153–6.

Etzioni, Amitai (1985) "The Political Economy of Imperfect Competition," *Journal of Public Policy*, **5** (2), 169–86.

Finger, Michael J. (ed.) (1993) *Antidumping: How it Works and Who Gets Hurt*, Ann Arbor: University of Michigan Press.

Finger, Michael J., H.K. Hall and D.R. Nelson (1982) "The Political Economy of Administered Protection," *American Economic Review*, **72** (3), 452–66.

GATT (1947) General Agreement on Tariffs and Trade, Geneva.

Griffith, Spencer S. and Ronald P. Phipps (1996), "Honey Talks Yield Sweet Results; Import Duties on Chinese Honey," *China Business Review*, **23** (January), 48–52.

Herander M.G. and R.L. Pupp (1991) "Firm Participation in Steel Industry Lobbying," *Economic Inquiry*, **29** (January), 134–47.

Hindley, Brian (1988) "Dumping and the Far East Trade of the European Community," *The World Economy*, **11** (December), 445–63.

Hirsch, Seev (1988) "Anti-Dumping Actions in Brussels and East–West Trade," *The World Economy*, **11** (December), 465–84.

Hunt, Shelby D. (1983) *Marketing Theory: The Philosophy of Marketing Science*. Homewood, IL: Richard D. Irwin.

Kodama, Fumio (1992) "Technology Fusion and the New R & D," *Harvard Business Review*, **70** (July–August), 70–78.

Kreinin, Mordechai E. (1987) *International Economics: A Policy Approach*, 5th ed., Orlando, FL: Harcourt Brace Jovanovich.

Lytle, David (1990) "Keeping the Playing Field Level: United States International Trade Commission Rules in Favor of Wyatt Technology in Unfair Pricing Dispute with Otsuka Electronics Co.; The Government Factor," *Photonics Spectra*, October, 18.

Matsumoto, Hiroshi (1993) "Legal Harassment of Foreign Firms: The Case of the U.S. Steel Industry," *Pacific Basin Quarterly*, Fall.

Norall, Christopher (1986) "New Trends in Anti-dumping Practice in Brussels", *The World Economy*, **9**, 1 (March) 97–111.

Rehbein, Kathleen and Stephanie Lenway (1993) "Industry Signals and Political Success: An Analysis of the U.S. International Trade Commission's Escape Clause Investigations," Paper presented at the Annual Conference of the Academy of International Business.

Ritt, Adam and Bryan Berry (1994) "Leave the Lawyers at Home. Let's Talk," *New Steel*, April, 20–25.

Rugman, Alan M. and Andrew Anderson (1987) *Administered Protection In America*, New York: Croom Helm.

Salorio, Eugene (1993) "Strategic Use of Import Protection: Seeking Shelter for Competitive Advantage." In: *Research in Global Strategic Management*, A. Rugman and A. Verbeke (eds), Greenwich, CT: JAI Press, 103–124.

Schott, Jeffrey (1994) *The Uruguay Round: An Assessment*. Washington DC.: Institute for International Economics.

Sykes, Alan O (1990) "GATT Safeguards Reform: The Injury Test." In: *Fair Exchange: Reforming Trade Remedy Laws*, M. Trebilcock and R. York (eds), Toronto, C.D.: Howe Institute, 203–30.

U.S. General Accounting Office (1990a) *International Trade: Use of the GATT Antidumping Code*. Washington DC.: GAO/NSIAD-90-238 FS, (July).

U.S. General Accounting Office (1990b) *International Trade: Comparison of U.S. and Foreign Antidumping Practices*. Washington D.C.: GAO/NSIAD-91-59 (November).

U.S. International Trade Commission (1980–1992) *Collection of Trade Assistance Cases*. U.S. Government Printing Office, Washington, D.C.

U.S. International Trade Commission (1985) *Proceedings before the U.S. International Trade Commission*. Meeting of the commission, June 12.

U.S. International Trade Commission (1994) *The Year in Trade: 1993 Operations of the Trade Agreements Program*. Washington D.C.: U.S. ITC Publication 2769, June.

U.S. International Trade Commission (1995) *The Economic Effects of Antidumping and Countervailing Duty Orders and Suspension Agreements*, Publication 2900, U.S. Government Printing Office, Washington D.C., p. 2–15ff.

Vernon, Raymond (1992) *Ascendancy of the Private Sector in Developing Countries: Trend or Pendulum?* Washington D.C.: International Finance Corporation, (December 10).

White, Alice P (1983) *The Dominant Firm: A Study of Market Power*. Ann Arbor, MI: UMI Research Press.

7

A National Export Assistance Policy for New and Growing Businesses

MICHAEL R. CZINKOTA
GEORGETOWN UNIVERSITY

Exporting is one of many market expansion activities of the firm. As such, exporting is similar to looking for new customers in the next town, the next state, or on the other coast; it differs only in that national borders are crossed, and international accounts and currencies are involved. Yet, these differences make exports special from a policy perspective.

From a macro perspective, exports are special because they can affect currency values and the fiscal and monetary policies of governments, shape public perception of competitiveness, and determine the level of imports a country can afford. Abroad, exports augment the availability and choice of goods and services for individuals, and improve the standard of living and quality of life. On the level of the firm, exports offer the opportunity for economies of scale. By broadening its market reach and serving customers abroad, a firm can produce more and do so more efficiently, which is particularly important if domestic sales are below break-even levels. As a result, the firm may achieve lower costs and higher profits both at home and abroad. Through exporting the firm benefits from market diversification, taking advantage of different growth rates in different markets, and gaining stability by not being overly dependent on any particular market. Exporting also lets the firm learn from the competition, makes it sensitive to different demand structures and cultural dimensions, and proves its ability to survive in a less familiar environment in spite of higher transaction costs. All these lessons can make the firm a stronger competitor at home. Finally, since exporting is only one possible international marketing strategy, it may well lead to the employment of additional strategies such as direct foreign investment, joint ventures, franchising or licensing – all of which contribute to the growth and economic strength of the firm, and, on an aggregate level, to the economic security of a nation.

The Export Competitiveness of New and Growing Businesses

Many see the global market as the exclusive realm of large, multinational corporations. It is commonly explained that almost half of U.S. exports are made by the 100 largest corporations, and that 80 percent of U.S. exports are carried out by only 2,500 firms. Overlooked is the fact that thousands of smaller sized firms have been fueling a U.S. export boom, which has supported the economy in times of limited domestic growth. A large portion of export shipments from the United States are for less than $10,000 and there are more than 100,000 U.S. firms that export at least occasionally.

The reason for this export success of smaller firms lies in the new determinants of competitiveness, as framed by the wishes and needs of the foreign buyers. Other than in the distant past, where price alone was at the forefront, buyers today also expect an excellent product fit, high levels of corporate responsiveness, a substantial service orientation, and high corporate commitment. New and growing firms stack up well on all these dimensions compared to their larger brethren, and may even have a competitive advantage.

Take the issue of product fit. In today's era of niche marketing, where specialization rather than mass production is prized, the customization of operations is often crucial. In a large corporate system, changes are often subject to delays as various layers of management are consulted, costs recalculated, and multiple communication levels exercised. In a smaller operation, procedures can more easily be adapted to the special needs of the customer or to local requirements.

Smaller firms can offer clearer lines of accountability since the decision maker can be more visible and responsive to the customer. During negotiations, or later on, if something does not go according to plan, the customer knows who to contact to fix the problem. Smaller firms are better equipped to handle exceptions. Since international sales situations have high variability, either in terms of the timing or the nature of the sale, a smaller firm can provide a more flexible framework for the decision process. Exceptions can be handled when they occur rather than after waiting for concurrence from other levels of the organization. Smaller firms offer their customers better inward and outward communication linkages, which are direct between the provider of a service or product and its user. The result is a short response time. If a special situation should arise, response can be immediate, direct, and predictable to the customer, providing precisely those competitive ingredients that reduce risk and costs.

Smaller firms also have the most to gain from the experience curve effects of exporting. Research by the Boston Consulting Group has shown that each time cumulative output of a firm doubles, the costs on value added decrease between 20 to 30 percent. Due to the small original base, it is much easier for a new or growing business to double cumulative output and reap the resulting benefits than it is for a large established firm. Most importantly, once a small firm goes international, it usually does so with the full commitment of the owner and top management. The foreign customer therefore knows that this is activity which has management's heart and soul behind it. In today's times where we are moving, on a global level, away from transaction marketing and toward relationship marketing, such a perception may be crucial in providing the winning edge.

Coping with Obstacles

All these advantages do not remove the existing obstacles to international market prosperity. Smaller firms in particular tend to encounter five types of export-related problem areas (Kotabe and Czinkota 1992). One of these concerns logistics – arranging transportation, determining transport rates, handling documentation, obtaining financial information, coordinating distribution, packaging, and obtaining insurance. Another one consists of legal procedures and typically covers government red tape, product liability, licensing, and customs/duty issues. The servicing of exports is a third area, where the firm needs to provide parts availability, repair service, and technical advice. Sales promotion is a fourth area; firms need to cope with advertising, sales effort, and the obtaining of marketing information. The fifth problem area concerns foreign market intelligence, which covers information on the location of markets, trade restrictions, and competition overseas.

These obstacles, both real and perceived, often prevent firms from exporting. Many managers often see only the risks involved in exporting rather than the opportunities that the international market can present. As a result, the United States still under-exports when compared to other nations. U.S. merchandise exports comprise only 7.5 percent of GNP, compared to 24.1 percent for Germany and 23 percent for Canada. On a per capita basis, the United Kingdom exported in 1992 $3,250 for every man, woman, and child. The figure for Japan is $2,660; for the United States, it is only $1,750. Given the plenitude of benefits to be derived from exporting, it therefore seems worth while and necessary to increase the export activities of U.S. firms.

A Perspective on Export Promotion

Even though exports are important, in times of tight budget constraints and competing public priorities, it is important to ask why firms should be enticed into exporting through the use of public funds. Given the motivation of business activity by profit, one could argue that the profit opportunities for exporters should be enough of an incentive to motivate firms to export.

THE EXPORT DEVELOPMENT PROCESS

To explore this issue, it is helpful to understand the export development process within the firm. Typically, firms evolve along different stages to become experienced exporters (Czinkota and Ronkainen 1993). These stages start out with a firm being uninterested in things international. Management frequently will not even fill an unsolicited export order. Should such orders or other international market stimuli continue over time, however, a firm may move to the stage of export awareness, or even export interest. Management will begin to accumulate information about foreign markets and may consider the feasibility of exporting. At the export trial stage, the firm is likely to fill selected export orders, serve few customers, and expand into countries that are geographically close or culturally similar to the home country. At the export evaluation stage, firms consider the impact of exporting on overall corporate activities. If expectations placed in exporting are not met, the firm is likely to discontinue its export efforts and either seek alternative international growth opportunities or restrict itself to the domestic market. If the evaluation is positive, the firm

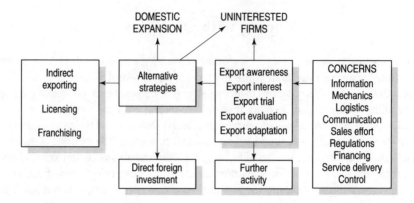

Figure 7.1 The export development process

will, over time, move on to become an export adapter, make frequent shipments to many customers in more countries, and incorporate international considerations into its planning.

In each one of these stages, firms have different concerns. For example, at the awareness level, firms worry mainly about information on foreign markets and customers. At the interest stage, firms become concerned about the mechanics of exporting. During the export try-out, communication, logistics, and the sales effort become key problems. At evaluation time, government regulations and financing take on greater importance. In the adaptation stage, service delivery and control are major issues. Figure 7.1 describes this export development process and summarizes these stages and concerns.

A DIVERGENCE OF PROFIT AND RISK

As a firm moves through these stages, unusual things can happen to both risk and profit. In light of the gradual development of expertise, the many concerns, and a firm's uncertainty with the new environment it is about to enter, management's perception of risk exposure grows. In its previous domestic expansion, the firm has gradually learned about the market, and therefore managed to have its risk decline. In the course of international expansion, the firm now encounters new factors such as currency exchange rates and their vagaries, greater distances, new modes of transportation, new government regulations, new legal and financial systems, new languages, and cultural diversity. As a result, the firm is exposed to increased risk. At the same time, due to the investment needs of the exporting effort, in areas such as information acquisition, market research, and trade financing, the immediate profit performance may deteriorate. Even though international market familiarity and diversification effects are likely to reduce the risk below the previous "domestic only" level, and increase profitability as well, in the short and medium term, managers may face an unusual and perhaps unacceptable situation – rising risk accompanied by decreasing profitability. In light of this reality, and not knowing whether there will be a pot of gold at the end of the rainbow, many executives either do not initiate export activities or discontinue them. A temporary gap in the working of market forces seems to exist. Government export assistance can help firms over this rough patch to the point where profits increase and risk heads downward.

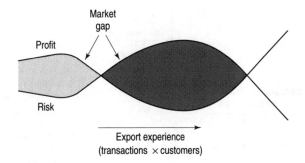

Figure 7.2 Profit and risk during export initiation

Bridging this short-term market gap may well be the key role of export assistance, and the major justification for the involvement of the public sector. Figure 7.2 illustrates this process.

LINKAGES AMONG ASSISTANCE COMPONENTS

If export assistance and promotion are to be rendered, it becomes important to consider how budgets and efforts should be expended in order to be most effective. Figure 7.3 provides a structural perspective of the linkage between export assistance, the firm, the international market and, eventually export performance. The firm is separated into its organizational and its managerial dimensions. Organizational key determinants of business and export success are size, human and financial resources, technology, service and quality orientation, information system, research capabilities, market insights and connections, and the firm's capabilities to manage regulations. The managerial characteristics that research has most closely linked to export success are education, international exposure, expertise, international orientation, and commitment. These corporate dimensions, subject to the opportunities and constraints of the international market environment, determine the degree of the firm's export involvement. This involvement in turn will result in export performance, which can be measured in three different ways. Efficiency refers to the relationship between corporate input employed and the resulting outputs achieved. Typically, efficiency is measured through the proxy of export profitability. Effectiveness refers to relative business success when compared to other competitiors in the market, and is often measured in terms of market share and export sales growth. Competitive position addresses the overall strength of a firm arising from its distinct competencies, management style, and resource deployment. Typical indicators here are the overall quality and competence of a firm's export activities.

Export assistance can aim at the organizational characteristics and capabilities of the firm and try to improve those. It can also work with the managerial characteristics and contribute to their positive change. All this is subject to continued involvement on the part of providers of export assistance with the international market environment, both in terms of learning from as well as shaping the environment. Export assistance will be most effective when it either reduces the risk to the firm or increases its profitability from export operations, particularly when the stage-specific concerns of firms are taken into account. For example, providing information on market potential abroad is likely to decrease the risk (both real and perceived) to the firm. Offering low-cost credit is likely to

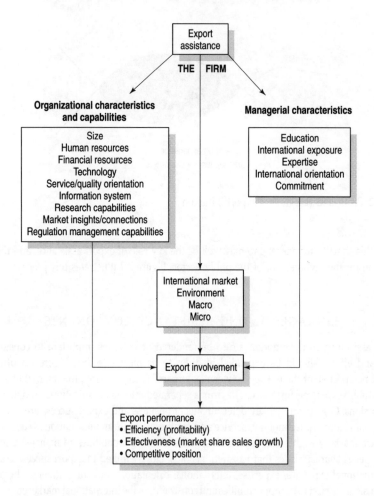

Figure 7.3 Export assistance and performance – a structural model

increase the profitability. Macro assistance in the foreign market environment can consist of international trade negotiations designed to break down foreign barriers to entry. Micro assistance consists of learning from the foreign market and its customers, and passing on that knowledge to enable domestic firms to adjust to that market.

AN INDUSTRY EXAMPLE

It is important to recognize the linkages between these efforts and the need for them to occur simultaneously. Otherwise there will be more results like the ones obtained from the U.S.–Japan wood products initiative. In that particular case, which the author researched with the U.S. General Accounting Office (U.S. GAO 1993), U.S. trade negotiations with Japan were conducted for more than a decade, so that more U.S. solid wood products could enter the Japanese market.

High-level meetings, ongoing negotiations, government financial support, and industry demonstra-tion projects were to achieve that goal. Japanese building codes and product certification procedures were changed and tariffs were lowered. The Foreign Agricultural Service spent more than $17 million to promote U.S. wood-product sales to Japan. The result? Canadian lumber companies are the leading wood exporters to the Japanese market. There were only marginal increases in U.S. exports and export-related jobs.

There are reasons for this outcome. U.S. products were not tailored to the Japanese market. Japanese builders prefer post-and-beam construction, which requires 4 × 4 inch lumber and 3 × 6 foot modules to match the standard tatami mats that cover floors. But U.S. companies were either unaware of those requirements or unwilling to meet them. Instead, the U.S. producers focused on the standard 2 × 4 products used in the United States, even though only 7 percent of new homes in Japan use that standard. In effect, U.S. negotiators and companies focused their energies on increasing the U.S. presence in the smallest part of the market, rather than pursuing the biggest market. This focus was the result of trying to sell what is produced, rather than producing what foreign customers want to buy. In addition, some of the U.S. firms that did enter the Japanese market did so with only limited enthusiasm and commitment. In contrast to the Canadian firms, many companies paid little attention to product quality and appearance and did not deliver after-sales service. Few firms translated their product information into Japanese or wrote manuals describing the new type of construction. Those U.S. companies that did try to vigorously pursue the new market encountered major problems in obtaining information about specific market requirements. They also had trouble adjusting their production processes to meet Japanese product specifications and obtaining financing to pay for new equipment and larger export inventories. Without these resources, their efforts were severely handicapped.

In sum, a well-intended approach did not achieve its deserved success since the focus rested on the wrong opportunities, the needs of customers were not sufficiently taken into account, firms were unable or unwilling to adjust to market requirements, and the linkages between all these compo-nents were not taken into account.

Some Policy Implications and Issues

Here then are some conclusions about the dimensions that should guide export assistance efforts, in particular where new and growing businesses are concerned. There are only six of them, but each one is crucial.

1. CLARITY OF PURPOSE

Agreement needs to be reached on what export assistance is to achieve. Some of the objectives currently competing with each other are global fairness, the opening of world markets, and economic activity and jobs in the United States. Public funds are too scarce, as is our capacity to negotiate, and our capability to achieve negotiation success – to invest funds and government attention solely to right wrongs or for the sake of fairness. There needs to be explicit recognition of the fact that the times are over when the United States opened foreign markets simply for the well-being of the world. Though it might be a delightful side effect to also see other nations' trade increase after the United States has broken down trade barriers, the key focus should rest on U.S. employment.

Clarification is also needed for the time frame involved. Given a short-term orientation, emphasis on a temporary increase in the export sales of multinational corporations will be most desirable. A more long-term orientation will concentrate efforts on introducing more and new firms to the global market.

2. TIGHTNESS OF FOCUS

Export assistance needs to achieve either a specific reduction of risk or an increase in profits for firms. It should be concentrated primarily in those areas where profit and risk inconsistencies produce market gaps, and be linked directly to identifiable organizational or managerial character- istics that need improvement. Otherwise, assistance supports only exports that would have taken place anyway. Such a focus, of course, requires the implementation of evaluation criteria and measurement mechanisms, which determine the effectiveness of export assistance (Cavusgil 1990; Seringhaus and Rosson 1990). I believe that for policy purposes, such measurement should not be based on the firm's export performance, which is mainly controlled by the corporation. Rather, the measurement should be based on the export involvement of the firm, focusing on the number of customers, transactions, and countries served.

3. COORDINATION OF APPROACHES

Coordination must occur both within and outside the government. Within government, it will be crucial to set overall effectiveness priorities and to trade off export assistance programs across agencies. Otherwise, an economic sector with relatively low employment effects could consume resources in an over proportionate fashion while priority industries would suffer from insufficient support. The fact that the agricultural sector spends about 74 percent of total federal export promotion outlays may serve as an example (U.S. GAO 1992). Externally, export assistance must be directly linked to domestic industries to ensure that the policy gains abroad can be taken advantage of by firms. Doing so must include collaboration for both product and process technologies, which now play a crucial role in attaining global competitiveness, similar to the much supported field of science. For example, the issue of quality performance can well become the focus of a cooperative effort throughout an entire industry, its suppliers, and customers alike. Rather than concentrate only on the well-entrenched industries, it is particularly important here to include a focus on sunrise industries.

4. EMPHASIS ON STRENGTHS

Within government, export assistance should emphasize those areas where government can bring a particular strength to bear – such as contacts, prowess in opening doors abroad, or information collection capabilities. Externally, programs should aim at the large opportunities abroad. As far as firms are concerned, attention should not just concentrate on assisting or bailing out industries in trouble, but also on helping successful firms do better.

5. TARGETING OF CRUCIAL FACTORS

Export assistance is likely to have the greatest impact when it serves the needs of companies. Programs therefore should start out by analyzing the current level of international involvement of the firm and then deliver assistance appropriate to the firm's needs. For example, help with after-sales service delivery is most appropriate for firms at the adaptation stage; firms at the awareness stage worry much more about information and mechanics. Assistance must also take foreign market conditions and foreign buyer preferences into account, and communicate the resulting constraints and opportunities to domestic firms. It is easier to sell what is in demand.

6. BOLDNESS OF VISION

In spite of the need to improve ongoing programs, there should be a spark of boldness which goes beyond ensuring that things are done right, but checks whether one can do more right things. One could, for example, think about domestic and international efforts to set standards for technology and quality. One could go beyond products in such an effort and also include services and agriculture. One could even include the grading of enzymes, meats, hormones, and other products developed by biotechnology firms. There could be efforts to develop the domestic mentoring services of a senior executive corps to provide much needed international experience to new and growing firms. Or one could think about the development of a national forfeiting institution to be of major assistance in handling the financial and documentation aspects of exporting.

In a world of rapidly changing global realities, the future is shrouded in much uncertainty. Yet the likelihood of continued and closer global linkages and interdependence is high. Our firms need to be prepared for the global marketplace. If we can help them to grow and successfully meet the competition on foreign shores as well as on ours, we will have strengthened them and the nation.

References

Cavusgil, S. Tamer (1990) "Export Development Efforts in the United States: Experiences and Lessons Learned." In *International Perspectives on Trade Promotion and Assistance*, S.T. Cavusgil and M.R. Czinkota (eds), 173–83. New York: Quorum Books.

Czinkota, Michael R. and Ilkka A. Ronkainen (1993) *International Marketing*, 3rd edn. Fort Worth: The Dryden Press.

Kotabe, Masaaki and Michael R. Czinkota (1992) "State Government Promotion of Manufacturing Exports: A GAP Analysis," *Journal of International Business Studies*, 4, 637–58. (See chapter 8.)

Seringhaus, Rolf F.H. and Philip J. Rosson (1990) *Government Export Promotion: A Global Perspective*. London: Routledge.

United States General Accounting Office (1993) *Agricultural Marketing: Export Opportunities for Wood Products in Japan Call for Customer Focus*. Washington, D.C.: Government Printing Office, May.

United States General Accounting Office (1992) *Export Promotion: U.S. Programs Lack Coherence*. Washington D.C.: Government Printing Office, March.

8

State Government Promotion of
Manufacturing Exports: A Gap Analysis

MASAAKI KOTABE

THE UNIVERSITY OF TEXAS AT AUSTIN

AND

MICHAEL R. CZINKOTA

GEORGETOWN UNIVERSITY

The United States still suffers from a large trade deficit in the 1990s, let alone the record trade deficit of over $152 billion in 1987 (Korth 1991; Murad 1991). Prospects of the edging-up of the dollar against major foreign currencies have fueled renewed concern about a further deterioration of the U.S. trade position in the future (Farrell and Mandel 1991).

The trade deficit is not simply the nation's problem, but is also a major economic issue to be dealt with at the state level. Export promotion has become a matter of urgent necessity throughout the United States (Bello and Williamson 1985) and has received an increasing amount of research attention (Cavusgil and Czinkota 1990; Eisinger 1988; O'Rourke 1985; Samiee and Walters 1990; Seringhaus and Botschen 1991). As domestic economic growth slows, export promotion activity by state governments has become an important component of the states' economic development programs.

Some research indicates that the firms' export involvement occurs in stages and that their progression from one stage to the next encounters different problems (e.g. Bilkey 1978; Cavusgil 1980; Czinkota 1982). Therefore, it is expected that exporters in different stages of export involvement will require different types of state export assistance. However, little is known empirically about the appropriateness of public assistance for exporters and as to how adequately state export promotion activity is allocated among firms in different stages (Czinkota 1982; Seringhaus 1986). To improve the effectiveness of state export promotion, a match between export assistance desired by firms and state export promotion activities should be expected.

The authors gratefully acknowledge the support from the Center for International Business Education and Research at the University of Texas at Austin, Dean's Office at the University of Missouri-Columbia, and the Missouri Department of Economic Development. The authors also thank three anonymous *JIBS* reviewers for their constructive comments and suggestions on earlier drafts of the article.

"State Government Promotion of Manufacturing Exports: A Gap Analysis," by Masaaki Kotabe and Michael R. Czinkota, *Journal of International Business Studies*, Fourth Quarter 1992. Used by permission.

Objectives of the Study

Given the growing role of state export promotion, this study examines a number of questions that have remained unanswered to date:

- What are the key export assistance requirements of firms in different stages of export involvement?
- Do these requirements necessitate assistance from the public sector?
- Are state export development agencies focusing their resource allocation on the needs of their client firms?

Population Under Study

A midwestern state was selected for this study for a number of reasons. This state has become increasingly export-oriented in recent years. Roughly 14 percent of the manufacturing firms in this state are exporters, comparable to the national average (Keegan 1989, p. 528). Other export-related profiles of the state economy also reflect the national scene. Export-related manufactures are an important part of the state economy, accounting for 10.2 percent of total manufactured goods production. Manufacturers of export-related goods provided employment for an estimated 43,300 manufacturing workers, comprising 10.4 percent of all manufacturing jobs in the state. In addition, 40,200 workers were employed in non-manufacturing industries as a direct result of the export-related manufactures. On all these dimensions, this state is fairly representative of the nation's export involvement (U.S. Department of Commerce 1988).

The Role of the State Governments

During the 1980s, state governments have stepped up their participation in export promotion (even though such efforts may have declined recently due to drastic state budget cuts) (Singer 1990, pp. 69–70). Although the International Trade Administration (ITA) has a national network of district offices, these offices are limited in the number of local businesses they can serve. In light of federal budget cuts and as a supplement to the ITA's trade promotion efforts, state governments have significantly increased their staff and budgets for export assistance, particularly, in nurturing small local businesses (Cavusgil 1990; Eisinger 1988). In 1988, about 56 percent of the state governments' budgets for international trade promotion was appropriated for activities to increase exports (Association of State Development Agencies 1988). These export promotion efforts are intended to help increase job opportunities and tax revenues for the states, and indirectly reduce the nation's trade deficit.

Export promotion activities generally comprise (1) *export service programs* (e.g. seminars for potential exporters, export counseling, how-to-export handbooks, and export financing) and (2) *market development programs* (e.g. dissemination of sales leads to local firms, participation in foreign trade shows, preparation of market analysis, and export news letters) (National Governors' Association 1985; Lesch, Eshghi and Eshghi 1990). In addition, program efforts can be differentiated as to whether the intent is to provide informational or experiential knowledge (Singer 1990). Informational knowledge typically would be provided through "how-to" export assistance, workshops and seminars, while experiential knowledge would be imparted through the arrangement of foreign buyers' or trade missions, trade and catalog shows, or participation in international market research.

On the surface, state government expenditures on export promotion make sense. One billion dollars worth of exports creates, on average, 22,800 jobs (Davis 1989). In 1988, over ten million U.S. jobs depended on trade. It has been estimated that $2 billion of GNP are generated per billion dollars of exports, together with $400 million in state and federal tax revenues (Shaw 1977). More recently, the National Governors' Association has reported that the doubling of the value of U.S. exports in the first half of the 1980s generated more than 1.5 million new jobs, accounting for over 80 percent of employment increases in the manufacturing sector and a third of the growth in private-sector employment. Thus, exports may be considered a major engine of economic growth in the U.S. economy.

Furthermore, many U.S. firms do not export. Estimates by the U.S. Department of Commerce indicate that "[h]alf of all U.S. exports of manufactured products are made by only 100 companies, and that 80 percent are made by 2500 companies" (House of Representative 1988). Many firms, particularly small to medium-size ones, appear to have developed a fear of international market activities. Their management tends to see only the risks – informational gaps, unfamiliar conditions in markets, complicated domestic and foreign trade regulations, the absence of trained middle managers for exporting, and lack of financial resources (Cavusgil 1980; Czinkota 1982) – rather than the opportunities that the international market can present. Yet, these very same firms may well have unique competitive advantages to offer which may be highly useful in performing successfully in the international market.

For example, small and medium-size firms can offer their customers shorter response times. If some special situation should arise, there is no need to wait for the "home office" to respond. Responses can be immediate, direct and predictable to the customer, therefore providing precisely those competitive ingredients that increase stability in a business relationship and reduce risk and costs. These firms often can also customize their operations more easily. Procedures can be adapted more easily to the special needs of the customer or to local requirements (Czinkota 1991). One could argue that in a world turning away from mass marketing and towards niche-marketing, these capabilities may well make smaller firms the export champions of the future.

In spite of all these reasons speaking in favor of export promotion by state governments, the empirical evidence providing a substantiated rationale for and information about the effectiveness of export promotion efforts is limited and mixed. One nationwide study suggests that for every increase of $1 in state expenditures for export promotion (all states taken as an aggregate), approximately $432 in increased exports were generated in 1980 (Coughlin and Cartwright 1987). As this study neither examined the lag effect of promotional expenditure on resultant increase in exports nor controlled for private and federal export promotion expenditures, this estimate should thus be interpreted with caution. Other research reports some skepticism about the effectiveness of state export promotion as small firms tend to make limited use of government programs (O'Rourke 1985; Reid 1984; Samiee and Walters 1991a). Indeed, adequate measures of export promotion program impact on users are difficult to establish and very little can be said conclusively about the effectiveness of export promotion (Seringhaus and Rosson 1990, p. 189).

Even the government is suspicious. In congressional testimony, the U.S. General Accounting

Office stated that "evaluations [of export promotion programs] to date generally do not appear to focus on the 'bottom line' – the effectiveness of the [Foreign Commercial Service]'s overall or individual trade programs – but on more narrow, administrative issues, such as [its] compliance with budgeting and fiscal procedures" (Mendelowitz 1989).

In times of tightening budget constraints, and competing public priorities, the question then still remains as to why it should be through the use of public funds and public efforts that firms should be enticed into exporting. Given the motivation of business activity by profit, one could argue that the profit retention of exporters should be enough of an incentive to motivate export efforts. Therefore, the expenditure of public monies on export promotion may be inappropriate. Even if such funds are spent, a secondary question then concerns the issue of how the allocated budget can be used most effectively.

It is therefore more necessary than ever to systematically examine the need for and appropriateness of government export promotion programs (Objective 1). A benefit analysis is used to determine the appropriateness of government expenditures for export promotion (Objective 2). Subsequently, a gap analysis is employed to measure the extent to which state promotion programs match assistance sought by firms (Objective 3). It is expected that the findings of this research will assist in ensuring the relevance of state export promotion programs in a rapidly changing international business climate (Goodnow and Goodnow 1990).

STAGES OF EXPORT INVOLVEMENT

A systematic evaluation of export promotion programs mandates identification of firms' export-related skills and needs for improvement. Various alternatives exist to differentiate firms and their level of export expertise. Given the increased research attention the export activities of firms have received, segmentation schemes abound. Some authors, for example, have focused on managerial attitudes (Wiedersheim-Paul, Olson, and Welch 1978; Cavusgil, Bilkey, and Tesar 1979). Other scrutinized the size of the firm (Bilkey 1978; Bilkey and Tesar 1977), its service orientation (Kahn 1978), or differentiated between sporadic and regular exporters (Samiee and Walters 1991b). Johansson and Vahlne (1977) suggested that firms' export involvement is a gradual learning process, which develops from a series of incremental decisions and over time draws some firms into the international market. Since export stages have been shown to segment most successfully between firms (Czinkota and Johnston 1981), it was decided, for purposes of this research, to evaluate the classification of firms by stage of export involvement. By using an a priori classification scheme, this study will also test the appropriateness of export stages.

Table 8.1 summarizes the stages of internationalization or export involvement, as initially proposed by Bilkey (1978), Cavusgil (1980), and Czinkota (1982), among others. Although the number of discrete stages differs across the classification schemes, the description of the evolutionary pattern of export involvement is essentially identical. Therefore, a five-stage model is employed for this study (see table 8.1).

In the early stage of export involvement, the internationalization process is a consequence of incremental adjustments to the changing conditions of the firm and its environment, *rather than* a result of its deliberate strategy. Such a pattern is due to the consequence of greater uncertainty in international business, higher costs of information, and the lack of technical knowledge about international marketing activities.

Some firms progress to a more involved stage of internationalization once three conditions are

Table 8.1 Stages of export involvement

Stage 1: Partial interest in exporting	Would fill an unsolicited export order, but make no effort to explore the feasibility of exporting
Stage 2: Exploring exports	Actively explore the feasibility of exporting, but currently exporting less than 5% of total sales
Stage 3: Experimental exporter	Exporting on an experimental basis to countries that are geographically close or that share a culture similar to the U.S.; export sales represent a volume greater than 5% of total sales
Stage 4: Experienced exporter with limited scope	Experienced exporter, with an export sales level greater than 5% of total sales, that adjusts export offerings optimally with changes in the foreign environment (e.g. exchange rates, tariffs, etc.) although still only exports to countries that are geographically close or have a similar culture
Stage 5: Experienced exporter	Experienced exporter with an export sales level greater than 5% of total sales, currently exploring the feasibility of exporting to additional countries that are farther away than previous exports, or have a very different culture

Sources: Warren J. Bilkey (1978) "An attempted integration of the literature on the export behavior of firms," *Journal of International Business Studies*, **9** (Spring/Summer): 33–46; S. Tamer Cavusgil (1980) "On the internationalization process of firms," *European Research*, **8** (November): 273–79; and Michael R. Czinkota (1982) *Export development strategies: U.S. promotion policy*. New York: Praeger Publishers.
Non-exporters who are in a pre-export stage of "No Interest in Exporting" were not included in the present investigation.

satisfied. First, the management of the firm obtains favorable expectations of the attractiveness of exporting based on experience. Second, the firm has access to key resources necessary for undertaking additional export-related tasks. Such availability of physical, financial, and managerial resources is closely associated with firm size. Particularly, small firms may have few trained managers, and little time for long-term planning as they are preoccupied with day-to-day operational problems, and consequently find it difficult to become involved in exporting. Third, management is willing to commit adequate resources to export activities. A high level of export commitment is evident in various ways, such as (1) existence of an export department or personnel, (2) development of direct export channels, and (3) frequent executive trips to foreign markets (Cavusgil 1980).

The long-term commitment of the firm to exporting depends on how successful management is in overcoming various barriers encountered in export activities. These barriers can be distinguished from those faced by firms in the earlier stage of internationalization. An experienced exporter has to deal with difficulties in maintaining and expanding export involvement. These difficulties include import/export restrictions, cost and availability of shipping, exchange rate fluctuations, collection of money, and development of distribution channels, among others (Cavusgil 1980).

Overall, favorable experience appears to be a key component in moving firms along the internationalization continuum. To a large degree an appropriate measure of favorableness for firms consists of profits. An increase in profits due to a certain activity is likely to increase management's interest in such activity. Since profits are largely the compensation for the risk incurred by the firm, degrees of profitability should vary with the amount of risk taken, in order to produce similar levels of profit.

In the context of internationalization, one should be able to compare degrees of profitability of domestic operations with those of international operations. Since international activities tend to involve greater distances, more complexity, and new factors, such as currency exchange rates, they are likely to be seen by firms as resulting in greater uncertainty. Such a rise in uncertainty is likely to lead to a perception of greater risk, which in turn requires compensation through higher degrees of profitability. In order for a firm to be enticed into international business rather than domestic expansion, international operations must produce at least the same level of profit as domestic activities. Therefore, the degree of profitability of international operations must be higher than of domestic operations.

Data

THE SAMPLE

A sample of 500 exporting manufacturers in the midwestern state was randomly selected by computer from the most comprehensive database provided by the Harris Publishing Company in 1990. This database comprised a population of 8,761 manufacturing firms (SIC 20–39), of which 1,212, or 13.8 percent, were exporters. Export stages could not be identified a priori from this database. Firms' annual sales ranged from $15,000 to over $10 billion with an average of $140 million. Total employment ranged from one person to over 10,000. During our pretest, the presidents of 20 exporters representing a wide range of firm sizes (in terms of either employment or annual sales or both) were interviewed. They indicated that they were either chiefly responsible for executing/participating in export decision-making (75 percent) or fully informed of export-related decisions made by export managers (25 percent). Without such major involvement of top management, the focus on and interest in exporting necessary for planning activity is highly unlikely (Czinkota and Ronkainen 1990, p. 223). Thus, an endorsement letter by the state's export development office and a questionnaire were subsequently sent to the president (or owner) of each of the randomly selected 500 firms in 1990.[1] Although the database was the most recent, our research established that a certain percentage of the sample of firms could not participate in the survey for a number of uncontrollable reasons, including 1) undeliverable addresses and 2) firms no longer in business. Based on a method suggested by Wiseman and Billington (1984), the maximum usable sample was estimated to be 450.[2]

Approximately 2 weeks after the survey instrument was mailed out, a follow-up reminder notice was sent out. A total of 176 responses were received. Fourteen of these responses were later deemed unusable, resulting in 162 usable returns with an effective adjusted response rate of 36.0 percent.

THE RESPONDENTS

Almost all of the respondents were in executive positions. About 80 percent of them were in the cadre of top management: chief executive officers, presidents, or owners (65 percent); and vice presidents or directors (15 percent). Middle-management ranks (i.e. functional managers and treasurers) represented the remaining 20 percent of the sample. The participation of these executives (key informants) who are involved in important export decision-making assures the reliability of

Table 8.2 Average profile of sample of firms

Characteristic		Export stage					
		1	2[a]	3	4	5	
	Sample size	(n=51)	(n=61)	(n=17)	(n=8)	(n=25)	F-value
Employment							
Total employment		18.8	82.2	40.1	398.1	696.8	3.11*
Expected loss of employment without export business		0.0%	0.6%	1.1%	10.1%	21.4%	14.18***
Export experience							
Number of countries exported in 1989		0.8	2.0	5.3	7.5	19.4	22.11***
Expected number of countries exported in 1992		0.7	5.1	8.6	10.8	25.2	24.05***
Number of years exported		5.2	4.3	7.5	7.4	10.3	6.26***
Sales							
Share of export in total sales in 1989 (A)		1.2%	1.9%	7.9%	17.9%	23.5%	34.94***
Expected share of export in total sales in 1992 (B)		1.1%	8.8%	12.1%	22.4%	28.2%	39.76***
Expected growth of export share (ratio of B/A)		0.9	4.6	1.5	1.3	1.2	5.10***
Executives in charge of export							
Education level (in years)		15.5	15.6	15.6	16.8	16.1	0.61
							χ^2-value
Percentage traveled abroad		43.2%	53.6%	94.1%	100.0%	95.8%	36.42***
Percentage interested in foreign culture		53.5%	77.2%	88.2%	75.0%	87.0%	18.49**

* $p < 0.05$
** $p < 0.01$
*** $p < 0.001$
[a] Two firms, respectively, with employment of 3,000 and 7,600, were excluded from analysis as they were outliers (i.e. exceptions) in this category of exporters. For this phase of analysis, the sample of firms in Stage 2 is 59. Inclusion of the two firms inflates absolute values (e.g. total sales) dramatically, but not ratio values (e.g. share of exports in total sales).

information provided (Huber 1985). Key informant bias would not likely have occurred as managers responded to questions within their level of responsibility (Phillips 1981; Schwenk 1985). Furthermore, as the job position of the respondents was found to have no significant impact on the way they responded to the questionnaire, the position would not likely bias the findings of the study (Armstrong and Overton 1977).

Results

PROFILE OF FIRMS IN THE SAMPLE

It was necessary to examine whether the five-stage classification of exporters was adequate for use in this study. At the outset of the survey, respondents were asked to identify their export stage from the list of five stages (as defined in table 8.1). Since the initial categorization was based on an "aided" self-selection process, a series of questions regarding exporters' characteristics was also asked in various places of the survey instrument for validation purposes.

Table 8.2 presents the average profile of firms in different stages of export involvement. ANOVA was employed to see if there was any significant difference across the five stages in each of the demographic characteristics. As expected, the firm size (measured by total employment) generally becomes larger as the stage of export involvement progresses ($p < 0.05$). It suggests that large firm size may be a necessary condition for high involvement in exporting (Czinkota and Johnston 1983; Samiee and Walters 1990, 1991a). However, one anomaly is also observed. The average size of firms in Stage 2 (i.e. exploring the feasibility of exporting, with exports less than 5 of total sales) is larger than the average size of firms in Stage 3 (i.e. experimental exporter, with exports more than 5 percent of total sales), even after excluding two firms with employment of 3,000 and 7,600 as outliers in Stage 2. Casual conversation with some executives of larger firms in Stage 2 indicates that they were reactively drawn into exporting due to competitive pressures. It appears that these pressures come from smaller competitors who have gained economies of scale from international marketing activities (Czinkota and Ronkainen 1990, pp. 214–15).

The other characteristics of the firms follow the internationalization process as described in the literature. The importance of export business to the firm is observed in the expected loss of employment if export business were held off. It increases from 0 percent in Stage 1 to over 21 percent in Stage 5 ($p < 0.0001$). This is due to the fact that firms gradually switch from indirect to direct mode of exporting as they increase export involvement, and demonstrates the major in-house employment multiplier of export activity.

Generally consistent with the internationalization process, a number of observations can be made. First, the number of countries to which the firms exported in 1989 continually increases from no more than one in Stage 1 to 19 in Stage 5 ($p < 0.0001$), consistent with Samiee and Walters (1990). Firms in Stage 2 and above of export involvement also plan to increase the number of countries they will export to over the next 2 years. Firms in Stage 1 fail to show such interest. Similarly, the share of exports in total sales in 1989 increased from 1.2 percent in Stage 1 to 23.5 percent in Stage 5 ($p < 0.0001$), while the expected share of exports 2 years hence ranges from 1.1 percent in Stage 1 to 28.2 percent in Stage 5. In other words, while firms in Stage 1 do not show any expected increase in export sales share (i.e. 1.2 percent in 1989 to 1.1 percent in 1992), firms in higher stages expect their export sales share to increase. Firms in Stage 2 expect the highest growth rate in export sales share (1.9 percent in 1989 to 8.0 percent in 1992 or 4.6 times in 3 years). The expected growth rate in export sales share declines as export involvement progresses to maturity. This is not surprising because an incremental increase in export sales constitutes a smaller portion of the export share as the base share of exports in total sales becomes larger along the export involvement continuum.

The profile of executives in charge of export business also shows a similar pattern of progression. Their average education levels seem to be slightly higher, the higher the export involvement stage. While the average education level is not significantly different for managers across stages of export

Table 8.3 Technical requirements and benefits of export involvement

	Export stage					F-value
	1	2	3	4	5	
Export procedural expertise (1 ... 5)[a]	1.5	2.1	2.4	3.1	3.4	21.73***
Importance of ___ for export involvement (1 ... 5)[b]						
Availability of financing and market information[c]	3.4	3.2	2.9	2.8	3.2	0.59
Managerial ability[d]	2.9	3.5	3.5	3.0	3.7	1.35
Profitability relative to domestic business (1 ... 5)[e]	2.1	2.6	2.6	3.0	3.1	3.45**
Competitive benefit of exporting (1 ... 5)[f]	1.9	3.0	3.6	4.0	4.1	23.90***

* $p < 0.05$
** $p < 0.01$
*** $p < 0.001$

[a] Mean of the seven areas of expertise measured on a five-point scale (not at all knowledgeable = 1 ... 5 = extremely knowledgeable): 1) overseas shipping and transportation arrangement; (2) how to structure transactions to ensure payment from abroad; (3) foreign demand for products; (4) regulations and paperwork for foreign marketing; (5) international marketing services available from public and private sources; 6) tax implications of exporting; and (7) antitrust regulations.
[b] Nine items were measured on a five-point scale (not at all important = 1 ... 5 = extremely important). They were submitted to principal components analysis with varimax rotation. Two factors were identified.
[c] Mean of the five items representing the availability of financing and market research: (1) Financing to cover the time lag between shipping and payments; (2) in-house financing for offering credit to buyers; (3) external financing for offering credit to buyers; (4) in-house market research on foreign markets; and (5) external market research on foreign markets.
[d] Mean of the four items representing managerial ability: (1) maintaining management control over export operations; (2) domestic production capabilities, (3) availability of transportation; and (4) protecting trade secrets.
[e] One item measuring the current export sales' profit contribution to the firm, relative to that of domestic sales (much less than domestic = 1 ... 5 = much more than domestic).
[f] Mean of the four benefits gained from exporting measured on a five-point Likert scale (strongly disagree = 1 ... 5 = strongly agree): (1) contribution to the firm's sales growth; (2) contribution to the overall quality of management; and (3) more competitive firm.

involvement, the increase in their personal foreign travel experience and interest in foreign culture along the export involvement stage are revealing ($p < 0.01$ for both). More than 90 percent of the executives of firms in Stage 3 and above have traveled abroad for non-business reasons. Similarly, three-quarters or more of the executives of firms in Stage 2 and above expressed interest in foreign culture. These personal factors strongly suggest the importance of education level and cultural awareness for executives' interest in, and commitment to, exporting (Cavusgil and Nevin 1981; Johansson and Vahlne 1977; Reid 1981).

TECHNICAL REQUIREMENTS AND BENEFITS OF EXPORT INVOLVEMENT

Table 8.3 summarizes findings regarding technical requirements and benefits of exporting. As a result of principal components analyses with varimax rotation, two categories of technical requirements and two categories of export benefits were identified. Technical requirements for successful exports were examined in two ways: 1) *export procedural expertise* and 2) *corporate resources for export involvement*. The second technical requirement is further divided into availability of financing/market research information and managerial ability. Similarly, two types of benefits of export involvement were considered: 1) *relative profitability* and 2) *competitive benefit*. The variables used to define the types of technical requirements and benefits of export involvement are presented in the footnote section of table 8.3. ANOVA was also employed to investigate whether technical requirements and benefits of export involvement would differ across the five export stages.

TECHNICAL REQUIREMENTS

Export procedural expertise

The first technical requirement is export-related procedural expertise measured on a five-point scale (not at all knowledgeable = 1 . . . 5 = extremely knowledgeable), consisting of: (1) overseas shipping and transportation arrangement; (2) how to structure transactions to ensure payment from abroad; (3) identification of foreign demand for products, (4) regulations and paperwork for foreign marketing; (5) international marketing services available from public and private sources; (6) tax implications of exporting; and (7) antitrust regulations. Principal components analysis indicated that these seven areas of export procedural expertise constituted one factor. Thus, the mean of the seven items was computed to represent management's export procedural expertise (Cronbach's *alpha* = 0.93).

It is not surprising, as shown in table 8.3, that the level of export procedural expertise significantly increases as the firms' export involvement rises ($p < 0.0001$). The expertise level is measured at 1.5 on a five-point scale for firms in Stage 1, suggesting that firms that have just filled unexpected export orders have little export procedural expertise, as expected. However, firms in the highest stage of export involvement (Stage 5) rated their expertise level on the average at as low as 3.4. It was not expected that even the most experienced exporters were not confident about shipping arrangements, payment procedure, and various regulations, and so on. This finding clearly shows that regardless of the export stage, the firms' export procedural expertise is less than adequate. Obviously, firms see a strong need for strengthening their export procedural expertise.

Availability of corporate resources

The second technical requirement is availability of corporate resources. Nine items related to financing/market information and managerial ability were considered and measured on a five-point scale (not at all important = 1 . . . 5 = extremely important). Two factors were extracted by principal components analysis with varimax rotation. The mean of items with factor loading exceeding 0.40 was computed for each of the two factors, representing availability of financing/market information (five items; Cronbach's *alpha* = 0.82) and managerial ability (four items; Cronbach's *alpha* = 0.75), respectively.

First, the availability of financing and market information is perceived to be weakly important across all stages of export involvement (a mean of 3.42 on a five-point scale; $p > 0.20$). Second, managerial ability seems to be also equally important across all stages of export involvement (a mean of 3.17 on a five-point scale; $p > 0.20$). It appears that managerial ability is somewhat more important than the availability of financing and market information for firms in all stages except for those in Stage 1.

BENEFITS OF EXPORTING

Relative export profitability

The first type of benefit is current profitability of exports relative to domestic business (one item measured on a five-point scale). The importance of relative profitability significantly increases across stages of export involvement ($p < 0.01$). However, contrary to expectations, the relative export profitability of export operations is rated relatively low by firms in all stages. Only those firms in Stages 4 and 5 indicated that exporting is as profitable as domestic business.

Competitive advantage

The second type of benefit considers how exporting improves sales, management, and firms' competitive position (three items measured on a five-point scale). Principal components analysis showed that these three items make up one construct, i.e. competitive advantage. Competitive advantage refers to the overall strengths of a firm arising from its choice of served markets, its distinctive competences, and pattern of resource deployment, among others, and affects its long-term profitability (Buzzell and Gale 1987). The mean of the three items was used to represent competitive advantage of exporting (Cronbach's *alpha* = 0.90). As table 8.3 shows, the competitive advantage of exporting rating increases dramatically as the stage of export involvement progresses (1.9 at Stage 1 to 4.1 at Stage 5). This unequivocally confirms that exporting significantly benefits the firm's competitiveness ($p < 0.0001$).

Based on these two types of benefits that can be gained from exporting, it is clear that exporting primarily helps firms become more competitive by improving sales growth and managerial skill, among others, although it may not necessarily lead to higher profitability, particularly in the early stages of internationalization. Our post hoc interview with several exporters further confirmed this view. These exporters indicated that while their initial expectation of higher profitability from exporting than from domestic business usually did not materialize, they have become more flexible and resilient competitors in the domestic market than non-exporters, thanks chiefly to economies of scale in production, ease of weathering sales fluctuations at home, and prospect of foreign sales increase in the near future.

EXPORT ASSISTANCE DESIRED BY LOCAL FIRMS VS. STATE EXPORT ASSISTANCE EFFORT ALLOCATION: A GAP ANALYSIS

In this section, we will develop indices reflecting the extent of export assistance desired by local firms and those showing the allocation of state export assistance efforts across various problem areas by export stage. Both indices will be developed such that the total sums to 100, respectively, to facilitate direct comparison between the two indices.

Table 8.4 Export-related problems

Logistics	1.	Arranging transportation
	2.	Transport rate determination
	3.	Handling of documentation
	4.	Obtaining financial information
	5.	Distribution coordination
	6.	Packaging
	7.	Obtaining insurance
Legal procedure	8.	Government red tape
	9.	Product liability
	10.	Licensing
	11.	Customs/duty
Servicing exports	12.	Providing parts availability
	13.	Providing repair service
	14.	Providing technical advice
	15.	Providing warehousing
Sales promotion	16.	Advertising
	17.	Sales effort
	18.	Marketing information
Foreign market intelligence	19.	Locating markets
	20.	Trade restrictions
	21.	Competition overseas

Initially, a list of 19 export-related problems identified earlier by Czinkota (1982, p. 57) had been considered for this study. However, during the pretest, executives from exporting companies interviewed indicated eight additional problems, which were also included in the questionnaire. Respondents were asked to rate the difficulty of these problems relative to their domestic business on a five-point scale (much less of a problem = 1 ... 5 = much more of a problem). This way, a firm would have its domestic business activities as a basis for comparison to its international business activities.[3] Subsequently, executives were asked to rate the extent of assistance they would expect from the export promotion agency on a five-point scale (could be of no help = 1 ... 5 = could be of much help).

Principal components analysis with varimax rotation was subsequently used to reduce the number of dimensions on the first set of questions. Seven factors were extracted, of which the first five factors were interpretable and accounted for 82.2 percent of the variance. Those five factors were used for subsequent analysis. The mean of items with factor loading > 0.40 was computed for each of the five factors, representing: (1) *logistics* (i.e. arranging transportation, transport rate determination, handling of documentation, obtaining financial information, distribution coordination, packaging, and obtaining insurance: seven items, Cronbach's *alpha* = 0.93); (2) *legal procedure* (i.e. government red tape, product liability, export licensing, and customs duty: four items, Cronbach's *alpha* = 0.91); (3) *servicing exports* (i.e. providing parts, repair service, technical advice, and providing warehousing: four items, Cronbach's *alpha* = 0.90); (4) *sales promotion* (i.e. advertising, sales effort, and marketing information: three items, Cronbach's *alpha* = 0.82), and (5) *foreign market intelligence* (i.e. locating markets, trade restrictions, and competition overseas: three items, Cronbach's *alpha* = 0.84). The five areas of export-related problems are summarized in table 8.4.

Table 8.5 Export assistance desired by local firms vs. state export assistance effort allocation: a gap analysis[a]

Export-related problem	Export stage					Row total	F-value[b]
	1	2	3	4	5		
Logistics	6.1	6.3	5.9	4.8	4.4	27.5	2.86*
	(1.5)	(3.8)	(3.8)	(3.8)	(2.3)	(15.0)	
Legal procedure	5.0	5.0	4.6	3.8	3.7	22.0	2.28*
	(0.5)	(1.3)	(1.3)	(1.3)	(0.8)	(5.0)	
Servicing exports	2.8	3.1	2.5	2.4	2.5	13.2	1.30
	(0.5)	(1.3)	(1.3)	(1.3)	(0.8)	(5.0)	
Sales promotion	3.2	4.2	3.8	3.3	2.8	17.3	3.43**
	(5.0)	(12.5)	(12.5)	(12.5)	(7.5)	(50.0)	
Foreign market intelligence	4.0	4.4	4.5	3.4	3.7	20.0	2.63*
	(6.3)	(6.3)	(6.3)	(6.3)	(2.3)	(25.0)	
	21.2	23.0	21.2	17.6	17.0	100.0	2.63*
	(10.0)	(25.0)	(25.0)	(25.0)	(15.0)	(100.0)	

* $p < 0.05$
** $p < 0.01$
[a] Indices for EDO export assistance efforts are in parentheses.
[b] Results of the analysis of variance for each of the five areas of assistance by export stage.

Subsequently, an index was developed to measure the value of export promotion assistance as perceived by firms. The value of export promotion assistance to firms would be higher, the more difficult the export-related problems are and the higher the firms' expectation of export promotion assistance is. The value index represents the anticipated value of five areas of assistance as perceived by firms in different export stages (Stages 1 to 5). It was computed as follows:

$$Assistance\ value\ index_{ij} = DIFF_{ij}\ EXPECT_{ij}\ /\Sigma\Sigma(DIFF_{ij} \times EXPECT_{ij}) \times 100$$

such that

$$\Sigma\Sigma(Assistance\ value\ index_{ij}) = 100$$

where: $DIFF$ = difficulty rating in each of the five areas of assistance (mean of the items representing each area) (much less of a problem = 1 ... 5 = much more of a problem), and

$EXPECT$ = level of firm's expectation of export promotion assistance (could be of no help = 1 ... 5 = could be of much help),

i = each of the five identified areas of assistance, and

j = export stage.

Meanwhile, the director of the export promotion agency was contracted to obtain information on its effort allocation across the five identified areas of assistance by export stage. He indicated that it was not possible to identify budgeted dollar amounts across various export promotion activities, and instead he suggested that the agency's allocation of efforts and human resources could be assessed. Therefore, the director and his staff of trade specialists in his office were asked to brainstorm among themselves to allocate 100 points among the five areas of assistance identified above to reflect the export promotion agency's allocation of efforts and resources. As a second step, they were also asked to allocate 100 points among the export stages to reflect the agency's distribution of efforts and resources for firms in each export stage. They also indicated that they would not target any particular assistance to any particular group (export stage) of firms. Therefore, the allocation of assistance efforts was independent of the stage that the firms were in. Based on this information, the export promotion effort index was computed as follows:

$$Effort\ index_{ij} = PROB_i \times STAGE_j / 100$$

such that

$$\Sigma\Sigma(Effort\ index_{ij}) = 100$$

where: $PROB$ = allocation of efforts in each of the five areas of assistance, and
$STAGE$ = allocation of efforts in each of the five export stages,
i = each of the five identified areas of assistance, and
j = export stage.

The value indices and the export promotion effort indices (in parentheses) are presented in table 8.5. The row totals suggest the value of export promotion assistance desired by firms across all stages of export involvement. It is clear that logistics-related problems are the most pressing area of assistance desired (27.5 out of 100), followed closely by legal procedure (22.0) and foreign market intelligence (20.0). Servicing of exports is not strongly considered to be in the realm of state export assistance across all export stages (13.2). The row totals in parentheses represent the export promotion agency's effort allocation by area of assistance. For example, the agency allocates 50 percent of its export promotion efforts to sales promotion and 15 percent to logistics-related problems. The contrast of the row totals of the two indices suggest that the agency's assistance in sales promotion appears to be by far overbudgeted, while its assistance in legal procedure is severely underbudgeted.

The column totals represent the value of export assistance desired by firms across all areas of export assistance by export stage. The column totals in parentheses, on the other hand, show the export promotion agency's effort allocation by export stage. The agency does not allocate any effort to firms with no interest in exporting (in the pre-export stage). Three-quarters of its total assistance efforts are provided equally to firms in Stages 2 to 4. The remaining quarter of its efforts is split between firms in Stage 1 and those in Stage 5. It appears that the export promotion agency's assistance effort to those firms in Stage 2 is somewhat lower than desired by them (i.e. 10.0 allocated vs. 21.2 desired). This misallocation of promotion efforts is due to the slightly more than desired level of allocation given to firms in Stages 2 to 4.

Comparisons and contrasts can be made for firms in each export stage by area of export assistance. ANOVA was used to see if there is a significant difference in the perceived value of assistance in various export-related problem areas across the five export stages. Results show that firms' export stage is significant in explaining the variation in the perceived value of assistance in all export-related problem areas except for servicing of exports. Servicing of exports is not strongly considered to be in the realm of state export assistance in any stage of export involvement ($p >$ 0.20). As a rule, the perceived value of state export assistance peaks at Stage 2 of export involvement and gradually declines thereafter. This is reasonable as more experienced exporters are able to rely more on in-house export expertise (e.g. Cavusgil 1980; Czinkota 1982).

Conclusions and Policy Implications

The major purpose of this study was to identify various problems exporters face in export business, appropriateness of government assistance with these problems, and the match between the type of government assistance desired with the assistance delivered. This identification of expertise, problems, and government assistance needs can help government agencies such as the midwestern state's export promotion agency understand their mission, and identify existing gaps between their offerings and client firms' assistance needs. Based on the findings of this study, a number of conclusions can be made with respect to both local firms along the internationalization continuum and the role of the state government's export assistance agencies such as the Export Development Office. On a tentative basis, since not fully generalizable, policy implications are also explored.

FIRMS AND EXPORT INVOLVEMENT

First, firms generally fit the internationalization continuum as explained in the literature. The growth in firm size appears to be a necessary condition for increased export involvement. In addition, executives' commitment to exporting demonstrated by cultural awareness manifested in their foreign travel experience and interest in foreign cultures appears to be an underlying force to get their firms involved in export business. Interestingly, firms in Stage 2 (i.e. actively exploring the feasibility of exporting, with current export sales being less than 5 percent of total sales) initially seemed somewhat anomalous. They are much larger in average size than those in the earlier stages and in Stage 3. However, it is easily reconciled by the fact that many of larger firms in Stage 2 have recently started exporting with a high average annual growth rate of over 21 percent in export sales from ground up. It may also suggest that recent export promotion by federal and state agencies has encouraged what would otherwise have been domestically minded firms to actively consider exporting.

Second, local firms' export-related procedural expertise is alarmingly limited. While it is true that experienced exporters have higher levels of export procedural expertise, the absolute level of expertise seems inadequate even for the most experienced exporters. Export procedural expertise includes: (1) overseas shipping and transportation arrangement; (2) how to structure transactions to ensure payment from abroad; (3) foreign demand for products; (4) regulations and paperwork for foreign marketing; (5) international marketing services available from public and private sources; (6) tax implications of exporting; and (7) antitrust regulations.

Third, the availability of export financing and foreign market information is crucial for firms in the early stages of export involvement. Since many of the firms in the early stages (in particular, Stages 1 to 3) are relatively small, they may not have adequate resources to obtain foreign market intelligence and execute export transactions on their own. In addition to these problems, firms that did not export in 1989 (mostly in Stage 1) expressed government red tape as another problem.

Fourth, exporting does not necessarily result in higher profitability relative to domestic business. However, profitability is just one measure of the firm's competitiveness. Many exporters indicated that exporting makes their firms more competitive domestically as a result of increased sales opportunities overseas and improved quality of management, among others. Increased foreign sales mean that manufacturing operations will not be as much affected by domestic demand fluctuations as they would be without exports. Overall, executives of local firms become more aware of the competitive benefits of exporting, the more involved they are in exporting.

ROLE OF THE EXPORT DEVELOPMENT OFFICE

The fact that the prime export benefit to firms appears to accrue in the area of competitiveness, rather than profitability, may be a key tentative justification for government involvement in export promotion. U.S. firms in general, and smaller sized firms in particular, often are said to suffer from a short-term perspective and are subject to the need for immediate profit. The findings reported here indicate that, particularly in the early stages of internationalization, export activities produce lower levels of profit than do domestic business activities. Combined with the relatively low levels of procedural export expertise across the international stages, exporting appears to be a high-risk activity with insufficient profit rewards. Under those conditions, exporting would not appear to be an attractive alternative for firms, save for those with unrealistic expectations. The public sector, however, is much more interested in competitiveness issues, since those will determine the future levels of job creation and tax revenue. There appears to be a legitimate gap in the market mechanism addressed by the government through its export promotion efforts, which either lower the risk of international activities and/or increase their level of profitability. The existence of this gap may then well justify the expenditure of public funds on export promotion.

The question then becomes how these public monies are best employed. A gap analysis has shown that a wide discrepancy may exist between local firms' assistance needs and the export promotion agency's provision of assistance. While logistics, legal procedure, and foreign market intelligence are the problematic areas for local exporters, in particular, in early stages of export involvement, the state export promotion agency focuses half of its export assistance effort on sales promotion. The gap analysis also suggests that it should redirect some more assistance effort to firms in Stage 1 of export involvement from those in Stages 3 to 5.

This research addressed the issue of export promotion on a state-specific basis. It has shown the appropriateness of the export stage conceptualization for governmental efforts. It has presented some tentative evidence – well worth following up in future research – that public sector export promotion may be necessary due to the competitiveness rather than the profitability aspects of exporting. It has also developed a methodology to assess the effectiveness of governmental programs via a gap analysis, which identifies differences between "client" needs and governmental efforts. Given the need for budget containment, this methodology can be crucial in improving promotional effectiveness without incurring a major additional financial burden. Use of these findings may enable existing and future government programs to extend their reach and expand U.S. exports even more. As of yet, many firms are still waiting for assistance without knowing where to go for help.

Limitations

Our research findings and conclusions should be interpreted in light of the following limitations. First, the study is cross-sectional. The results provide a "snapshot" of various firms in various stages of export involvement, and are interpreted as if they represented what was essentially a dynamic process. Indeed, the characteristics of exporters in the sample amply suggested dynamism in the expected changes in the number of countries to which they exported, the export share in their total sales, and the number of years of export experience. However, a cross-sectional study may not have captured all the implications of a dynamic process.

Second, the sample of firms was taken within a single stage. While many characteristics of the state are representative of those of other states, generalization of the findings should be made cautiously. Replications of the study with samples from other states should provide more generalizable implications.

Notes

1 The presidents (or owners) were requested to forward the questionnaire to the most appropriate executive directly responsible for export business.
2 The adjustment was made on the basis of the estimated rate of three reasons identified in the text. A random sample of 50 addresses was verified through telephone calls to the addresses.
3 The role of the export promotion agency is to provide special assistance to exporters if they experienced difficulty in exporting above and beyond what should be expected in domestic sales. For items like export licensing and trade restrictions, where there may be few direct counterparts in domestic sales (except for, say, liquor licensing in interstate commerce), exporters would face new problems they have not experienced before. For items like customs duty, on the other hand, there are fairly similar domestic equivalents such as sales and excise taxes. Finally, locating markets and competition overseas involve essentially the same activities as in domestic marketing although there are locational differences between them.

References

Armstrong, J. Scott and Terry S. Overton (1977) "Estimating nonresponse bias in mail surveys," *Journal of Marketing Research*, **14** (August), 396–402.

Association of State Development Agencies (1988) *State export program database*. Washington, D.C.

Bello, Daniel C. and Nicholas C. Williamson (1985) "The American export trading company: Designing a new international marketing institution," *Journal of Marketing*, **49** (Fall), 60–69.

Bilkey, Warren J. (1978) "An attempted integration of the literature on the export behavior of firms," *Journal of International Business Studies*, **9** (Spring/Summer); 33–46.

—— and George Tesar (1977) "The export behavior of smaller-sized Wisconsin firms," *Journal of International Business Studies*, **8** (Spring/Summer); 93–98.

Buzzell, Robert D. and Robert T. Gale (1987) *The PIMS principles*. New York: Macmillan.

Cavusgil, S. Tamer (1980) On the internationalization process of firms. *European Research*, **8** (November); 273–79.

Cavusgil, S. Tamer (1990) "Export development efforts in the United States: Experiences and lessons learned."

In S. Tamer Cavusgil and Michael R. Czinkota (eds) *International perspectives on trade promotion and assistance*, 173–83. New York: Quorum Books.

—— and Michael R. Czinkota (eds) (1990) *International perspectives on trade promotion and assistance*. New York: Quorum Books.

—— and John R. Nevin (1981) "Internal determinants of export marketing behavior: An empirical investigation," *Journal of Marketing Research*, **28** (February), 114–19.

—— Warren J. Bilkey and George Tesar (1979) "A note on the export behavior of firms: Exporter profiles," *Journal of International Business Studies*, **10** (Spring/Summer), 91–97.

Coughlin, Cletus C. and Phillip A. Cartwright (1987) "An examination of state foreign export promotion and manufacturing exports," *Journal of Regional Science*, **27** (August), 439–49.

Czinkota, Michael R. (1982) *Export development strategies: U.S. promotion policy*. New York: Praeger Publishers.

—— (1991) "Export promotion and competitiveness: The case of small and mid-sized firms." In Ali Abbas (ed.) *International competitiveness and managerial action*. Haworth Press.

—— and Wesley J. Johnston (1981) "Segmenting U.S. firms for export development," *Journal of Business Research*, **9** (December), 353–65.

—— (1983) "Exporting: Does sales volume make a difference?" *Journal of International Business Studies*, **14**, (Spring/Summer); 147–53.

—— and Ilkka A. Ronkainen (1990) *International marketing* 2nd edn. Chicago: Dryden Press.

Davis, Lester A. (1989) *Contribution of exports to U.S. employment: 1980–87*. Washington, D.C.: U.S. Government Printing Office.

Eisinger, Peter (1988) *The rise of the entrepreneurial state: State and local economic development policy in the United States*. Madison, WI: University of Wisconsin Press.

Farrell, Christopher and Michael J. Mandel (1991) "At last, good news: The stunning turnaround in trade is no fluke," *Business Week*, June **3**, 24–25.

Goodnow, James D. and W. Elizabeth Goodnow (1990) "Self-assessment by state export promotion agencies: A status report," *International Marketing Review*, **7** (3); 18–30.

House of Representatives, 101st Congress, 2nd Session (1988) Hearings on small business obstacles to exporting before the committee on small business. October 4.

Huber, George P. (1985) "Temporal stability and response-order biases in participant descriptions of organizational decisions," *Academy of Management Journal*, **28** (December); 943–50.

Johansson, Jan and Jan-Eric Vahlne (1977) "The internationalization process of the firm – A model of knowledge development and increasing foreign market commitments," *Journal of International Business Studies*, **8**, (Spring/Summer), 22–32.

Kahn, Silkander M. (1978) "A study of success and failure in exports." A paper presented at the Annual Meeting of the European International Business Association, December 14–16.

Keegan, Warren J. (1989) *Global marketing management* (4th edn). Englewood Cliffs, NJ: Prentice Hall.

Korth Christopher M. (1991) "Managerial barriers to U.S. exports," *Business Horizons*, **34** (March–April), 18–26.

Lesch, William C., Abdolreza Eshghi and Golpira S. Eshghi (1990) "A review of export promotion programs in the ten largest industrial states." In S. Tamer Cavusgil and Michael R. Czinkota (eds) *International perspectives on trade promotion and assistance*, 25–37. New York: Quorum Books.

Mendelowitz, Allen I. (1989) Director, United States General Accounting Office, testimony before the subcommittee on commerce, consumer and monetary affairs, Committee on Government Operations, U.S. House of Representatives, 102nd Congress, Oct. 18.

Murad, Howard. (1991) "U.S. international transactions: Second quarter of 1991," *Survey of Current Business*, **71** (September), 39–64.

National Governors' Association. (1985) "States in the international economy." Paper prepared for the 77th Annual Meeting of the National Governors' Association, Washington, D.C.

O'Rourke, A. Desmond (1985) "Differences in exporting practices, attitudes and problems by size of firm," *American Journal of Small Business*, **9** (Winter), 25–29.

Phillips, Lynn W. (1981) "Assessing measurement error in key informant reports: A methodological note on organizational analysis in marketing," *Journal of Marketing Research*, **18** (November), 395–415.

Reid, Stan D. (1981) "The decision-maker and export entry and expansion," *Journal of International Business Studies*, **12** (Fall), 101–12.

—— (1984) "Information acquisition and export entry decisions in small firms," *Journal of Business Research*, **12** (June); 141–57.

Samiee, Saeed and Peter G.P. Walters (1990) "Influence of firm size and export planning and performance," *Journal of Business Research*, **20** (May), 235–48.

—— (1991a) "Rectifying strategic gaps in export management," *Journal of Global Marketing*, **4** (1), 7–37.

—— (1991b) "Segmenting corporate exporting activities: Sporadic versus regular exporters," *Journal of the Academy of Marketing Science*, **19** (Spring), 93–104.

Schwenk, Charles R. (1985) "The use of participant recollection in the modeling of organizational processes," *Academy of Management Journal*, **10** (3); 496–503.

Seringhaus, F.H. Rolf (1986) "The impact of government export marketing assistance," *International Marketing Review*, **3** (2), 55–66.

—— and Guenther Botschen (1991) "Cross-national comparison of export promotion services: The views of Canadian and Austrian companies," *Journal of International Business Studies*, **22** (First Quarter), 115–33.

Seringhaus, F.H. Rolf and Philip J. Rosson (1990) *Government export promotion: A global perspective*. London: Routledge.

Shaw, Robert G. (1977) *Commerce and state department's export promotion programs*. Washington, D.C.: U.S. Government Printing Office.

Singer, Thomas O. (1990) "The role of export promotion in export management: The case of the Minnesota trade office." Unpublished doctoral dissertation, George Washington University.

U.S. Department of Commerce. (1988) "U.S. manufactured exports and export related-employment: Profiles of the 50 states and 35 selected metropolitan areas for 1984." Study prepared by the International Trade Administration.

Wiedersheim-Paul, Finn, H.C. Olson and L.S. Welch (1978) "Pre-export activity: The first step in internationalization," *Journal of International Business Studies*, **9** (Spring/Summer), 47–58.

Wiseman, Frederick and Maryann Billington (1984) "Comment on a standard definition of response rates," *Journal of Marketing Research*, **21** (August), 336–38

III

MANAGEMENT DIMENSIONS

The current decade is characterized by increasingly contested business environments, with more competition from around the world than ever before. As a result, many U.S. executives are feeling much more competitive urgency today in product development, materials procurement, manufacturing, and marketing around the world. The same competitive pressure equally applies to executives of foreign companies. For example, due to cost pressure in its home country, Hoechst, the German chemicals giant with annual revenues larger than those of Dow Chemical and Union Carbide combined, is de-Germanizing its operations by reducing its German workforce to only 30 percent of its worldwide total in 1997, 30 percent less than three years earlier, and beefing up its U.S. operations from less than 6 percent of its annual revenues to 40 percent by the year 2000.[1]

In such a highly competitive environment where the product life cycle is very short and cost pressure is relentless, successful strategy increasingly requires risk-sharing and cooperation. Not many companies can go it alone; they have to pool limited capital resources and technical capabilities for operational viability. Whether they like them or not, cooperative strategies have become a fact of life for most companies.

Chapter 9 explores how cooperating companies can build a trustworthy relationship. Without trust, many cooperative strategies, such as joint ventures, tend to fail. In spite of the increasing popularity of international joint ventures, managers express a high level of dissatisfaction with them. It is argued that overemphasis on the outcome has resulted in a neglect of the social processes underlying the outcome. This chapter also helps understand a shift in focus from ownership-based strategy development to relational dynamics.

Chapter 10 deals with new product development. In the last decade, a large number of new products have been developed by a group of cooperating firms rather than by single companies. Some 905 new product innovations are examined that have been introduced since September 1988 to determine the influences on product innovativeness, with a specific interest in cooperative strategies. Findings suggest that horizontal (e.g. R&D to R&D) cooperative strategies, cross-industry product offerings, and cross-industry cooperations are used for the development of significantly more innovative products. However, truly innovative products seem to be developed by single companies. Strategic implications are sought.

Chapter 11 examines the hidden strengths of Japanese business practices that emphasize customer satisfaction. Ito-Yokado Co. Ltd. of Japan, the long-time licensee of the Southland Corp.'s 7-Eleven store chain, has come back to the U.S. to acquire its parent company and has begun to implement the Japanese firm's management techniques at 7-Eleven stores in the U.S. The key to the campaign, called the Vanguard Program, is a shift in focus from the historical emphasis on volume sales to an emphasis on customer satisfaction. As the Japanese licensee's takeover of the American convenience-store parent company suggests, the next generation of Japanese competition may come unexpectedly from service sectors such as retailing.

Note

1   Greg Steinmetz and Matt Marshall, "How A Chemicals Giant Goes About Becoming A Lot Less German," *Wall Street Journal*, February 18, 1997, A1, A18.

9

Revisiting Multinational Firms' Tolerance for Joint Ventures: A Trust-based Approach

ANOOP MADHOK

UNIVERSITY OF UTAH

International joint venture activity has been increasing in recent years, both in terms of frequency and strategic importance (Geringer and Hebért 1991). In spite of the rising popularity of joint ventures (JVs), there is significant dissatisfaction with their performance (Beamish 1988). This is intuitively inconsistent and indicates that, though firms perceive the need for JVs, they find them difficult to manage. Considering their increasing popularity, it is important to address this inconsistency.

Investigation of JVs has tended to stress the outcome of collaboration (e.g. survival, control, performance) and does not adequately recognize the inseparability of the outcome from the process (Parkhe 1993a; Hebért and Geringer 1993). Parkhe (1993a) has criticized past empirical work on JVs for being haphazard in that researchers have not effectively built upon each other's work if the outcome being investigated was different. He argues that such an orientation ignores critical issues pertaining to the relationship process that have the potential to link and bridge disparate work on JVs through core concepts like trust, reciprocity, opportunism, and forbearance. These concepts, which are interrelated, encompass behavioral variables at the heart of voluntary interfirm cooperation, and have a significant influence on the dynamics and eventual performance within interorganizational collaborations like JVs. In this regard, Beamish (1985) found that the social dimension governing JV relationships was instrumental in explaining part of the dissatisfaction that managers experience with JVs.

The author would like to thank Karin Fladmoe-Lindquist, Steve Tallman, Louis Hebért, Jan Jorgensen, and three anonymous reviewers whose comments significantly improved this paper. Steve Tallman's suggestions were especially helpful.

Ownership and Relationship-centered Approaches Towards Joint Ventures

A major cause for dissatisfaction with JVs is that a dual hierarchy, arising as a result of shared ownership, results in a high potential for conflict. Conflicts of interest due to divergent objectives and operational asymmetries may adversely affect a firm's flexibility in decision making and its ability to coordinate globally (Harrigan 1985; Berg and Friedman 1980; Porter and Fuller 1986). This hampers the efficient conduct of its operations. One approach towards overcoming the difficulties inherent in managing JVs is oriented primarily towards the issue of formal control through owner-ship (Stopford and Wells 1972; Franko 1971; Gomes-Casseres 1989). In this chapter, this approach is referred to as the ownership-centered approach. It suggests that a wholly owned subsidiary provides the firm with the desired flexibility to coordinate activities globally and facilitates decision making through more direct means of control, such as hierarchical fiat (Williamson 1975), available as a result of ownership. In this way, it avoids the problem of managing conflict in JVs. Stopford and Wells (1972) refer to this as unambiguous control.

Other studies (Beamish 1985; Schaan 1983; Tomlinson 1970) focus more closely on the social dimension within which the relationship is embedded in order to attain the desired flexibility. This approach, referred to as the trust-centered approach in this paper, revolves primarily on the notion of trust, and related issues such as reciprocity, commitment and mutual forbearance. Here, owner-ship and control are not viewed as commensurate with one another. Beamish and Banks (1987) argue that the ownership-centered approach tends to neglect the social context surrounding the JV relationship. This prevents the exploitation of the full potential benefits of shared resources, and hampers recognition of the potential for effective reduction of the costs inherent in shared owner-ship through nurturing the social quality of the relationship. Furthermore, it also hinders the attainment of coordination efficiencies. These efficiencies are facilitated by a mutual orientation towards one another, which is based on trust (Johanson and Mattson 1987; Jarillo 1988). Further-more, a cooperative attitude manifests itself in a higher level of flexibility within the relationship (Beamish 1985; Tomlinson 1970). These arguments suggest that, even in the case of majority ownership, the dominant partner would be better off paying attention to the venture's social relations and gradually building up trust since forcing decisions by virtue of sheer ownership would be a pyrrhic victory and ultimately threaten the venture (Friedmann and Beguin 1971; Killing 1983).

Although their focus differs, the common factor underlying both the ownership-centered and the trust-centered approaches is the objective of flexibility and efficiency in the conduct of the operation (Madhok 1995). One emphasizes the attainment of flexibility and efficiency through hierarchical relations while the other emphasizes this through social relations. Given this commonality of interest, it would be useful to understand how the two approaches inform one another. That this has not been done may reflect the different orientations of the two approaches. Ownership-centered approaches are outcome oriented, relatively static and do not address the critical role of social phenomena in interorganizational relationships (Parkhe 1993a; Hebért and Geringer 1993; Ring and Van de Ven 1992). Furthermore, ownership-centered approaches are primarily investigating phe-nomena from within a more structural framework. An overemphasis on the structural features of interorganizational exchange results in a neglect of important process issues which add value to the exchange (Zajac and Olson 1993). For example, Stopford and Wells (1972) and Franko (1971) investigated multinational strategy, structure and consequent control and coordination require-ments and related these to ownership preferences and tolerance for JVs. In studying the issues at this more macro strategy–structure–ownership level, some of the subtle and fine-grained insights that can be obtained from more in-depth studies are difficult to capture. Such in-depth studies (e.g. Schaan 1983, Beamish 1985) investigated specific JV relationships with a micro-level orientation towards control and coordination. For example, in his clinical study of ten JVs in Mexico, Schaan (1983) found that a fit between the objectives of the multinational firm, the focus of control, and the mechanisms to operationalize this control was critical for JV success.

The purpose of this chapter is to show how the trust-centered approach can provide additional insight and enrich current understanding of multinational ownership preferences and the tolerance for JVs. The paper first examines the dynamics of trust, which is crucial to the trust-centered approach, and then discusses it in the context of JV relationships. Following this, some of the key findings of Stopford and Wells (1972) and Franko (1971), two influential and insightful early studies which systematically examined multinational ownership preferences and the tolerance for joint ventures, are reexamined. In the subsequent section, the need for greater attention to the social dynamics of the relationship is reemphasized, and some research implications are discussed.

Two points need to be made clear at the outset. Firstly, it is not the intention in this chapter to single out Stopford and Wells' and Franko's studies (hereafter referred to as the SWF studies) but, rather, to refer to them in the sense of an especially lucid representation of the arguments of the ownership-centered approach. Secondly, the scope of the chapter is explicitly limited to multinational firm–local partner JVs. The reason for this is that the chapter purports to reexamine the ownership-centered approach, as represented by the findings of the SWF studies. These dealt specifically with multinational–local JVs. However, the issue of collaborations between multinational firms for global markets is addressed later on in the chapter. These are too important today to be ignored.

Trust and Its Role in Joint Venture Relationships

THE STRUCTURAL AND SOCIAL DIMENSIONS OF TRUST

In order to explore the dynamics of trust in explaining the tolerance for JV relationships, it is important to understand what trust is and why actors would have a trusting orientation towards each other. Trust is based on a set of mutual expectations or anticipations regarding each other's behavior and each actor's fulfillment of its perceived obligations in light of such anticipation (Thorelli 1986). Trust does not mean the "naive belief in the honesty of other actors but rather the probability of violation of implicit or explicit agreements" (Bromiley and Cummings 1993:10). In other words, trust is the perceived likelihood of the other not behaving in a self-interested manner.

Trust has two components – the structural and the social – each of which reinforces the other. The structural component refers to the complementarity of the resources contributed. Synergy through resource complementarity provides the value added and the consequent inducement to contribute toward the relationship.

With regard to the social component, the quality of the relationship has a strong impact on the nature and value of exchange within it (Jones 1983). Ouchi (1980) argues that trust, arising from the perception of long-term equity within the relationship, is essential for continued benevolent exchange. This perception of equity, by increasing overall goal congruence, induces behavior in the interest of the relationship and reduces the need for monitoring. Trust is especially important in situations of uncertainty since, in its presence, less stringent contracting can occur in the expectation that the social dimensions of the relationship will occasion mutually desirable behavior. Where performance is difficult to measure, as in the team production characteristic of many JVs, trust becomes critical to the relationship since performance need not be so directly measurable in a situation of mutual trust and commonality of interests.

The pattern of interaction provides the social "glue" within which economic exchange occurs. By providing the motive to cooperate and the mutual orientation that determines which action is in the best interest of the relationship, a regime of trust induces reciprocity and coordinates action (Blau 1964; Ouchi 1980). Investment in building trust through mutually oriented actions can then be interpreted as the creation of a stock of goodwill from which an actor can draw when the need arises. Such action also signals a commitment to the relationship (Camerer 1988). It conveys a long-term intent and creates reciprocal obligations. Such reciprocal obligations encourage flexibility within the relationship, although an approximate balance is required over the longer term for its sustenance (Blau 1964; Ouchi 1980). Here, each round of interactions need not be equally satisfactory to both parties provided that, on average, both actors are satisfied by the general pattern of interaction within the relationship over time. Since overall goal congruence facilitates the tolerance of both partial goal conflict and temporary periods of inequity within the relationship, trust creates flexibility within a relationship and has efficiency implications (Wilkins and Ouchi 1983). It reduces friction and is "the behavioral lubricant that can improve a system's operating efficiencies" (Parkhe 1993b: 307).

It is important to recognize the difference in orientation between the structural and social dimensions of trust within a relationship. For the former, the incentive to abstain from behaving in a self-interested manner, i.e. to mutually forbear (Buckley and Casson 1988), is that it would be costly to do otherwise. Here, both firms are in a mutual hostage situation. Opportunistic behavior would deplete the potential value added arising from the partners' complementarities to the detriment of both parties. On the other hand, from the social perspective, mutually oriented behavior is more positive in nature and occurs not to prevent value depletion but to enhance the relationship's value. The two together lower the perceived probability of opportunistic behavior or, conversely, increase trust.

The structural dimension is essential for the creation of the relationship but not sufficient for its continuation. It is necessary since, unless both parties are benefiting from the relationship, it is inherently unstable. It is not sufficient for two reasons. Firstly, a weak social foundation undermines the potential value of the synergy that can be gained by two firms pooling their assets together, since contributions become much more tentative. The partners would also tend to discount the future stream of benefits from the operations more heavily. Furthermore, the cost of the operation increases since greater expectation of opportunism by a partner causes the other to bear higher costs of installing safeguards against opportunism (Parkhe 1993c; Hill 1990; Ring and Van de Ven 1992). A breakdown of the regime of trust and a consequent increase in uncertainty therefore weakens the mutual orientation and diminishes the perceived value of the relationship, making it unsustainable.

Secondly, contributions cannot be continuously evenly matched. This is where the social dimension stabilizes the relationship. It cements the relationship and provides the tolerance through the social "glue" to tide over temporary periods of disequilibrium.

A strong social foundation enhances the potential value of the synergy that can be gained by two firms pooling complementary assets. Where the structural basis of trust is weak, the relationship becomes unstable. The social basis of trust does not play the role of a "super glue" to patch together all differences but, rather, facilitates the continuation of the relationship during intermittent periods of inequity. It makes the relationship more resilient and, consequently, durable. The critical notion here is that inequity is often temporary, and the durability of the relationship is dependent on the social quality within which it is embedded. Therefore, during a period of flux in a relationship, the social aspect of trust acts to prevent a hasty or premature rupture that would sacrifice significant potential future benefits. In other words, the band of tolerance for inequity is wider in the presence of more deeply embedded social relations.[1]

However, the social basis of trust is not adequate in and of itself. Tomlinson and Willie (1978) distinguish between the existence of compatible capabilities and the willingness to provide them, with both being critical to the success of a relationship. These, in our terms, are parallel to the structural and social aspects of a relationship. The social aspects facilitate the attainment of the objectives of the collaboration through more sustained and higher quality inputs and lower conflict and coordination costs. Therefore, investment in trust-building becomes important. The underlying synergistic potential, however, lies in the structural aspects. Tomlinson (1970) found a high correlation between the motivation underlying the formation of JVs and partner complementarities, even amongst partners where there had been a history of successful cooperation. This suggests that, just as the structural component is necessary but not sufficient, neither are the social aspects sufficient in and of themselves. The two do not substitute for one another but rather supplement and reinforce one another.

Proposition 1: The structural component of trust is necessary but not sufficient for the sustained continuation of interfirm relationships.

Proposition 2: The social component of trust is necessary but not sufficient for the sustained continuation of interfirm relationships.

Proposition 3: A relationship will be more durable when the social component is strong than when it is weak.

Proposition 4: Where the structural component is equally strong, differences in the social foundation underlying relationships will result in different rates of stability.

A trustful relationship does not just happen. It evolves gradually over time through repeated successful interaction and has to be carefully nurtured through various forms of hard and soft commitments. A major implication of this is that creating a foundation of trust is a slow, time-consuming and expensive process (Ouchi 1980; Jaeger 1983; Ring and Van de Ven 1992) requiring a significant investment of resources – financial, temporal and managerial. In this regard, the structural and social components of trust have the potential for a positive feedback effect upon one another. As mentioned, successful interfirm cooperation requires a relationship that has both a potential for synergistic creation of value and a more mutually oriented behavior in order to tap and enhance this potential. This value outcome provides the ability or means to invest in the value creation process while the social component provides the willingness to do so.

Proposition 5: Interfirm relationships characterized by both a strong structural and a strong social component of trust will be characterized by a greater investment in trust-building expenditures than those relationships that are not so characterized.

The presence of both components of trust is therefore important. The positive feedback effect between the two components of the relationship, by influencing the ability or means and the willingness to invest in the relationship, builds resilience into a relationship and strengthens it by making it more self-sustaining.

An effective collaboration smoothens the interface between partners and is characterized by trust and understanding. In this way, it confirms the partners' importance to one another. A couple of prominent examples are illustrative. One is the GE–Snecma JV. Originally brought together by product–market complementarities in jet engine technology, this JV enjoyed strong top-level commitment. When lower level personnel in GE would attempt to engage in self-interested behavior, these issues were always resolved at a higher level in the spirit of the partners mutual commitment (Lewis 1990). Success in the initial phase of the relationship resulted in continued cooperation over a family of engines that has lasted to the present. Such cooperation has been facilitated by a demonstration of flexibility over the duration of the relationship. For example, in order to be fair, GE and Snecma have periodically readjusted their contractual revenue-sharing formula due to unexpected changes in inflation and exchange rates (Lewis 1990). This is not to suggest that the relationship has not been occasionally stormy. However, due to their structural complementarities and the social quality of the relationship, the arrangement has survived these moments. Such conflict, if handled properly, plays a positive role in that it tests the resolve and strengthens the resilience of the relationship. In discussing the GE–Snecma JV, Roehl and Truitt (1987) argue that such conflict results in better "real" relationships and provides the experience and sophistication to deal with dynamic environments characterized by uncertainty without destroying the commitment to the venture.

Another example is the collaboration between Boeing, the dominant partner, and a Japanese consortium for the development of jet aircraft. The two sides needed one another to share massive development costs and to realize synergies between the design experience of Boeing and the manufacturing efficiencies of the Japanese. In this venture, the Japanese had to undertake a significant degree of risk in terms of loss of income should the expected sales of the 757 fail to materialize. When this happened, Boeing allocated some work on other planes as a compromise gesture, even though there was no contractual commitment to do so. This gesture of integrity created a level of good will that facilitated resolution of later conflicts (Moxon, Roehl and Truitt 1988). The collaboration has now lasted into the next generation of aircraft with the Japanese being permitted a much more constructive role than in the earlier phase of the relationship.

APPLICATION TO THE JV

Partner commitment and compatibility is a critical issue in JV relationships. Friedman and Beguin (1971) argue that ownership arrangements are not as important for successful JV performance as the similarity of outlook and objectives, i.e. compatibility. Greater compatibility increases the probability of balance between inducements and contributions with temporary imbalances being smoothed by trust. Greater compatibility manifests itself in greater commitment to the JV, which enables broader "bands of tolerance" and makes the partners more flexible with respect to the JV's operations. In such cases, they would be more willing to accept minority ownership, adapt products to local markets, accept the partner's personnel in important positions, adapt systems to accommodate the partner's needs, etc. (Beamish 1985). Such ventures are characterized by a greater allocation of time and effort towards trust-building and knowledge transfer, greater interaction through more regular meetings and visits, and an open communication system (Schaan 1983), all of which results in clear mutual expectations and enables more efficient coordination.

Beamish's (1985) identification of a positive correlation between commitment and need for the partner, and a negative correlation between commitment and extent of control desired, reflects both dimensions of trust in a JV relationship. The former addresses the mutual complementarities which underlie the structural dimension of trust while the latter addresses the social aspects, where the existence of commitment mitigates the desire for formal control measures. Tomlinson (1970) and Beamish (1985) argue that the extent of concern over control reflects the nature of a firm's attitudes toward the partner's contributions, with lower concern being symptomatic of a more positive evaluation of the relationship and a lower tendency to act solely in one's own interest. Such a positive evaluation, and consequent commitment, is facilitated by a high level of structural compatibility between the partners' inputs. Positive attitudes result in a greater ability to tap and benefit from partners' resources. (Beamish 1985; Tomlinson 1970).

The implicit assumption by authors such as Davidson and McFetridge (1985) that wholly owned subsidiaries are more efficient than JVs is not necessarily true. Depending on the nature of resources needed, the initial stock of commitment and the interaction between these two factors, JVs can be both a revenue enhancing and a more efficient mode of organizing (Beamish and Banks 1987). In this respect, mutual need for the partner's resources makes shared ownership more conducive towards encouraging participation while the presence of commitment curbs the transaction costs arising from opportunism, small numbers bargaining and uncertainty, and also facilitates information sharing. Under these conditions, the additional costs faced in the management of JVs can be contained at a level where benefits are greater than the costs. Development of the relationship over time leads to lower costs of transacting (Jarillo 1988; Ring and Van de Ven 1992).

Arguments against the use of JVs due to the associated problems of coordination and control imply that internalization would solve these problems. However, this does not recognize that headquarter–subsidiary relationships are also mixed-motive dyads similarly characterized by independent and interdependent interests (Ghoshal and Nobria 1989). Accordingly, depending on the role and strengths of different subsidiaries, the multinational firm faces governance problems and related costs in control and coordination of different operations, even when fully owned. Therefore, the assumption of such a direct inverse relationship between ownership and coordination and control costs is questionable, and it would be more appropriate to approach the issue in a comparative manner, where the coordination and control costs of JVs are compared with those of wholly owned subsidiaries (Gomes-Casseres 1987).

The incremental costs of managing JVs arise partially from the costs of maintaining safeguards against the possibility of self-seeking behavior arising from divergent objectives. As noted above, ownership-centered approaches inadequately recognize the scope for reduction of opportunistic behavior which is available through addressing the social context of the relationship. A positive social dynamic between partners is important, since it facilitates the building of trust within a relationship. Jarillo (1988) argues that where a relationship is value laden due to its social properties, it can manifest the advantages of hierarchies identified by Williamson (1975). According to Jarillo (1990), neither pure market nor pure hierarchical relations are critical for sustaining a relationship: trust is.

The argument that nurturing the social dimension increases flexibility and tolerance, especially in a situation of ambiguity, is especially relevant in entities such as JVs, which involve team production by two actors contributing their respective inputs for mutual benefits. Here, Beamish's (1985) observation of dissatisfaction with the JV's performance in cases where one partner had greater than two avenues over the other for earning income is significant. This shows that the perception of equity within the relationship does not automatically arise from the formal aspects of ownership. The alignment of incentives through the sharing of ownership is not adequate to ensure desirable action by the partner. Through income earning avenues like royalties for technology supplied, monopoly over the supply of inputs, management fees etc., the multinational firm can capture the bulk of the value added prior to the formal sharing of gains through the ownership structure. Therefore the critical issue is not that of the formal distribution of the residual income in line with the percentage of equity ownership but, rather, that of equity and fairness with respect to the process of the relationship itself. This perception of equity is important to encourage mutually oriented action, beyond the very minimum under the terms of the agreement. Without it, the base of trust would be violated.

In this regard, Cory's (1982) statement that JVs are a mixture of contract and commitment is relevant. Here, the critical initial decisions are agreed to contractually in the negotiation phase, but sustenance of the relationship is based on trust and commitment. This commitment develops through interaction, and results in a trust-based relationship that more closely resembles an internalized mode than a contractual one (Cory 1982). This implies a shift from control through the ownership structure to influencing behavior through interaction and the nurturing of relationships (Beamish 1988).

The need for control is positively correlated with lack of information which then heightens the level of risk perceived by an actor and consequently affects the choice of governance structure (Ring and Van de Ven 1992). A successful pattern of interaction results in not only a trustful orientation, where relationship-specific routines as a result of greater experience with each other facilitate coordination and lower the proclivity to be opportunistic, but also greater knowledge about each other as a result of a more open sharing of information. This lowers information asymmetries and consequent scope for opportunism and perceived risk. This then lowers the perceived probability of opportunism and, combined with a lower perceived necessity for maintaining safeguards, explains why a successful cooperative history was found to be the most important criterion in the selection of JV partners (Tomlinson 1970).

The various propositions by Ring and Van de Ven (1992), and the support for various hypotheses by Parkhe (1993c), regarding the impact of the perceived level of opportunism or trust within an interfirm relationship upon the nature of behavior and performance are in line with the arguments discussed in this paper. For example, Ring and Van de Ven (1992) proposed that reliance on trust emerges gradually though repeated rounds of interaction by both parties observing the norms of equity. Similarly, they proposed that the perceived level of risk is lower where a relationship is characterized by greater trust, and that this has direct implications for the elaborateness of safeguards. Parkhe found support for his hypotheses that: (1) the elaborateness of safeguards and the perception of opportunistic behavior are directly related; (2) the extent of commitment that a firm is willing to make is directly related to the perception of opportunistic behavior; and (3) the perceived level of opportunistic behavior is negatively related to the history of cooperation between two actors.

In concluding this section on trust, trust has efficiency implications, and its potential cost reduction and value enhancing properties need to be recognized. Trust is dynamic in nature and changes over the life of the relationship. It is both input into and output of a relationship and infuses the relationship with value. Creation and sustenance of trust in a relationship requires a significant commitment of hard and soft resources. The cost reduction and value-enhancing properties of trust make available valuable resources for investing and reinvesting in the relationship for its continued sustenance. Opportunistic behavior, or expectation of such by the other, depreciates this asset of trust while mutually oriented behavior leverages it.

Revisiting the Multinational Firm's Tolerance for Joint Ventures

So far, the dynamics of trust and the importance of paying attention to the social dimension in JV relationship has been discussed. This section reexamines the key ownership-centered arguments regarding multinational ownership preferences and the tolerance for JV relationships, most lucidly explained by Stopford and Wells (1972) and Franko (1971).

PRODUCT AND MARKET STANDARDIZATION STRATEGIES

The extent of ownership has always been a critical issue in multinational operations. Stopford and Wells (1972) and Franko (1971) argued that market or product standardization strategies, occurring in the mature stages of an industry when there is greater homogeneity of tastes and stiffer competition, are characterized by pressures to lower both production and administrative costs through consolidation and rationalization. This increases the desirability of tighter coordination between units and, by centralizing the locus of decision making, results in a lower tolerance for JVs. JVs increase the potential for friction and adversely effect the flexibility in decision making required for overall system optimization. In other words, strategies requiring centralized control result in a more cautious attitude towards JVs. On the other hand, a strategy based upon product diversification or market expansion results in a higher tolerance for JVs since, when a firm's resources are allocated towards introduction of new products rather than cost minimization and strategic coordination, JVs provide a desirable complementarity.

These arguments can be interpreted in a different light. JVs by definition are more complicated to manage because of dual hierarchies. One way to manage the greater potential for friction is to influence the social context of interaction. As mentioned earlier, creating a foundation of trust is a slow, time-consuming and expensive process. Creation and sustenance of trust requires both structural compatibility as well as the willingness to invest in the relationship to enable more effective realization, on a continual basis, of the potential benefits of such compatibility. The requirements for investment in trust-building are greater in the formative period of a relationship in order to absorb the initially higher costs of creating commitment, including any possible losses from self-interested behavior in the initial stages. However, once the foundation has been secured, extraordinary expenditures for relationship sustenance are minimal, though normal expenditures are still necessary to enable continued enhancement and realization of value from the relationship.

One principal source of resources for investment into the relationship is above-normal returns. Greater competition during the more mature stages of an industry, when firms pursue standardized strategies, makes the attainment of above normal returns difficult. This is not the case in an earlier stage characterized by less competition. This argument addresses the issue of scarcity and munificence of environments (Aldrich 1975) where, in lean environments characterized by more intensive competition and dissipation of excess rents, there is less slack and coordination and cost minimization become more important. Furthermore, in cases where the scope of the operation is global, as is often the case in world-wide consolidation and rationalization strategies, while the JV partner is strictly local, coordination at a more centralized level is preferred by the multinational firm and communication flows at a local level are largely of an implementing nature. The weaker structural foundation, due to relatively insubstantive inputs from the local unit, results in lower commitment towards building a long-term stable relationship. Therefore, both the structural and the social basis of the relationship are undermined. In such environments, firms are less able to undertake, and less tolerant of, the investments necessary for trustbuilding in JVs.

PRODUCT DIVERSIFICATION

With respect to product diversification, the SWF studies found that most product diversification strategies were in related products. According to them, product diversification strategies involved uncertainty for multinational firms since these firms were usually product-oriented and lacked the market orientation that was equally important for the success of such strategies. These strategies required greater decentralization and flexibility to adapt to local markets, which increased the tolerance for JVs. In such cases, the need for complementary resources was greater than the cost of reduced levels of control. Stopford and Wells (1972) argued that the provision of an ownership stake in recognition of the partner's contribution was expected to provide incentives to the partner to act in the interest of the JV.

The argument was made earlier, however, that a mere ownership stake is not sufficient in a JV, and needs to be supplemented by a belief or trust that each partner is acting in the best interest of the relationship. A perception of equity, aside from the ownership structure, is all the more important in strategies of related product diversification. This is because the relatedness makes it difficult for the value of the firm's contribution to be accurately measured and reflected in a contract (Jones and Hill 1988), since shared activities are difficult to disentangle and cost separately. This increases coordination costs and opportunities for conflict (Jones and Hill 1988).

In a situation characterized simultaneously by the desirability of the partner's contributions and greater scope for conflict, investment in trust-building expenditures is critical in order to exploit more effectively the synergies due to product–market complementarities. Under related diversification strategies, economies of scope arising from the relatedness between products result in more efficient utilization of firm resources (Teece 1982). Such economies are unlikely to be available in the case of single or unrelated products (Mahoney and Pandian 1992) where there is little scope for sharing costs across activities. Moreover, first-mover advantages of new product introduction into new markets provide scope for initial monopolistic rents. This first-mover advantage is further enhanced in the case of JVs oriented towards local markets of limited capacity. All these factors enable the firm to undertake the investments necessary to create and realize a more sound relationship with their JV partners.

PRODUCT INNOVATION

Stopford and Wells (1972) found that product innovation strategies, being dominated by fears of technology leakage, free riding, and problems of technology pricing, were characterized by a desire for greater control. This resulted in a strong apprehension regarding JVs and a preference for subsidiaries over JVs.

Product innovation strategies are characterized by a high degree of uncertainty due to the technological and task complexity and the uncertainty of returns. Furthermore, product innovation mostly occurs in the early stages of the product life cycle when the environment is more volatile (Harrigan 1985) and the routines less codified. Greater complexity and a more volatile environment in these stages lower firms' ability to respond to situations through a fixed set of routines (Aldrich 1975), and consequently increases the scope for conflict. This lowers the tolerance for decision making through JVs. In situations characterized by such uncertainty and ambiguity, the contract would be increasingly incomplete, consequently heightening the firm's concerns regarding opportunistic behavior by a partner. In such situations, a high level of trust would be required to mitigate such concerns. The resources required, whether temporal, managerial or financial, for creating such a high level of trust would make the firm reluctant to enter into a locally oriented JV, which provides limited scope to generate a sufficiently high level of gain. Furthermore, as in the case of product and market standardization strategies, a local partner's contribution is not so significant. This weakens the commitment toward building a long-term stable relationship. All these factors undermine the relationship and result in a lower tolerance for JVs.

Briefly speaking, the SWF studies found the highest tolerance for JVs when the strategy and the scope of the operation was local in nature. Here, both partners were able to make valued contributions. Where the JV is such that the local partner does not make a significant contribution, there is little incentive to enter into a JV except for defensive or passive reasons, such as financing needs or benefits of local identity. Here, the partner's contribution is valued more as a convenience than a contribution, resulting in little commitment on both sides and a greater incentive to free ride by the local partner. Furthermore, any opportunistic behavior by the local partner is less likely to be tolerated by the multinational, since the asset contributed by the partner to the venture is not so firm-specific. In other words, a small numbers situation does not exist, resulting in a lack of incentive to nurture the relationship and, simultaneously, little patience for shirking and free riding by the local partner (Beamish 1988). A weak structural foundation and such a negative social atmosphere lowers tolerance for JVs and makes sustenance of the relationship improbable. This further explains the SWF studies' finding of low tolerance for JVs in the case of product innovation, marketing standardization, and production rationalization.

ABILITY TO MANAGE CHANGE

From the above discussion, it is clear that the scope of a particular operation, deriving from the multinational firm's strategy, is critical to the tolerance for JVs. Franko (1971) observed a peaking in JV instability in line with changes in strategy and accompanying changes in structure, though there were differences in the lags between the change and the instability, as well as differences in stability rates. For example, with increasing significance of international operations and other exogenous environmental changes, like demand convergence and technological developments, a shift from a decentralized strategy through an international division to a more centralized one through worldwide product divisions or geography-based regional structures resulted in a lack of tolerance for existing JVs and consequent increase in failure rates.

This can be understood more clearly when one considers Granovetter's (1985) argument that it is the nature and pattern of interaction within a relationship, rather than its institutional properties, which are critical for the efficient conduct of an activity. We argued earlier that trust is a dynamic concept and that the structural and social aspects underlying the relationship strongly influence the nature and pattern of interaction. A major cause of conflict in JVs is that the relative contributions and comparative advantages of the venture partners change continually, whether due to exogenous events or due to internal dynamics, for example differential rates of learning by both partners (Hamel 1991). This influences the evaluation of a firm's contributions.

Regarding Franko's finding of a peak in JV instability, the change in strategic scope or purpose of the operation and concomitant change in structure and systems changed the nature and desirable pattern of interaction within the relationship. The perceived propensity for trust or opportunism depends upon the nature and pattern of interaction (Jones and Hesterly 1993). In this case, the need for strategic coordination and control of the operation increased and the locus of strategic decision making moved to a supranational level. Consequently, the role of the local operation changed from a relatively substantive one to that of an implementor, where the erstwhile contributions of the JV partner are less valued, reducing the structural bonding properties of the relationship. In other words, the structural foundation of the relationship became weakened in a manner creating not a temporary but a long-term disequilibrium. Furthermore, increased interdependence among various units under such closely coordinated strategies increased the negative externalities of self-interested behavior. In a relationship with a more tightly coordinated and interdependent system, where the structural foundation of the relationship is weakened and, simultaneously, there is a greater potential for negative externalities, the potential for, and probability of, self-interested behavior is perceived to be higher, i.e. lower trust. This in turn influences the evaluation of the relationship and destabilizes it (Parkhe 1993c), since there is a lack of correspondence between the incentive or payoff structure and the new reality. Such a correspondence between the relatively inflexible incentive system and the variable importance of partners' respective inputs is difficult to maintain, and is a major source of strain in the relationship (Berg and Friedman 1980).

Structural changes in firm complementarities can therefore strain a relationship and consequently influence tolerance for JVs. Where the basis for such conflict is long-term structural disequilibria in contributions, the bonding properties of the social dimension become inadequate. Clearly, there are limits to trust. At the same time, the underlying social properties of the relationship would be manifest in different degrees of flexibility in managing these strategic disjunctures, and would be reflected in differences in lags before failure and differential survival and failure rates in the face of similar strategic changes.

The above discussion of the peaking phenomenon noticed by Franko suggests that comparative costs need to be evaluated not just against another governance structure, for instance a subsidiary versus a JV, but also with regard to costs within the same form before and after a change in strategy that alters the scope or purpose of the activity to be undertaken. It is worth mentioning, however, that where the social foundation of a relationship is strong, a demise of one venture due to structural weaknesses need not equate with the end of the relationship between two actors. There are numerous instances of partners being engaged in multiple partnerships, simultaneous or sequential, which have been built around a successful cooperative history. Here the relationship, the process and not the outcome, is viewed as a value-bearing asset in its own right (Jarillo and Stevenson 1991).

The ability to build and maintain trust is a critical component of understanding tolerance for JVs. Clearly, however, there are differences in actors' abilities to invest in trust building expenditures and to pursue a cooperative strategy. In the presence of significant size asymmetries, it is easier for a larger firm, being less dependent on the venture, to nurture a positive atmosphere. This is due to both a higher tolerance for losses, in case of opportunistic behavior, and to the normally higher stakes and greater vulnerability of the smaller partner. Such would be the case in many of the multinational operations studied by Stopford and Wells and Franko. Similarly, a well-diversified firm has a greater ability to make trust-building gestures, since resources from other activities can both be tapped for investment in trust building as well as provide the firm with the buffering capacity to absorb violations of trust in any single activity. This is much more difficult for firms with more limited sources of income based on a single critical sphere of activities. This reinforces Franko's findings that undiversified firms pursuing functional strategies had a lower tolerance for JVs.

Discussion and Research Implications

The stability of cooperative agreements is a combination of the structural and social aspects of a relationship. The structural dimension underlying interfirm relationships is necessary but not sufficient, and needs to be complemented by a greater attention to the social component within which the relationship is embedded. The SWF studies were most original and insightful, and have made major contributions towards our understanding of multinational ownership preferences, especially in the environment of that time. Their focus, however, is primarily on the formal and structural aspects of the relationship and, consequently, the informal and social dimension is neglected.

Both these dimensions have the common objective of obtaining flexibility and efficiency in the conduct of the multinational firm's operations. The important issue perhaps is *not* that of ownership per se but, rather, that of superior coordination and conflict resolution. Refocusing the pivotal issue away from ownership has important implications. The core of the argument shifts the emphasis from hierarchical governance mechanisms to "relationship management". It extends the extant strategy–structure–ownership approach towards multinational operations to include the process of coordination and conflict resolution through microlevel and process-oriented mechanisms. Furthermore, by deemphasizing ownership (the distinctive feature of JVs *vis à vis* other collaborative forms), and by encouraging a deeper appreciation of relational dynamics, the basic underlying arguments, revolving around notions of trust, reciprocity, forbearance, and opportunism, can be extended beyond JVs and applied to all collaborative relationships, such as strategic alliances. This takes on added importance in today's business environment where, in the face of the exigencies of technological complexity and global competition, firms are increasingly engaging in a wide variety of collaborative agreements.

The shift in focus from ownership to relational dynamics has a number of important research implications. One potentially fruitful area of research would be the nature and mechanisms by which firms build and maintain a relationship characterized by trust. For example, do firms invest more resources in trust building in the initial stages of a relationship, when mutual trust is usually lower? If so, how? An example would be staffing policy. The multinational firm may initially choose to rotate personnel less frequently so that social relationships have greater continuity and boundary personnel can acquire greater mutual confidence. Another significant gesture would be the secondment of a more prominent person, which would signal a higher level of commitment to the operation. What is the nature and pattern of interaction in relationships characterized by trust? Is it more personal and more dense in the initial stages? This has the potential both to generate greater confidence and to enable the formation of norms, which would facilitate coordination and lower the need for interaction later. In an ongoing relationship, is the pattern dynamic, for example a flurry of interaction during periods of conflict in order to demonstrate commitment and contain it? What are the differences in trust-building expenditures and mechanisms between firms that are satisfied and those that are dissatisfied with their JV relationships? Under what circumstances are firms willing to commit to such investments? What characterizes more durable relationships and makes them more resilient? Is there a difference in the emphasis on ownership versus relationship dynamics? How do conflict resolution mechanisms differ between satisfied and dissatisfied firms? In this regard, how dominated are the partners by the contract in contrast to the ongoing relationship? Research into such process issues would be fruitful since they are inextricably intertwined with the outcome.

In line with the scope of the SWF studies, this paper has primarily addressed multinational–local JVs. Another important area of research is that of collaborations, both JVs and strategic alliances, between two multinational firms. Such collaborative activity has become increasingly popular in global and knowledge-intensive industries, where firms encounter high uncertainty and limits to their capabilities. Such collaborations, especially those with a broad scope, in terms of product–market coverage and a multiplicity of objectives and functions, and a more volatile environment, are confronted with increased task complexity and uncertainty of returns. In such operations, potential for both conflict and contribution is high. The ample scope for a wide range of behavior, both positive and negative, then influences each other's evaluation of the relationship (Buckley and Casson 1988). Such collaborations, if successful, require flexibility in conduct and would be expected to be characterized by high levels of both risk and trust (Killing 1988).

It would be naive to overemphasize trust and to neglect the competitive elements of the interaction between two partners. Interfirm collaboration is clearly a mixed motive game where the relationship is characterized by a spirit of collaboration (for creation of the pie) and competition (for distribution of the pie). It is important to know when to collaborate and when to compete. An important research issue would be that of the strategies pursued by firms to manage different combinations of risk and trust. Firms may undertake a strategy of complexification (Schoemaker 1990) through continuous investment in know-how in order to make the source of advantage less transparent. Firms may resort to more complex governance structures to manage the risk (Ring and Van de Ven 1992). An example would be nested arrangements where a core technology is licensed within a JV, e.g. the collaboration between Ericsson and Honeywell, as described by Kogut (1988). In this case, joint research and development in the JV, drawing on the expertise of both the firms, not only resulted in sharing risk, but also through shared research efforts enabled coordination and was instrumental in building trust (Kogut 1988). Through cleverly crafted agreements, safeguards can be maintained, even if there is trust. Firms may choose to maintain selective control over critical activities, rather than overall control through equity. This also provides scope for economizing on coordination and control costs, as well as signalling an intention or commitment not to dominate all aspects of the relationship. These issues, and others related to the process and mechanisms for managing risk and building trust, need to be researched.

If the conceptual framework discussed in this chapter holds across different kinds of interfirm agreements and across different kinds of partners, then the implication would be that it is fairly robust. For example, Hladik (1985) found a number of R&D-driven JVs between two multinational firms where greater information sharing occurred due to first-mover advantages (e.g. setting of technological standards), since the benefits of joint technological development and rapid market penetration were greater than the negative externalities from leakage. In line with the underlying logic of this chapter, it can be argued that the monopolistic advantages, along with the low price elasticity characterizing new products, generate excess rents in the short term. Such potential rents are enhanced by the global scope of the operation. Thus, value creation through complementary capabilities can be used to enhance the relationship and absorb any additional costs of collaboration, with the excess resources generated being used for investments in building trust. Moreover, where complementary capabilities are mutually valued, the possibility of future team production would curtail opportunistic behavior. The examples of the GE–Snecma and the Boeing–Japanese consortia relationships clearly illustrate this.

Basically, careful attention needs to be paid to the process of the relationship with the partner in order to reduce the costs and increase the gains from the collaboration, and issues such as control and leakage may need to be managed and, at times, traded off against the benefits of complementary resources (Mody 1993). For example, on one hand may be the risk of unintended technological spill-overs (Hamel 1991) while, on the other, concomitant with the greater risks may be the potential for greater returns. When do managers decide to make such trade-offs? Under what circumstances? How do they manage them? These are issues that are ripe for further research.

Conclusion

The simultaneous popularity of international JVs and dissatisfaction with their performance indicates the need for greater attention to, and a more sophisticated understanding of, the process of governing them. "Relationship management" is increasingly important in today's business environment where the forces of global competition and technological dynamism compel even the strongest firms to enter collaborative relationships in order to remain competitive. This chapter elaborated upon a trust-centered perspective and discussed key process issues pertaining to relational dynamics, embedded in notions of cooperation and opportunism, which Parkhe (1993a) has suggested are critical to theoretical development and a more complete understanding of JV relationships. We also reexamined the structural arguments of the ownership-centered approach by revisiting Stopford and Wells' (1972) and Franko's (1971) studies of multinational firms' ownership strategies and tolerance for JVs, and showed that relationship-oriented reasoning, revolving around trust, is largely consistent with their ownership-centered arguments. This then links strategy–structure–ownership issues with more dynamic social exchange issues. A focus on dynamic processes underlying the relationship provides additional insights into multinational ownership preferences and the JV process. A structural orientation treats interfirm relationships as largely predictable (Zajac and Olson 1993). Greater attention to the social dimension not only enriches understanding but, additionally, can explain some of the variance in JV instability rates that ownership-dominated approaches are not able to capture.

I would like to conclude with a caveat. This chapter has focused on the social dynamics underlying the tolerance for JVs. However, I fully recognize that there are other reasons why JVs may continue to exist even when the structural and social foundation is weak. These include, among others, legal restrictions on ownership, government incentives and disincentives (e.g. tax breaks) and high exit costs making the reversal of the JV decision difficult. All these would distort the cost–benefit calculus and result in continued tolerance for JVs, at least in form if not in spirit.

Notes

1   The structural and social components of trust are somewhat analogous to the two types of diversity within firms identified by Parkhe (1991). Type I referred to the "harder" differences in the complementary contributions that

occasioned the relationship in the first place, or what we refer to as the structural component of trust. Type II referred to the "softer" differences that arose from differencs in firms' culture and systems. Broadly speaking, the role of the social component of trust is that of smoothening the relationship by reducing the disruptive influence of Type II diversity through a more developed mutual orientation, while making it more resilient in the face of temporary fluctuations in Type I diversity.

References

Aldrich, Howard (1975) "An organization-environment perspective on cooperation and conflict between organizations in the manpower training system." In Anant R. Negandhi (ed.) *Interorganization Theory*. Kent, Oh. Kent State University Press, 49–71.

Bartlett, Christopher A. (1986) "Building and managing the transnational: The new organizational challenge." In Michael E. Porter (ed.) *Competition in Global Industries*. Boston, Mass.: Harvard Business School Press, 367–401.

Beamish, Paul W. (1985) *Joint Venture Performance in Developing Countries*. Unpublished Ph. D. dissertation. University of Western Ontario, London, Ontario.

—— (1988) *Multinational Joint Ventures in Developing Countries*. New York: Routledge.

—— and John C. Banks (1987) "Equity joint ventures and the theory of the multinational enterprise," *Journal of International Business Studies*, **18** (2); 1–16.

Berg, Sanford V. and Phillip Friedman (1980) "Corporate courtship and successful joint ventures," *California Management Review*, **22**, 85–91.

Blau, Peter M. (1964) *Exchange and Power in Social Life*. New York: Wiley.

Bourgeois, Lawrence J. (1981) "On the measurement of organizational slack," *Academy of Management Review*, **6** (1), 29–39.

Bromiley, Phil and Larry L. Cummings (1993) "Organizations with trust: Theory and measurement." Paper presented at the Academy of Management Conference, Atlanta.

Buckley, Peter J. and Mark Casson (1988) "A theory of cooperation in international business." In Farok J. Contractor and Peter Lorange (ed.) *Cooperative Strategies in International Business*. Lexington, Mass: Lexington Books, 31–54.

Camerer, Colin (1988) "Gifts as economic signals and social symbols." In C. Winship and S. Rosen (eds) *Organizations and Institutions: Sociological and Economic Approaches to the Analysis of Social Structure*. Chicago: University of Chicago Press, 180–214.

Cohen, Wesley M and Daniel A. Levinthal (1990) "Absorptive capacity: A new perspective on learning and innovation," *Administrative Science Quarterly*, **35**, 28–52.

Cory, Peter F. (1982) "Industrial cooperation, joint ventures and the multinational enterprise in Yugoslavia." In Alan M. Rugman. (ed.) *New Theories of the Multinational Enterprise*. London: Croom Helm, 133–71.

Davidson, William H. and Donald G. McFetridge (1985) "Key characteristics in the choice of international technology transfer mode," *Journal of International Business Studies*, **16** (2); 5–21.

Franko, Lawrence G. (1971) *Joint Venture Survival in Multinational Corporations*. New York: Praeger.

Friedmann, Wolfgang G. and John-Pierre Beguin (1971) *Joint International Business Ventures in Developing Countries*. New York: Columbia University Press.

Geringer, J. Michael and Louis Hebért (1989) "Control and performance of international joint ventures," *Journal of International Business Studies*, **20** (2), 235–54.

—— (1991) "Measuring performance of international joint ventures," *Journal of International Business Studies*, **22** (2), 249–64.

Ghoshal, Sumantra and Christopher A. Bartlett (1988) "Creation, adoption and diffusion of innovations by subsidiaries of multinational corporations," *Journal of International Business Studies*, **19** (4), 365–388.

Ghoshal, Sumantra and Nitin Nobria (1989) "Internal differentiation within the multinational corporation,"

Strategic Management Journal, **10**, 323–37.

Gomes-Casseres, Benjamin (1987) "Joint venture instability: Is it a problem?" *Columbia Journal of World Business*, **22** 97–102.

—— (1989) "Ownership structure of foreign subsidiaries: Theory and evidence," *Journal of Economic Behavior and Organization*, **11**, 1–25.

Granovetter, Mark (1985) "Economic action and social structure: The problem of embeddedness," *American Journal of Sociology*, **91** (3), 481–510.

Hamel, Gary (1991) "Competition for competence and interpartner learning within international strategic alliances," *Strategic Management Journal*, **12** (special issue), 83–103.

Harrigan, Kathryn R. (1985) *Strategies for Joint Ventures*. Lexington Mass: Lexington Books.

Hebért, Louis and J. Michael Geringer (1993) "Division of control and performance outcomes in international joint ventures: A social exchange framework." Paper presented at the Academy of Management Conference, Atlanta.

Hill, Charles W.L. (1990) "Cooperation, opportunism, and the invisible hand: Implications for transaction cost theory," *Academy of Management Review*, **15** (3), 500–13.

Hladik, Karen J. (1985) *International Joint Ventures: An Economic Analysis of US–Foreign Business Partnerships*. Lexington, Mass.: D.C. Heath.

Jaeger, Alfred M. (1983) "The transfer of organizational culture overseas: An approach to control in the multinational corporation," *Journal of International Business Studies*, **14** (3), 91–114.

Jarillo, Jose-Carlos (1988) "On strategic networks," *Strategic Management Journal*, **9** 31–41.

—— (1990) "Comments on 'transaction costs and networks'," *Strategic Management Journal*, 11, 497–99.

—— and Howard H. Stevenson. (1991) "Cooperative strategies – The payoffs and the pitfalls," *Long Range Planning*, **24** (1), 64–70.

Johanson, Jan and Lars-Gunnar Mattson (1987) "Interorganizational relations in industrial systems: A network approach compared with the transaction cost approach," *International Studies of Management and Organization*, **17** (1), 34–48.

Jones, Candice and William S. Hesterly (1993) "Alternatives in coordinating economic exchange: Markets and networks in the American film industry." Paper presented at the Academy of Management Conference, Atlanta.

Jones, Gareth R. (1983) "Transaction costs, property rights and organizational culture: An exchange perspective," *Administrative Science Quarterly*, **28**, 454–67.

—— and Charles W. L. Hill (1988) "Transaction cost analysis of strategy structure choice," *Strategic Management Journal*, **9**, 159–72.

Killing, J. Peter (1983) *Strategies for Joint Venture Success*, London: Croom Helm.

—— (1988) "Understanding alliances: The role of task and organizational complexity." In Farok J. Contractor and Peter Lorange (eds) *Cooperative Strategies in International Business*. Lexington, Mass.: Lexington Books, 55–68.

Kogut, Bruce (1988) "A study of the lifecycle of joint ventures." In Farok J. Contractor and Peter Lorange (eds) *Cooperative Strategies in International Business*. Lexington, Mass.: Lexington Books, 145–68.

Lewis, Jordan D. (1990) *Partnerships for Profit: Structuring and Managing Strategic Alliances*. New York: The Free Press.

Madhok, Anoop (1995) "Opportunism and trust in joint venture relationships: An exploratory study and a model," *Scandinavian Journal of Management*, **11**, 1–5.

Mahoney, Joseph T. and J. Rajendran Pandian (1992) "The resource-based view within the conversation of strategic management," *Strategic Management Journal*, **13**, 363–81.

Mody, Ashok. (1993) "Learning through alliances," *Journal of Economic Behavior and Organization*, **20**, 151–70.

Moxon, Richard W., Thomas W. Roehl, and J. Frederick Truitt (1988) "International cooperative ventures in the commercial aircraft entry: Gains, sure, but what's my share?" In Farok J. Contractor and Peter Lorange (eds) *Cooperative Strategies in International Business*, Lexington, Mass: Lexington Books, 255–78.

Ouchi, William G. (1980) "Market, bureaucracies, and clans," *Administrative Science Quarterly*, 25: 129–41.

Parkhe, Arvind (1991) "Interfirm diversity, organizational learning, and longevity in global strategic alliances," *Journal of International Business Studies*, **20**, 579–601.

—— (1993a) " 'Messy' research, methodological predispositions, and theory development in international joint ventures," *Academy of Management Review*, **18** (2), 227–68.

—— (1993b) "Partner nationality and the structure-performance relationship in strategic alliances," *Organization Science*, **4** (2), 301–24.

—— (1993c) "Strategic alliance structuring: A game theoretic and transaction cost examination of interfirm cooperation," *Academy of Management Journal*, **36** (4), 794–829.

Porter, Michael E. and Mark B. Fuller (1986) "Coalitions and global strategy." In Michael E. Porter, (ed.) *Competition in Global Industries*. Boston, Mass.: Harvard Business School Press, 315–42.

Ring, Peter S. and Andrew H. Van de Ven (1992) "Structuring cooperative relationships between organizations," *Strategic Management Journal*, **13**, 483–98.

Roehl, Thomas W. and J. Frederick Truitt (1987) "Stormy open marriages are better: Evidence from US, French and Japanese cooperative ventures in commercial aircraft," *Columbia Journal of World Business*, **22** (2), 87–95.

Schaan, Jean-Louis (1983) *Parent Control and Joint Venture Success: The Case of Mexico*. Unpublished Ph.D. disseration. University of Western Ontario, London, Ontario.

Schoemaker, Paul J. H. (1990) "Strategy, complexity and economic rent," *Management Science*, **36**, 1178–92.

Stopford, John M. and Louis T. Wells (1972) *Managing the Multinational Enterprise*. New York: Basic Books.

Teece, David J. (1982) "Toward an economic theory of the multiproduct firm," *Journal of Economic Behavior and Organization*, **3**, 39–63.

Thorelli, Hans B. (1986) "Between markets and hierarchies," *Strategic Management Journal*, **7**, 35–51.

Tomlinson, James W. C. (1970) *The Joint Venture Process in International Business*. Cambridge, Mass.: MIT Press.

—— and C. S. W. Willie (1978) *Cross Impact Simulation of the Joint Venture Process in Mexico*. Research Report for the Technological Innovation Studies Program. Ministry of Industry, Trade and Commerce, Ottawa, Canada.

Wilkins, Alan L. and William G. Ouchi (1983) "Efficient cultures: Exploring the relationship between culture and organizational performance," *Administrative Science Quarterly*, **28**, 468–81.

Williamson, Oliver E. (1975) *Markets and Hierarchies: Analysis and Antitrust Implications*. New York: Free Press.

Zajac, Edward J. and Cyrus P. Olson (1993) "From transaction cost to transaction value analysis: Implications for the study of interorganizational strategies," *Journal of Management Studies*, **30**, 131–45.

10

The Role of Strategic Alliances in High-Technology New Product Development

MASAAKI KOTABE

THE UNIVERSITY OF TEXAS AT AUSTIN

AND

K. SCOTT SWAN

COLLEGE OF WILLIAM AND MARY

Innovative decision processes have been the subject of extensive theorizing, modeling, and empirical testing (D'Aveni 1994; Dickson 1992; Gatignon and Robertson 1991; Hirschman 1980; Rogers 1962). While researchers in marketing have focused on the adoption and diffusion of innovation along with similar behavioral constructs, the economics and management literature have presented a rich exploration of product innovativeness (Acs and Audretsch 1988; Ettlie and Rubenstein 1987; Mahajan, Muller, and Bass 1990; Myers and Marquis 1969; Scherer 1980; Utterback 1974). Additionally affecting this research stream, strategic alliances, or new cooperative organization forms, are replacing simple market-based transactions and traditional bureaucratic hierarchical organizations (Harrigan 1988; Nielsen 1988; Webster 1992). However, the role that this new organizational arrangement has on product innovativeness is left unexplored. Global and increasingly key organizational forms are being created through cooperative ventures (Perlmutter and Heenan 1986; Terpstra and Simonin 1993). This article seeks to further innovation research with an exploration of product innovativeness within the context of cooperative strategies and hypercompetition.

Gold (1981) observed that changes in the diffusion rates "may be due in large measure to the extent of technological changes in the innovations being studied rather than changes in the receptiveness of perspective adopters." Though a market economy relies on this dynamic technical advancement of products, the competitive environment and marketing strategy are ignored by the dominant diffusion of innovation paradigm (Gatignon and Robertson 1991). Additionally, examining the inherent innovativeness of the product manifests different implications than the traditional behavioral innovation adoption model.

Different levels of innovation (degree and rate) have been explored along with product, industry, and firm-specific variables but never all in concert (Buckley and Casson 1988; Ettlie and Rubenstein

1987; Robertson 1967). Consequently, there has been a clear gap in understanding how technological change affects organizational decisions to utilize cooperative strategies, especially with regard to competitive pressure over time. With the increasing use of cooperative arrangements between competing firms and the convergence of many high-technology fields, a broad longitudinal investigation is needed to provide insight into the innovativeness of new products by examining the attributes of the firm, the firm's new products, and the circumstances in which the products are introduced. Further, dynamics of the marketplace are crucial to strategic theory (Porter 1990).

In recent years, dynamic models of competition, such as theory of competitive rationality (Dickson 1992) and theory of hypercompetition (D'Aveni 1994), have begun to emerge with emphasis on competitive urgency as a result of rapid technological change and competitive pressure. These models share in common similar origins of the Schumpeterian economics emphasizing the role of innovation (Schumpeter 1939). We begin by reviewing prior research in management, marketing, and economics on innovation. Drawing from recent dynamic models of competition, research hypotheses are developed and subsequently tested. We conclude with a discussion of the relevant research findings and alert managers to the important implications of pursuing particular strategies to increase product innovativeness.

Literature Review and Hypotheses Development

While there has been a long history of inquiry into the degree of product innovativeness (Schumpeter 1939; Barnett 1953), one of the greatest obstacles to understanding innovation has been the lack of meaningful measures (Capon *et al.* 1992; Gatignon and Robertson 1991; Kuznets 1962; Utterback 1987). Popular proxy measures of innovation have involved R&D and patents but both have been criticized as biased. In addition, they engender problems that affect both within-industry and between-industry comparisons (Griliches 1990). In a scheme that has come to dominate diffusion research, Rogers (1962) described innovation as an idea that was perceived as new by the individual. One framework that has been suggested classifies innovation by its effect on established patterns: continuous, discontinuous, and dynamically discontinuous (Robertson 1967). The extent to which the new product changes the customer's habits or usage patterns would indicate the degree of product innovativeness. While we would prefer to capture the consumer's perceptions of product "newness," perceptual variation confounds measuring the consumers' roles as innovators and the causes of an individual's innovativeness preference remain obscure (Hirschman 1980).

Extant literature suggests that innovativeness be investigated from a perspective of inherent product attributes through three schemata: "newness to the market," "newness to the firm," or a combination thereof. First, a "newness to the market" framework for classifying innovations by their effect on established usage patterns was originally developed by Robertson (1967) and has been widely used along with its tripartite variants (e.g. Drucker 1991; Kotabe 1990; Leroy 1976). Similarly, other studies sought to differentiate the types of innovation by how drastically the product was changed: either evolutionary vs. revolutionary innovation (Utterback 1987) or radical vs. incremental innovation (Ettlie, Bridges, and O'Keefe 1984). Thus, product innovations can be defined as either continuous, dynamically continuous, or discontinuous. Each category is clearly distinct and all three types of innovations can be the result of programmatic development (Drucker 1985).

In the second schema, a "newness to the firm" framework is typically made up of three levels: 1)

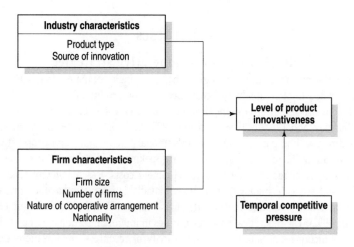

Figure 10.1 Industry, firm, and temporal factors influencing the level of product innovation

minor change of previous product; 2) major change of previous product; and 3) totally new to the firm. This firm-based framework has not been used independently as it fails to reflect a product's impact on either competitors or consumers. But from a broader perspective, the measure captures the ability of the firm to service and continue to update the technology which are key consumer concerns.

In the third schema, Booz, Allen & Hamilton, Inc. (1982) combined "newness to the market" and "newness to the firm" frameworks into a six-level scale to reflect a dynamic interaction between the firm and the marketplace. The six levels of product innovativeness include: 1) *cost reductions* – new products that provide similar performance at lower cost; 2) *repositionings* – new products that are targeted at new markets or new market segments; 3) *improvements in/revisions to existing products* – new products that provide improved performance or greater perceived value and replace existing products; 4) *additions to existing product lines* – new products that supplement a firm's established product lines; 5) *new product line* – new products that allow a firm to enter an established market for the first time; and 6) *new-to-the-world product* – new products that create an entirely new market. While all these product development and introduction options have been implemented, there has been no empirical research suggesting that one option results in, or results from, increased product innovativeness.

In this study three dimensions of product innovativeness will be developed based on the previously discussed measures of innovativeness: 1) newness to the market; 2) newness to the firm; and 3) Booz, Allen, & Hamilton's innovativeness scale. Additionally, from a review of the literature, a conceptual model (figure 10.1) and eight hypotheses are developed concerning the effect that the number of firms involved, nature of the strategic linkages, firm size, industry, temporal order, and nationality have on a product's degree of innovativeness.

HYPOTHESES

Number of firms/cooperative strategies

In industries experiencing rapid technological change, a single company rarely has the full range of expertise needed to offer timely and cost-effective new product innovations (Teece 1987). In fact, a turbulent, uncertain environment serves to increase the motivation to cooperate and innovate (Buckley and Casson 1988; Dickson 1992; Lengnick-Hall 1992). Alternatively, it is difficult to attract willing partners because revolutionary innovations and cooperative ventures are fragile, vexatious to manage, and often fail (Spekman and Salmond 1992). Despite these problems, strategies to reduce enormous development costs, lessen inherent risks of product introduction, and access technology/know-how unavailable internally have led firms to shift to strategic alliances or cooperative ventures (Hamel, Doz, and Prahalad 1989; Kogut 1988; Ohmae 1989; Webster 1992). The theoretical basis for this lies in interorganizational exchange behavior in which, given functional specialization and a scarcity of resources, organizations exchange resources for mutual benefit (Bucklin and Sengupta 1993; Frazier 1983). This view complements the clear resource and institutional constraints on a firm's behavior and motives of interfirm technology cooperation inherent in dynamic models of competition (Hagedoorn 1993).

Additionally, interorganizational linkages may help firms cope with problems faced at different stages of industry evolution (Roberts and Berry 1985) or span boundaries which are positively associated with organizational innovativeness (Kimberly 1978). A natural aperture through which cooperation could progress is across product development, manufacturing, and marketing (Ouchi 1980). New product development increasingly requires the integration of R&D, marketing, engineering, and design (Kotabe 1992; Kotler and Rath 1984). Interdisciplinary development increases the complexity of introducing the new product while corporate limitations require focusing on internal resources (Prahalad and Hamel 1990). Thus, firms need to source some knowledge and technology externally in order to concentrate on its competitive advantage (Teece 1987; Ohmae 1989). Successful firms employ their resources to focus on their relative competitive advantage and then leverage the skills and knowledge outside the firm to maximize this advantage (Dickson 1992). Cooperating firms' cumulative resources, complementary skills, and boundary-spanning activities are likely to increase the level of innovativeness of products. Therefore:

Hypothesis 1: Products of cooperating firms tend to be more innovative than products of a single firm.

Strategic linkage

Vertical linkages occur when firms cooperate across different levels of the value-added chain whereas horizontal linkages are across the same level. Vertical linkages are distribution or outsourcing arrangements, while common horizontal linkages would include R&D consortia, patent swaps, technology transfers, and joint ventures which would be more likely to supplement the internal technology base. Hagedoorn (1993) estimates that R&D joint ventures and research cooperations, along with joint R&D agreements and equity investments, are over 85 percent motivated to improve the long-term technological prospect of the product–market combinations of the companies. On the other hand, only a small portion of vertical linkages such as customer–supplier relationships and distribution agreement are designed for such a purpose. Thus, horizontal linkages are more likely to be strategically motivated to improve long-term product technology development, while vertical linkages tend to be more concerned with cost economizing rather than with product innovation. Through similar logic of external linkages, single firms are considered an internal vertical linkage (Williamson 1979).

Additionally, interdepartmental conflict erects barriers to innovation through differences in time horizons, communication depth, and contact infrequency (Roussel, Saad, and Erickson 1991). While horizontal cooperation would help eliminate or reduce the cultural and technical barriers, barriers to innovation within the firm would be unlikely to change in a vertical cooperation between firms. In fact, physical distance between cooperating firms could decrease the level of contact, therefore requiring each communication to be all the more important and giving horizontal linkages a decided advantage. Also, a firm makes better use of outside resources if it has its own general expertise. A broad internal technology base allows the firm to be more efficient in acquiring and implementing new core complementary knowledge (Granstrand and Sjolander 1990; Hamel *et al.* 1989) over the benefits of seeking new peripheral knowledge from a vertical linkage. Therefore:

> *Hypothesis 2:* The products of cooperating firms using a horizontal linkage tend to be more innovative than products introduced using a vertical linkage between cooperating firms.

Firm size

Ambiguity as to the role of firm size in innovativeness is still evident (Acs and Audretsch 1988; Ettlie and Rubenstein 1987; Scherer 1980). Large firms have a stable of products that could be extended through continuous improvements. Also, large firms may be more efficient innovators because of larger, more diverse resources and skills, better-developed marketing channels, and economies of scale (Baldwin and Scott 1987). On the other hand, small companies must be highly innovative to attract attention, interest investment, and more importantly overcome larger competitors' advantages to attract customers (Utterback and Abernathy 1975). These smaller, less integrated, and underfunded companies with new technological innovations cooperate with established companies to gain access to the latter's complementary assets of reputation and distribution channels, customer bases, and possible acceptance as dominant design in subcategory markets. It is wholly conceivable that products successfully introduced by large firms are the result of small firms' innovations (Granstrand and Sjolander 1990), since large firms are in a better position to learn and imitate with manufacturing and distribution advantages over a small innovator (Miles and Snow 1978). Thus, size may also play a role in that diversity of firm size, a mixture of large and small firms, was supported as most conducive to innovation (Scherer 1980). So, in the Schumpeterian tradition of the dynamic models of competition, small firms normally need dynamically continuous or discontinuous innovations to break into the market and to sustain competitive lead. Therefore:

> *Hypothesis 3:* The product of a small firm tends to be more innovative than a product introduced by a large firm.

Industry effect

At the heart of new technologies is a diverse range of basic and applied research requirements and sectoral convergence or "technology fusion" (Hagedoorn 1993; Kodama 1992). Kodama (1992), for example, differentiates between two types of technology fusion. The first type is identified as mechatronics or Type M products. Type M products are essentially assembled from mechanical and electronic components. Second, biotechnology, pharmaceutical, and chemical, or Type B, products are the result of genetic engineering and biochemistry. Type B products are created at the molecular level and are inseparable from their process. Hagedoorn (1993), focusing on the industry level, empirically affirms the differences between industries' innovativeness due to convergent technologies.

Contrary to the studies of Myers and Marquis (1969) and Utterback (1974), which did not find significant differences between industries, reverse engineering and inventing around are technically easier with type M products (e.g. microelectronics) than with the Type B products (e.g. pharmaceuticals). Furthermore, these studies did not have a similar industry segment as in our study and, more importantly, environmental and technological changes have transformed whole industries in response to the demands of hypercompetition (D'Aveni 1994). A single or group of industries' level and rate of innovativeness may become more pronounced during a period because of technological, structural, and competitive characteristics having a differential effect. Also, for those Type B products, not only the product *per se* but also inventive processes are protected by patent, making it more difficult to imitate (Levin *et al.* 1987). Given the nature of these products and the relative difficulty of reverse engineering and inventing around, Type B products tend to be more innovative than Type M products in order to break into the market.

Hypothesis 4a: The products introduced in Type B industries tend to be more innovative than products introduced in Type M industries.

Calantone, Di Benedetto, and Meloche (1988) found that successful product innovations frequently were revolutionary and originating from outside the industry. A discontinuous change in a product from outside the industry requires firms to update old technology or gain access to new technology through external acquisition (Cooper and Schendel 1976). This suggests that it may be necessary for firms to partner with other firms to complement each other's strengths and weaknesses – small with large firms and interindustry cooperations – although the dynamic models of competition suggest that cooperation might be temporary.

While incremental innovations often originate from inside the firm and are derived largely from the experience of people within the firm (Czinkota and Kotabe 1990; Dickson 1992; Utterback 1987), a major innovation is often viewed as disruptive to established investments (D'Aveni 1994). A major change would affect the goals and the control systems which are the bases for authority, leaving change often without a constituency (Tushman and Anderson 1986). Incremental innovation often reinforces the existing structure. This bias of an industry toward conservatism and incremental change offers opportunities for invasions of the existing market by substitute products from firms outside the industry (Abernathy and Clark 1985; Porter 1980). The convergence of technology and industries creates enormous cross-industry innovation subsidies. Therefore, firms associated with an industry outside an existing product's industry are likely to offer more innovative products than firms within the industry (Kodama 1992).

Hypothesis 4b: Products introduced by firms associated with an industry outside an existing product's industry tend to be more innovative than products introduced by firms associated with the product's *industry.*

Hypothesis 4c: The products introduced by firms that are cooperating across industries tend to be more innovative than products introduced by firms that are cooperating within the same industry.

Temporal aspects

Time (i.e. competitive imitation, intensification of competition, and knowledge accumulation) renders nearly all advantages obsolete (Fardoust and Dhareshwar 1990; Stalk 1988). Since new products determine many firms' competitive strengths (Booz, Allen, & Hamilton 1982), there are considerable pressures to innovate as a result of the shortened product life cycle, rapid price reduction, and eroding profit margins. Firms must improve their speed and chance of introducing successful innovations (Davidson and Harrigan 1977; Hagedoorn 1993). This accelerated techno-logical environment further demands a more significant innovation and a faster implementation for a firm to stay ahead of competition than in the past (D'Aveni 1994; Dickson 1992). As a result, increasingly innovative products are introduced in a shorter time interval.

Hypothesis 5: Product innovativeness tends to increase with time.

Nationality

Growth and profits come largely from new products (Booz, Allen, & Hamilton 1982). Additionally, there has been a renewed interest in manufacturing process innovation, which was long ignored in traditional considerations of strategy development as a competitive weapon (Cohen and Zysman 1987). While firms of the Triad place emphasis on manufacturing and concomitant product quality (Kotabe 1990; Utterback 1987), different innovation biases and technology demands exist between firms of different national origin (Franko 1976; Pavitt 1969). Though comparative marketing studies have shown that different marketing strategies can be associated with countries (Boddewyn 1981; Kotabe and Duhan 1991), it has not been determined how cross-national cooperations affect innova-tion.

Increasingly, global products are becoming standardized and world dominant designs are being sought by both firms and customers (Kotabe 1990). Convergence of high-technology fields, degree of expertise needed, and pace of knowledge also push firms to cooperate (Ohmae 1989). Porter (1990) argues, however, that despite the globalization of competition and urgency of technology acquisi-tion, the sustainability of firms' competitive advantage depends strongly on national characteristics of competitive rivalry, supporting industries, demand conditions, and productive factor avail-ability in their home country. While the dynamic models of competition do not directly address national differences in innovativeness, they do state that structural and transactional disequilibrium in markets to be addressed by multinational firms.

An important factor in the endurance of a global alliance is compatibility between partners with a common set of values, style, and culture (Perlmutter and Heenan 1986). All elements of the organization, including competitive rationality, are potentially constrained by the cultural environ-ment (Farmer and Richman 1965; Terpstra and David 1991). Many U.S. managers still regard cooperation with skepticism and suspicion while the Japanese and Europeans are more culturally familiar to shared enterprises (Perlmutter and Heenan 1986). In addition, all firms would rather have a partner of their own nationality (Montgomery 1993). Cultural incompatibility and lack of trust can produce enormous difficulties. As a result, many "alliances" between U.S. companies and their Asian or European counterparts tend to be little more than sophisticated outsourcing arrange-ments (Hamel *et al.* 1989). Therefore, new products introduced by single firms or cooperating firms from the same country are likely to be more innovative than those introduced by cross-nationally cooperating firms.

Hypothesis 6: Products introduced by firms of the same Triad region tend to be more innovative than products introduced by cross-nationally cooperating firms.

In the following sections, the methodology for collecting the data and conducting the analysis is presented. This is followed by a discussion of the results, from which conclusions and recommendations are drawn.

Content Analysis

TECHNIQUE AND CONSIDERATIONS

Major innovations come to fruition over a span of years; so cross-sectional and survey data do not adequately capture how innovation occurs (Utterback 1979). Longitudinal research adds considerable insight and permits the researcher to determine underlying temporal linkages between competitive environment, organizational and industry characteristics, and innovativeness. Our data base consists of 905 new product introductions in the United States by firms from the Triad regions (the United States, Western European countries, and Japan) announced in the *Wall Street Journal* over a 5-year period (since the *inception* of the "Technology" section in September 1988). Because of the prevalence of "vapor ware" (i.e. proactive announcements of nonappearing products meant to disrupt sales of competitors), only products that have been or were to be introduced within 1 month were included in the study. Care was taken not to double count products. Finally, software was excluded from the study because of infrequent and relatively incomplete coverage of the category.

Each article was examined using the "content analysis" technique – the objective, systematic, and quantitative description of the manifest content of communication (Berelson 1954). Content analysis is used in a variety of disciplines and has been applied, for example, to analyze the sources of satisfaction and dissatisfaction in service encounters (Bitner, Booms, and Tetreault 1990) and retail store image (Zimmer and Golden 1988), as well as international partnerships (Porter and Fuller 1986; Terpstra and Simonin 1993).

A reliable and objective analysis requires that the experiment be replicable and systematic, and that categorizations be according to consistently applied rules to avoid researcher bias (Holsti 1968). Content analysis has the same advantages and disadvantages of other inductive procedures such as factor analysis, cluster analysis, and multidimensional scaling (Hunt 1983). The product's effect on established usage patterns and inherent product competitive advantages, namely the degree of innovativeness, is well-suited to content analysis and can supply external validity to the results (Kolbe and Burnett 1991).

SAMPLE AND CLASSIFICATION OF PRODUCT INTRODUCTIONS

After an initial agreement on concepts and their operational definitions, three judges independently completed the coding instrument for the product introduction articles. Interjudge agreement (based on the average of a three independent judge group consisting of a technology researcher with a PhD degree, a product designer with an MBA degree, and a product engineer with a graduate engineering degree) was 92 percent, which compares favorably with past interjudge reliability of 60–97 percent (Zimmer and Golden 1988; Kolbe and Burnett 1991). Thus, there were few differences in the placement of the articles in the categories. In total, 905 product introduction articles remained after contentious articles were jointly evaluated to obtain unanimous agreement in categorization. In the next section, we analyze the data and discuss the results. Then, implications and future research directions are suggested.

Measures

Initially, Robertson's (1967) tripartite "newness to the market", the three-part "newness to the firm," and Booz, Allen, & Hamilton's (1982) six-part "Level of innovation" were individually employed as dependent variables; all three models were found to be significant ($p < 0.0001$) with consistent results. Since the three items of innovativeness were highly correlated and in an effort to capture as many dimensions and interactions as possible, they were combined to increase measurement reliability, as follows: as the first two items were measured on a three-point scale and the third item was on a six-point scale, these items were respectively standardized to have a mean of 0 and a standard deviation of 1, and the mean of the three standardized items were computed to represent "product innovativeness" (INNOV: Cronbach alpha = 0.82). Excluding any of the three items of innovativeness served to reduce the alpha coefficient. The independent variables were the number of firms that were involved in the product introduction (NO_FIRM), strategic linkage between cooperating firms (LINKAGE: vertical vs. horizontal),[1] size of the firm (SIZE: large = *Fortune* 500 or *Fortune International* 500, small = otherwise, and mixed = at least one in each firm size category), product type (PRODUCT: Type B vs. Type M), agreement between the firm's industry and the product's industry (MATCH), month in which the product was introduced (DATE: i.e. September 1988 = 1, with an increment of 1 per month onward), and nationality of the firm (NATION).

There were too few cases of three or more cooperative firms introducing a product, so the NO_FIRM variable for the number of firms introducing a product was collapsed into two categories: 1) cases of a single firm offering a new product; and 2) cases of multiple firms offering a new product. For the NATION variable, European–Japanese cooperations and U.S.–European–Japanese cooperations categories were deleted as there were too few cases. Thus, the NATION categories analyzed were 1) European, 2) Japanese, 3) U.S., and 4) cross-national (U.S. with one or more foreign partners).

Because of the longitudinal nature of this study,[2] the whole data set is analyzed as well as the split of the data set to uncover any trends. This split-half analysis allowed us to ascertain that the stability of the results was very high across phases and time frames. In conducting this comparison, we offer a measure of internal validity. While internal validity does not strictly allow us to extend or generalize our findings, it may suggest venues for future research.

Analysis

The study was accomplished in two phases. Phase 1 includes all product introductions and is designed to examine the difference between product innovativeness of (a) single vs. multiple cooperating firms and (b) horizontal vs. vertical linkages. Phase 2 includes only product introductions by cooperating firms. The results of the ANCOVA are shown in table 10.1.

Table 10.1 Industry, firm, and temporal factors influencing the level of product innovation

	Expected sign	1988–89 coefficient estimate		1990–92 coefficient estimate		Aggregate coefficient estimate	
		Phase 1	Phase 2	Phase 1	Phase 2	Phase 1	Phase 2
Intercept		−0.28 (−1.42)	−0.67[a] (−3.52)	−1.35[a] (−5.98)	−1.50[a] (−6.19)	−0.62[a] (−5.31)	−0.86[a] (−6.99)
H1: NO-FIRM							
Multiple	(+)	−0.29[b] (−2.28)		−0.21[c] (−1.75)		−0.19[b] (−2.21)	
Single		−		−		−	
H2: LINKAGE							
Horizontal	(+)	0.31[b] (2.17)	0.23[c] (1.68)	0.32[a] (2.62)	0.23[b] (2.14)	0.35[a] (3.77)	0.29[a] (3.34)
Vertical		−	−	−	−	−	−
H3: SIZE							
Small	(+)	0.52[a] (5.58)	0.55[a] (5.86)	0.45[a] (4.92)	0.48[a] (5.19)	0.49[a] (7.37)	0.51[a] (7.72)
Mixed		0.11 (0.77)	0.05 (0.35)	0.27[b] (2.26)	0.23[b] (1.93)	0.17[c] (1.83)	0.14 (1.59)
Large		−	−	−	−	−	−
H4a: INDUSTRY							
Type-B	(+)	0.32[a] (3.32)	0.34[a] (3.49)	0.30[a] (3.25)	0.31[a] (3.28)	0.37[a] (5.46)	0.38[a] (5.56)
Type-M		−	−	−	−	−	−
H4b: MATCH							
Industry ≠ Product	(+)	0.16[c] (1.65)	0.13 (1.32)	0.14[c] (1.63)	0.14 (1.53)	0.17[a] (2.56)	0.15[b] (2.29)
Industry = Product		−	−	−	−	−	−
H4c: COOP							
Interindustry	(+)		0.30[b] (2.27)		0.10 (0.84)		0.18[b] (2.03)
Intraindustry			−		−		−
H5: DATE	(+)	−0.007 (−1.41)	0.006 (−1.21)	0.02[a] (6.10)	0.02[a] (5.89)	0.01[b] (4.77)	0.01[a] (4.73)
H6: NATION							
Europe	(+)	0.75[a] (2.57)	0.84[a] (2.97)	0.01 (0.06)	0.10 (0.48)	0.32[c] (1.85)	0.38[b] (2.26)
Japan	(+)	0.12 (0.60)	0.20 (1.06)	0.02 (0.09)	0.11 (0.61)	0.07 (0.52)	0.14 (1.04)
U.S.A.	(+)	0.13 (0.92)	0.17 (1.30)	−0.02 (−0.15)	0.04 (0.36)	0.09 (1.00)	0.13 (1.45)
Cross-national		−	−	−	−	−	−
n		440	139	465	168	905	307
R^2		0.16[a]	0.16[a]	0.16[a]	0.16[a]	0.13[a]	0.13[a]

[a] $p < 0.01$; [b] $p < 0.05$; [c] $p < 0.10$.

Note: Corresponding t-statistics are shown in parentheses.

Interpretation: The level of product innovativeness was measured as a standardized Z score with a mean of 0 and a standard deviation of 1. The actual level of product innovativeness observed in the data set varied from −1.74 to 2.19, with a total range of 3.93 standard deviations. Therefore, the estimated coefficients are expressed in standard deviation units.

For example, in the aggregate model, a coefficient for NO_FIRM suggests that the level of innovativeness of products introduced by cooperating firms is −0.19 standard deviation, or about 5% (−0.19 divided by a range of 3.93), below that by single firms.

Similarly, a coefficient for DATE (in months) for the aggregate model shows that the level of product innovativeness is estimated to increase by 0.01 per month, or 0.12 standard deviation in 1 year (0.01 × 12 months), which translates to an increase in product innovativeness by 3.1% (0.12 divided by a range of 3.93) per year, or 15.3% during the entire 1988–93 period.

PHASE 1

The number of firms involved in the product introduction turned out to be significant ($p < 0.05$) for the first period, for the second period ($p < 0.10$), and subsequently for the aggregate period ($p < 0.05$), although in the opposite direction than hypothesized in hypothesis 1. There appears to be a disadvantage to cooperating with other firms in developing and introducing more innovative new products. Cooperating firms seeking to reduce the risk inherent in the more innovative products, sharing in the development and introduction costs, or pooling resources for other benefits, may be penalizing their innovative activities. We cannot rule out the possibility that poor performance can cause firms to seek additional cooperation with competitors (Burgers, Hill, and Kim, 1993). Our data base fails to lend support for hypothesis 1. This point will be discussed further under "Conclusions and implications."

The strategic linkages were classified into two categories: vertical cooperations (links were not between similar functions, i.e. distribution arrangements) and horizontal cooperations (links were between similar functions, i.e. R&D consortium). The relationship between innovativeness and strategic linkage was significant ($p < 0.05$ in the first period, and $p < 0.01$ in the second period and in aggregate), which is consistent with hypothesis 2. This finding suggests that horizontal cooperative relationships tend to increase the level of innovativeness of their product more than vertical cooperative or single-firm strategies.

Firm size was a strongly significant variable ($p < 0.01$) in both periods as well as in aggregate, with small firms being more innovative than large firms. Small firms also displayed strong positive coefficients. Small and large firms cooperating were also significantly likely to introduce more innovative products than large firms in the second period ($p < 0.05$) and in aggregate ($p < 0.10$) but coefficients were considerably less than those for small firms. Thus, hypothesis 3 was supported. These findings endorse the notion that small firms possibly unencumbered by the bureaucracy and conservative approach of large firms tend to come up with more innovative products to attract investors and customers. Additionally, cooperating firms of differing sizes (mixed cases of large and small firms) also seem to introduce more innovative products than large firms. The higher level of innovativeness of small and mixed-size firms substantiates the small firm's appeal to larger firms as a source of products and partners.

As hypothesized, type B industries were more innovative than type M industries ($p < 0.01$) in both periods and in the aggregate. With strong positive coefficients, hypothesis 4a is supported. Our finding endorses the claim that revolutionary developments such as gene splicing and other biotechnological advancements transform the biochemical industry through "technology fusion." This finding seems to support the dynamic assertions of Auster (1992) that peak rates of technological linkages are highest in emerging industries, and of Schroeder (1990) that technology waves are at different levels or stages within industries. Hence, a life cycle relationship may exist between the level of innovativeness and specific industries or industry segments.

The match between the firms' industry and the product's industry yielded significant ($p < 0.10$) findings in both periods. In aggregate, MATCH was highly significant ($p < 0.01$). Products introduced in industries outside the firms' industry have a tendency to be more innovative than products introduced within the firms' industry. Support was found for hypothesis 4b.

While the first period showed no significance ($p > 0.10$), the temporal intensity of innovativeness (DATE) has increased within our data set for the second period and in aggregate, exhibiting a strong, significant relationship ($p < 0.01$) between the level of innovativeness and the progression of time. Thus, hypothesis 5 was supported. This finding is possibly the most ominous and suggestive of a hypercompetitive nature of competition for firms that do not nurture an environment that promotes not only continuous innovation but also continuously increasing innovativeness (D'Aveni 1994; Dickson 1992). With the progression of time comes an intensification of competition which is manifested by an increase in the speed of product replacement and levels of innovativeness. As explained in table 10.1, the level of product innovativeness is estimated to have increased, on average, by 15.3 percent during the 1988–93 study period. This finding appears consistent with the notion that lead time is becoming more effective than patents in protecting a firm's competitive advantage (Levin *et al.* 1987).

The nationality of the firm seemed to be little related to the innovativeness of the product except in the case of European products, which exhibited a significant result in the first period ($p < 0.01$) and in the aggregate ($p < 0.10$). The idea that new products introduced by firms of single-country origin might be more innovative than those introduced by cross-nationally cooperating firms was partially supported for European firms. While not conclusive, cultural difficulties might seem to affect cross-national cooperative strategies. Hypothesis 6 found partial support but does little to enlighten our understanding of the nature of nationality's effect on innovativeness.

The models for product innovativeness were highly significant in both the first period ($p < 0.01$) and the second ($p < 0.01$). The R^2 of the first period was 0.16 and remained stable at 0.16 in the second period. The aggregate model, with an R^2 of 0.13, was highly significant ($p < 0.01$) but explained slightly less of the variance than either of the disaggregated models. While relatively low, the R^2 values were consistent over time, suggesting that structural, rather than random, patterns exist in determining the level of innovativeness of products.

PHASE 2

The purpose for the second phase of this study was to explore specifically the changes of cooperating firms' product innovativeness between the two periods (single-company product introductions were discarded so the variable NO_FIRM was unnecessary). The total number of cases of cooperating firms was 307. The independent variables, LINKAGE, SIZE, PRODUCT, MATCH, DATE, NATION, remained and a variable was added to represent agreement or accord between the cooperating firms' industries (COOP: intraindustry vs. interindustry cooperation). There was a question of a relationship between MATCH and COOP, so the analysis was run independently for each of these variables with the other dependent variables and then run with MATCH and COOP together. The findings remained stable, so MATCH and COOP were found to be fairly independent and both variables were maintained in the study.

The results of the ANCOVA for this phase were consistent with the first phase of the study. Therefore, only the newly added COOP variable needs to be discussed. The relationship between COOP and the level of innovativeness was significant ($p < 0.05$) in the first period and in the aggregate. The coefficient for interindustry cooperation indicated a likelihood of an increased level of innovativeness over products of intraindustry origin. For the second period, the coefficient estimate exhibited a positive coefficient but was not significant ($p > 0.10$). Hypothesis 4c was generally supported. This finding agrees with Killing's (1980) evidence that joint ventures undertaken with diversified partners have greater success than those with similar partners.

The phase 2 model for product innovativeness was significant in the first and second periods ($p < 0.01$). The R^2 of the first period was 0.16 and remained constant in the second period at 0.16, as in the first phase. Again the aggregate model was significant ($p < 0.01$) and explained slightly less of the variance ($R^2 = 0.13$) than the models for period one or two. Overall, these results show consistency and stability over time.

Conclusions and Implications

This chapter has explored the impact of cooperating firms, firm size, industry, strategic linkages, temporal aspects, and nationality on the innovativeness level of new products. Cooperative strategies were examined to refine and extend the understanding of innovativeness of high-technology product introductions, especially within the theory of competitive rationality and hypercompetition. The use of actual product introductions, inclusion of a consumer orientation, and development of multiple dimensions of the innovation construct produced a degree of external validity. However, our findings should be interpreted cautiously as the explanatory power (R^2) of the models is relatively weak. Strictly from a statistical point of view, the use of categorial variables reduces the model's explanatory power, but generates more conservative results than the use of quantitative variables. Therefore, our findings should be considered conservative.

The general findings suggest that small firms, horizontal linkages, and type B (e.g. biochemical) products are the strongest contributors to the level of product innovativeness. Additionally, single firms, mixed-size firms, cross-industry product offerings, cross-industry cooperations, and cooperating European firms are intermediate indicators of higher product innovativeness. The increasing intensity of competition as measured by the general progression of time also signaled a significant, positive effect on the level of innovativeness.

To understand the study's implications, a firm can be viewed as a collection of technologies ranging from simple administrative procedures to applied sciences (Porter 1980). Cooperative strategies seek to coordinate two or more firms' technologies while eliminating the redundancies. Cooperating strategies are undertaken at the most efficient level to capture the maximum profits and market opportunities for the product (Dickson 1992). Communication, coordination, and a multidisciplinary effort between and within firms is key to building trust and superior performance but must be balanced against the burden of these additional tasks, which could decrease the level or rate of innovation. Our research suggests that cooperating firms' efforts to achieve other benefits from the alliance negatively affected the innovativeness of their products. On the other hand, cooperating European firms' product innovativeness held out the possibility that cooperating firms can develop innovative synergy for their products.

One possible reason why cooperating firms' efforts had a negative impact on the products' innovativeness is their failure to balance competing demands. Management's orientation toward the primacy of either technology or strategy will affect the innovativeness of the products (Petroni 1983a, 1983b). A complementary fit is needed between technology and strategy. It is also necessary to establish a shared perception of the relative value of each firm's contributions and a mutually acceptable division of profits (Spekman and Salmond 1992). The results of our study could suggest that firms have had difficulty in finding the equilibrium point between the competing demands of cooperation and competition. Another possible explanation may be found in the inherent difficulty in recognizing the commercial potential and convincing other firms to cooperate in a venture involving a dramatic innovation. Therefore, cooperating firms may tend to introduce less innovative products.

One of the principal forces driving competition is technological change. The gathering pace of technological change has demonstrated its power to influence the environment and create a competitive advantage for firms that can keep abreast and place technology in the context of their competitive strategy (Hayes and Abernathy 1980). Rapid technological change leads to stunted diffusion curves resulting from inhibited diffusion rates as prospective adopters seek to avoid products which are quickly superseded (Gold 1981). Apple Computer's announcement of the impending release of Newton more than a year ahead of its actual introduction had profound effects on the sales of competitors' palmtop computers and personal data assistants (PDAs). Diffusion researchers will increasingly find that diffusion models must account not only for contingent relationships (i.e. Bayus 1987) and a decreasing time interval between successive generations (i.e. Norton and Bass, 1987), but also for increasing innovativeness and the effect of expectant, albeit non-existent, products.

A firm can use its innovative skills to shape the environmental conditions in its favor, to attract more competent partners, to communicate the greater benefits of the firm's products to the consumer, and to extract more favorable gains from cooperative strategies. Incrementally more innovative products and incrementally greater revenues compound in the long term to substantial advantages for the firm. Successful innovation generates change in the organization which can trigger the unraveling of a firm's existing strategy as new capabilities, structures, and relationships are frequently required to exploit innovation (Jelinek, 1986; Lengnick-Hall, 1992). Alternatively, organizations that are not actively involved in innovation may lose their ability to keep abreast of and deal with technological evolution (Kotabe 1992; Tushman and Anderson 1986).

Another managerial recommendation includes a warning that a company should constantly monitor within its own industry but even more importantly outside its industry for product technology. If a company is small, it can go it alone or attract a large partner without overly compromising the innovativeness of its efforts. If the firm is large, good sources for acquiring innovative products and partners are small firms. Industry differences occur and in this data set firms in the biotechnology industry have the greatest product innovativeness hurdle to overcome. Additionally, horizontal and cross-industry cooperative arrangements have contributed to the increase of product innovativeness but the overall tendency toward negative effects of cooperative strategies demands managers' attention.

Finally, it is not clear, however, whether increased product innovativeness is necessarily the most productive route to enhanced performance in all situations. Rapid product and process incremental innovation geared toward satisfying customer needs is vastly easier to maintain and less risky than committing the firm to a strategy of discontinuous product development (Czinkota and Kotabe 1990). While the difference between the two may be reduced if the innovative effort is directed toward solutions to customer problems rather than corporations committed to an aggressive program of basic research, it is more likely that a balance must be struck between developing continuous and discontinuous innovations. The effect on innovativeness of technological push as opposed to market pull is unclear.

Limitations and Future Directions

Unfortunately, we cannot determine if the product introduction was successful on the market. Between one-third (Booz, Allen, & Hamilton 1982) and as high as three-fifths (Silk and Urban 1978) of product introductions are rated as failures or of doubtful success. Seventy percent of the resources spent on new products are allocated to products that are not successful in the market (Booz, Allen, & Hamilton 1982). These dismal figures are for products that get to the introduction phase. Managerial relevance and implications for diffusion research would be greatly enhanced if factors of success for products could be included among the predictor variables. A follow-up study is recommended to clarify which combination of innovation types and product strategic advantages were more aligned with success of products after introduction.

Second, while simultaneous pursuit of multiple types of innovation for one product or of multiple strategies was not directly studied, exceptional companies manage both radical breakthrough and incremental technology change (Marquis 1972). While only the dominant product attributes generate our findings, cross-boundary research as to how synergies between levels of innovation would arise and their effects would illuminate this area. Other research questions are whether simultaneous innovation on all levels is better than concentration on a single innovation, whether companies that have lost manufacturing ability can achieve long-term success, and whether strategic alliances allow these firms to continue to complete or allow competitors to appropriate their technology. Also, the level of resource investment tied to interdependence and commitment of the cooperation, explored by Auster (1992), would be an interesting variable with which to study product innovativeness.

Third, a more representative sample of product introductions over a longer period of time should be examined. A more accurate representation of the population of product introductions could solve possible biases such as the tendency toward computers, electronics, pharmaceuticals, and biochemicals. More innovative products are probably more newsworthy and might have been overrepresented in the sample. Other possible biases could include a slightly greater tendency to cover products introduced by large firms that have an interest to investors, although there are more small companies than large listed on the stock exchange. Finally, it is possible that cooperating firms are more newsworthy than single firms, although until a product is introduced the collaboration would not be included in the data set. While such biases may limit the range of the finding's application, the results of the study are robust, with important implications for product development, cooperative strategies, and theory refinement.

Notes

1 Single-firm cases are essentially a form of vertical cooperation within the company and are thus considered vertical in terms of LINKAGE.

2 We examined a potential heteroskedasticity problem in our longitudinal data. Based on residuals plotted against the predicted values of the level of product innovativeness, no significant heteroskedasticity was detected. Further, we examined the potential impact of outliers that might exist in our data set. Based on residual and Cook's D statistic criteria (Cook 1979), about 5 percent, or 45 cases out of the sample of 905 cases, exceeded the Studentized residual criterion, although Cook's D statistic criterion suggested that their impact was negligible. Subsequently, analyses were performed both on the full sample and on the reduced sample (without those 45 cases). The difference observed in the reduced-sample results was a slightly improved R^2 by about 2 percent across the board, without any measurable change in the estimated coefficients and their statistical significance. For these reasons, heteroskedasticity and outliers do not appear to cause any undue strain on the estimated parameters.

References

Abernathy, W. and K.B. Clark (1985) "Innovation: Mapping the winds of creative destruction," *Research Policy*, **14**, pp. 3–22.

Acs, Z. and D.B. Audretsch (1988) "Innovation in large and small firms: An empirical analysis," *American Economic Review*, **78**, pp. 678–90.

Auster, E.R. (1992) "The relationship of industry evolution to patterns of technological linkages, joint ventures, and direct investment between U.S. and Japan," *Management Science*, **38**, pp. 779–92.

Baldwin, W.L. and J.T. Scott (1987) *Market Structure and Technological Change*. Harwood Academic Publishers, Chur, Switzerland and New York.

Barnett, H.G. (1953) *Innovation: The Basis of Cultural Change*. McGraw-Hill, New York.

Bayus, B.L. (1987) "Forecasting sales of contingent products: An application to the compact disc market," *Journal of Product Innovation Management*, **4**, pp. 243–55.

Berelson, B. (1954) "Content analysis." In G. Lindzey (ed.) *Handbook of Social Psychology: Theory and Method*, Vol. 1. Addison-Wesley, Reading, MA, pp. 488–522.

Bitner, M.J., B.H. Booms and M.S. Tetreault (1990) "The service encounter: Diagnosing favorable and unfavorable incidents," *Journal of Marketing*, **54**, pp. 71–84.

Boddewyn, J.J. (1981) "Comparative marketing: The first 25 years," *Journal of International Business Studies*, **12**, pp. 61–79.

Booz, Allen, & Hamilton, Inc. (1982) *New Products Management for the 1980s*. Booz, Allen & Hamilton, Inc., New York.

Buckley, P.J. and M. Casson (1988) "The theory of cooperation in international business," In F.J. Contractor and P. Lorange (eds) *Cooperative Strategies in International Business*. Lexington Books, Lexington, MA, pp. 31–53.

Bucklin, L.P. and S. Sengupta (1993) "Organizing successful co-marketing alliances," *Journal of Marketing*, **57**, pp. 32–46.

Burgers, W.P., C.W.L. Hill and W.L. Kim (1993) "A theory of global strategic alliances: The case of the global auto industry," *Strategic Management Journal*, **14** (6), pp. 419–32.

Calantone, R.J., C.A. Di Benedetto and M.S. Meloche (1988) "Strategies of product and process innovation: A loglinear analysis," *R&D Management*, **181**, pp. 13–21.

Capon, N., J. Farley, D. Lehmann and J. Hulbert (1992) "Profiles of product innovators among large U.S. manufacturers," *Management Science*, **38**, pp. 157–69.

Cohen, S.S. and J. Zysman (1987) "Why manufacturing matters: The myth of the post-industrial economy," *California Management Review*, **29**, pp. 9–26.

Cook, R.D. (1979) "Influential observations in linear regression," *Journal of the American Statistical Association*, **74**, pp. 169–74.

Cooper, A.C. and D. Schendel (1976) "Strategic responses to technological threats," *Business Horizons*, **191**, pp. 61–9.

Czinkota, M. and M. Kotabe (1990). "Product development the Japanese way," *Journal of Business Strategy*, **11**, pp. 31–6. (See Chapter 12.)

D'Aveni, R. (1994) *Hypercompetition: Managing the Dynamics of Strategic Maneuvering*. Free Press, New York.

Davidson, W.H. and R. Harrigan (1977) "Key decisions in international marketing: Introducing new products abroad," *Columbia Journal of World Business*, **12**, pp. 15–23.

Dickson, P.R. (1992) "Toward a general theory of competitive advantage," *Journal of Marketing*, **56**, pp. 69–83.

Drucker, P.F. (1985) *Innovation and Entrepreneurship: Practice and Principles*. Harper & Row, New York.

Drucker, P.F. (1991) "New strategies for a new reality," *Wall Street Journal*, October 2nd, p. A12.

Ettlie, J.E. and A.H. Rubenstein (1987) "Firm size and product innovation," *Journal of Product Innovation Management*, **42**, pp. 89–108.

Ettlie, J.E., W.P. Bridges, and R.D. O'Keefe (1984) "Organization strategy and structural differences for radical versus incremental innovations," *Management Science*, **306**, pp. 682–95.

Fardoust, S. and A. Dhareshwar (1990) *A Long-term Outlook for the World Economy: Issues and Projections for the 1990s*. World Bank, Washington, D.C.

Farmer, R.N. and B.M. Richman (1965) *Comparative Management and Economic Progress*. Richard D. Irwin, Homewood, IL.

Franko, L.G. (1976) *The European Multinationals*. Greylock, Stamford, CT.

Frazier, G.L. (1983) "Interorganizational exchange behavior in marketing channels: A broadened perspective," *Journal of Marketing*, **47**, pp. 68–78.

Gatignon, H. and T.S. Robertson (1991) "Innovative decision processes." In T.S. Robertson and H.H. Kassarjian (eds) *Handbook of Consumer Behavior*. Prentice Hall, Englewood Cliffs, NJ, pp. 316–48.

Gold, B. (1981) "Technological diffusion in industry: Research needs and shortcomings," *Journal of Industrial Economics*, **29**, pp. 247–69.

Granstrand, O. and S. Sjolander (1990) "The acquisition of technology and small firms by large firms," *Journal of Economic Behavior and Organization*, **13**, pp. 367–86.

Griliches, Z. (1990) "Patent statistics as economic indicators: A survey," *Journal of Economic Literature*, **28**, pp. 1661–1707.

Hagedoorn, J. (1993) "Understanding the rationale of strategic technology partnering: Interorganizational modes of cooperation and sector differences," *Strategic Management Journal*, **14** (5), pp. 371–85.

Hamel, G., Y.L. Doz, and C.K. Prahalad (1989) "Collaborate with your competitors and win," *Harvard Business Review*, **67**, pp. 133–9.

Harrigan, K.R. (1988) "Joint ventures and competitive strategy," *Strategic Management Journal*, **9** (2), pp. 141–58.

Hayes, R.H. and W.J. Abernathy (1980) "Managing our way to economic decline," *Harvard Business Review*, **58**, pp. 67–77.

Hirschman, E.C. (1980) "Innovativeness, novelty seeking, and consumer creativity," *Journal of Consumer Research*, **7**, pp. 283–95.

Holsti, O.R. (1968). "Content analysis". In G. Lindzey and E. Aronson (eds) *The Handbook of Social Psychology: Research Methods*, Vol. 2. Addison-Wesley Reading, MA, pp. 596–692.

Hunt, S.D. (1983) *Marketing Theory: The Philosophy of Marketing Science*. Richard D. Irwin, Homewood, IL

Jelinek, M. (1986) "Organization structure; The basic conformation." In M. Jelinek, J.A. Litterer and R.E. Miles (eds) *Organizational by Design: Theory and Practice* (2nd edn). BPI, Plano, TX, pp. 125–39.

Killing, P. (1980) "Technology acquisition: License or joint venture," *Columbia Journal of World Business*, **15**, pp. 38–46.

Kimberly, J.R. (1978). "Organizational innovation: The influence of individual, organizational, and contextual factors on hospital adoption of technological and administrative innovations," *Academy of Management Journal*, **24**, pp. 689–713.

Kodama, F. (1992) "Technology fusion and the new R&D," *Harvard Business Review*, (July–August), pp. 70–78.

Kogut, B. (1988) "Joint ventures: Theoretical and empirical perspectives," *Strategic Management Journal*, **9** (4), pp. 319–32.

Kolbe, R.H. and M.S. Burnett (1991) "Content-analysis research: An examination of applications with directives for improving research reliability and objectivity," *Journal of Consumer Research*, **18**, pp. 243–50.

Kotabe, M. (1990). "Corporate product policy and innovative behavior of European and Japanese multinationals: An empirical investigation," *Journal of Marketing*, **54**, pp. 19–33.

Kotabe, M. (1992) *Global Sourcing Strategy: R&D, Manufacturing, and Marketing Interfaces*. Quorum, New York.

Kotabe, M. and D. Duhan (1991) "The perceived veracity of PIMS strategy principles in Japan: An empirical inquiry," *Journal of Marketing*, **55**, pp. 26–41.

Kotler, P. and G.A. Rath (1984) "Design: A powerful but neglected strategic tool," *Journal of Business Strategy*, **5**, pp. 16–21.

Kuznets, S. (1962) "Inventive activity: Problems of definition and measurement." In R.R. Nelson (ed) *The Rate and Direction of Inventive Activity*. Princeton University Press, Princeton, NJ, pp. 19–43.

Lengnick-Hall, C.A. (1992) "Innovation and competitive advantage: What we know and what we need to learn," *Journal of Management*, **18**, pp. 399–429.

Leroy, G. (1976) *Multinational Product Strategy: A Typology for Analysis of Worldwide Product Innovation and Diffusion*. Praeger, New York.

Levin, R.C., A.K. Klevorick, R.R. Nelson and S.G. Winter (1987). "Appropriating the returns from industrial research and development," *Brookings Papers on Economic Activity*, Issue 3, pp. 783–831.

Mahajan, V., E. Muller and F.M. Bass (1990) "New product diffusion models in marketing: A review and directions for research," *Journal of Marketing*, **54**, pp. 1–26.

Marquis, D.G. (1972) "The anatomy of successful innovations," *Managing Advancing Technology*, pp. 35–48.

Miles, R.E. and C.C. Snow (1978) *Organizational Strategy, Structure and Process*. McGraw-Hill, New York.

Montgomery, D. (1993) "U.S. vs. Japanese preferences in corporate alliances," working paper, Stanford University.

Myers, S. and D.G. Marquis (1969) *Successful Industrial Innovations*. National Science Foundation, Report no. 69–17, Washington, DC.

Nielsen, R.P. (1988) "Cooperative strategy," *Strategic Management Journal*, **9** (5), pp. 475–92.

Norton, J.A. and F.M. Bass (1987) "A diffusion theory model of adoption and substitution for successive generations of high technology products," *Management Science*, **33**, pp. 1069–1086.

Ohmae, K. (1989) "The global logic of strategic alliances," *Harvard Business Review*, **67**, March–April, pp. 143–54.

Ouchi, W.G. (1980) "Markets, bureaucracies, and clans," *Administrative Science Quarterly*, **25**, pp. 129–141.

Pavitt, K. (1969). "Technological innovation in European industry: The need for a world perspective," *Long Range Planning*, December, pp. 8–13.

Perlmutter, H. and D. Heenan (1986). "Cooperate to compete globally," *Harvard Business Review*, March–April, pp. 136–52.

Petroni, G. (1983a) "Strategic planning and research and development: Can we integrate them?" *Long Range Planning*, **2**, pp. 15–25.

Petroni, G. (1983b) "The strategic management of R&D part II: Organizing for integration," *Long Range Planning*, **16**, pp. 51–64.

Porter, M.E. (1980) *Competitive Strategy*. Free Press, New York.

Porter, M.E. (1990) *The Competitive Advantage of Nations*. Free Press, New York.

Porter, M.E. and M. Fuller (1986) "Coalitions and global strategy." In M. Porter (ed) *Competition in Global Industries*. Harvard Business School Press, Boston, MA, pp. 315–43.

Prahalad, C.K. and G. Hamel (1990) "The core competencies of the corporation," *Harvard Business Review*, **68**, pp. 79–87.

Roberts, E.B. and C. Berry (1985) "Entering new business: Selecting strategies for success," *Sloan Management Review*, **26**, pp. 3–17.

Robertson, T.S. (1967) "The process of innovation and the diffusion of innovation," *Journal of Marketing*, **31**, pp. 14–19.

Rogers, E.M. (1962) *Diffusion of Innovations*. Free Press of Glencoe, New York.

Roussel, P.A., K.N. Saad, and T.J. Erickson (1991) *Third Generation R&D*. Harvard Business School Press, Boston, MA.

Scherer, F.M. (1980) *Industrial Market Structure and Economic Performance* (2nd edn). Rand-McNally, Chicago, IL.

Schroeder, D.M. (1990) "A dynamic perspective on the impact of process innovation upon competitive strategies," *Strategic Management Journal*, **11**, (1), pp. 25–41.

Schumpeter, J.A. (1939) *Business Cycles*, Vol. 1. McGraw-Hill, New York.

Silk, A.J. and G.L. Urban (1978) "Pre-test market evaluation of new packaged goods: A model and measurement methodology," *Journal of Marketing Research*, **15**, pp. 171–91.

Spekman, R.E. and D. Salmond (1992) "A working consensus to collaborate: A field study of manufacturer-supplier dyads," *Marketing Science Institute*, working paper 92–134, pp. 1–35.

Stalk, G. (1988) "Time – the next source of competitive advantage," *Harvard Business Review*, **68** (4), pp. 41–51.

Teece, D.J. (1987) "Capturing value from technological innovation: Integration, strategic partnering, and licensing decisions," *Interfaces*, **18**, pp. 46–61.

Terpstra, V. and K. David (1991) *The Cultural Environment of International Business* (3rd edn). South-Western Publishing Co., Cincinnati, OH.

Terpstra, V. and B. Simonin (1993) "Strategic alliances in the triad: An exploratory study," *Journal of International Marketing*, **1**, pp. 4–25.

Tushman, M.L. and P. Anderson (1986) "Technological discontinuities and organizational environments," *Administrative Science Quarterly*, **31**, pp. 439–65.

Utterback, J.M. (1974) "Innovation in industry and the diffusion of technology," *Science*, **183**, pp. 620–626.

Utterback, J.M. (1979) "The dynamics of product and process innovation in industry." In C.T. Hill and J.M. Utterback (eds) *Technological Innovation for a Dynamic Economy*. Pergamon Press, New York, pp. 40–65.

Utterback, J.M. (1987) "Innovation and industrial evolution in manufacturing industries." In B.R. Guile and H. Brooks (eds) *Technology and Global Industry*. National Academy Press, Washington, DC, pp. 16–48.

Utterback, J.M. and W.J. Abernathy (1975) "A dynamic model of product and process innovation," *Omega*, **36**, pp. 639–56.

Webster, F.E., Jr. (1992) "The changing role of marketing in the corporation," *Journal of Marketing*, **56**, pp. 1–17.

Williamson, O. (1979). "Transaction-cost economics: The governance of contractual relationships," *Journal of Law and Economics*, **22**, pp. 233–62.

Zimmer, M.R. and L.L. Golden (1988) "Impressions of retail stores: A content analysis of consumer images," *Journal of Retailing*, **64**, pp. 265–94.

11

The Return of 7-Eleven . . . from Japan: The Vanguard Program

MASAAKI KOTABE

THE UNIVERSITY OF TEXAS AT AUSTIN

The convenience-store industry in the United States was successful in the 1970s and early 1980s, but began to stumble in the late 1980s and early 1990s. In the late 1980s, major oil companies, accustomed to the rigors of intense competition, entered the market and sent industry giants like Southland, Circle K Corporation and National Convenience Stores reeling. Competition was intense, and many retailers borrowed excessively to expand and diversify. As a result, 14 convenience-store companies filed for bankruptcy from 1989 to 1991.

In recent years, the industry has been beset by a host of difficulties. Among the industry's problems are a sluggish economy, declining sales of tobacco and beer, diminishing consumer preference for traditional snack foods, stiff competition from fuel-company-owned food marts and, most importantly, the inability of many store chains to adapt to changing customer needs.

Across the Pacific in Japan, the convenience-store industry is experiencing a revolution of a different kind . . . the kind of competition about which we rarely hear and that we have generally ignored. While still considered inefficient by many U.S. observers, the Japanese retail industry has undergone a quiet revolution at the hands of major retail and convenience-store chains that boast world-class efficiency and profitability, despite Japan's current recession.[1] Ito-Yokado, the largest retailer in Japan and the 7-Eleven licensee, recently took over its U.S. parent company, the Southland Corporation, known for its 7-Eleven store chains throughout the United States and in some 20 foreign countries. Indeed, this event could forebode that the next generation of Japan's formidable competition will come from its retail "transplants" in the United States.

This chapter examines how Ito-Yokado of Japan, with the charismatic leadership of Toshifumi Suzuki, its chief executive officer, is revising the story of the U.S. convenience-store industry through his experiment with new 7-Eleven stores. The implications of the changes are enormous, as evidenced by their huge success.

"The Return of 7-Eleven from Japan: The Vanguard Program," by Masaaki Kotabe, *The Columbia Journal of World Business*, Winter 1995, pp. 70–81. Reprinted by permission of Jai Press Inc.

Southland Corporation

In 1985, the Southland Corporation, owner of the 7-Eleven convenience-store chain, was the nation's seventh-largest retailer, with more than 7,500 stores, sales of $8.5 billion and net earnings exceeding $210 million. However, a series of problems soon besieged the corporation.

One of the first problems Southland experienced was an ill-timed restructuring of its labor force in 1986. A consulting firm was hired to undertake a study of the company's organizational makeup. Although Southland was showing record profits and company morale was high, the study concluded that Southland should lay off a number of employees. One former Southland vice president noted, "The company's forward momentum stopped abruptly. Discussion of who-will-get-it-next replaced brainstorming sessions . . . It was definitely the beginning of a malaise that has now ended with bankruptcy."[2] These layoffs destroyed the cohesion of the company, and the resulting lack of creative force helped push Southland into bankruptcy.

Financial problems that ensued were also very serious. One financial problem was Southland's expensive acquisition of Dallas's Cityplace Complex. By 1985, the bottom had dropped out of the Dallas land market, and Southland was stuck with a new building generating annual losses of over $85 million. Another financial problem arose from a takeover bid by a Canadian company. Southland raised $1.5 billion in junk bonds to repel the takeover, but the October 1987 crash of the New York Stock Exchange made these bonds almost worthless. This forced Southland to take out an expensive loan and plunge even deeper into debt in order to pay for their leveraged buyout. As a result, Southland Corporation was forced to file for bankruptcy protection under Chapter 11. In early 1990, Southland's sales began sagging, due in part to a shortage of funds with which to reposition and renovate its stores, competition from emerging regional chains and an inability to come to grips with changing trends and consumer demands in the retail business.

On March 5, 1991, after five months in bankruptcy, Southland Corporation was acquired by Ito-Yokado, the extremely successful licensee of 7-Eleven stores in Japan since 1973. The deal involved the purchase of 70 percent of Southland for $430 million by IYG Holding Co., wholly owned by Ito-Yokado Co. Ltd. and 7-Eleven Japan Co. Ltd. The purchase gave Ito-Yokado control of more than 7,000 American and Canadian stores as well as franchise authority in 20 other countries.

Southland emerged from Chapter 11 with its sales having slipped as a result of financial restructuring. In an ambitious move to recapture its past glory, Southland decided to take a page from its new Japanese owner and embark on a radical new campaign. The key to the campaign is a shift in focus from the historical emphasis on *volume sales* to an emphasis on *customer satisfaction*. Southland's strategy (heavily influenced by Ito-Yokado) primarily focuses on three key areas: 1) *pricing*; 2) *store remodeling and remerchandising*; and 3) *inventory management/new product development*.

Specifically, Southland chose to change the pricing strategy away from heavy discounting of merchandise and focus on selling products at "everyday fair prices." This new pricing policy contrasts greatly with Southland's former practice of heavily discounting merchandise from time to time to attract customers.

Another key area strategy was the remodeling and remerchandising of 7-Eleven stores. Store remodeling involved a general face-lift: lower shelves, new in-store signs, better lighting and uncluttering of the sales counter. Remerchandising involved the addition of a wide variety of new products, such as fresh foods, staples in preferred sizes and more upscale offerings.

Finally, one of the most important changes involved distribution management. The key to Ito-

Yokado's success with 7-Eleven Japan has been the use of its inventory and physical distribution management systems that result in lower on-hand inventory, faster inventory turnover and, most importantly, accurate information on customer buying habits.

The Vanguard Program

Since its acquisition, Ito-Yokado has tested its operational systems in 7-Eleven stores in the United States. This experiment is known as the Vanguard Program. The Austin, Texas, market was selected as the first test market because of its large and diverse consumer base, 7-Eleven's substantial market penetration in the area and its proximity to company headquarters in Dallas. The Vanguard Program was implemented in October 1991 in the 52 7-Eleven stores in Austin. During the first year, sales increased by 11.4 percent over a matched set of stores in the Dallas–Fort Worth area. Monthly sales have risen continuously since the inception of the Vanguard Program.

The main goal of the Vanguard Program was to make 7-Eleven stores more responsive to the needs of the consumer, the hypothesis being that sales and profits will improve as 7-Eleven improves its ability to respond to consumer needs.[3] The program had two basic components: a *new store concept* (store look, prices and product mix) and a *new customer-driven operating system*. The Vanguard Program takes a store/market-wide approach in addressing changing consumer needs (vs. the traditional piecemeal approach to change). The ultimate goal of the Vanguard Program goes well beyond specific sales targets and knowledge of the preferences of a particular store or market. It is to develop a system based on the same principle upon which 7-Eleven was founded more than 60 years ago: to give customers what they want, when they want it.

NEW STORE CONCEPT

The new store concept was designed to improve the customer's shopping experience while fulfilling more of the current customer's needs. The fundamental areas in which changes have been made are as follows.

Product selection

Significant changes were made in the choice of the products carried at Vanguard stores. More than 700 items were removed and more than 500 new items were added. Added to inventory were easy-to-prepare entrees, fresh produce and fresh fruit, preferred brands and sizes for many staples, condiments and grocery items and deli sandwiches and salads prepared fresh and delivered daily by 7-Eleven's new commissary in Austin, managed by CaterAir International, the largest airline-catering business in the world.

Competitive pricing

The pricing structure of more than 1,900 items was changed from discounting to "everyday fair pricing," the goal of which was to ensure product quality at competitive prices (i.e. modest premiums over supermarket prices). To aid the new policy, 7-Eleven hired an outside agency to check on supermarket prices and developed a procedure for routine price surveys.

Store appearance

Managers improved interior and exterior lighting (brighter lights), reduced gondola height and wider aisles, reduced air space between products and removed hanging signs to give the store a more open appearance and less clutter on checkout counters.

Store operations

Among the changes instituted were double coverage (a minimum of two clerks on duty at any time for quicker checkout and added security); a stricter dress code as well as new employee training programs; installation of credit-card readers at gas pumps; multiple payment options, including cash, checks, credit cards, coupons and food stamps; a 100 percent customer satisfaction program, empowering store personnel to respond to customer concerns on the spot; a redefined role for field consultants; development of new means of communication between field consultants and store managers and top-level management; and new tools for effective store-level communications and planning, such as Total Quality Leadership and the Individual Store Development Plan.

Distribution support

This involved an increase in the frequency of deliveries to the stores as well as modification of shipping procedures from shipping cases or half-cases to individual items.

Customer communications

One key element in informing customers about the sweeping changes was aggressive customer communications. The communications campaign involved an advertising campaign (television, newspapers, radio, billboards and direct mail), a public relations campaign to maximize news coverage and weekly ads focusing on improvements in pricing and product mix.

CUSTOMER-DRIVEN OPERATING SYSTEMS

To manage a retail business, both information and goods have to flow through distribution channels as efficiently as possible. At the heart of Ito-Yokado's new consumer-driven operating systems lies AIM (Accelerated Inventory Management), which is designed not only to accomplish streamlined just-in-time inventory management, but also to improve employee morale from the bottom up (see figure 11.1). To supplement AIM and further improve logistical efficiency, the Combined Distribution Center (CDC) concept has also been introduced.

Accelerated Inventory Management

AIM builds on Ito-Yokado's corporate philosophy and practice of customer orientation. The plan to use the AIM system stresses customer needs, as do the layout of the new stores and emphasis on quality and freshness. Choices of products sold in 7-Eleven stores will be tailored to the neighborhoods in which the stores are located. If many of the customers are children, a store will sell more candy. If a number of single working people visit the store, more premade fresh dinners will be made available.

Customer responsiveness also gives the manager more responsibility over what is being sold in his or her store. This strategy of giving store employees more responsibility is very important in the "new 7-Eleven" philosophy. Managers are responsible for choosing about 50 percent of the store's merchandise based on customer information collected from the AIM system. Under this system,

7-Eleven's spectacular success in Japan can be attributed to its management information system, which allows inventory to be turned over as many as 30 times a year, versus 12 times a year in the United States. The introduction of the Accelerated Inventory Management (AIM) system for 7-Eleven in the United States was the first step in building a customer-driven management inventory system. The objectives of AIM were to build a balanced inventory, improve store merchandising, manage inventory, improve ordering of products, identify "dead" items and introduce new products. Specifically, AIM would do the following:

- Build a balanced inventory by
    - identifying "core" products (400 national, 650 regional)
    - maintaining a minimum inventory of three units per product to maximize sales/minimize shortages and enhance product presentation
    - developing a list of optional items that the store can use to customize product mix to suit its target market (target marketing completed through the Individual Store Development Plans or ISDP)
- Improve store merchandising by
    - establishing consistent layout of product categories (determined by the merchandise manager)
    - implementing a flexible planogram [a] system
    - providing training programs to assist store operators and field consultants with product presentation, dead/new item evaluation and merchandising know-how
- Improve inventory management by
    - reducing on-hand inventory to no more than twice that amount required to satisfy sales during a delivery cycle with a minimum of three items each (aim to achieve 2 turns/month or 24 turns annually)
    - removing dead items and slow-selling items
- Improve ordering by
    - counting every item during every order cycle using standard count and order forms. Information on count sheet determines quantity on hand, delivered quantity, credits and write-offs, sales and order quantity. Frequency of counts depends on the product. Fresh products are counted every four hours.
    - assigning each store employee a section in the store to manage inventory. Employee takes responsibility for counting as well as ordering and identifying dead products and recommending new products. This process raises employee morale by encouraging ownership, establishing accountability and enriching the job.
    - providing forms to assist in analysis of data, such as dead items, ordering efficiency and new product sales
- Remove dead items by
    - developing predetermined sales hurdle rates for defining dead items
    - evaluating dead items based on the determined rates as well as other factors, after which an item may be adjusted and remain active or is disposed of through transfer to another store, return to seller, clearance or write-offs
- Introduce new products by
    - selecting new products based on a criterion called the "Southland Business Concept," according to which products must conform to and enhance the speed of service, quality, selection, price and store environment
    - sending new item information to stores and presenting new items to field management groups at weekly meetings
    - requiring field consultants to review new products, while giving store operators the final decision, unless products are to be carried in other corporate stores or are recommended to be carried in franchises

[a] A planogram system is a proprietary system by which to determine an optimal merchandise mix that helps reduce dead items and increase a proactive introduction of new product items.

Figure 11.1 Accelerated Inventory Management

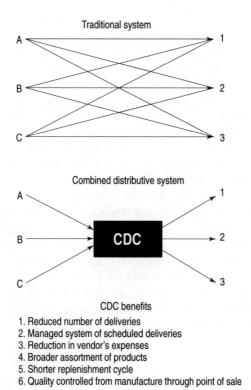

Figure 11.2 Combined Distribution Center

each store has about 3,000 SKUs (stock-keeping units), made up of core, regional core and optional items. Store managers help develop both the regional core and optional items. In any given year, about 25 percent of products are replaced with better-selling items. The goal is to achieve 24 inventory "turns" annually.

"Dead" items are removed from inventory, new items are introduced and current items are reordered through a rigorous analysis of inventory levels. Each item must be counted by hand for each order cycle. Data are recorded on a standard order form and reviewed. Each store employee is given responsibility for one section of the store. He or she must count the items, reorder if necessary and make the decision to cut an item if it is not selling well. The person responsible for inventory control not only evaluates how much is left on the shelves but also how much was sold in the previous order cycle. Factors such as weather, neighborhood events and holidays also enter into buying decisions.

Incentive programs have also been implemented throughout the company emphasizing efficiency and the importance of AIM. The objectives of the AIM system are to have a well-managed inventory, improved merchandise, item-by-item tracking of sales and the ability to purchase fresh foods just-in-time.

Combined distribution center

In keeping with its overall strategy of distribution efficiency, Ito-Yokado has made a number of changes in suppliers, distribution and operational procedures. One Southland spokesperson observed, ". . . in the past, our approach to increasing revenues was to build new stores. Now, in part with our renovations, the idea is to increase sales on a per-store basis." Southland plans to focus on improving the old stores and closing "less profitable" locations. In 1992, Southland closed 358 locations and opened only 34 new ones.

One of the biggest changes is in Southland's physical distribution system. CDCs allow vendors' products to be consolidated at a common dock and delivered daily to each store (see Figure 11.2). The manufacturer receives an order (either with the last delivery or electronically) and delivers the products to the distributor. The CDCs gather the products from the various manufacturers and deliver them to each store during off-peak hours. Store employees check the incoming products and place orders for the next day or next ordering cycle. The CDC system both improves efficiency and gives customers the freshest and highest quality products available.

Ito-Yokado sold Southland's distribution and food preparation centers in Orlando, Florida; Tyler, Texas; and Champaign, Illinois. Southland sold many of these facilities to its new distributor, McLane Co., from which it now obtains most of its perishable and nonperishable items. By changing its distribution system, Southland has been able to sell its old internal distribution system, thus streamlining operations considerably.

Sweeping Transformation, Textbook Style

There are a few success factors that explain the changes at Southland. The interplay among these factors has allowed Ito-Yokado to acquire its former American parent and to transform it into a successful part of the Japanese-based corporation. The first is the power of Ito-Yokado's image and the company's clear focus on customer satisfaction. Second, in order to practice its customer orientation, operational management has been decentralized to empower every employee. Third, management at Southland has been extremely successful in implementing all-encompassing feedback and accountability structures throughout its new distribution system.

Customer orientation

Instead of implementing a "cookie cutter" approach wherein all stores carry the same products, responsibility for product selection is shifted downward, allowing individual stores to be customized for specific target markets.[4] 7-Eleven also has shifted its pricing policy from frequent discounting to a moderate-pricing scheme. Finally, additional services such as ATMs, faxing, mailing and check-cashing have been gradually added to boost customer convenience, while cosmetic changes, such as lighting and store layout, served to complete the favorable shopping experience. The crucial point is that all these changes have been made in all stores, so that the "big picture" of 7-Eleven's strategy has become apparent.

A survey of 7-Eleven customers[5] showed the following:

• More than 90 percent of customers who shopped in stores in the Vanguard Program were satisfied with the speed of service and the ease of finding products;

- More than 85 percent were satisfied with the quality of fresh food (including sandwiches, salads and produce); and
- Seventy percent were aware of the increased selection of healthier foods.

Prices at 7-Eleven stores are also perceived to be comparable to those at supermarkets. These results are a far cry from the general customer dissatisfaction registered at the 7-Eleven stores prior to the inception of the Vanguard Program. While there is always room for improvement, customer orientation is no longer a philosophy of 7-Eleven stores just to talk about, it is being *practiced*.

Decentralized management

In an effort to improve its customer focus, one of the sweeping changes Southland Corporation undertook was in its management hierarchy. First, the number of 7-Eleven stores was reduced, so that only the profitable stores remained. This reduction freed financial and other resources to be used for improvements in the remaining stores.

The key to the reformed structure is the focus on each individual 7-Eleven store. Store managers were given more power in order to enhance the company's flexibility in a highly competitive environment. By decentralizing authority, Southland empowered the individual stores to react more effectively to changes in consumer demand.[6] Relocating much decision making to the store level has made 7-Eleven more responsive to both customer needs and store-level employee initiatives.

Another major change has been the sale of 7-Eleven's warehouse facilities, transferring them to McLane, enhancing 7-Eleven's flexibility as a convenience store rather than a distributor. Decentralized decision making and teamwork play major roles in 7-Eleven's daily operations.

One of the most encouraging changes is the openness with which communication presently occurs at the storewide level. Open communications within a company have become a strong motivator for employees. Achieving customer satisfaction requires that clerks, who are in close contact with the customer, gather, communicate and respond to customer feedback. In order to demonstrate 7-Eleven's concern about the customer's opinion, a formal dress code is maintained.

Taking into consideration that the employees in the stores are not highly paid, management style plays a major role in motivating people. 7-Eleven gives its employees responsibilities such as "ownership" or merchandising responsibility over a particular shelf. According to this arrangement, the initiative of store clerks directly affects sales since the clerks are responsible for counting, ordering and, to a certain extent, merchandising.[7] The result has been a better inventory system and more motivated employees. It is this sense of "ownership" that motivates employees because they feel that they are an essential part of the company and that their performance counts. Another change in style is the openess of store managers to ideas, comments, or suggestions from the staff.

AIM also has improved product selection. One of the benefits of regular counting of inventory was that store managers learned which products sold well and which collected dust. Based on this, store managers were permitted, actually encouraged, to drop slow-sellers and find better merchandise. With the exception of a set of designated core products, product decisions are made at the store level.

Another innovation requires store managers to submit reports to Southland so that communications extend beyond their immediate supervisor. This Individual Store Development Plan (ISDP) was important because, although Ito-Yokado was implementing proven strategies from Japan, some translation was undoubtedly required in order to implement them successfully in the American market.

Store managers report that ISDP has fostered more effective communication with field consultants and partially flattened the chain of command. Instead of merely issuing directives to store managers, field consultants now often act as a sounding board for store managers' ideas as well as a conduit for communication with Dallas. Field consultants meet with store managers weekly to review inventory and store appearance, current sales patterns, long-range planning and suggestions for Southland. One reported result was that store managers were more apt to support changes that required their approval and input first.

Not only are store managers able to interact more effectively with their field consultants, they also receive feedback from other store managers in their area at scheduled meetings to critique each other's stores. Store managers, accompanied by their field consultant, periodically visit another manager's store to assist in the implementation of recent innovations that the company is testing. If the focus is on eliminating air space between shelves, all the managers get their hands dirty redesigning the store. As a follow-up, store managers can discuss the benefits of the changes. If all agree that the changes have been successful, managers together implement them at other stores.

In summary, the style of management that 7-Eleven has adopted at the store level is "people-oriented," relying on open communication, positive reinforcement and motivation. The changes have attracted better qualified and more motivated employees, and employee morale has gone up. Additional training and "double coverage" (two clerks in a store at all times) have been important morale boosters, particularly on night shifts and among women employees.

Efficient distribution

In the fast-changing world of the convenience-store industry, accurate and timely information is a resource of capital importance. Having recognized the importance that information and open communication lines play, 7-Eleven focused its efforts on systematizing information and communication, especially at the store level, where market information is gleaned. One move was the introduction of the Weekly Communications Recap form under the ISDP. The forms systematize the flow of information from the store level to the field consultants and, if need be, to the headquarters in Dallas.

Each week, field consultants review their operations at the Division Communication Conference by way of video conferencing. Issues raised at individual field consultant/store manager meetings and store manager team meetings are raised for general discussion. If a field consultant has been unable to effect the change the store manager has requested, upper management can clear the way for easy resolution of the problem. This way, good ideas generated in one part of the company get passed around to all parts of the organization.

Another move was to implement subgroup meetings that are organized by the field consultants so as to enable store managers to exchange information and learn from each other. These small groups (about ten people) have proven to be more effective than former mass meetings.

7-Eleven's major skills are the management of distribution systems and logistics. The timely and efficient distribution of goods is a key competitive advantage of the company. 7-Eleven has a competitive advantage in getting the right merchandise to the right place at the right time. Although these skills already existed before 7-Eleven was acquired by Ito-Yokado, they were less developed in those days. Presently, corporate management builds on the expertise from the store operations in Japan and emphasizes the core competencies of the company reflected in all changes as they have been described above. The eye-catching AIM system enables the company to process large amounts of information on customer buying patterns and the products. Once systems like AIM are computerized, it will become a means of pooling the information produced by the individual stores, so that the

Table 11.1 Improvement in Southland Corporation's financial performance

	1994	1993	1992
Total revenue ($ millions)	$6,759.8	$6,814.2	$7,499.5
Earnings ($ millions)	$73.5	($2.6)	($119.9)
Average growth in store sale	2.0%	(2.7%)	(3.9%)
Average per-store gross profit change	2.1%	2.2%	(0.3%)
Earnings per share ($)	0.22	0.17	(0.32)

Source: SEC Report

company as a whole can capitalize on this resource. Changes in the ordering system allow managers and clerks to fill our "item request forms" to get new products to fill dead space. Otherwise, the merchandising department at Southland sends the new product ideas.

The crucial point is that 7-Eleven has proven itself capable of implementing innovative programs, such as AIM and the CDC, that are unique to 7-Eleven and have worked effectively. However, Toshifumi Suzuki, CEO of Ito-Yokado, initially decided against installing the Japanese company's much-lauded electronic customer-tracking and inventory devices at Southland. Reflecting his philosophy, Suzuki says, "The POS (point-of-sale) system does not automatically equal profits. It is in fact a calculator. It's up to management to do something with it." Instead, he has had employees do the same inventory tracking and evaluation by hand. While this is extremely time-consuming and inefficient, Suzuki feels that this will teach employees the actual purpose of collecting POS data. In the long run, according to this logic, understanding the importance of the POS information and correctly interpreting the data will lead to greater profits than an early decision to install price scanners in each store. Southland does plan to install these in time, as their proper use was viewed as one of the keys to 7-Eleven Japan's success.

As a result of Suzuki's methodical leadership, 7-Eleven stores have experienced a metamorphosis under the Vanguard Program. As presented in table 11.1, Southland's turnaround is illustrated vividly by the improvement in its financial performance for the 1992–4 period (the Vanguard Program was implemented in October 1991). While total revenue declined, this was mostly due to consolidation through the elimination of marginal stores and a lackluster U.S. economy. The company's net earnings have improved drastically due to cost cutting and implementation of AIM and the just-in-time inventory management. It was the first profitable year for Southland since 1989, when the company lost $1.32 billion. Sales growth, store profitability and earnings-per-share have consistently improved in the last three years.

Ito-Yokado/Southland Nexus

In the late 1980s, many Americans were under the impression that Japan was trying to take over the West economically. As *Time* magazine, the *Wall Street Journal*, and *The Economist* published many articles on the downfall of the American style of management, Japan's was treated in the

United States with envy and awe. Midway through this period, Southland Corporation agreed to its acquisition by its successful licensee to avoid a buyout by an unrelated company. Faced with the potential for disillusionment among employees and others with a stake in the company, Southland and Ito-Yokado decided on a bold move to introduce new management techniques. Over the next three years, everything from corporate style to consumer focus was modified. Today, stores in the U.S. function much as the stores in Japan do, and fears of backlash against the new Japanese owners and management style have not been realized.

There are two equally important factors to consider in 7-Eleven's turnaround. In a licensee-acquiring-a-licenser relationship, it would have been almost impossible to accomplish what Ito-Yokado and Southland Corporation have accomplished without charismatic leadership and what is referred to in Japan as *Kaizen* (continual improvement) effort.

CHARISMATIC LEADERSHIP

Southland was willing to accept the change because the company's financial position was weak and employees at all levels accepted the need for change throughout the firm. However, the basis for Southland Corporation's success was the way the Japanese parent company coordinated the changes. The charismatic leader, Toshifumi Suzuki, spearheaded this effort by creating an image for the company. He wanted to push three radical changes:

1. "Japanize" the U.S. 7-Eleven stores in terms of image and management style;
2. Infuse cash into Southland Corporation so the changes could be undertaken correctly; and
3. Change the infrastructure of the distribution system.

By defining and laying out the programs used in Japan's 7-Elevens for the American 7-Eleven managers, he received their support for the changes he saw as necessary. The American corporation's ability to see and be guided by a unifying vision ensured that the management programs introduced by Suzuki would work as a unified whole in the United States.

In addition to its guiding vision, Ito-Yokado also had a specific blueprint for success. The convenience stores in Japan served as a role model in store appearance, customer service, product selection and replenishment, training and development of staff and operational efficiency. Many of the information management programs implemented, such as AIM and POS, had already been tried, tested and refined in the stores in Japan.

KAIZEN (CONTINUAL IMPROVEMENT) EFFORT

The next essential element in the successful change process at Southland was in relationship building with Ito-Yokado. Ito-Yokado became the Japanese licensee for Southland in Japan in 1973. As with any venture between Japanese and American firms, both sides began the long process of getting to know one another long before the crisis ever arose at Southland. By 1989, the two organizations were probably very familiar with each other's operations. Thus, Ito-Yokado's plan to purchase Southland was seen as less adversarial.

After the sale and the initial implementation of the different management styles, the pace of change, though somewhat inconspicuous, contributed to the success of 7-Eleven's transformation. Store managers believed that the changes were made smoothly, and they looked forward to new programs.

Our analysis suggested that infrequent changes of small scale would reduce store manager motivation and enthusiasm and raise doubts concerning Southland's commitment to improvement. Infrequent changes of large scale would also likely damage employee morale because it is more difficult to work under such "feast or famine" conditions. The success of these programs would also be compromised because they would be implemented in haste with a "crush" mentality.

In the Vanguard Program, the scale and frequency of improvements were balanced to achieve optimum operational effectiveness and to provide ample motivation at the store level.[8] Ito-Yokado was able to direct changes of a challenging, yet reasonable, scale on a regular basis. Projects could also be evaluated quickly and regularly, so that feedback was both accurate and timely. Because the improvements were of an incremental nature, however, neither Southland nor store managers deviated much from the corporate vision, and only minor adjustments were needed to make programs complement each other and bring the company closer to its goals. In addition, store managers learned that they were expected to make improvements on a regular basis.

Challenges Facing 7-Eleven Stores and the Southland Corporation

There are a few issues and possible challenges that 7-Eleven faces. Specifically, these issues are in the area of store-to-management communication, resistance to change and competition from other convenience stores and similar outlets.

COMMUNICATION

One key to the success of 7-Eleven in Austin has been open communication. As 7-Eleven moves to replicate the successes of the Austin area in other parts of the country, the communication issue may arise, especially in parts of the country where 7-Eleven stores are owned by individual franchisees. Since all the Austin-area 7-Eleven stores are corporate owned, communication between head-quarters and individual stores has been relatively easy. With independently owned stores, however, it may be more difficult to maintain the enthusiasm and commitment needed to empower everyone from store managers to store clerks.

Another issue is the changing role of field consultants. In the Austin area, the field consultants served as change agents in close contact with the customer, store management and corporate headquarters. It may also be more difficult to maintain the same openness and enthusiasm for open communication among field consultants in other areas, especially if they are not familiar with their new role as change agents rather than order givers. Geography or the wide distances involved may hinder open communication between stores and headquarters.

RESISTANCE TO CHANGES

Another possible issue that may arise is frustration with the number of frequent changes that must be made in service and product selection. Although most Austin-area store managers welcomed improvement, there were some who resented the constant changes ordered by Dallas. This problem may be more manifest with independently owned 7-Eleven stores around the nation.

COMPETITION

The issue of competition is a serious one. First, many other convenience-store chains may attempt to replicate 7-Eleven's success by remodeling stores and offering better products and services. One can expect some flight of store and field-management talent to the competition. Larger stores, such as 24-hour supermarkets, may also pose increased competition as they offer similar products at lower prices.

Conclusion and Discussion

Customers once viewed 7-Elevens as unsafe, unclean stores that sold a limited range of low quality goods at high prices. The AIM system has expanded the range of quality items available. Store managers took steps to improve safety and cleanliness in their stores. In keeping with their focus on the customer, 7-Eleven now offers more services, such as mini post offices, automated teller machines and check cashing.

Ito-Yokado of Japan purchased 70 percent of Southland in 1991. Since that time, almost all of the over-arching goals of Ito-Yokado's Suzuki have been implemented in the Austin market. Notably, the AIM system will soon be automated, when an electronic POS system is installed at all 7-Eleven stores.

The success of Southland has been built upon the successful integration of programs and their adaptation to individual stores and areas. Within that lies the core of a good business: a guiding vision, regular and open communication and an unswerving dedication to discerning customer expectations and exceeding them.

The changes in Austin have proven successful with a 43 percent sales-volume growth in the past 3 years. In spite of the expense of the many changes in the Austin Vanguard 7-Eleven market, the corporation has also been profitable. Those changes have been gradually implemented in 7-Eleven stores throughout the United States. Thus, Southland has begun to achieve the profitability that eluded the company for so many years. In light of this success, Southland seems to have a blueprint for further strides in the future.

Implications Beyond the 7-Eleven Stores

The Southland experiment suggests that there is a lot to be learned from Japanese management practices in the convenience-store industry. In recent years, customer orientation has become a corporate buzzword in the United States. Research abounds concerning the superiority of Japanese to U.S. marketing practices. In the 1980s, many researchers discussed the superiority of Japanese marketing techniques in terms of soft-data gathering and distribution channels,[9] product development,[10] communication and problem-solving processes,[11] decision-making process[12] and organizational learning,[13] among others.

However, less than a decade later, Japanese companies once thought to be almost invincible are reeling from Japan's "post-bubble" economy as they face a weakened domestic market, skyrocketed yen and trade relations with the United States that have worsened. As a result, many U.S. business practitioners question the future competitiveness of Japanese companies.

This is a shortsighted view that fails to see the fundamental strengths of Japanese firms, as illustrated by Ito-Yokado's management of 7-Eleven stores in the United States. Americans should not be fooled by the seeming weaknesses of many Japanese companies today. In order to achieve organizational goals, firms have to determine the needs and wants of target markets and deliver the desired value more effectively than competitors. Japanese companies still appear to have an edge over U.S. firms in emphasizing customer value. While reeling from the Japanese recession and further battered by the overvalued yen, many Japanese firms will, in all likelihood, continue to emphasize the benefit of focusing on customer value and may emerge stronger than ever before.

To compete successfully, U.S. firms will need to go back to basics: how to keep improving customer value by focusing anew on the product they offer – its cost, its quality and its availability – and on service and flexibility in response to the market needs.

Japanese marketers view marketing primarily in human terms while American executives treat marketing mainly as impersonal sales and profit-oriented activities. Market orientation is a corporate philosophy that needs to be internalized within an organization, not something to be practiced only by marketing experts. Unfortunately, many U.S. companies have become too functionally divided and compartmentalized to adopt market orientation throughout their ranks. The organizational setup and practices of Japanese companies, on the other hand – an example is found in Southland's 7-Eleven stores in the United States – may be conducive to promoting a much-needed culture of market orientation in American businesses.

Ito-Yokado is the first Japanese retail company to introduce a Japanese-style market orientation in the United States. Indeed, the revival of 7-Eleven stores in the United States may herald the beginning of another type of Japanese competition based on service quality and strong customer orientation.

Notes

1 Michael R. Czinkota and Masaaki Kotabe (1993) *The Japanese Distribution System: Opportunities and Obstacles, Structures and Practices*. Chicago, IL: Probus Publishing Company.
2 Allen Liles (1992) "Road to Long-term Ruin," *Barron's*, January 27, p. 34.
3 John C. Narver and Stanley F. Slater, (1990) "The Effect of Market Orientation of Business Profitability." *Journal of Marketing* (October), pp. 20–35.
4 Changes at 7-Eleven stores were driven by changing consumer needs. The 7-Eleven chain grew up with the "baby boom" generation in the 1960s and 1970s. The needs of these customers, 18–34 years old, largely defined the way 7-Eleven did business. Today, 7-Eleven recognizes that their target customers are a little older and have made some fundamental changes in the way they live. For example, consumers are less tolerant of slow service; eat lighter, healthier foods; and are more value-conscious.
5 The survey was conducted March through April 1994. Personal interviews were conducted with 150 randomly selected customers at the three stores in Austin. The stores are located in socioeconomically distinct areas, the Ben White store in a largely working-class area, the Guadalupe store in a middle-class and student-populated area, and the Far West store in an upper middle-class area.
6 Southland's category managers frequently visit manufacturers and ask what new products are beginning

to take off on the market (i.e. in the growth stage of the product life cycle) in the hope that those products can be introduced early on at 7-Eleven stores. However, the final decision to acquire any new product is up to each store manager or even up to each clerk who has responsibility for his/her own shelf.

7 Further, Southland offers a graduated profit sharing program to 7-Eleven store clerks based on the length of their employment.

8 See Masaaki Imai (1986) *Kaizen*, New York: Random House Business Division. The "Kaizen" concept was originally employed for continual improvement in manufacturing operations. However, a similar continual-improvement effort can be equally adopted in non-manufacturing activities, such as in relationship building.

9 Johny K. Johansson and Ikujiro Nonaka (1987) "Marketing Research the Japanese Way," *Harvard Business Review* (May–June); pp. 16–22.

10 Michael R. Czinkota and Masaaki Kotabe (1990) "Product Development the Japanese Way," *Journal of Business Strategy* (November/December), pp. 31–36.

11 William Lazer, Shoji Murata and Hiroshi Kosaka, "Japanese Marketing: Towards a Better Understanding." *Journal of Marketing* (Spring 1985): 69–81.

12 Richard Pascale and Anthony Athos (1981) *The Art of Japanese Management*. New York: Warner Books.

13 Ikujiro Nonaka and Johny K. Johansson, (1985) "Japanese Management: What About the 'Hard' Skills." *Academy of Management Review* 2, pp. 181–91.

IV

MARKETING DIMENSIONS

The key objective of the marketing function is to develop an in-depth understanding of the business environment and the customer, in terms of requirements, needs, and wants. Given the country-and consumer-specific differences encountered in the international arena, marketing becomes a crucial function for the international business executive. In addition, marketing, as a social science, should not only follow and be responsive to existing circumstances, but should also take on a trail-blazing leadership function by setting new standards which aid in improving the standard of living and quality of life.

Chapter 12 offers a perspective of product development within Japanese firms. It highlights the approach to product development as a process of continuous technological improvements aimed at making an already successful product even better for customers. This process view also affects the way firms conduct their market research and how the findings from such research are disseminated within the firm. Chapter 13 investigates the issue of market orientation more closely by contrasting the marketing involvement of U.S. and Japanese managers. Japanese firms are under pressure from a domestic recession, high domestic costs, and a high currency value. In order to compete effectively, these firms stress the benefits they offer to the customer more than ever before. Their aim is not just to satisfy but rather to delight the customer through superior products and outstanding pre- and post-sales service. This aim is achieved by internalizing market orientation as a corporate philosophy within the organization rather than using market-ing simply as a compartmentalized corporate function. Chapter 14 discusses the transition of Central and Eastern Europe to a market economy. It presents an analysis of the economic shifts which have taken place in these countries, and develops alternative market entry and marketing mix strategies which accommodate these shifts. In addition, this chapter also highlights the corporate and social responsibility of marketers to implement a market orientation which is responsive to and respectful of existing societal conditions.

12

Product Development the Japanese Way

MICHAEL R. CZINKOTA
GEORGETOWN UNIVERSITY

AND

MASAAKI KOTABE
THE UNIVERSITY OF TEXAS AT AUSTIN

The 1980s saw a great surge in the global market success of Japan. Increasingly, there has been talk about the beginning of the Japanese century and the emergence of an overpowering Japanese economy.

Policy makers have responded to these visions by expressing concern about the trade competitiveness of the United States and taking actions designed to break down real or perceived trade barriers. Competitiveness, however, is driven and maintained to a large degree by individual firms and their marketing efforts. A quick review of the successes and inroads achieved by Japanese products confirms this perspective.

Japanese firms have been successful in established industries in which U.S. firms were once thought invincible, as well as in newly developing industries. They have been able not only to capture third-country market share from the U.S. competition but also to obtain major footholds in the U.S. domestic market. They supplied almost 20 percent of U.S. imports in 1989 and achieved their surplus in trade in manufactured goods on the basis of both high-technology and non-high-technology products.

As a result, U.S. producers' domestic market share for color televisions dropped from 90 percent in 1970 to less than 10 percent by the early 1990s, and the domestic share of semiconductor production declined from 89 percent to 60 percent. Even more startling are the developments in the newly emerging high-definition television (HDTV) technology, which harbors the promise of a new electronic age. Several Japanese electronics giants have developed HDTV technology commercially. U.S. producers, which previously balked at the idea of such technology because they did not see a ready market for it, are now seeking shelter behind standard-setting rules by the U.S. Government.

In spite of the expenditure of vast funds on R&D, a number of U.S. products do not seem to be able to perform sufficiently well in the marketplace. Yankee ingenuity once referred to the ability of U.S. firms to successfully imitate and improve on foreign technology.

"Product Development the Japanese Way," by Michael R. Czinkota and Masaaki Kotabe, *The Journal of Business Strategy*, Nov./Dec. 1990. Reprinted by permission of Faulkner & Gray.

For example, the British discovered and developed penicillin, but it was a small U.S. company, Pfizer, which improved the fermentation process and became the world's foremost manufacturer of penicillin. The Germans developed the first jet engine, but it was two American companies, Boeing and Douglas, that improved on the technology and eventually dominated the jet airplane market.

Yankee ingenuity seems to have vanished and reemerged in the form of Japanese marketing techniques, which appear to see what many others do not recognize and often are right on target in identifying market needs. Perhaps it is time that U.S. firms rediscover their former talents in order to compete with renewed vigor in the global market.

Incrementalism vs. the Giant Leap

Technology researchers argue that the natural sequence of industrial development comprises imitation (manufacturing process learning), followed by more innovations. In other words, continual improvements in manufacturing processes enables a firm not only to maintain product innovation-based competitiveness but also to improve its innovative abilities in the future. Failed innovators, in turn, lack the continual improvement of their products subject to a market-oriented focus.

During the postwar period, Japanese firms relied heavily on licensed U.S. and European technology for product development. Product quality was improved through heavy investment in manufacturing processes with the goal of garnering differential advantage over foreign competitors. Continued major investment in R&D earmarked for product innovation heralded the technological maturation within Japanese firms, where the quality and productivity levels began to match or even surpass those of the original licensor.

U.S.-style product innovation has placed major emphasis on pure research, which would allegedly result in "giant leap" product innovations as the source of competitive advantage. By comparison, incremental improvements in products and manufacturing processes were neglected and relegated to applied research. As Peter Drucker has argued, however, research success may very well require the end of the nineteenth-century demarcation between pure and applied research. Increasingly, a minor change in machining may require pure research into the structure of matter, while creating a totally new product may involve only careful reevaluation of a problem so that already well-known concepts can be applied to its solution.

By contrast, the Japanese incrementalist view of product development emphasizes continual technological improvement aimed at making an already successful product even better for customers. Take the case of Japanese very-large-scale integration (VLSI) technology. The origin of VLSI technology was the transistor. Recognizing consumers' unsatisfied need to tune in their favorite music anywhere at any time, Sony introduced small portable transistor radios in 1955. Other Japanese companies quickly followed suit. There was quick market acceptance of the product worldwide.

Mass-production made it possible to lower the cost and improve the quality of the product. In a short time, Japan reached a technological level at par with, and soon surpassing, that of the United States in transistor technology. As the age of integrated circuits (ICs) began, compact electronic calculators using this emerging technology boosted the growth of Japan's IC industry. The IC evolved into the large-scale integration (LSI) and now into VLSI.

These emerging technologies are used in consumer products, including personal computers, Japanese-language word processors, video cassette recorders (VCRs), compact disk players, and HDTVs. Many electronics products have sold in extremely large volumes, a fact which has subsequently made ongoing investment in production possible, as well as further technological development. Incremental improvements in IC technology have made it possible for Japanese firms to improve continually on a variety of products. In the end, emerging products such as HDTV are truly different from what they used to be both in form and in concept.

This incremental technological improvement is not limited to high-tech industries. Steel making is considered a mature or declining industry in most developed countries. However, Japanese steel makers are still moving toward higher levels of technological sophistication, for example by developing a vibration-damping steel sheet (i.e. two steel sheets sandwiching a very thin plastic film).

It is a small technological improvement that has a wide range of possible applications. Due to the growing popularity of quiet washing machines in Japan, this steel sheet has been used successfully as the outer panels of washing machines and is increasingly finding its way into other noise-reducing applications, such as roofing, flooring, and automotive parts.

The Marketplace as R&D Lab

Due to the incrementalist product-development approach, Japanese firms have also been able to increase the speed of new product introductions, meet the competitive demands of a rapidly changing marketplace, and capture market share. Japanese firms adopt emerging technologies first in existing products to satisfy customer needs better than their competitors. This affords an opportunity to gain experience, debug technological glitches, reduce costs, boost performance, and adapt designs to customer use.

In other words, the marketplace becomes a virtual R&D laboratory for Japanese firms to gain production and marketing experience as well as to perfect technology. This requires close contact with customers, whose inputs help Japanese firms improve their products on an ongoing basis.

In the process, they introduce newer products one after another. Year after year, Japanese firms unveil "not entirely new" products that keep getting better, more reliable, and less expensive. For example, Philips marketed the first practical VCR in 1972, three years before Japanese competitors did. However, Philips took seven years to replace the first-generation VCR with the all-new V2000, while late-coming Japanese manufacturers launched an onslaught of no fewer than three generations of improved VCRs in this five-year period.

The continuous introduction of "newer" products also brings greater likelihood of market success. Ideal products often require a giant leap in technology and product development and are subject to a higher risk of consumer rejection. Not only does the Japanese approach of incrementalism allow for continual improvement and a stream of new products, but it also permits quicker consumer adoption. Consumers are likely to accept improved products more rapidly than they accept very different products, since the former are more compatible with the existing patterns of product use and life-style.

Japanese firms also display a willingness to take the progress achieved through incrementalism and develop a new market approach around it. An excellent example is provided by the strategies used by different Japanese automobile manufacturers. After decades of honing refinements in their products, these firms, within a short period of time, developed the Infiniti, Lexus, and Acura brands, which were substantially different in the consumer's mind from existing cars.

Each of these new brands was introduced to the market through an entirely new distribution system. Even though pundits had argued that in the automotive sector the time for new brands was over, let alone the likelihood of success for new channels, the approach chosen seems to be crowned by greater success than the more traditional acquisition route taken by Ford (Jaguar) or General Motors (Saab).

Market research is a key ingredient for successful ongoing development of newer products. The goal is to provide customers with more "value" in the products they purchase. Product value is determined by cost and quality factors. In the United States, cost reduction and quality improvement are too often thought to be contradictory objectives, particularly when quality is perceived to be measured mainly by choice of materials or engineering tolerances.

Japanese firms, by contrast, see cost reduction and quality improvement as parallel objectives that go in tandem. The word *Keihakutansho* epitomizes the efforts of Japanese firms to create value by simultaneously lowering cost and increasing quality. *Keihakutansho* literally means "lighter, slimmer, shorter, and smaller" and thus implies less expensive and more useful products that are economical in purchase, use, and maintenance.

Furthermore, Japanese perceptions consider quality in a product to be generated as well by the contextual usage of the product. If a product "fits" better for a given usage or usage condition, it delivers better quality. That is why Japanese firms always try to emphasize both the "high-tech" and the "high-touch" dimension in their product innovations.

The market success of Sony's black-and-white TV sets in the early 1990s illustrates this point. Conventional market research failed to show that a market existed for such products in the United States. However, by studying the contextual usage of TV sets, Sony found that in addition to a family's main color TV set, Americans wanted a small portable TV to use in their backyards or to take away with them on weekends.

How Does Japanese Market Research Differ?

U.S. market researchers, after developing and insulated staff function of their own, have grown enamored of hard data. By processing information from many people and applying sophisticated data manipulations, statistical significance is sought and, more often than not, found.

Toru Nishikawa,[1] marketing manager at Hitachi, summarized the general Japanese attitude toward such so-called scientific market research. He provides five reasons against relying too much on a general survey of consumers for new-product development:

1. *Indifference*: Careless random sampling causes mistaken judgment, since some people are indifferent toward the product in question.
2. *Absence of responsibility*: The consumer is most sincere when spending, but not when talking.
3. *Conservative attitudes*: Ordinary consumers are conservative and tend to react negatively to a new product.
4. *Vanity*: It is human nature to exaggerate and put on a good appearance.
5. *Insufficient information*: The research results depend on the information about product characteristics given to survey participants.

Japanese firms prefer more "down to earth" methods of information gathering. Johansson and Nonaka[2] illustrate the benefit of using context-specific market information based on a mix of soft data (e.g. brand and product managers' visits to dealers and other members of the distribution channels) and hard data (e.g. shipments, inventory levels, and retail sales). Such context-specific market information is directly relevant to consumer attitudes about the product or to the manner in which buyers have used or will use specific products.

Several things stand out in Japanese new-product development (or in their continual product improvements). First, Japanese new-product development involves context-specific market research as well as ongoing sales research. Second, some of the widely observed idiosyncracies of the Japanese distribution system serve as major research input factors. For example, when a manufacturer dispatches his own sales personnel to leading department stores, not only are business relationships strengthened, but a direct mechanism for observation and feedback is developed as well.

Third, significant effort is expended on developing data, be it through point-of-sale computer scanners or the issuance of discount cards to customers, which also carry electronically embedded consumer profiles. Fourth, engineers and product designers carry out much of the context-specific research.

Toyota recently sent a group of its engineers and designers to southern California to nonchalantly "observe" how women get into and operate their cars. They found that women with long fingernails have trouble opening the door and operating various knobs on the dashboard. Toyota engineers and designers were able to "understand" the women's plight and redraw some of their automobile exterior and interior designs.

City, another highly acclaimed small Honda car, was conceived in a similar manner. Honda dispatched several engineers and designers on the City project team to Europe to "look around" for a suitable product concept for City. Based on the Mini-Cooper, a small British car developed decades ago, the Honda project team designed a "short and tall" car, which defied the prevailing idea that a car should be long and low.

Yet, hands-on market research by the very people who design and engineers a prototype model is not necessarily unique to Japanese firms. Successful U.S. companies also have a similar history. For example, the Boeing 737 was introduced about 25 years ago to compete with McDonnell-Douglas's DC-9. However, DC-9s were a somewhat superior plane; they had been introduced three years before the Boeing 737 and were faster.

Witnessing a growing market potential in Third World countries, Boeing sent a group of engineers to those countries to "observe" the idiosyncrasies of Third World aviation. These engineers found that many runways were too short to accommodate jet planes. Boeing subsequently redesigned the wings, added low-pressure tires to prevent bouncing on shorter landings, and redesigned the engines for quicker takeoff. As a result of these changes, the Boeing 737 became the best-selling commercial jet in history.

Hands-on market research does not negate the importance of conventional market research, emphasizing quantity of data and statistical significance. In developing the ProMavica professional still video system, which, unlike conventional 35 mm still cameras, records images on a two-inch-square floppy disk, Sony did extensive market research involving a mail survey, personal and telephone interviews, and on-site tests to elicit user response to the product during its development. What was unique was that the ProMavica task force included both engineers and sales/marketing representatives from Sony's medical systems and broadcast units. Sony's engineers gained insights from talking with prospects as much as did their marketing peers, and they incorporated user comments into product modifications.

It is clear that engineers and designers, people who are usually detached from market research, *can* and *should* also engage in context-specific market research side by side with professional market researchers. After all, these engineers and designers are the ones who convert market information into products.

Some Recommendations

Clearly, U.S. new-product development and market research are sophisticated and successful. Yet, in order to improve competitiveness further, several aspects of Japanese activities could be considered by U.S. firms.

First, the incrementalist approach to product development appears to offer advantages in the areas of costs, speed, learning, and consumer acceptance. Second, such an approach requires a continuous understanding of current and changing customer needs and of the shortcomings of one's own products and those of the competition. In order to achieve such understanding, market research is essential.

In order for such research to be successful, the contextual usage and usage conditions of products need to be investigated and, once found, acted upon. While extremely useful in their own right, hard data alone are not the answer. This type of information often provides only limited insights into these contextual conditions.

It is therefore important to include soft information based on down-to-earth market observation. Since the ability to recognize dimensions of context is not uniquely confined to market researchers, it is important to fully include product managers, designers, and engineers in the research process.

Marketing research should not be a "staff" function performed only by professional market researchers, but rather a "line" function executed by all participants in the product development process. Not only will such an approach permit the discovery of more knowledge, but it will also immediately achieve the transformation of gleaned market data into information that is disseminated and applied throughout the entire organization.

Notes

1   Nishikawa, T. (1989) "New Product Planning at Hitachi," *Long Range Planning*, **22**, pp. 20–24.
2   Johansson, J.K. and Nonaka, I. (1987) "Marketing Research the Japanese Way," *Harvard Business Review*, **65** (May–June), pp. 16–22.

13

The "Depth" of the Japanese Market Orientation: A Comparison Across Ranks and Functions with U.S. Firms

MASAAKI KOTABE

THE UNIVERSITY OF TEXAS AT AUSTIN

AND

ALDOR R. LANCTOT, JR.

ADVANCED TECHNOLOGY GROUP, DELL COMPUTER CORPORATION

The 1980s saw a great surge in the global market success of Japanese firms. There was talk about the beginning of the Japanese century and the emergence of an overpowering Japanese economy. U.S. policy makers, in particular, responded to these visions by expressing concern about the trade competitiveness of the United States and taking actions designed to break down Japan's trade "barriers" and reduce the United States' massive trade deficits *vis-à-vis* Japan. U.S. policy makers allegedly have found the root of the Japanese competitiveness in its trade barriers. Thus, various solutions to the trade deficit problem have been proposed.

Depreciation of the U.S. dollar was one solution (Brownstein 1990; Johnson 1987). Indeed, the dollar depreciated against the Japanese yen from 239 yen/dollar in 1985 to as low as 80 yen/dollar in 1995, or by almost 70 percent over the past ten or so years. The dollar depreciated similarly against other key currencies of the world. That depreciation has allowed the U.S. trade deficits with many countries to decline. While this has been true particularly with Western Europe, the trade deficit with Japan still remains a sticky problem that has not been sufficiently corrected despite the dramatic depreciation of the U.S. dollar against the Japanese yen (Platt 1994).

Another solution that is often proposed is the removal of Japanese import restrictions (*Business America* 1990; Norton 1989). While many formal trade restrictions existed in Japan into the 1970s, U.S. trade deficits with Japan over the past 10 years do not appear to be due strictly to various trade barriers in Japan (Czinkota and Kotabe 1993; Kotabe 1985). Data from GATT and other sources strongly suggest that the United States has as many tariff and non-tariff barriers as does Japan (see, for example, Bergsten and Cline 1985; Onkvisit and Shaw 1988).

A decade later, Japanese firms, once thought to be almost invincible, are reeling from Japan's post-bubble economy as they face the imploded domestic market, the skyrocketed yen, and worsened trade relations with the United States. As a result, many U.S. business practitioners have begun to discount the future competitiveness of Japanese firms.

However, we feel it is their short-sightedness that fails to see the fundamental strengths of Japanese firms. We argue that because of the inherent similarities of the U.S. and Japanese macroeconomic structure, answers to Japan's (and Japanese firms') competitiveness in the past two decades cannot be found completely in macroeconomics alone. Rather, the real answers may be found in the superior global corporate strategies and technological prowess of Japanese firms, which are currently shadowed in Japan's post-bubble economy.

One component of the Japanese model that has received considerable attention is the way the Japanese design and implement marketing strategies. The Japanese have demonstrated their superior ability to provide consumers with what they want, when they want it, and at a price they are willing to pay. In simpler terms, the Japanese have proven to be superior marketers (Kotler, Fahey, and Jatusripitak 1982). To those who have kept up with the stream of articles that have attempted to explain the success of Japanese business, the fact that the Japanese have proven to be superior marketers is not a revelation (Czinkota and Kotabe 1990; Kotabe and Duhan 1991).

Research abounds concerning the superiority of Japanese over U.S. marketing practices. More specifically, researchers have discussed the superiority of Japanese marketing techniques in terms of soft-data gathering and distribution channels (Johansson and Nonaka 1985); product development (Takeuchi and Porter 1986; Czinkota and Kotabe 1990); communication and problem-solving processes (Lazer, Murata, and Kosaka 1985); decision-making process (Pascale and Athos 1981; Ouchi 1981); price setting (Ohsone 1988); and organizational learning (Nonaka and Johansson 1985), among others. These and other studies have suggested that Japanese businesses approach the marketing function from a different perspective than that taken by U.S. businesses.

The common U.S. approach has been to decrease the emphasis on manufacturing and to increase the emphasis on marketing (Buffa 1984). This change in emphasis may have been in response to the perceived superiority of the Japanese marketers. Ironically, the Japanese marketing departments have never had the power that their U.S. rivals currently possess. In fact, our visits to various Japanese companies have made us aware that many Japanese firms do not even have a marketing department. Then, how can Japanese firms which are reportedly more market-oriented than U.S. firms not have a marketing department? It has been suggested that the reason this can occur is because the entire Japanese corporation is market-oriented (Morishima 1982; Nakane 1970). Thus, the need for a specific department to champion the marketing concept cause within the corporation is eliminated. Research further suggests that differences in the roles and power of the marketing department have resulted from a difference in the implementation of the marketing concept (Lazer, Murata, and Kosaka 1985; Kohli and Jaworski 1990).

In this study, we explore how Japanese firms accomplish the implementation of the marketing concept as a corporate-wide driving force. The study promises to offer some insight into why the Japanese have been more successful in the implementation of the marketing concept than their U.S. competitors. In the next section, the concept of market orientation is reviewed in the context of U.S. and Japanese firms. Four hypotheses are developed.

Implementation of the Marketing Concept

THE MARKETING CONCEPT

The marketing concept is the business management philosophy which causes all management decisions to be pursued with the consumer as "the end and object of all business effort" (Bartels 1988). Kotler and Armstrong (1991) state that the marketing concept "holds that achieving organizational goals depends on determining the needs and wants of target markets and delivering the desired satisfactions more effectively than competitors." The three central themes of the marketing concept are a customer focus, coordinated marketing, and firm profitability. Only once the marketing concept has been implemented can a firm be called "market-oriented" (Barksdale and Darden 1971; Kohli and Jaworski 1990; McNamara 1972).

Market orientation "is the very heart of modern marketing management and strategy" (Narver and Slater 1990). A market orientation provides the firm with the culture required to create value for the consumers and prosperity to the firm (Narver and Slater 1990; Kohli and Jaworski 1990). A market orientation is different, however, from a marketing orientation. This difference will be discussed in the next section.

BENEFITS OF MARKET ORIENTATION

Kohli and Jaworski (1990) summarize three benefits to a firm adopting a market versus marketing orientation. First, a market orientation suggests that a variety of departments can participate in its implementation. Second, the term "market-oriented" is less politically charged than its rival term, "marketing-oriented," and is therefore more likely to be accepted by non-marketing departments. Finally, a market orientation focuses the firm's attention on markets (customers and competitors).

To be considered market-oriented, a firm must display three orientations: consumer, competitor, and interfunctional (Narver and Slater 1990). The consumer and competitor orientations are obvious to most firms. They require the firm to monitor their customers and competitors. The third orientation, interfunctional, is not as obvious. Briefly, an interfunctional-orientation requires the firm to coordinate across departments the use of the information derived from the monitoring of its consumers and competitors.

The ultimate reward for achieving an organization-wide market-orientation should be greater profitability for the firm. Narver and Slater (1990) empirically found that a market-orientation "is an important determinant of profitability" (p. 32). Thus, it is critical that firms have a market orientation if they are to be successful. The market orientation is itself dependent upon an organization-wide acceptance of its philosophy.

ORGANIZATION-WIDE ADOPTION OF MARKET ORIENTATION

Kohli and Jaworski (1990) describe a market orientation as the "*organization-wide* (italics added) generation, dissemination, and responsiveness to market intelligence." As discussed previously, Narver and Slater's (1990) definition states that an *interfunctional-orientation* is one of the three components of a market orientation. These two market orientation definitions clearly proclaim that serving customers is not just a marketing function. As David Packard of Hewlett-Packard said, "Marketing is too important to be left to the marketing department" (Kotler and Armstrong 1991, p. xix).

Japanese firms

Japanese marketers view marketing activities "to be primarily units of human activity," while American executives perceive them mainly as impersonal business, sales, and profit activities. Furthermore, the adhering to the marketing concept is "not solely the responsibility of the marketing department . . . It is a group responsibility, with a group approach for the performance of marketing activities resulting" (Lazer, Murata, and Kosaka, 1985; Nakajima 1981; Takezawa and Whitehall 1981; Tanouchi 1983; Morishima 1982; Nakane 1970). Further proof of the organization-wide acceptance of the marketing concept is provided by Ouchi (1981) in his description of the Japanese Type Z organization in which "the division between one department and another is . . . unclear." Ouchi describes the perfectly integrated organization as one that "has no organizational chart, no divisions, no visible structure at all." Akio Morita, Chairman of the Sony Corporation, writes: "At Sony we at times have scientists participate in sales for a while because we don't want our scientists to live in ivory towers" (1986).

The infusion of the marketing concept throughout the organization strongly indicates that the firm has a market-orientation. Clearly, the Japanese seem to have infused the marketing concept throughout the organization to a greater degree than has generally been practiced in the United States. Consistent with Narver and Slater's (1990) finding, spectacular Japanese business performance around the world may indeed be reflective of their adoption of a market orientation.

U.S. firms

Despite its plausible merit, many U.S. firms seem to have failed to implement the market orientation organization-wide (Bell and Emory 1971; Lavidge 1966; Lear 1963; Lundstrom 1976). When faced with decreasing market share in the 1970s, due primarily to Japanese inroads, the first response of many U.S. businesses was to surrender that particular niche. The Americans reasoned that Japanese were successfully penetrating only the low-end markets in cars, consumer electronics, copiers, and computer chips. It was further considered that the low end of the market was quite low in profitability and not worth the effort to retool to meet the Japanese challenge. As time progressed, American businesses became alarmed at the progress the Japanese were making. Not only were the Japanese exploiting a market the Americans had underestimated, but the Japanese were also rapidly "trading up" the quality of their product offerings into the medium- and high-ends of the market. The Japanese were capturing market share to the point where many American businesses either had to clamor for government protection (via tariffs, quotas, voluntary export restraints and other non-tariff barriers) or had to exit the market. Meanwhile, many of these same firms attempted organizational changes to confront the Japanese inroads.

Many U.S. firms reacted to the Japanese challenge in one of two different ways. First, for those firms which were convinced by repeated successful Japanese product introductions in the United States that they had lost touch with consumers, they increased the relative power of the marketing department over other departments within the organization in an attempt to bring the organization closer to the customer (as the Japanese were presumed to have done). However, the Japanese version of a marketing department does not appear to have the clout within their own organizations that U.S. businesses have long suspected that they did. Hence, the U.S. response to increase the relative power of their marketing departments may have had an opposite effect to that which was intended – the U.S. firms have become marketing-oriented instead of market-oriented.

Other U.S. firms had not sought to enhance the role of the marketing department or the role of marketing to solve their problems. Instead, because they diagnosed their problems as financial, they had instead increased the relative power of the finance department (Buffa 1984). That particular remedy to the threat of Japanese competition led to the so-called "paper entrepreneurship" of leveraged buyouts, junk bonds, acquisitions, and mergers to improve short-term financial positions. This practice is critized as having contributed very little to increasing the competitiveness of U.S. businesses (Reich 1983). Therefore, we expect that:

> *Hypothesis 1:* More non-marketing personnel in Japanese firms have a vested interest in marketing than those in U.S. firms.

SENIOR MANAGEMENT FACTORS

Kohli and Jaworski (1990) find that the role of senior management is "one of the most important factors in fostering a market orientation." They further state that "the commitment of top managers is an essential prerequisite to a market orientation . . ." If that commitment is genuine, the responsibility of the marketing department for ensuring organizational compliance is unnecessary and may in fact interfere with the complete acceptance. Webster (1988) likewise argues that top management must originate the market orientation and be responsible for it. These views have stood the change in business climate over the years and are consistent with Felton (1959) who concluded more than three decades ago that a market orientation is possible only if "the board of directors, chief executive, and top-echelon executives appreciate the need to develop this marketing state of mind." Therefore, we expect that:

> *Hypothesis 2:* More top executives in Japanese firms have a vested interest in marketing than those in U.S. firms.

JOB ROTATION

One reason that may account for hypothesis 2 is the noted practice of job rotation in Japan (Ouchi 1981). The Japanese practice of job rotation is pervasive throughout employees' life-long career as part of their continual on-the-job training to make general managers as opposed to specialized functional managers within the company. What is distinctive in the Japanese organization is that there are many cross-functional job assignments, as if in a project team. Czinkota and Kotabe (1990) and Morita (1986), among others, have described the practice of converting scientists, engineers, and finance personnel into salespeople and market researchers, at least for a time, in order to give them "experience in the front lines (i.e., marketing-related activities) of the business." Marketing-related tasks are not only performed but also appreciated by all functional managers. Therefore, we expect that:

> *Hypothesis 3:* Fewer managers in Japanese firms have had a formal marketing/sales management position than those in U.S. firms.

MARKETING PLANNING

It has been argued by Johansson and Nonaka (1987) that the Japanese rely more on instincts and "hands-on research" versus the quantitative data that American managers prefer. The Japanese prefer to gather information directly from the consumer and channel members rather than to rely on research reports "that are too remote from actual consumer behavior to be useful." Furthermore, Lazer, Murata, and Kosaka (1985) observe that the "marketing functions and responsibilities tend to be loosely defined, with the existence of overlapping responsibilities." These two observations lead us to expect that:

> *Hypothesis 4:* Executives in Japanese firms allocate less time to formal marketing planning than those in U.S. firms.

Methodology

THE SAMPLE

The sample employed to test the first two hypotheses is from two sources: 1) the Japanese Marketing Association (JAMA) Directory, and 2) the American Marketing Association (AMA) Directory. From these two sources we extracted the business practitioner membership in the manufacturing sector. In our study we suggest the use of these two sources to indicate the degree to which marketing is consequential to marketing, non-marketing, and executive personnel. It is proposed that membership in these two organizations is an indication of the importance of marketing to these employees.

The JAMA Directory includes the company name, industrial group classification, member's name and self-reported position within the firm. The directory was translated from Japanese to English by a third party. One hundred and fifty-six Japanese companies and 1,128 employees were present in the sample. The 156 companies were classified into 10 different industries. The employees were classified into one of 25 specific positions and then assigned to one of three groups. These groups were "top executive," "non-marketing position," or "marketing position."

The AMA Directory was the second source utilized to test the first two hypotheses. The information we received from the AMA included only the name of the firm and the self-reported position of the AMA member. We then extracted from the master list those members who worked for a company in the 1991 *Fortune* Industrial 500 because of the similarity of those companies with the Japanese companies represented in the JAMA Directory. The sample was further reduced by the elimination of those *Fortune* 500 firms which did not have at least three employees who were members of the AMA. This was done in order to more closely match the JAMA sample. The resulting AMA sample was 101 firms comprising 815 employees. The AMA members were then classified into 35 specific positions and then into the same three groupings as in the JAMA sample.

Table 13.1 reveals the industry groupings into which both samples were placed. The table also shows for each country the number of firms in each industry grouping and the average number of employees in that industry that are members of their respective marketing associations.

The sample used for testing the third and fourth hypotheses utilizes data collected but unreported in a previous study by Kotabe and Duhan (1991) and provided to us at their courtesy. Their sample was chosen to mirror the characteristics of the businesses represented in the PIMS database. The

Table 13.1 Industry and membership comparison

Industry	Japan		U.S.	
	No. of firms	Average no. of JAMA members	No. of firms	Average no. of AMA members
Metals	5	5.8	2	11.0
Chemicals	10	5.6	6	8.5
Food	32	7.6	16	8.8
Beverages	21	10.9	7	12.9
Electronics	21	6.0	20	8.7
Motor vehicles	7	5.4	8	5.8
Pharmaceuticals	30	8.2	15	9.0
Precision machinery/computers	5	5.2	8	10.3
Forest products	7	5.3	6	6.5
Home supplies	17	5.6	5	7.4
Total	155	6.6	93	8.9

questionnaire had been filled out by an executive directly in charge of the business, with 202 responses for the U.S. sample and 193 for the Japanese sample. Demographic characteristics of both the U.S. and Japanese executives in the samples are similar. The average age of executives who responded to the questionnaire was 47 years for the Japanese executives, and 46 years for the U.S. executives. The average level of formal education was 16 years for the Japanese executive and 17 for the U.S. executives. On average, the participating executives, both Japanese and U.S., held their current position for about 6 years.

Results

Hypothesis 1 states that more non-marketing personnel in Japanese firms have a vested interest in marketing than those in U.S. firms. As shown in table 13.2, the distribution of the job positions of marketing association members significantly differs between the JAMA and the AMA ($\chi^2 = 381.8, p < 0.0001$). A larger percentage of non-marketing membership is observed in the JAMA sample. Thirty-four percent of the JAMA membership is composed of non-marketing personnel while only 24 percent of the AMA membership is likewise composed of non-marketing personnel. Therefore the results lend support to hypothesis 1, suggesting that the notion of market orientation may be more widely practiced across functional lines in Japanese firms than in U.S. counterparts.

Hypothesis 2 states that more top executives in Japanese firms have a greater vested interest in marketing than those in U.S. firms. Once again, table 13.2 reveals that a larger percentage of Japanese top executives belong to their country's marketing association than for the American sample, in support of hypothesis 2. Thirty-five percent of Japanese executives belong to the JAMA as compared with only 4 percent of the American executives who belong to the AMA. If Kohli and Jaworski (1990) are correct in their assertion that the involvement of senior management is a critical factor in

Table 13.2 Number of personnel in the JAMA and AMA by job position in the firm

	Japan		U.S.	
	Number	Percent	Number	Percent
Top executive	400	35	39	4
Marketing	340	30	580	71
Non-marketing	388	34	196	24
Total	1128		815	

[$\chi^2 = 381.8, p < 0.0001$

Table 13.3 Country by marketing experience

	Marketing experience	
Country	Yes	No
Japan ($n = 93$)	55.4%	44.6%
USA ($n = 202$)	98.0%	2.0%

$\chi^2 = 101.7, p < 0.0001$

Table 13.4 Percent of time spent in market planning

Country	Percent	t	p-value
Japan	20.94	4.40	< 0.0001
U.S.	30.95		

fostering a market orientation in the organization, then these results appear to indicate the difficulty U.S. firms will have in their quest to become more market-oriented.

Hypothesis 3 states that fewer managers in Japanese firms have had a formal marketing/sales management position than managers in U.S. firms. The results of the questionnaire survey presented in table 13.3 reveals that while only 55.4 percent of the Japanese managers who head their businesses have had a formal marketing/sales management position, 98.0 percent of the American managers have had a marketing/sales management position. The difference is very significant ($\chi^2 = 101.7, p <0.0001$), thus lending support to hypothesis 3.

Finally, hypothesis 4 states that executives in Japanese firms allocate less of their time on formal marketing planning than those in U.S. firms. The questionnaire results summarized in table 13.4. show that on the average, U.S. and Japanese executives spend about 31 percent and 21 percent of their time for marketing planning, respectively. In other words, U.S. executives allocate approximately 50 percent more time for market planning than Japanese counterparts. This finding, when compared with the results of the tests of the three previous hypotheses, give some insight into the behaviors of a market-oriented manager. To have a true market orientation, managers may need to rely more on instincts and "hands-on research" as Czinkota and Kotabe (1990) and Johansson and Nonaka (1987) already observed of Japanese managers.

Conclusions and Implications

U.S. policy makers have spent an inordinate amount of their time looking for the "cause" of the current trade deficit and U.S. competitive position with Japan over the years. In the meantime, the precipitous depreciation of the dollar has failed to produce as dramatic an improvement in U.S. export position with Japan or in competing with the Japanese on the U.S. market as economic theory would have predicted. Consequently, these U.S. policy makers feel all the more convinced that they have found the cause and have consequently turned to blaming Japan for unfair trade practices. Many U.S. businesses have lent their voices to the U.S. government to blame Japanese for their own less than satisfactory market performance *vis-à-vis* the Japanese.

The results of this study could imply that the cause of the fall may lay elsewhere. Based on our preliminary study which compared the JAMA and AMA membership, U.S. firms do not seem to be as market-oriented as their Japanese competitors. Considering the results of Narver and Slater's (1990) empirical findings that a market orientation is an important determinant of profitability and Buzzell, Gale, and Sultan's (1975) findings that market share is a key to profitability, then our findings are particularly revealing. Our findings suggest that the blame for the relatively poor performance of many U.S. firms over the years rests more appropriately with U.S. businesses themselves which fail to achieve the levels of market orientation that their Japanese competitors have achieved.

U.S. firms have not considered the fluctuating exchange rate explicitly as part of their costing/pricing strategy. When the dollar was overvalued in the mid-1980s, many U.S. firms had difficulty both exporting their products – as they were overpriced abroad – and competing with foreign imports on the U.S. domestic market. Now that the dollar has depreciated drastically, many U.S. firms are now enjoying price advantage at home and abroad. In other words, price has been considered a major determinant of U.S. firms' competitiveness over time. The ups and downs of U.S. firms' competitiveness are analogous to those of people living in a flood-prone lake shore. When the water rises, their houses get flooded; when the water recedes, they enjoy a picturesque lifestyle. Now the major question is what would happen to U.S. firms if the dollar appreciated again? Would the result be a repeat of the mid-1980s?

We argue that those firms with a strong market orientation can *and* are willing to shield themselves from much of the macroeconomics impact of the exchange rate fluctuation. After all, the bottom line is that to achieve organizational goals, firms have to determine the needs and wants of target markets and deliver the desired satisfactions more effectively than competitors. What customers want is value, which conceptually is the benefit divided by the price.

In the 1980s when the dollar was overvalued, many U.S. firms failed to stress the benefit side of the customer value, nor did they make any measurable effort to lower prices. When the Japanese yen began appreciating against the U.S. dollar, many U.S. firms' initial reaction was to increase their prices to make more money as the Japanese products became more expensive in dollars and less price competitive in the United States. On the other hand, many Japanese firms reacted by *not* passing on their price increases to U.S. customers as much as the yen appreciated. Their objective was to maintain the benefit/price ratio to the extent possible. Simply stated, U.S. firms tend to focus more on price factors, while Japanese firms concentrate more on benefit factors in determining customer value.

The bottom line is that to achieve organizational goals, firms have to determine the needs and wants of target markets and deliver the desired value and satisfactions more effectively than competitors. Japanese firms seem to have an edge over U.S. firms in market orientation emphasizing customer value. While reeling from the burst of the bubble economy and a resultant recession, further battered by the overvalued yen, many Japanese firms will in all likelihood emphasize the benefit side of the customer value all the more and come out of the doldrums again to be better competitors than before – benefits derived from superior products that *delight* customer needs and from superior pre- and post-sales services to the customer. On the other hand, an impending task that we see for U.S. firms is how business practitioners can go back to basics: Can they keep improving customer value by refocusing on what they produce, its cost, its quality, its availability, and on the service and flexibility of the production system in response to the market needs, unbaffled by of the fluctuating exchange rate?

Market orientation is a corporate philosophy that needs to be internalized within the organization. It is not something that needs to be practiced only by marketing practitioners; rather it needs to be shared and practiced by all members of the organization irrespective of their functional belonging and job ranks. Unfortunately, many U.S. firms have become too functionally divided and compartmentalized to adopt market orientation throughout the organization. Part of the blame may probably be attributed to the way U.S. business schools teach functional courses and train functional specialists. On the other hand, U.S. MBA-type business schools did not exist in Japan until 15 or so years ago; to this day, there are only four schools, including Keio, Kobe, Hitotsubashi, and International University of Japan (IUJ). Obviously, market orientation had been planted in the minds of Japanese business men and women before those business schools were established. Market orientation being so basic and fundamental to business, we are not even sure whether it can be taught in a business school. We feel that Japanese firms' organizational setup and practices, examined in this article, may be conducive to promoting a market orientation culture.

We are fully aware that our study is far from conclusive, but rather raises many more fundamental issues than it has addressed. Two major limitations of this study should be noted. The study has relied on membership in the AMA and JAMA to investigate the existence of a market orientation. While the results presented here may be supportive of the hypothesis that the Japanese are more market-oriented than their American competitors, the results are circumstantial in nature and should not be considered conclusive. Another limitation of this research is its failure to control for differences in the two cultures in attitudes or motivations for membership in organizations such as the AMA and JAMA. With these two particular organizations it should be determined what differences may exist in the benefits offered by membership that would explain the dramatically different membership percentages we found. This information could also be found via a survey of U.S. and Japanese managers.

References

Barksdale, Hiram C. and William Darden (October 1971) "Marketers' Attitude toward the Marketing Concept," *Journal of Marketing*, **35** (4), 29–36.

Bartels, Robert (1988) *The History of Marketing Thought*. Columbus, OH: Publishing Horizons, Inc.

Bell, Martin L. and C. William Emory (June 1971) "The Faltering Marketing Concept," *Business Horizons*, **22** (3), 76–83.

Bergsten, C. Fred, and William R. Cline (October 1985) *The United States–Japan Economics Problem*. Washington, D.C.: Institute for International Economics.

Brownstein, Vivien (April 23, 1990) "A Weaker Dollar Will Help Keep the Deficit Shrinking," *Fortune*, 23.

Buffa, Elwood S. (Spring 1984) "Making American Manufacturing Competitive," *California Management Review*, **26** (3), 29–46.

Business America (March 7, 1990) Statement of President Bush, Secretary Mosbacher on Super 301 Decisions, 6.

Buzzell, Robert D., Bradley T. Gale, and Ralph G.M. Sultan (January–February 1975), "Market Share – A Key to Profitability," *Harvard Business Review*, **53**.

Czinkota, Michael and Masaaki Kotabe (November–December 1990) "Product Development the Japanese Way," *Journal of Business Strategy*, **11** (6), 31–6. (See Chapter 12.)

Czinkota, Michael and Masaaki Kotabe (1993). *The Japanese Distribution System: Opportunities and Obstacles, Structures and Practices*. Chicago, IL: Probus Publishing Company.

Felton, Arthur P. (July–August 1959) "Making the Marketing Concept Work," *Harvard Business Review*, **37** (4), 55–65.

International Directory of the American Marketing Association and Marketing Services Guide. Chicago: American Marketing Association.

Japanese Marketing Association Directory. Tokyo: Japanese Marketing Association.

Johansson, Johny K. and Ikujiro Nonaka (May–June 1987) "Marketing Research the Japanese Way," *Harvard Business Review*, **65** (3), 16–22.

Johnson, Omotunde E. G. (March 1987) "Currency Depreciation and Export Expansion," *Finance and Development*, **24** (1), 23–26.

Kohli, Ajay K. and Bernard J. Jaworski (April 1990) "Market Orientation: The Construct, Research Propositions, and Managerial Implications," *Journal of Marketing*, **54** (2), 1–18.

Kotabe, Masaaki (Fall 1985) "The Roles of Japanese Industrial Policy for Export Success: A Theoretical Perspective," *Columbia Journal of World Business*, **20** (3), 59–64.

—— (First Quarter 1992) "A Comparative Study of U.S. and Japanese Patent Systems," *Journal of International Business Studies*, **23** (1), 147–68.

—— and Dale Duhan (January 1991) "The Perceived Veracity of PIMS Strategy Principles in Japan: An Empirical Inquiry," *Journal of Marketing*, **55** (1), 26–41.

Kotler, Philip, L. Fahey, and S. Jatusripitak (1985) *The New Competition*. Englewood Cliffs, NJ: Prentice Hall.

Kotler, Philip and Gary Armstrong (1991) *Principles of Marketing*, (5th edn). Englewood Cliffs, NJ: Prentice Hall.

Lavidge, R. J. (October 1966) "Marketing Concept Often Gets Only Lip Service," *Advertising Age*, **37** (10), 52.

Lazer, William, Shoji Murata, and Hiroshi Kosaka (Spring 1985) "Japanese Marketing: Towards a Better Understanding," *Journal of Marketing*, **49** (2), 69–81.

Lear, Robert W. (September–October 1963) "No Easy Road to Market Orientation," *Harvard Business Review*, **41** (5), 53–60.

Lundstrom, William J. (Fall 1976) "The Marketing Concept: The Ultimate in Bait and Switch," *Marquette Business Review*, **20** (3), 214–230.

McNamara, Carlton P. (January 1972) "The Present Status of the Marketing Concept," *Journal of Marketing*, **36** (1), 50–57.

Morishima, Michio (1982) *Why Japan Has Succeeded?* Cambridge: Cambridge University Press.

Morita, Akio (1986) *Made in Japan*. New York: E.P. Dutton.

Nakajima, Masaki (1981) "The Roots of High Productivity in Japan," *Journal of Mitsubishi Research Institute*, **10**, 7–11.

Nakane, Chie (1970) *Japanese Society*. University of California Press.

Narver, John C. and Stanley F. Slater (October 1990) "The Effect of a Market Orientation on Business Profitability," *Journal of Marketing*, **54** (4), 20–35.

Nonaka, Ikujiro and Johny K. Johansson (1985) "Japanese Management: What About the 'Hard' Skills?" *Academy of Management Review*, **10** (2), 181–191.

Norton, Robert E. (June 19, 1989) "Unfair Traders: A Passing Storm," *Fortune*, 16.

Ohsone, Kozo (1988) *The Case of the Walkman: Innovation in Management*. Tokyo: Sony Corporation.

Onkvisit, Sak and John J. Shaw (May–June 1988) "Marketing Barriers in International Trade," *Business Horizons*, **31** (3), 64–72.

Ouchi, William (1981) *Theory Z: How American Business Can Meet the Japanese Challenge*. Boston: Addison-Wesley.

Pascale, Richard and Anthony Athos (1981) *The Art of Japanese Management*. New York: Warner Books.

Platt, Gordon (July 18, 1994) "Dollar to Set New Lows Against Yen on Wider U.S. Trade Gap," *Journal of Commerce and Commercial*, p. 2A.

Reich, Robert B. (1983) *The Next American Frontier*. New York: Times Books.

Takeuchi, Hirotaka and Michael E. Porter (1986) "Three Roles of International Marketing in Global Strategy." Michael E. Porter (ed.) *Competition in Global Industries*, Boston, MA: Harvard Business School Press, 111–46.

Takezawa, Shin-Ichi and Arthur M. Whitehall (1981) *Work Ways Japan and America*. Tokyo: Japan Institute of Labor.

Tanouchi, Koichi (July 1983) "Japanese Style Marketing Based on Sensitivity." *Dentsu Japan: Marketing/Advertising*, **23**, 77–81.

Webster, Frederick E., Jr (May–June 1988) "Rediscovering the Marketing Concept," *Business Horizons*, **31** (3), 29–39.

14

A Perspective of Marketing in Central and Eastern Europe

MICHAEL R. CZINKOTA

GEORGETOWN UNIVERSITY

HELMUT GAISBAUER

WIRTSCHAFTSUNIVERSITÄT WIEN

AND

REINER SPRINGER

WIRTSCHAFTSUNIVERSITÄT WIEN

Successful international marketing requires the development and implementation of marketing strategies responsive to different environments. In the emerging democracies of Central Europe and the new countries of the former Soviet Union, the economic, social, and political dimensions differ in major ways from the environment Western marketers are used to at home. In light of the transitions taking place, marketers should sense an obligation to help restructure society and improve the standard of living in this region. At the same time, the opportunities for change are constrained by decades of ideological pressures fundamentally opposed to the core aspects of marketing. Therefore, marketers must design strategies which work within existing economic structures yet also contribute to the emergence of new societal orientations.

The objective of this paper is to offer a perspective on strategic international marketing options for companies entering the markets of Central and Eastern Europe. The discussion is based on the experience accumulated by the authors after developing and leading several university programs in the region, structuring a training center for the employees of large multinational corporations investing there, offering seminars to more than 400 local executives, and advising many new market entrants into the region over the last 10 years.

It can be expected that, over time, a continued transition will lead to a growing similarity in the market environment of West and East. Systemic differences of the past may eventually disappear. In the short run, however, there continue to be substantial variations in the focus, objectives and techniques of marketing, making it imperative for companies entering the region to understand the existing disparities and to respond to them in their marketing activities. We distinguish between three strategy fields: 1) fundamental strategic outlook; 2) market entry strategies; and 3) marketing mix strategies. For each one of these fields we develop a framework of direction and alternatives.

Fundamental Strategic Outlook

Whether or not to become active in Central and Eastern Europe depends mostly on a firm's underlying motives and objectives for internationalization. In the main, firms go abroad to achieve corporate growth, sustainable competitive advantages, and the roll-back and neutralization of competitors. These motives are valid for the international move to Central and Eastern Europe as well. Frequent additional motives for an engagement in these markets are:

- a high cultural and historical affinity with some of the countries in the region
- the ability to acquire companies with an "Eastern" expertise
- simultaneous preferential market access to both the European Union and the former centrally planned economies.

The decision to enter the region is also driven by the current strengths and weaknesses of its countries. Some of the strengths are large populations, low wages, geographic proximity to Western Europe, privatization opportunities, low market-entry costs and long-term growth potential. On the other hand, low per capita income, limited management skills, low productivity, overdrawn expectations, poor infrastructure, an unstable business environment, large bureaucracies and short-term decline and crises represent some of the weaknesses (Kostecki 1993).

Strengths and weaknesses differ from country to country and from industry to industry. Central and Eastern Europe is not an economically homogeneous bloc and disparities in the pace and depth of ongoing transformation continue to widen the differences between countries. Therefore, strategies must be differentiated to satisfy the heterogeneous market requirements and customers in these countries, rather than standardized. Another strategic consideration concerns the competitive orientation of a company entering this market. The still existing demand overhang in the region combined with the weak purchasing power of many potential customers suggests the adoption of a cost leadership strategy. Firms can also prolong the life cycle of their existing products by implementing market penetration and market development strategies. Strategies of product development and diversification can often be delayed until competition is increasing.

A targeted marketing effort (i.e. concentration on specific market segments within each country) is the preferred option to reach customers in an efficient way. As for market entry timing, the train is leaving the station. Many opportunities in these markets can be explored best through a pioneer strategy. By entering these markets before competitors do, existing, but rapidly shrinking knowledge, technology, and process gaps can yield an advantageous investment position and high payoffs.

Low wages in the transition economies can also enable Western companies to pursue cost leadership by shifting labor intensive production to them. Average wages in Central and Eastern Europe are only 15 percent or less of the wages in the European Union (see figure 14.1). Nevertheless, it is important to view this difference in the context of the qualifications, skills, and productivity of the Eastern European workforce, which in some areas corresponds more or less to the Western

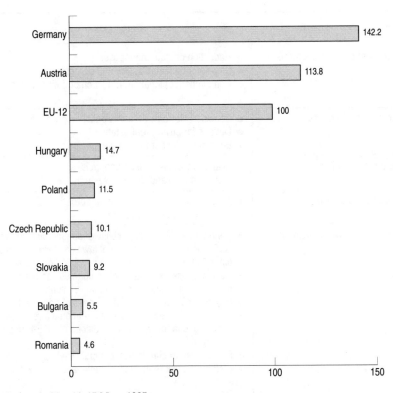

Source: *Industrie*, No. 46, 15 Nov. 1995

Figure 14.1 Costs per labor hour in manufacturing industry in 1994 (figures in % compared with EU-12).

standards, while falling far short in others. In addition, the gradual decrease of the labor proportion in the total cost of manufacturing may impose limits on this alternative.

Of major overall importance is the choice between adapting to the marketing environment in the host country and working towards changing it. The decision will be a function of the time horizon and resources of the firm. When using a long-term perspective, Western firms may find it beneficial to pursue a strategy of altering the marketing environment step by step in order to move it closer to a functioning market economy. Such an approach, however, requires an understanding of current societal weaknesses, accompanied by a willingness not to exploit them to the detriment of individuals. In addition, significant investments are necessary into employee training programs which focus not only on achieving knowledge transmission but also facilitate behavioral change (Czinkota 1997). Furthermore, programs need to be developed which educate and assist suppliers, customers and policy makers to understand the workings of a market and enable them to make better decisions. While such an approach to new market opportunities may appear to be overly cautious and expensive, it is crucial to take these steps in order to gain gradual acceptance for a market orientation in the former centrally planned economies. Rapid changes and substantial economic dislocations have imbued many private individuals and policy makers with suspicion and weariness towards

Criteria	Dimensions
Progress of economic reforms	• Reduction of state monopolies • Degree of decentralization and deregulation • Containment of inflation, reduction of deficits in the state budget
International openness	• Conditions for outside participation in privatization • Options for buying real estate • Equal treatment of foreign companies
Distribution conditions	• Availability of distribution channels • Transportation and logistics systems
Competitive platform	• Acceptance of competition from abroad • Structure for fair competition
Assessment of commercial risks	• Contract risk (non-compatibility of commercial laws in C&E-Europe with international laws, implementation of different trade rules; existence of arbitration system) • Customer risk (liquidation of companies can cause disturbances in supplier customer relations) • Payment risk (bankruptcy in process of privatization) • Credit risk (limited access to international foreign trade financing; change in credit conditions of C&E-European banks) • Product risk (technological compatibility) • Distribution risk (efficiency of national distribution systems) • Price risk (price regulation in response to resistance to economic reforms) • Inflation risk (hyperinflation and difficulties in calculating prices on a long-term basis) • Acceptance risk (mistrust and aversion to Western products, companies, and managers)

Figure 14.2 Specific commercial criteria for market selection in Central and Eastern Europe

marketing. Unless Western marketers are able to convincingly demonstrate how competition, variety, and freedom of choice can improve the quality of life, one of the great opportunities for marketing to become a discipline which transforms society will have been lost. Such a loss would also damage severely the long-term prospects for Western corporate success in the region.

Market Entry Strategies

Market entry deals mainly with market selection and the determination of suitable market entry modes. By analyzing potential customers and competitors, the firm expects to identify those markets which best satisfy company objectives. Typically, one uses checklists, evaluative screens, scoring models, and country portfolio analyses to make a market selection. Markets are evaluated based on one or several criteria, which allow for rankings and facilitate the selection decision (Cavusgil 1985). Aside from general selection criteria such as market potential, market growth, market volume and market access, an assessment of the transformation process and of specific commercial risks is useful when evaluating markets in Central and Eastern Europe. Among other factors, one needs to assess the progress of economic reforms, the extent to which state monopolies have been abolished and the direction of the governmental budget deficit. Figure 14.2 provides more detail on some of the commercial factors to consider.

In addition to these commercial factors, however, the firm should also deliberate the extent to which its market selection will hasten the economic transition. It should be understood that economic change in Central and Eastern Europe does not take place in isolation from outside factors. Rather, the change will be encouraged or retarded by the actions of external forces. Each corporate market entry decision will therefore have an effect on the rate and success of change, which firms should take into account. This is not to say that firms should ignore the results of their traditional analyses of market entry, but rather that they should be cognizant of an important additional dimension. The German Treuhandgesellschaft, the institution in charge of privatizing East German state property, considered the profitability of a corporation, the burden of privatization on the public purse, and the employment plans of prospective owners, along with any privatization proceeds in making a final decision about the disposition of assets. Similarly, Western marketers in Central and Eastern Europe should consider an evaluation of those non-traditional factors which may have a bearing on the long-term success of their activities.

With regard to market entry modes, the region could in the past only be entered via exports or, in some countries (Poland, Hungary, Romania), through joint ventures. Now, export, direct investment, licensing, franchising, contract manufacturing, and management contracts can all be pursued. Yet, many Western companies still favor the traditional approach. In general, they prefer to use the low-risk market entry modes of exporting and the establishment of sales subsidiaries. High-risk entry modes such as production subsidiaries are used much less often. Firms persist with such patterns even in those countries which are considered to be more aggressive reformers in the transition process, as confirmed by a study of the market entry behavior of German subsidiaries based in Austria, which have entered the markets in Central and Eastern Europe (see figure 14.3). As a result, many firms deprive themselves and their target markets of the investment benefits mentioned earlier. They also demonstrate a lack of presence and commitment which, in the long run, may place them at a disadvantage against their more enterprising competitors.

Buying Behavior

Development of a marketing mix strategy requires an understanding of the changes in consumer and organizational buying behaviour which have accompanied the transformation from a planned economy to a market economy. Historically, the buying behavior of consumers was shaped somewhat by limited purchasing power, but mainly by continuous shortages in supply. Due to very limited access to substitutes, consumers hardly compared quality and prices, and bought products as soon as they reached the shelves in order to buy something. Price played a subordinated role in the buying decision, since purchasing power was larger than supply, and prices were the same in all retail outlets.

These conditions have changed. Now supply is expanding, prices are varied, but money is the

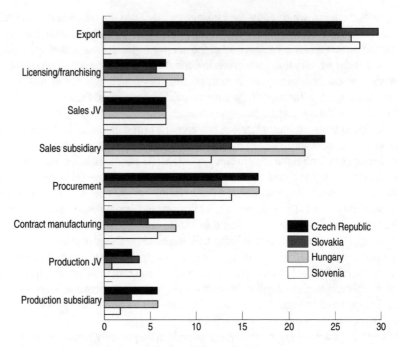

* Frequency of entry modes used in absolute numbers based on a sample of 55 companies.
Source: Moser, R., Springer, R. and Gaisbauer, H. (1996) *Östkompetenz Osterreichs in der EU* Wien: Studie im Auftrag des Kuratoriums der Deutschen Handelskammer in Österreich, p. 80

Figure 14.3 Entry modes of companies with German parent company in the countries Czech Republic, Slovakia, Hungary and Slovenia*

bottleneck. Price has therefore become a decisive buying factor. The main features of the buying behavior of consumers in Central and Eastern Europe are:

● reduced consumption due to price increases and limited purchasing power
● thorough price observation and careful comparison of different offers
● avoidance of risky or impulse purchases
● preparation of buying decisions in the family
● growing brand consciousness (Shama 1992).

With regard to organizational buying, the decisions formerly taken by the central planning apparatus, are now made by newly independent companies. Changes in the organizational buying behavior can be demonstrated by the results of a study of the buying behavior of end users and importers of industrial equipment in the former Czechoslovakia. During the summer of 1991 we questioned 18 industrial companies which were a representative sample of Czech and Slovak firms importing industrial products from the West. Their most important buying criteria were product quality, followed by price and guarantee conditions. After-sales service, time of delivery and stability of the relationship were also seen as important. On the selling side, interviews conducted with Western purchasers during 1992 and 1996 indicated that to them three dimensions were at once the most important and the most problematic. Western firms purchasing products from the Central and Eastern European region considered timely delivery, the delivery of the agreed upon quality, and the delivery of the agreed upon quantity as the most critical dimensions.

In the context of organizational buying it is worth reiterating that all the countries in the region have a history of treasuring the personal relationship. Business typically is not done between organizations but between individuals. Personal contacts and connections have long been an important organizational resource. The same continues to hold true today. Therefore, the development, building, and maintenance of long-term relationships are basic preconditions for long-term corporate success (Lehtinen 1996).

Marketing Mix Strategies*

PRODUCT POLICY

The product policy for the markets in Central and Eastern Europe is heavily influenced by the technological gap between Western industrialized nations and the former socialist countries. This gap is largely the result of the export control policy implemented by the West during the period of the Cold War, which was designed to preserve the technological advantage of the West (Czinkota and Dichtl 1995). In spite of today's openness of markets and rapid diffusion of innovation, most firms in the region are still a decade or more behind the technological standard of the West. As a result, product policy decisions for markets in Central and Eastern Europe can focus on the selection of products from the existing company portfolio for export to or production in these markets. In the early years of market opening, concentrated research of user needs and problems in order to find ideas for new products was of secondary importance for initial market entry. However, growing competition from indigenous firms which are close to their customers increases the importance of such research.

In positioning established products in these markets, branding is a very important tool. So far, brand awareness has been underdeveloped, since most products were sold as generics or local brands. The few international brands which used to be offered only in special restricted shops acquired an aura of very high prestige. Early on in the transition, Western brands in general were seen as being of higher quality and preferable to domestic products. More recently, however, consumers have discovered that Western products are not necessarily better than their domestic counterparts. A resurgence of domestic pride and fond memories of the olden days have translated into renewed demand for domestic products, be they soft drinks, bread, or soap.

To a large extent, however, branding in the markets in Central and Eastern Europe is still an empty field. Most brands still lack character and personality and remain interchangeable to the consumer. Investing in brand positioning can greatly enhance brand loyalty, especially if companies pursue a pioneer strategy. Focused branding strategies combined with a positive country-of-origin

---

* This section draws on Reiner Springer (1995) "Market Entry and Marketing Strategies for Eastern Europe," *Journal of East–West Business*, 1 (3), pp. 67–104.

image are very effective because brand awareness can be developed quickly and at relatively low cost (Schweiger and Frieders 1994). The branding strategy must, however, be accompanied by a truly superior product in order to achieve consumer loyalty.

MARKETING COMMUNICATION

Both companies and consumers typically still have insufficient information on potential partners and products from the West to make decisions. Marketers have to take into account that most Eastern individuals and companies have been separated from the world market for generations, and that privatization has created new companies that are considering internationalization for the first time. Marketing communication must therefore, above all, aim to reduce the information deficit of potential customers and partners. Yet it must do so in ways which are seen as honest and appropriate. It must be remembered that public messages in Eastern Europe used to consist mainly of propaganda, designed for ulterior motives, and despised by many. Today, in virtually all countries, communication instruments such as advertising, personal selling, public relations, and sales promotion can be used and a wide variety of media channels is available.

The most important communication instrument is advertising. In the development of advertising campaigns for consumer goods, the following guidelines apply:

- Customers in Central and Eastern Europe react more sensitively to advertising messages than customers in industrialized countries.
- Consumers are interested in rational advertising which clearly states its message. They expect advertising to help them in sorting through numerous and confusing offers, and they prefer information about products to efforts at persuasion. Hyperbole engenders mistrust and builds up a psychic distance to the product and its seller. A survey of consumers in the eastern states of Germany provides insightful findings: 87 percent of Easterners believed that advertising makes them buy things they don't need; 64 percent believed that advertising gives a misleading impression of products; and 59 percent believed that advertising takes advantage of them (Lipman 1991).
- Advertising on television is not as accepted as advertising in the daily press. TV advertising often does not meet the information requirements of customers. Ads in papers, especially with informative and well-structured arguments, are seen as most useful to prepare buying decisions.
- Advertisers need to remember that not all domestic brands have a poor image, and that some of them are increasingly being rediscovered and valued. In such cases, sensitive treatment of domestic brands is necessary in order not to offend customers.

One question often raised is whether special advertising campaigns should be designed for the region or whether campaigns successfully implemented in Western markets can be transferred. Both approaches are possible, as long as the advertising strategy takes into account the information needs of the customers in Central and Eastern Europe. Practical experience shows that adjusted Western strategies can be implemented very successfully. However, it is useful to rely on local talent, which is best able to judge local reactions, to modify existing advertisements and to create new ones for this market.

With local input into the design of advertising compaigns, care must be taken to understand the still existing limitations. Useful as local agencies are for local companies, firms may be ill served if they use locals to develop campaigns for Western customers. While local experts may be able to copy the West, they do not necessarily understand the underlying dimensions. For example, Aeroflot, the major Russian airline, produced an advertising compaign to attract new customers from the West. But even though planes were shown off and the staff wore new uniforms, no fun of flying was conveyed in the advertisement. Rather, the advertisement transmitted an image of the Russian army.

Finally, the importance of personal communications should not be underestimated. Relationships matter! This point is driven home when one observes the success in the region of direct marketers such as Avon, Mary Kay, Tupperware, and Amway. For example, without any advertising, Amway has 94,000 representatives in Hungary, which move more than $39 million of product (Muraskin 1994). A focus on personal orientation therefore may well become a prime tool for marketing communication.

CHANNEL MANAGEMENT

The abolishment of the foreign trade monopoly and the right of companies in Central and Eastern Europe to engage in foreign trade on their own has opened new options for Western companies in channel management.

IMPORTS FROM CENTRAL AND EASTERN EUROPE

In the past, the Western buyer was not permitted to choose between several suppliers. Now, companies can choose between various import channels such as:

- direct import from the manufacturer
- import through trading houses
- import through export cooperatives or trade associations of small and medium-size companies.

The opportunities for direct imports will increase if manufacturers in Central and Eastern Europe develop the prerequisite capabilities to satisfy their clients. Many buyers have found that selling is still not part of the economic culture in the region. Available descriptive materials are often poorly written and devoid of useful information. Obtaining additional information about a product may be difficult and time-consuming. The quality of the products can also be a major problem. In spite of their great desire to participate in the global marketplace, many producers still tend to place primary emphasis on product performance and, to a large extent, neglect style and product presentation. In many instances, the international customer needs to forge agreements that require the manufacturer to improve quality, provide for technical control, and ensure prompt delivery in order to develop a satisfactory relationship. It may be necessary for the buyer to provide personnel and process assistance to the seller in order to improve performance to desirable levels. Alternatively, companies will have to source from trading houses or cooperatives, which, for a price, can take on some of these preparatory functions.

EXPORTS TO THE REGION

Several export channels are open to Western suppliers:

● *Direct export to the end user, especially for industrial products.*

Many customers, especially buyers of industrial products, have an interest in buying directly. Domestic intermediaries, above all the Foreign Trade Organizations (FTOs), which the state had placed in charge of all international trade during the decades of central planning, are often avoided. Therefore, the establishment of direct links to users is not difficult. A problem that arises is that some of the users do not have any experience with foreign trade. If this is the case, then direct links can be risky and be subject to misunderstandings, particularly when it comes to exchange rate management and interest payments. In case of doubt, the services of a trading house should be used.

● *Export through trading houses, which operate as intermediaries (dealer or agent) and establish direct contacts between foreign suppliers and domestic users.*

For both options, one has to be aware of the differing sophistication of private wholesalers and retailers in the countries of Central and Eastern Europe (Iwinska-Knop 1992). For example, in the successor states of the former USSR, a functioning wholesale trade system still does not exist. Commodity exchanges are taking over the functions of wholesalers, as well as those of retailers. Some retail systems are very underdeveloped. For instance, per capita, only half as many shops exist in the former USSR as in Hungary.

● *Export to wholesalers and/or retailers, whereby trading houses can be part of the distribution chain.*

● *Export through subsidiaries or joint ventures of Western companies in Central and Eastern Europe, which serve end users or function as channel members.*

Channel management must also take into account the shortcomings of the current logistics systems in the region. For example, in the United States, 40 percent of shipments are under a just-in-time/quick response regime. For the U.S. economy, the total cost of distribution in 1995 was close to 11 percent of GNP. By contrast, some of the countries in the region are battling poor lines of supply, insufficient warehousing facilities, a lack of distribution and service centers, limited rolling stock, and inadequate transportation systems. Producers are uninformed about issues such as inventory carrying costs, store assortment efficiencies, and replenishment techniques. The need for information development and exchange systems, for integrated supplier–distributor alliances, and for efficient communication systems is poorly understood. As a result, distribution cost in some countries of Eastern and Central Europe remain at well above 30 percent of GNP (Czinkota 1994). These infrastructure constraints also often mean that Western firms initially may only be able to reach major cities. In addition, criminal elements in these societies in upheaval endanger the distribution system. Lenders and insurance providers are wary about supporting distribution in areas where the tendency of shipments is to disappear, sometimes in part, sometimes altogether, sometimes temporarily, sometimes forever (Canna 1994). Western companies exporting to these markets must therefore be prepared to shoulder the burden of a whole range of distribution functions, such as financing, risk management, product assortment structure, transportation, storage, packaging, security, communication, and after-sales services.

CONTRACTUAL AND PRICE POLICY

The ongoing transformation means that the framework for contractual and pricing decisions is constantly changing. Customer and supplier relations are being reorganized. New customers are entering the market. Stable supplier–customer relationships have yet to be developed. The new legal framework is opening the way towards a wide variety of contract types and contract conditions. But even though most countries now have a property rights framework, bankruptcy laws and other commercial legislation, they often have not been applied sufficiently widely and consistently to yield any consensus concerning their practical content. Weak implementation has been paralleled by jurisdictional conflicts that have resulted in outright confusion as to which laws have precedence.

In addition, many government authorities have not as of yet become convinced of the inviolability of contracts (Banerjee *et al.* 1995). On the corporate level, one additional major problem of contractual policy is to find mutually agreeable financial arrangements. In many countries, particularly those of the former Soviet Union, classical forms of foreign trade financing are available only on a limited scale. Restricted access to convertible currencies, limited liquidity, and systemic weaknesses in the banking sector continue to pose major problems. As a result, countertrade often remains an important instrument of contract policy.

The rapid changes also require the constant observation of customers in order to recognize upcoming difficulties early on. It is important to have steady and direct contact with one's trading partner in the East. Personal contact with top management creates a basis for trust. Very important also is the ongoing evaluation of the reliability and creditworthiness of customers. Doing so should include asking for banking references with regular updates.

Pricing decisions must be based on the specific market conditions, the target groups envisioned, and the company objectives. For most standardized mass products, a low-price strategy seems to be the most market-oriented one in light of limited purchasing power, decreases in the standard of living, and a high-price sensitivity on part of consumers. However, a growing number of customers are ready and able to pay higher prices, especially for high-quality technical products which offer substantial benefits. For example, in Hungary, the cellular telephone company WESTEL decided not to sell phone instruments on a subsidized basis, as is done in the U.S., but rather sold the instruments with a relatively high markup. In light of a very outmoded land-line telephone system with long installation delays, the resulting high price was no deterrent, but rather led to the attraction of customers with heavy use. The social desirability of cellular phones, combined with growing business needs have led to deep market penetration and high profitability. Such high-price strategies need to be seen of course in the context of demand, but also in light of growing purchasing power in the future.

Conclusions

The strategy patterns of marketers working in Central and Eastern Europe will vary depending on corporate goals and the specifics of the marketing environment. Basic strategic options are summarized in figure 14.4. The shadowed cells illustrate the strategy path implemented by Henkel Austria. Key elements of the Henkel strategy are an early presence in markets (pioneer strategy), market entry by majority joint ventures with the option of complete takeover, product mix of local and

Strategy dimension	Match of single strategy options with the marketing environment in Central and Eastern Europe		
	very likely	**likely**	**less likely**
Focus on competitive advantage	Cost leadership	Quality leadership	Mix of cost and quality leadership
Scope of strategy variation	Differentiation adapation	Standardization combined with local adaptation	Plain standardization
Product–market Combinations	Market penetration	Market development	Product development, diversification
Concentration on specific market areas	Segmentation by country markets	Regional segmentation in country markets	Market segmentation by purchasing power
Market entry timing	Pioneer strategy	Follower strategy	Late-comer strategy
Market entry modes	Export	Direct investments exploiting the opportunities offered by privatization (buy-strategy, build-strategy)	Contractual market entry * contractual manufacturing * Licensing * franchising
Product policy	Product selection	Product modification	Product innovation
Channel policy	Direct control of channel	Design and make of own channel	Use of independent channel members working for different suppliers
Communication policy	Informative product related national advertising based on differentration	Brand based advertising based on a combination of standardization and differentiation	Highly standardized advertising, focus on emotional advertising messages
Contractual policy and pricing	Risk-minimizing contracts, low-price strategy	Combination of low- and high-price strategies based on a corresponding product mix	Standardized world-wide price strategy

Source: Stara, F. (1994) "Henkel Austria. Aufbruch in den Osten – Strategien und Erfahrungen," *Werbeforschung & Praxis*, 3, p. 117.

Figure 14.4 Marketing strategy alternatives in Central and Eastern Europe

international brands, informative product related advertising, and newly developed distribution channels controlled by Henkel (Stara 1994).

The economic region of Central and Eastern Europe is characterized by growing differences between countries with regard to their political, economic, legal, and institutional conditions. The "old" and the "new" countries of Central and Eastern Europe cannot be treated as a unique economic bloc for which a standardized marketing strategy can be implemented. Rather, marketing strategies have to be tailored to the specific requirements of each country market. Yet there are commonalities in the areas of market selection, and marketing mix development which can be of use to firms desiring to enter these markets and to researchers who wish to pursue further work in this field.

Both companies and researchers should investigate the extent to which preexisting business practices in the East can be of value in furthering the marketing concept. For example, the development and maintenance of close, personal relationships are of major importance in the region.

Conservation and recycling are much more ingrained in the minds of customers in the former centrally planned economies than in the West – albeit for reasons of shortage and not because of environmental awareness. Some might even go so far as to claim that the socialist tradition of primacy of society over the individual is increasingly permeating the "capitalist" economies. In light of the fact that in the West the notion of ownership appears to be gradually replaced by temporary possession (e.g. leasing of cars, stockholding in mutual funds which continuously change their portfolios, renting rather than buying a home), perhaps even the traditional key issue of private property, which separated the East from the West, may not remain such a core issue at all. For the marketer, all this means that rather than simply aiming for a total replacement of previous practices, it may well be worthwhile to investigate the usefulness of some of them for further progress in the societal aspects of marketing.

Overall, it must be remembered that both the economies in transition as well as the market economies of the West are faced with an unprecedented situation, for which there are few guide posts. Both parties are only gradually gaining experience in how to adjust to the new realities. Until the time comes where both systems are closely intertwined, it is important to listen to each other, carefully observe environmental change, and to attempt to develop new approaches which are beneficial to and in harmony with society.

References

Banerjee, Biswajit, Koen, Vincent, Krueger, Thomas, Lutz, Mark S., Marrese, Michael, and Saavalainen, Tapio O. (1995) *Road Maps of the Transition: The Baltics, the Czech Republic, Hungary, and Russia*, International Monetary Fund, Occasional Paper 127, Washington D.C., September, p.63.

Canna, Elizabeth (1994) "Russian Supply Chains," *American Shipper*, June, pp. 49–53.

Cavusgil, Tamer S. (1985) "Guidelines for Export Market Research," *Business Horizons*, **28** (November–December).

Czinkota, Michael R. (1994) "Global Neighbors, Poor Relations," *Marketing Management*, **3** (1), pp. 46–52. (See Chapter 3.)

Czinkota, Michael R. (1997) "Russia's Transition to a Market Economy: Learning About Business," *Journal of International Marketing*, **5** (4).

Czinkota, Michael R. and Dichtl, E. (1995) "Export Controls: Providing Security in a Volatile Environment," *The International Executive*, **37** (5), pp. 485–97. (See Chapter 5.)

Iwinska-Knop, K. (1992) "Distribution as a Barrier to Application of Marketing in the Centrally Planned

Economy (Case Study of Poland)," *Journal of Business Research*, **24** (1), January, p.19.

Kostecki, M. M. (1993) "Doing Business in Eastern Europe: Opportunities and Threats for Western Firms," *Journal of Euromarketing*, **2** (4), p. 77.

Lehtinen, Uolevi (1996) "Relationship Marketing Approaches in Changing Russian Markets," *Journal of East–West Business*, **1** (4), pp. 35–39.

Lipman, Joanne (1991) "Eastern Germans Deeply Distrust Western World's Ad Campaigns," *The Wall Street Journal*, October 4.

Muraskin, Robert (1994) "Workers of Hungary Unite – in Amway," *The Washington Post*, August 6, p. D1.

Schweiger, G. and Frieders, G. (1994) "Markenaufbau in Osteuropa", *Markenartikel*, **11**, pp. 512–15.

Shama, Avraham (1992) "Transforming the Consumer in Russia and Eastern Europe," *International Marketing Review*, **9** (5), pp. 43–59.

Stara, F. (1994) "Henkel Austria. Aufbruch in den Osten – Strategien und Erfahrungen," *Werbeforschung & Praxis*, **3**, p. 117.

V

FINANCIAL AND ACCOUNTING
DIMENSIONS

Traditionally, many companies have suffered from three myopic views on financial resources. First, they have accepted fluctuating exchange rates as a fact of life. When the U.S. dollar appreciates, U.S. exporters face difficulty exporting their products overseas as the foreign currency-denominated prices of their products have increased. And when the dollar depreciates, they enjoy an export boom. Consequently, U.S. companies had difficulty competing in foreign markets in the late 1980s when the dollar was highly valued, and enjoyed an export success in the first half of the 1990s when the dollar depreciated. Now, in the second half of the 1990s, the dollar has again started appreciating, gradually affecting U.S. exporters with another round of harsh realities of the dollar appreciation.

A second myopic view is that capital investment is supposed to be made only when the predicted cash flow and profits are clearly positive. Unfortunately, this financial logic applies only when futures are predictable, reinforcing a short-term orientation of capital investment. Particularly, international business ventures tend to be fraught with higher levels of uncertainties – uncertainties magnified by fluctuating foreign exchange and unforeseen political and economic risks. For example, organizing workers in new ways of rationalized production in an era of global competition requires experimentation and massive financial investment without a clear assurance of success. Financial criteria presently taught in business schools and practiced in industry could not validate investment in such a "risky" venture.

A third form of myopia is that accounting tools are designed to be used only to record financial transactions and allocate costs as accurately as possible. Japanese companies made us aware that accounting tools could be used to *proactively* manage manufacturing operations rather than simply to record their cash flows on a *de facto* basis. Out of their practices originated *activity-based* cost accounting, which is gaining in popularity for managerial control.

In this section, we allocate three chapters to address those weaknesses with traditional views of financial and accounting tools. Chapter 15 addresses the first type of myopia by introducing the notion of "pass-through" – a practice exercised most effectively by Japanese companies to contain the impact of exchange rate fluctuations for the sake of maintaining their market share. While counter-intuitive, not increasing the foreign currency-denominated price at a time of a domestic currency appreciation is shown to increase profits rather than reduce them.

Chapter 16 presents a way not to be short-changed by the second myopic outlook. A major casualty of myopic rules is the underinvestment in new capabilities, such as increasing the speed to the market. Investments in new capabilities are investments in opportunity. The costs of short-term rules are analyzed and an evaluation technique based on option pricing is proposed as a way to demonstrate the value of long-term investments in new capabilities as platforms into new markets. The value of platforms as options ultimately comes down to viewing organizational capabilities as investments in learning and acquiring a broad-based expertise. Investments in core technologies, joint ventures, flexible manufacturing, and entry into foreign markets are examined in terms of their platform value.

Chapter 17 presents a way of using cost accounting proactively for managerial control. Patterns that have emerged from the study of cost accounting systems at companies in Japan differentiate certain aspects of Japanese cost accounting from established practices in the U.S. Firms in Japan tend to use their accounting systems to support and reinforce their manufacturing strategies. They also seem to utilize these systems more to motivate employees to act in accordance with long-term manufacturing strategies than to give senior management precise data on costs, variances, and profits. Japanese accounting reflects and reinforces an overriding commitment to market-driven management.

15

Exchange Rate Fluctuations, Pass-through, and Market Share

KENICHI OHNO

INTERNATIONAL MONETARY FUND

The overvaluation of the dollar and its subsequent decline in the 1980s revealed a marked difference in the pricing behavior of Japanese and U.S. manufacturing firms in response to large swings of the exchange rate, U.S. firms tend to pass through fluctuations of the dollar more or less completely to the foreign-currency price of their products, whereas Japanese firms absorb a significant part of a yen fluctuation in the form of flexible profit margins, keeping the foreign-currency price of their products far less volatile than the yen.

Some commentators have criticized the behavior of Japanese export firms, especially when the yen was appreciating, as being predatory, reflecting a single-minded obsession with market share with little regard for profit maximization. But this observation is at odds with economic rationality. Under many market structures, profit maximization requires adjustment of the domestic-currency price of exports to the exchange rate in order to smooth the foreign-currency price. For example, using the Cournot duopoly model, Dornbusch (1987) has shown that the pass-through of import prices depends on the relative number of foreign and domestic firms that are competing in the domestic market.

This paper also makes use of the Cournot model, but offers a different explanation for varying degrees of pass-through. The existence of hysteresis and firms' planning horizons are emphasized as important determinants of tradable prices. The model also attempts to link the concept of pass-through with such quantitative variables as the volume of exports and average market share. By considering the effect of a fluctuating exchange rate on firms' profits, it is hoped that new light may be shed on a neglected aspect of international trade under floating exchange rate regime.

Following a review of the asymmetry in the pricing behavior of Japanese and U.S. manufacturing firms, the second section discusses hysteresis and the corporate planning horizon. The third section presents the duopoly model, which incorporates these discussions, and the model is given solutions under alternative assumptions in the fourth section. The final section presents some conclusions.

The author thanks Karl F. Habermeier for comments on an earlier draft.

Asymmetry in Pricing Behavior

The concept of pass-through is related to the degree to which import prices reflect movements in the exchange rate. From the foreign exporter's viewpoint, it is the extent to which he "passes through" exchange rate fluctuations to the sales price abroad, rather than absorbing them by adjusting the home-currency price. If the exporter does not alter the shipping price at home, it is the foreign sales price that reflects the exchange rate, and pass-through is said to be complete. In contrast, if the exporter tries to stabilize the sales price abroad by "pricing to market," it is the exporter's shipping price that bears the brunt of exchange rate changes, and there is no pass-through.

To clarify this explanation, consider a Japanese manufacturer who sells merchandise both in Japan and in the United States. Let the unit cost of production be c yen and the yen/dollar exchange rate be e, yielding the following:

domestic sales price (in yen)	$p_d = (1 + m_d)c$
export price (in yen)	$p_x = (1 + m_x)c$
export price (in dollars)	$p_x^* = (1 + m_x)c/e$

where m_d and m_x are the markups for domestic and export sales, respectively. (These markups will later be determined as part of the equilibrium.) With respect to these relationships, existing evidence suggests the following for Japanese manufacturing industries. First, the yen-denominated unit cost (c) rises and falls with the yen/dollar rate to the extent that production cost includes imported raw materials. This cost effect of the exchange rate varies among industries: it is important in materials

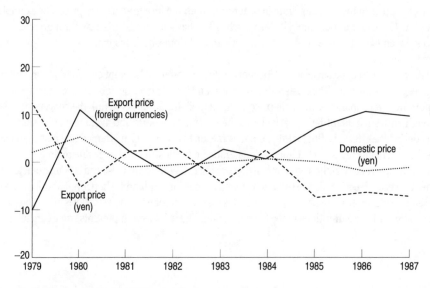

Sources: Bank of Japan and International Monetary Fund

Figure 15.1 Changes in domestic and export prices: Japanese general machinery (percent)

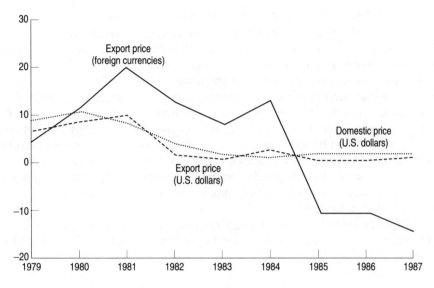

Sources: U.S. Department of Labor and International Monetary Fund

Figure 15.2 Changes in domestic and export prices: U.S. general machinery (percent)

industries such as chemicals and steel, less so in machinery industries, where the raw material content of the final product is usually 10 percent or less. For high-technology industries, the cost effect of the exchange rate is almost negligible (Ohno, 1989). Second, the domestic markup (m_d) does not respond systematically to the yen/dollar rate, whereas the export markup (m_x) is significantly affected by the yen/dollar rate.

Figure 15.1 plots the annual changes in the domestic and export (f.o.b.) prices of Japanese general machinery industry. In this figure, "foreign currencies" denotes the currency basket reflecting the destinations of Japanese manufactured exports, with weights derived from the International Monetary Fund's multilateral exchange rate model (MERM). The stable domestic price is in clear contrast to the variable export prices in yen and foreign currency, each of which accounts for roughly half of the exchange rate variation. This contrast further implies that Japanese manufacturers practice price discrimination between domestic and overseas markets. When the yen appreciates, this practice tends to generate "dumping," whereby the same goods are sold more cheaply abroad than at home. When the yen is undervalued, as in 1983–4, many Japanese goods are often cheaper in Japan than in the United States.

The pricing behavior of U.S. manufacturing firms is fundamentally different from that of their Japanese competitors – both domestic and export markups are virtually unaffected by the fluctuations of the dollar. Furthermore, U.S. manufacturers normally do not practice price discrimination between domestic and foreign customers. As a result, there is no systematic dumping as the exchange rate swings, and pass-through tends to be complete. Figure 15.2 demonstrates this point. The movement of the dollar rate appears to be reflected entirely in the foreign-currency price of U.S. exports.[1]

Many hypotheses have been advanced to explain the striking difference in pricing behavior between U.S. firms and firms in other industrial countries, but none seems to be completely satisfactory. One theory emphasizes the dollar's dominant role as an international invoice currency, which tends to keep contracted dollar prices constant in the face of exchange rate fluctuations. However, since contracts can be revised, this explanation would be plausible only for a short run of a few months. Another related view points to the substantial market power U.S. goods have in the rest of the world – but so do Japanese machinery, consumer electronics, and automobiles. Finally, one popular argument is that, with a huge domestic market, U.S. firms do not rely as heavily on exports as Japanese firms do; they can thus afford to be insensitive to exchange rate fluctuations. Looking at the 1980 or 1981 input–output tables of the two economies, one finds that, indeed, Japan recorded a higher export dependency – defined as the ratio of exports to total sales – than the United States in primary metals, electrical and transportation machinery, and precision instruments. In paper, chemicals, and general machinery, however, the export dependency ratios of the United States were higher than Japan's.

In the remainder of this paper a new model is proposed for explaining the asymmetry in pricing behavior between Japanese and U.S. firms, and the quantitative implications of this asymmetry are explored.

Hysteresis and the Planning Horizon

Given the resource endowment, technology, and taste of each country, the trade pattern is further determined by two important factors: the existence and degree of hysteresis, and the corporate planning horizon. The dynamic problem of cyclical exchange rate variation and the profit squeeze it generates under the floating exchange rate regime is an aspect of international trade that the traditional Ricardo and Heckscher-Ohlin models do not address directly.

HYSTERESIS

Hysteresis is a concept taken from physics of certain nonlinearity, whereby the relationship between two or more variables crucially depends on past history. Consider the experiment of first magnetizing a piece of iron by placing an electric magnet around it and then reversing the process. When the electric current is increased gradually from zero, the iron is at first slow to be magnetized, but after a while it becomes more susceptible, and then magnetizes quickly to a saturation point. Then, as the electric current is gradually decreased to zero, the iron remains magnetized for some time, but then becomes rapidly demagnetized afterwards. Since the iron "resists" the force to alter its present magnetic state, the amount of magnetization depends not only on the electric current applied, but also on whether it is rising, falling, or has turned around halfway.

Resistance to changes from the status quo also exists in economics. Consider two companies, A and B, which produce and market highly substitutable goods – different brands of aspirin, toothpaste, soft drinks, laundry detergents, and so on. If firm A first lowers its price sufficiently to drive out (partially or completely) the product of firm B and then raises the price, it is likely to end up with a larger market share than if it had first set the price high, lost most of its customers, and then lowered the price, even if the final prices happen to be the same. When the market exhibits inertia, the sales of firm A cannot be captured as a simple regression on distributed lags of income and prices.

How can this happen? There are both supply-side and demand-side reasons; together, they impart stickiness to the market share of many manufactured goods.

On the supply side, the cause of market inertia can be attributed to increasing returns to scale. A firm that already has a large market share is in a better position with regard to cost than a firm with a small market share or a firm contemplating entry. First of all, the current market leader has already invested in the "sunk costs" required to start or expand the business – sales and service networks, training, advertising and other promotional efforts to improve the brand image, consumer research, and so on. An upstart firm or a firm with an insignificant market share that must invest in these activities in the future cannot hope to compete with the giant firm and be equally profitable. Second, given the advantage of (static) large-scale production or the (dynamic) learning effect, the mere fact of a firm's being the first to dominate the market ensures its cost advantage over its followers, thus perpetuating its leading position. This entrenched lead makes it all the more difficult for other firms to carve out a larger share of the market.

On the demand side, brand loyalty is another independent cause of market stickiness. For consumer goods like automobiles and stereos or investment goods like machinery and equipment, the buyer does not necessarily choose different brands each time he repurchases the good.[2]

This is partly because the buyer is simply unaware of other brands, partly because of uncertainty about the quality of an unfamiliar brand, and partly because of the accumulation of human and nonhuman capital associated with the use of the present brand. For instance, someone who owns a personal computer manufactured by firm A is likely also to possess peripherals, software, operational knowledge, and a rapport with a certain dealership that would become useless or less useful if this consumer purchased another brand. Unless this person is dissatisfied with the present model, he or she is likely to replace or upgrade the present machine with another manufactured by firm A.

In a market where hysteresis prevails, whether because of the supply-side or the demand-side reason, additional expenditure becomes necessary to overcome the market inertia and recapture the previously lost market segment. Such "promotional costs" will probably be higher the longer the firm has been out of the market – requiring entirely new efforts in corporate planning, development of an appealing product or design, market research, advertising, and other promotional activities.

Under the circumstances described above, let us assume the existence of a *differentiated* shock, where a group of firms temporarily incur higher costs of production than before, while the production costs of the remaining firms are unchanged. Firms that belong to the first group now face a trade-off between current and future profit. If, on the one hand, they decide to raise their price sufficiently to maximize current profit, the second group of firms could expand operation at the expense of the first group, making the comeback of the latter all the more difficult even if these firms were prepared to lower their price in the next period. If, on the other hand, they choose not to raise their price at all, they would not lose any market share, but they would be forced to accept a loss of potential profit today. In general, a rational firm would raise its price but not to the extent of maximizing its short-term profit when its production costs were temporarily higher than other firms; or it would lower its price but not to the extent of maximizing short-term profit when its production costs were temporarily lower than others. This strategy has the effect of smoothing the market share over time and thereby reducing the other "promotional" costs required to expand business from the previous period.

Fluctuations of the yen/dollar exchange rate are a good example of a differentiated cost shock, whereby the relative production costs of Japanese and U.S. firms competing in the world market are altered. It is therefore not surprising to observe Japanese firms not fully lowering the dollar prices of their exports by their increasing profit margins when the yen is weak, and not fully raising them by accepting lower profits or even net losses when the yen is strong.[3]

THE PLANNING HORIZON

Why, then, do U.S. firms not adopt a similar pricing strategy? The hypothesis advanced here is that their corporate planning horizon is much shorter in time (that is, their discount rate is much higher) than that of their Japanese competitors. Explanations for the well-known preference of U.S. firms for short-term profit are often based on speculation about national psychology or corporate culture, which are beyond the purview of economics. However, there are many economic conditions that promote such corporate behavior in the United States.

First, the role of the stock market is fundamentally different between Japan and the United States. In Japan most stocks are owned by other companies belonging to a corporate group or *keiretsu*, which share the same business interest as the issuer company. In contrast, U.S. stocks are held by individuals and institutional investors who are mainly interested in capital gains. These investors are ready to sell the stock the moment the market perceives financial trouble for its issuer. Although this feature may be advantageous for market liquidity, it draws the attention of business people toward quarterly profits rather than long-term viability.

Second, as noted by HatsoPoulos, Krugman, and Summers (1988), U.S. firms' preference for short-term profit can be attributed to the high cost of capital in the United States relative to Japan. According to these authors, the erosion of U.S. competitiveness is caused by saving and investment rates that are too low, which in turn are the result of policies that raise the rate of time discount and favor consumption over saving – including the fiscal deficit and various aspects of social welfare and income tax systems.

Third, as McKinnon (1989) has noted, high *nominal* interest rates in the United States shorten the term structure of business decision making relative to a low-interest rate country like Japan, even though the differences are due purely to higher inflationary expectations in the United States. This is because the effective "duration" of finance, as defined in any standard textbook, would be reduced in inflationary countries. For any given term-to-maturity structure, the "real" amortization schedule would be more front-end loaded and the "real" payback time would be shorter the higher is the structure of nominal interest rates – even if *real* interest rates were the same.

When hysteresis is present, the constraint of short-term profit maximization placed on U.S. firms can explain the behavioral difference between them and their foreign competitors, as will be seen in the description of the Cournot duopoly model, which follows.

The Model

Consider a Japanese export firm and a U.S. domestic firm competing in the U.S. market.[4] The products of these firms are in fact perfect substitutes, but are perceived to be different by consumers as a result of packaging or brand image. Color film, cassette tapes, and floppy diskettes could fit this description. The Japanese firm, with yen-denominated costs and dollar-denominated revenues, maximizes profit in terms of yen. The U.S. firm maximizes profit in dollars, and both its costs and revenues are in dollars. Because of the reasons considered in the last section, the market is assumed to exhibit hysteresis. Each firm incurs promotional costs in addition to production costs when it expands production from the previous period. The assumption of perfect certainty is applied to the alternation of the yen/dollar rate between two levels.

Let the output of each firm be x (Japanese firm) and x^* (U.S. firm), and let p^* be the dollar price in the U.S. market received by both firms. For simplicity, assume a linear (inverse) demand function:

$$p^* = 1 - x - x^* \tag{15.1}$$

Next, assume that technology is subject to constant returns to scale. The unit cost of production is c yen for the Japanese firm and c^* dollar for the U.S. firm. The yen/dollar exchange rate takes the value e_0 (high yen, low dollar) in even-numbered periods, and the value e_1 (low yen, high dollar) in odd-numbered periods, with $e_0 < (c/c^*) < e_1$. Since c/c^* is the cost-based competitiveness parity rate, this inequality implies that Japan has an *absolute* advantage over the United States in producing this product in one period, and vice versa in the next period. Furthermore, due to hysteresis, each firm incurs the promotional cost of z yen (japanese firm) or z^* dollar (U.S. firm) for each additional unit sold over the previous period. However, no cost or gain is incurred when a firm reduces the size of its operation. Finally, each firm takes the output of the other firm as given in maximizing (short-term or long-term) profit.

With this setup, let us first consider the behavior of the Japanese firm corresponding to different planning horizons. Continuing to use subscript 0 for even-numbered periods and subscript 1 for odd-numbered periods, one can express the yen-denominated profit of the Japanese firm as

$$\Pi_0 = x_0 \left[e_0 \left(1 - x_0 - x_0^* \right) - c \right] \tag{15.2a}$$

$$\Pi_1 = x_1 \left[e_1 \left(1 - x_1 - x_1^* \right) - c \right] - z \qquad \max \left(x_1 - x_0, 0 \right) \tag{15.2b}$$

The profit for the high-yen period is simply the difference between revenue and production costs; the profit for the low-yen period must also include promotional costs z if the firm is to expand operation.

The planning horizon can be incorporated in this framework as follows. Suppose the Japanese firm ignores tomorrow and decides to maximize today's profit. In this case, the reaction function for each period can be obtained separately by maximizing equation (15.2a) with respect to x_0 and maximizing (15.2b) with respect to x_1, yielding

$$x_0 = [1 - x_0^* - c/e_0]/2 \tag{15.3a}$$

$$x_1 = [1 - x_1^* - (c + z)/e_1]/2 \tag{15.3b}$$

This is the (extreme) case where the rate of time preference is infinite.

Alternatively, consider the other extreme case where the firm does not differentiate current and future profits, and its rate of time preference is therefore zero. Although there are potentially an infinite number of periods in this model, each two adjacent periods are like any other under the assumption of perfect certainty. The only dynamic complication in the model comes from hysteresis associated with business expansion from period 0 to period 1, which does not spill over to any other periods. The condition for long-term profit maximization can therefore be derived by considering any even-numbered period and the subsequent odd-numbered period. Maximizing $\Pi_0 + \Pi_1$ with respect to both x_0 and x_1 yields

$$x_0 = [1 - x_0^* - (c - z)/e_0]/2 \tag{15.4a}$$
$$x_1 = [1 - x_1^* - (c + z)/e_1]/2 \tag{15.4a}$$

These are the reaction functions of the Japanese firm when it maximizes long-term profit. Comparison of equations (15.3a), (15.3b) and (15.4a), (15.4b) reveals that the only difference between short-term and long-term profit maximization is the extent of the production cutback in period 0. Long-term planning requires that the cutback be more modest than when the firm is more interested in short-term results. Note, however, that the simplicity of these reaction functions is due to the original assumptions – in particular, linear promotional costs. Generalizing them would complicate the solution without necessarily modifying the basic conclusions.

Notice that reaction functions in (15.3a), (15.3b) and (15.4a), (15.4b) are valid only if $x_1 > x_0$. If the solution obtained from these equations were $x_1 < x_0$, actual outcome would be $x_1 = x_0$, since potential gain from expanding output in period 1 would be more than offset by promotional costs. In this instance, the fixed output level would still be dependent on the firm's planning horizon.[5]

Next, the behavior of the U.S. firm is similarly specified. The U.S. firm is different from the Japanese firm in that it is not affected by the exchange rate directly; the yen/dollar rate matters only to the extent that the rival firm's output responds to it. The dollar-denominated profit of the U.S. firm is

$$\Pi_0^* = x_0^* (1 - x_0 - x_0^* - c^*) - z^* \quad \max (x_0^* - x_1^*, 0) \tag{15.5a}$$
$$\Pi_1^* = x_1^* (1 - x_1 - x_1^* - c^*) \tag{15.5b}$$

where the last term in (15.5a) is the promotional cost incurred if the firm decides to expand in period 0.

If the U.S. firm maximizes short-term profit, the corresponding reaction functions can be obtained by maximizing (15.5a) with respect to x_0^* and maximizing (15.5b) with respect to x_1^*:

$$x_0^* = (1 - x_0 - c^* - z^*)/2 \tag{15.6a}$$
$$x_1^* = (1 - x_1 - c^*)/2 \tag{15.6b}$$

whereas, if it maximizes long-term profit, maximizing $\Pi_0^* + \Pi_1^*$ with respect to x_0^* and x_1^* simultaneously yields

$$x_0^* = (1 - x_0 - c^* - z^*)/2 \tag{15.7a}$$
$$x_1^* = (1 - x_1 - c^* + z^*)/2. \tag{15.7b}$$

As before, the two strategies differ only in how deeply output is cut when the firm faces an unfavorable exchange rate. And if the solution implied $x_0^* < x_1^*$, actual output would be constant over time as discussed above.

Equilibrium output and price are derived by combining reaction functions of the Japanese and U.S. firms under varying assumptions about planning horizons as well as the size of exchange rate fluctuations. As an illustration, consider the case where exchange rate fluctuations are such that both firms adjust output every period – that is, $x_1 > x_0$ and $x_0^* > x_1^*$ (alternative cases are classified in the next section). It is easy to show that the solution takes the following general form:

output = [1 + (rival's marginal cost) − 2(own marginal cost)]/3

price   = [1 + (rival's marginal cost) + (own marginal cost)]/3

where all marginal costs are expressed in dollars.

The solution further depends on whether firms regard only production costs (c or c^*) as marginal cost or they include promotional costs (z or z^*) as well. This, in turn, of course depends on what planning horizons are adopted. For example, assume the Japanese firm maximizes long-term profit, while the U.S. firm maximizes short-term profit. Then, applying the above formula – or alternatively from equations (15.1), (15.4a), and (15.6a) – the solution for period 0, on the one hand, is found to be

$$x_0 = [1 + c^* + z^* - 2(c - z)/e_0]/3 \qquad\qquad (15.8a)$$

$$x_0^* = [1 + (c^* - z)/e_0 - 2(c^* + z^*)]/3 \qquad\qquad (15.8b)$$

$$p_0^* = [1 + c^* + z^* + (c - z)/e_0]/3 \qquad\qquad (15.8c)$$

where both firms take promotional costs (z and z^*) into account. (The U.S. firm, even though assumed to be myopic, must necessarily face promotional costs in expanding output.) The solution for period 1, on the other hand, is from equations (15.1a), (15.4b), and (15.6b):

$$x_1 = [1 + c^* - 2(c + z)/e_1]/3 \qquad\qquad (15.9a)$$

$$x_1^* = [1 + (c + z)/e_1 - 2c^*]/3 \qquad\qquad (15.9b)$$

$$p_0^* = [1 + c^* + (c + z)/e_1]/3 \qquad\qquad (15.9c)$$

where the U.S. firm no longer takes promotional costs (which would be incurred in the future) into consideration as it retreats. Hence, z^* appears in none of the above three equations.

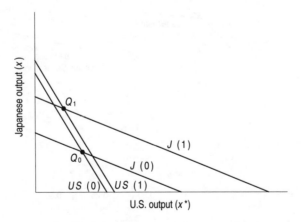

Note: $J(0)$ and $J(1)$ are Japanese reaction functions corresponding to equations (15.4a) and (15.4b); $US(0)$ and $US(1)$ are U.S. reaction functions corresponding to equations (15.6a) and (15.6b); Q_0 and Q_1 represent equilibrium output

Figure 15.3 Equilibrium output: Japanese and U.S. firms

Figure 15.3 graphically presents these solutions in which the Japanese firm pursues long-term profit and the U.S. firm maximizes current profit. The vertical axis measures output of the Japanese firm, and the horizontal axis measures output of the U.S. firm. $J(0)$ and $J(1)$ are Japanese reaction functions corresponding to equations (15.4a) and (15.4b); and $US(0)$ and $US(1)$ are U.S. reaction functions corresponding to equations (15.6a) and (15.6b). The slope of $J(0)$ and $J(1)$ is $-1/2$, and the slope of $US(0)$ and $US(2)$ is -2. Equilibrium output for each period is given by the intersection of $J(0)$ and $US(0)$, and $J(1)$ and $US(1)$, respectively (calculated in equations (15.8a), (15.8b), (15.8c) and (15.9a), (15.9b), (15.9c)). The two equilibria are stable.

Pass-through and Market Share

In a hysteretic environment, two factors determine the degree of pass-through and the relative market shares of export and domestic firms: 1) the magnitude of exchange rate fluctuations; and 2) planning horizons – short or long – adopted by the two firms. There are four possible combinations of corporate strategies: 1) Japan, short; United States, short; 2) Japan, long; United States, short; 3) Japan, short; United States, long; and 4) Japan, long; United States, long.

Assume that the yen/dollar exchange rate alternates around the competitiveness parity rate (c/c^*) by the same percentage amount in either direction. This upward or downward deviation from the average can be denoted by $\dot{e} = (e_1 - e_0)/(e_0 + e_1)$. For each of the four combinations of corporate strategies, pass-through, output, and the average market share of the Japanese firm vary as the amplitude of the exchange rate is increased.

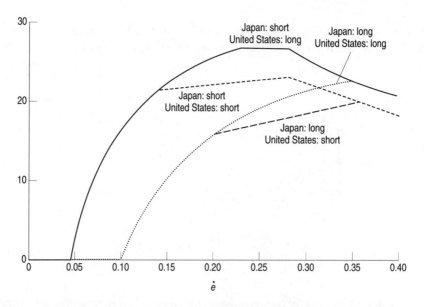

Note: $\dot{e}$ denotes the deviation from the mean; percentages are based on the numerical examples in the text

Figure 15.4 Pass-through under four planning-horizon scenarios (percent)

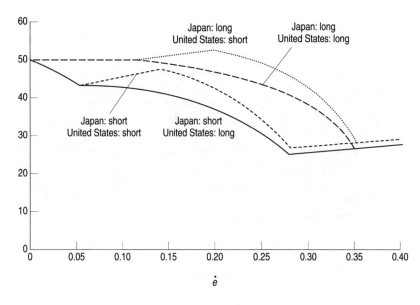

Note: $\dot{e}$ denotes the deviation from the mean; percentages are based on the numerical examples in the text

Figure 15.5 Average share of Japanese firm under four planning-horizon scenarios (percent)

In every case, the behavior of output and price goes through four phases as exchange fluctuations are magnified. First, when the exchange rate fluctuates insignificantly, neither firm responds to the exchange rate, and output and price therefore remain constant over time. This is because potential gain from output adjustment is more than offset by the promotional cost. Second, as the exchange rate becomes sufficiently unstable, the Japanese firm that is directly affected by the exchange rate begins to adjust output.[6] Third, as exchange fluctuations intensify, both firms adjust output according to the exchange rate. (See figure 15.3, which shows this phase.) Finally, as the fluctuation becomes extreme, the Japanese firm completely retreats from the U.S. market when the yen is high.

Planning horizons affect the critical points at which these changes take place, as well as pass-through and relative market shares associated with each phase. The latter can be seen more clearly if pass-through (defined as the percentage of exchange fluctuations reflected in changes in p^*) and the average market share of the Japanese firm (defined as simple average of the shares in two periods) are plotted, as in figures 15.4 and 15.5. The following numerical assumptions have been adopted: production cost, $c = ¥80$, $c^* = \$0.6$; promotional cost, $z = ¥8$, $z^* = \$0.06$. The competitiveness parity rate is therefore ¥133 to \$1.

In every case, pass-through remains zero for a while, then increases and finally decreases as exchange fluctuations become larger. However, pass-through is always lower in case 2 where Japanese firms are long-term maximizers and U.S. firms are short-term maximizers, than in case 3 where the opposite is assumed. Similarly, regardless of exchange fluctuations, the average presence of the Japanese firm is never smaller in case 2 than in case 3. The more forward-looking the export firm is relative to the domestic firm, the lower is pass-through and the higher the export penetration. These figures vividly illustrate the role hysteresis plays in determining price and output under the floating exchange rate regime.

Conclusions

Even without any change in technology or tastes, exchange rate fluctuations, which act as a differential cost shock, can alter not only the variances of output and price but their means as well. The model developed here has shown that, in imperfectly competitive markets such as duopoly, the existence of hysteresis, combined with various degrees of time preference, determines pass-through and the trade pattern in the floating exchange rate regime.

The model could be expanded to take further complications into account, without necessarily invalidating the general conclusion. For example, some framework other than the Cournot duopoly could be adopted; uncertainty about the exchange rate might be introduced; and the learning effect could be incorporated, whereby the production cost becomes a decreasing function of cumulative output rather than a constant as assumed here.

Notes

1 Many empirical studies corroborate these findings. See, for example, Woo (1984), Krugman (1987), Hooper and Mann (1987), and Ohno (1989). United States (1988) also offers a good review.
2 This argument is in contradiction to the Dixit-Stiglitz model where the consumer values variety. Although this may be true for food, drinks, and other entertainment goods and services, a majority of durable manufactured goods seem to be purchased as described in the text.
3 Various models have been constructed to explain incomplete pass-through based on the concept of hysteresis, including Baldwin (1988a, 1988b), Dixit (1987, 1989), Foster and Baldwin (1986), and Froot and Klemperer (1988). The present model, however, is unique in its formulation of linear promotional costs and its emphasis on the corporate planning horizon.
4 Marston (1989) shows that when home and foreign countries are two separate markets and when marginal cost is constant (as is assumed here), one can consider the pricing of Japanese goods abroad independently of that at home. The Japanese market is therefore ignored in this model.
5 If the firm is a short-term maximizer, output will be equal to x_0, which is set when the yen is strong. If the firm is a long-term maximizer, x will be chosen so as to maximize $\Pi_0 + \Pi_1$ in equations (15.2a) and (15.2b) after $x_1 = x_0$ is set.
6 The opposite asymmetry, where only the U.S. firm adjusts output, will never take place. It can be seen from equation (15.5) that, if $x_0 = x_1$, the U.S. firm faces identical profit-maximization problems in both periods, and therefore $x_0^* = x_1^*$ must hold.

References

Baldwin, Richard E. (1988a) "Some Empirical Evidence on Hysteresis in Aggregate U.S. Import Prices," NBER Working Paper 2483. Cambridge, Massachusetts: National Bureau of Economic Research, January.
—— (1988b) "Hysteresis in Import Prices: The Beachhead Effect," *American Economic Review*, **78** (September), pp. 773–85.
—— and Paul R. Krugman (1986) "Persistent Trade Effects of Large Exchange Rate Shocks," NBER Working Paper 2017. Cambridge, Massachusetts: National Bureau of Economic Research, September.
Dixit, Avinash (1987) "Entry and Exit Decisions of Firms Under Fluctuating Real Exchange Rates" (unpub-

lished) Princeton University, October.

—— (1989) "Hysteresis, Import Penetration, and Exchange Rate Pass-Through," *Quarterly Journal of Economics*, **104** (May 1989), pp. 205–28.

Dornbusch, Rudiger, (1987) "Exchange Rates and Prices," *American Economic Review*, **77** (March), pp. 93–106.

Foster, Harry, and Richard E. Baldwin (1986) "Marketing Bottlenecks and the Relationship Between Exchange Rates and Prices" (unpublished) October.

Froot, Kenneth A. and Paul D. Klemperer (1988) "Exchange Rate Pass-Through When Market Share Matters," NBER Working Paper 2542. Cambridge, Massachusetts: National Bureau of Economic Research, March.

HatsoPoulos, George N., Paul R. Krugman, and Lawrence H. Summers (1988) "The Problem of U.S. Competitiveness," paper presented at the Fourth International Symposium of the Economic Planning Agency, Tokyo (March).

Hooper, Peter and Catherine L. Mann (1987) "The U.S. External Deficit: Its Causes and Persistence," International Finance Discussion Paper 316. Washington: Board of Governors of the Federal Reserve System, November 1987.

Krugman, Paul R. (1987) "Pricing to Market When the Exchange Rate Changes." In S.W. Arndt and J.R. Richardson (eds) *Real-Financial Linkage Among Open Economies*. Cambridge, Massachusetts: MIT Press.

Marston, Richard C. (1989) "Pricing to Market in Japanese Manufacturing" (unpublished). Philadelphia: University of Pennsylvania, March.

McKinnon, Ronald I. (1989) "Toward a Common Monetary Standard Through the Regulation of Exchange Rates," paper presented at the Conference on Global Disequilibrium, held in Montreal, Quebec on May 17-19 (Montreal, Quebec: McGill Economics Centre, May 1989).

Ohno, Kenichi (1989) "Export Pricing Behavior of Manufacturing: A U.S. – Japan Comparison," *Staff Papers*, International Monetary Fund (Washington), **36** (September), pp. 550–79.

United States (1988) *Economic Report of the President with The Annual Report of the Council of Economic Advisers*. Washington: Government Printing Office.

Woo, Wing T. (1984) "Exchange Rates and the Prices of Nonfood, Nonfuel Products," *Brookings Papers on Economic Activity*: 2. Washington: The Brookings Institution.

16

Options Thinking and Platform Investments: Investing in Opportunity

BRUCE KOGUT

UNIVERSITY OF PENNSYLVANIA

AND

NALIN KULATILAKA

BOSTON UNIVERSITY

The world is witnessing a new era of competition with the development of new principles of organizing work, radical technologies, and globalization. For many firms, these transformations have biased managerial action towards myopic behavior and indecision. These transformations are similar to the changes that swept across the world at the turn of the century. In the United States and other countries, success was achieved through the willingness of entrepreneurs, firms, financial institutions, and government to invest capital for long-term payoffs. The building of the infrastructure in telecommunications, roadways, and electrical grids required massive amounts of invested capital. Organizing workers in the new ways of rationalized production required extensive experimentation and financial expense.

It is ironic that this willingness to invest is not validated by many of the financial criteria presently taught in business schools and practiced in industry. The problem is not that financial criteria have come to dominate decision making, but that there is a systematic bias towards the short term in the kind of decision heuristics that managers and financial analysts apply to evaluating major investments. Even popular strategic planning tools, such as industry structural analysis, bias action away from making investments with long-term payoffs. The myopia that currently plagues American industry has its source in the financial criteria, planning tools, and especially in the incentives attached to managers' performance.

Over the past few years, there have been two streams of thought aimed at correcting this bias. One has been the formulation of strategic investments as real options. By real, it is meant that the

The authors thank the anonymous referees for their constructive criticism, and their colleagues, especially Chris Ittner and Alan Marcus, for valuable discussions.

investment is in physical and human assets, as opposed to financial instruments. This stream of thinking has its origins in Stewart Myers' observations that the cash flows of many investments consists of income from the assets in their current use, plus a growth option to expand into new markets in the future.[1]

The second stream consists of recent works on organizational capabilities and core competence.[2] This approach seeks to redirect the orientation of strategic planning from the exploitation of current resources to an emphasis on the creation of capabilities with long-term payoffs. It is, in fact, a prominent feature of current competitive conditions that the battle for survival in many industries concerns the speed by which new organizational practices are adopted (e.g. quality programs, kanban systems, or value-based activity analysis).

The formal apparatus of option valuation has been criticized as being too narrow and demanding to be applied practically to strategic decisions. In contrast, the notion of organizational capabilities has been accused of being too vague to further useful analysis. We seek to bridge these two streams of thought by developing a set of heuristics that view an organizations's capabilities as generating platforms to expand into new but uncertain markets. These capabilities are considered options because they are investments in opportunity. Without making the initial stake, the firm would be unable to act to its advantage when opportunity does strike. Furthermore, these options are valuable for a broad range of applications. The techniques for analyzing platforms as options have developed rapidly over the past ten years. The problem is not so much analytical as it is conceptual.

Platform Investments as Options

Over the past few years, a wide body of applications of mathematical techniques has been developed to evaluate financial options. These techniques permit a price to be calculated for the value of the flexibility to exercise a given right, such as that of a being able to buy the stock of a company at a fixed price in the case of a call option. This flexibility is, obviously, more valuable when there is more uncertainty about the best investments to make.

Consider the case of a biotechnology company and an electric company. The shares of both companies are selling at a price of $30. If an investor were to be given the right to buy shares of either company at $32 within 30 days, holding the option to buy the stock of a biotechnology company is more valuable than that to buy the stock of an electric company. Either stock may finish the period at below $32; the worst the investor can do is not exercise and receive, effectively, a payment of 0 for holding the option. In this case, the option has turned out to be of no value. But the biotechnology stock, because its price is more variable, has a better chance to be "in the money"; that is, its price has more upside potential because it is more volatile. The option on the biotechnology company is a more valuable play on the upside potential, with the worst case being not to exercise at all, as in the case of the electric company option.

A common observation has been that the techniques used for valuing financial options of this sort are particularly well-suited to analyzing the complex and uncertain investment decisions facing managers. Indeed, many decisions have a straightforward option interpretation. Should a major oil company pump to full capacity today? If it pumps today, it has less oil in the future. If prices should rise, it would have oil to sell and to exploit the opportunity. Since more volatile oil prices increase the likelihood that it may pay to wait until the market takes off, the "option to wait" is more valuable when there is more price uncertainty.

Many options of this nature are *inherent* in an investment. If you are running a business, you have the option to abandon it. Should you abandon it now or wait? Obviously, it pays to wait if there is a higher chance that the market will be more valuable tomorrow and if it costs too much – as it always does – to close down an operation. If it turns out to be worse, the option to abandon is always there; it is inherent in any operating business.

We are concerned in this article with a more *proactive* kind of option, one that is not inherent but must be designed and planned. We call such options "platform investments" in order to cover two types of investment decisions. The first is the question of the design of an operating flexibility, such as whether it pays to buy robotics in order to automate a factory to produce many kinds of models depending on (uncertain) demand. The second is the growth option, as discussed earlier, which gives a firm the right to expand in the future into new product or geographic markets. This kind of investment captures the importance of investing rapidly in the opportunities critical to the growth and success of new business.

Platform investments are options on the future. This simple insight suggests that their value will be determined by the same factors that determine the price of a financial options. But because platform investments are real options, there are a few additional considerations which, in practice, turn out to be very messy for the purpose of arriving at easy methods of valuation. For example, whereas financial market expectations regarding the level and volatility of future oil prices can be easily gleaned from accessible trading data on crude oil future contracts, such data must be generated by the informed guesses of operating and staff managers for most kinds of investments. Many major investments, because they have an option-like quality, are more valuable than they appear in terms of simple discounted cash flows.[3] Such undervaluations are to be expected when the investments are in new ways of doing things.

The Problem of Myopic Heuristics

Applying option models to operating and investment decisions would not be as difficult if there existed a set of explicit methods by which to evaluate option opportunities. Such methods could then be embodied in the strategic planning tools and decision rules that serve as heuristics reflecting the prevailing wisdom on how to arrive at "best" performance. By heuristics, we mean the techniques used to identify and analyze problems. "Choose the project which has the highest net present value" is one heuristic; "enter markets only when you can win the most share of sales" is another.

There is no strategy that is best for all industries or at all times, but heuristics are often surprisingly robust. The choice of a heuristic is a compromise between ease of use and accuracy. Not everything can be measured and analyzed. Consequently, this compromise reflects the understanding of what rules support the achievement of best practices.

A common problem is that the notion of best practice changes more quickly than decision heuristics. Thomas Johnson and Robert Kaplan argue that accounting systems were developed during the first third of this century to track the cost of labor in the new mass systems of production.[4] Even though the importance of labor expenditure relative to quality and speed of production has fallen dramatically since then, many managerial accounting systems still emphasize direct labor costs as a primary concern of measurement.

There is good reason to suspect that today's heuristics are biased towards the short-term due to the evolution of particular institutions, ways of organizing, and rules developed during this century. Consequently, they ignore or undervalue platform investments. While these practices made good sense at one time, alterations are now required.

The following four sources of myopia are the most telling.[5]

FINANCIAL INSTITUTIONS

A common complaint of managers is that financial institutions compel boards of directors and top management to focus on short-term profits. This complaint has, until recently, received little credence among academics convinced that equity markets properly weigh current and expected cash flows. Moreover, this skepticism has been reinforced by the gradual emergence in the U.S. and Japan of similar patterns of equity financing with financial institutions (e.g. through pension fund management) as the dominant holders of equities. Today, both Japan and the United States have approximately the same levels of debt to equity financing.[6]

The analysis of the short-sightedness of American financial institutions has, however, become more subtle. The issue is not so much the differences in the cost of finance among countries (especially since capital costs are much more similar among countries in today's environment of integrated financial markets); rather, the factors affecting managers' investment horizons lie more in the differences among countries regarding the role of financial institutions (especially banks) in the governance of corporations. In this regard, Japan and Germany look very different from the United States. In these two countries, banks and insurance companies are permitted to hold substantial positions in the debt and equity of industrial corporations.

In Japan, a "main bank" serves as the primary adviser to firms belonging to an industrial group. Estimates for holdings in 133 Japanese manufacturing firms in 1984 show that the largest debtholder (either a bank or insurance company) owns on average 22.3 percent of the debt and 6.2 percent of the equity. Because the main bank and institutions hold debt and equity positions in each other, consideration of the crossholdings would increase the centrality of the main bank.[7]

In Germany, three banks serve as the largest sources of capital to industry. Due to a custom whereby individuals give proxy voting rights to banks ("Depotstimmrecht"), their influence is substantially enhanced beyond their direct ownership of equity and debt. This influence is further strengthened by the veto rights of any major investment given to minority owners controlling more than 25 percent of the votes. In 1975, the three major banks controlled 43.2 percent of the voting rights for the 74 largest non-financial corporations with traded stocks; all banks (including investment companies) controlled 92.5 percent. Since little debt is raised through bonds (and when it is, banks are often the issuers), most firms rely upon loans from banks. Banks serve as the primary provider of loans to firms, and own and control equity positions in the largest companies.[8]

The concentration of financial power in Japan and Germany has certain benefits. One, it more clearly aligns the interests of debt and equity holders. In the U.S., in the event of bankruptcy, dissolution of assets will first be used to cover senior debt, which is often held by banks; hence, there is less incentive to maintain the firm as a going concern and bankruptcy is used as a way for senior claimants to recover the value of their loans. Two, banks have not only greater access to information, but they also disseminate information which improves the quality of strategic decisions. As a result, Japanese firms belonging to a *keiretsu* (industrial grouping) are less financially constrained than other independent Japanese firms.[9]

While the Japanese and German financial systems are not without their pitfalls, the incentives for investing for a longer horizon is greater in these two countries. Prior to regulations limiting the equity shares of banks and insurance companies in the United States, certain investment houses (such as J.P. Morgan) played a similar role in the American economy at the turn of the century to the one of German and Japanese banks today.[10] At the present, the U.S. is struggling to change the current regulatory framework of financial institutions.

BUDGETING RULES

The method of discounted cash flows (DCF) diffused widely among corporations in the post World War II period. While there is no doubt that DCF is superior to such alternatives as pay-back or internal rate of return as ways to evaluate investments, DCF also has severe problems. The principal problem is that DCF provides the wrong answer in the wrong direction just when the need for a good way to evaluate an investment is the greatest. In stable environments, DCF provides an easy and instructive way to analyze the decision whether to commit resources to a new investment. It is mostly likely to fail in cases where the investment presents a platform for future expansion in highly uncertain environments. As shown below, the weakness of DCF is its failure to account for how uncertainty, rather than implying a higher discount rate, can increase the value of an investment.

STRATEGIC PLANNING

One of the activities encompassed by strategic planning is the application of heuristics by which to identify profitable businesses for investment and expansion. One of the most well-known tools is the Boston Consulting Group (BCG) growth matrix, which was developed in the 1960s. In this matrix, an attractive business is indexed by its growth rate. Competitive advantage is driven by the share of the market held by a firm. Market share is a proxy measurement of a firm's cost position; thus, due to scale economies and experience effects, a firm with the largest market share will have the lowest costs.

This planning heuristic has the advantage of being simple; it is easier to measure relative market share than actual costs. Its success was driven by its compatibility with the expansion of mass-production systems into new industries and markets. Volume strategies and low cost positions are inevitably linked to the concept of relative market share.

The technique of industry structural analysis, which was developed and diffused in the 1970s and 1980s, is more sophisticated.[11] By emphasizing the unique constellation of competitive pressures from rivals, suppliers, and buyers in a particular industry, this technique encourages the consideration of a wider menu of strategies. This approach focuses on exploiting a firm's resources in the context of specific market structures.

No matter how faulty the BCG growth matrix may be for some industries, it has the merit of encouraging the allocation of resources to new business for the long-term purpose of eventual market domination. Industry structural analysis places the stress more upon the exploitation of resources in a given market structure than upon the creation of new capabilities. It tends to underestimate, however, the importance of developing generalized resources (which not only provide entry into future markets, but also shape their evolution).

STRATEGIC BUSINESS UNITS

Along with the development of planning techniques for the analysis of discrete businesses, corporations have created corresponding organizational divisions. These divisions, called "strategic business units" (SBUs), are delegated responsibility for the formulation of business strategy and for operations. The managers of the SBUs usually have their compensation linked to performance.

Though there are many merits to SBUs, they frequently lead to an underinvestment in projects with long-term growth. This problem may be more acute for many American firms than for their international counterparts, since the higher turnover rates among managers in the United States conflicts with the tracking of results over a long period of time. The recent trends towards strengthening divisionalization by "flattening" the organization and by increasing the role of short-term incentives in compensation have exacerbated this orientation towards the short-term.

A more subtle problem is that the divisionalization of business will interfere with the identification and exercise of the underlying growth options. An SBU may view an investment as unattractive, even though it creates a platform valuable for other businesses. There is less incentive in this system to invest if the value of the platform accrues to other SBUs.

The SBU structure discourages the development of "corporate assets." New technologies are invariably valuable for many different business. Product divisions conflict with the broad implications of developing new capabilities. In many cases, no SBU can make the case for investment in expensive and risky new technologies. A corporate "buy in" is required to relieve any single SBU of bearing the burden of developing corporate-wide capabilities. The failure is not of the SBU system itself, it rests instead with corporate management.

Underinvestment

In some industries, myopic rules may be reasonable. What works today will work tomorrow; the extra cost of planning for the future may drown out the minor benefits. However, most industries do not fall in this category, and myopic biases will hurt when it matters the most. As a rule, the hard-nosed policy of accepting projects only on the basis of a hurdle rate will guarantee failure in any fast-growth industry.

The competitive implications of myopia can be seen through a simple simulation. Consider two firms in the same industry: one myopic and one far-sighted. The myopic firm uses the distribution of next period's net cash flows to forecast the future. The far-sighted firm recognizes that the decision to invest creates a platform to expand in the future. We let each firm increase its investment capacity by one unit, and we let supply equal demand, a not unreasonable assumption for fast-growing industries.

We trick the simulation to look as if there is an option to expand by using a log normal distribution of net cash flows. The log normal has the property of a fat upper tail, which is a good way to represent the "option" value as a play on the upside. This tail also increases for the projection of cash flows further out in time, which captures the importance of looking into the more distant future. In the simulations, the far-sighted firm decides to invest or not depending upon a forecast which incorporates a forecast of the value of the investment if the market should grow rapidly. The myopic firm forecasts the future on the basis of next period's cash flows.

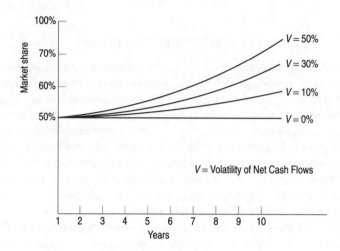

Figure 16.1 Market share of firms with foresight

In a stable environment, the performances of myopic and far-sighted firms do not differ. In figure 16.1, the simulated relationship between volatility of net cash flows and market share is graphed. Setting the volatility to 0, there is no difference in market shares after ten periods. These results underline the intuition that myopic behavior does not pay a penalty in stable and certain environments.

As the volatility of the net cash flows is allowed to increase, the penalty attached to myopia curves dramatically upward. With a volatility set to 50 percent of mean cash flows, the myopic firms are eliminated from the market. Far-sighted firms, even though constrained to invest only by increments, quickly come to dominate the market. Platform investments, like financial options, are more valuable in volatile environments.

What generates these results? The primary culprit is the aggregate underinvestment by the myopic firms in an industry where early investments generate the potential to expand and to earn increasing profits in later periods. In this industry, uncertainty actually favors more rather than less investment.

The issue is not that myopic policies fail under uncertainty; they fail when uncertainty represents opportunity. If the worse a firm can do is receive 0 net cash flows, then there is a fundamental asymmetry in profits and losses. The greater the uncertainty, the more likely will be the chance that the market will generate large profits; the worst case always remains 0. The only way to exploit this opportunity is to invest in the first place.

These results provide an interesting insight into two heuristic rules. In growing but uncertain markets, a heuristic that says accept projects that promise to pay 20 percent on invested assets (or on operating income) conveys the message, "Exit the market when uncertain." The heuristic that says "invest to capture dominant market share" is simple-minded but consistent with a far-sighted vision of the evolution of industry profits.

But is the rule to grab dominant share always right when there is high uncertainty? The answer is obviously no. This is a bad rule if there is no advantage to early investment. And it is a bad rule if all competitors blindly follow the same policy. Ignoring competitors is trading one kind of myopia for another.

Heuristics for Platform Investments Formulation

Rules must be developed for the identification of potential platforms in investment alternatives. Sometimes these rules can be formalized to arrive at rather exact valuations. More often, however, they will serve to guide how opportunities should be identified and framed for analysis.

Platforms, as options, are valuable due to four conditions: uncertainty, opportunity, time dependence, and discretion (see figure 16.2). Obviously, flexibility is valuable only when there is uncertainty, yet understanding the source and properties of the uncertainty is a substantial problem. For example, it is difficult to describe the probabilities attached to the arrival of new technologies.

The value of a platform is related directly to the breadth of opportunities. It stands to reason that an investment with many potential applications is more valuable than one with a narrow set of opportunities. At the same time, some opportunities are more valuable than others because their potential market is more lucrative. An investment in some platforms leads to products and services that are more valued by customers.

A more subtle feature is time dependence. The application of option analysis to investments is important, because it captures the value in the dependence of decisions over time. Having the ability to switch production from one kind of vehicle to another is only possible if an investment has been made earlier in flexible manufacturing systems. The issue of time dependence is one of the most complex problems in understanding the value of a platform investment. If the investment strategy can be quickly imitated, then there is no advantage for investing early. Similarly, if there is a high chance that a competitor will act first by preempting a market, then the value of investing in an option runs the threat of being eradicated over night.

A critical issue in the valuation of a platform is whether the investment is accompanied by the discretion to exercise the option. Many firms complain that they have more technologies than they use. It is not uncommon to hear the complaint that the benefits of investment in a technology were

---

- *Uncertainty*

- *Venue into multiple opportunities*
  A broad opportunity set
  Customers' perception of the value of derived products and services

- *Time dependence*
  Proprietary and difficult to imitate
  Risk of preemption

- *Managerial discretion to exercise the option*

Figure 16.2 What determines the value of a platform?

reaped by other firms. Witness the efforts of Texas Instruments and Honeywell, both of whom had to resort to the courts to collect on patented technologies. Competitors can sometimes have better incentives and information on how to apply a company's own technology to new markets.

Firms investing in platforms frequently face "windows of opportunities" during which they must act to exploit their investments. Appropriate information systems are necessary to identify these opportunities in a timely way. Incentives must be in place in order to reward managers for acting promptly. Failure to benefit from platform investments is often due to deficiencies in the design of information flows and managerial incentives. New heuristics without proper information and incentives are of no value.

Platform Investments as Capabilities

Organizational capabilities – e.g. creating quality, being more flexible, and responding to the market quickly – are the most important platforms that a firm can build, because they support investment strategies into a wide spectrum of opportunities.

Investing in opportunity is important in businesses where the capability to expand is not easily acquired. The capability to expand is linked to reputation and to technologies. Reputation is hard to build quickly; similarly, the ownership of particular technologies is not easily attained. It is easy to advise a firm that it should compete by increasing the perceived quality-to-price performance; the hard part is learning "how" to achieve the reputation for performance. Similarly, the important aspect of technological expertise is not simply the possession of a patent, but the capability to engineer new products consistently over time. Capabilities represent the accumulated skills of what corporations become best at doing.

These observations lead to a very simple point. The value of platforms as options ultimately comes down to viewing organizational capabilities as investments in learning and acquiring a broad-based expertise.[12] Prahalad and Hamel have suggested that these capabilities be understood as "core competencies" in particular technologies.[13] These capabilities need not be restricted to technologies, but to the wider organizational capacity to develop new products and services, to bring them quickly to the market, or to market and distribute them effectively.

Organizational capabilities essentially consist of how a firm develops the expertise of its employees, through the way in which they are organized and rewarded and through the way in which information is gathered and disseminated. As shown in figure 16.2, these capabilities represent the most important kind of options. They provide a platform into a wide number of opportunities. The ability to create new technologies is likely to generate a more vast potential than the opportunity associated with any one technology.

Organizational capabilities are important because they are hard to imitate or preempt. A competent group of engineers can reverse engineer and imitate many kinds of technologies. The hard part is learning how to build this group and coordinate product delivery to market. This capability is difficult to acquire, as it is often poorly understood and inadequately described in operating manuals.

The difficulty many corporations have had with adopting new capabilities has been that the benefits are often hard to measure. The benefits of new quality programs have been especially difficult to gauge, with estimates rarely being made and usually varying widely. No wonder that efforts to implement programs often appear as missionary. Not only are the data missing; there is not an understanding of what costs and benefits need to be measured to evaluate the investment in quality programs.

FOUR EXAMPLES

Organizational capabilities are unlikely to be subject to the careful financial evaluation of other kinds of investments. Often, new capabilities are learned due to survival pressures. Most firms in the auto industry have adopted the capability to lower inventories by just-in-time systems and to speed product delivery by reliance on external sourcing. Yet, the investment in new capabilities and platforms is often delayed or neglected due to the failure to understand the option value. Consider the following examples.

Core technologies

A popular Silicon Valley adage is that certain products are important as "technology drivers." The manufacturing of memory semiconductors has played the role of driving the accumulation of experience in design and high-volume production. Learning that is gained in the product development of one memory generation serves as a basis for lowering the costs of subsequent generations.

This experience is not only useful for subsequent memory products, but also serves as a platform for diversification into other industries. In a study of the diversification of start-up companies in the semiconductor industry, Dong-Jae Kim found that firms with experience in the design of memory devices expanded significantly into other related areas. Start-ups in certain markets, such as application-specific integrated circuits (ASICs), not only did not diversify; they were also far more likely to fail or be acquired.

These results fit well with what we know of larger semiconductor firms that withdrew from memory production to stem their losses in this highly competitive market, only to discover the harmful effects on their other products. In the case of Motorola, it withdrew and later reentered. Other firms withdrew and continued on a downward spiral. However, even if a firm makes the decision to reenter, the competition has already moved on.

Technology drivers are platforms. They generate proprietary learning and they serve as points for expansion into other markets. The failure to recognize core technologies can lead to devastating results. A large electronics firm scrapped its cellular business in the 1980s, only to reenter by acquisition a few years later. If it had kept the option "alive" by maintaining a small research and development activity, the capability to expand when the market turned-up would have been in place. The operating costs to keep the group running would have been low, at least in comparison with the high premium paid for the subsequent acquisition.

Joint ventures

An alternative to scrapping a project is to share the costs of running the activity with a partner. Frequently, the advantage of a joint venture is that the partners bring different capabilities to the cooperation. Motorola's reentry into the manufacturing of memory semiconductors was aided through a joint venture with Toshiba in exchange for microprocessor technology. As the Nummi joint venture between General Motors and Toyota indicates, the learning of new skills is facilitated by replicating the organization in the form of a joint venture.[14]

There is one complicating feature to joint ventures: they often do not last very long. The median life of a manufacturing joint venture in the United States is about 6 years. This gloomy figure is

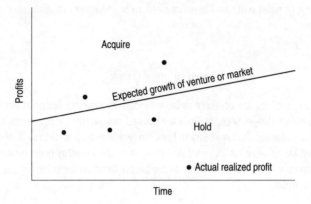

Figure 16.3 Timing of exercise to acquire joint venture

misleading, however, for most of these ventures terminate by acquisition. Figure 16.3 illustrates the relationship between profitability and the acquisition of the venture. The line indicates the expectation of profit based on a historical growth rate. (In this sense, this line corresponds to the expectation of the myopic firm, given in our earlier simulation.) Joint ventures tend to terminate when the industry begins to show unusual growth and the profits to early entrants increase. In this case, the joint ventures are not dissolved, but rather are acquired by the one of the partners. When the industry does poorly, however, the partners neither dissolve nor acquire it. They maintain a hold position since there is no reason to throw away an already-bought option and since it is often better (if the holding and operating costs are not too high) to wait and see what opportunities present themselves in the future.

Joint ventures often carry an important option value. They are frequently used in high growth markets when neither partner has the necessary skills nor wants to bear the full risk. When the industry begins to grow quickly, the partners must invest more in order to exercise the option to expand with the market. It is at the moment of new investment that the partners realize they put different valuations on the opportunity. One partner buys it; the other one is bought out with capital gains.

These kinds of joint ventures are platform investments. They transfer and develop capabilities which serve as points of entry into uncertain markets. That they are so frequently acquired underscores their value for the development of organizational capabilities.[15]

Flexible manufacturing systems

One of the most important dimensions of competition is the capability to respond flexibly. There are many ways to achieve flexibility, from sub-contracting policies to product design. Some investments are made, however, with the sole purpose of achieving the flexibility to respond to uncertain markets. Flexible manufacturing systems are an example of a decision to purchase the ability to reprogram industrial machinery in order to increase the variety produced by the same capital equipment. This flexibility makes it possible to respond to shifts in customer demand as well as to offer greater customization of the product.

Installing flexible manufacturing systems appears to be relatively easy. The number of vendors willing to sell the hardware and provide software services is staggering. Yet, the experience with flexible manufacturing systems has often proven to be disappointing.

Robert Stempel of General Motors has commented:

> We've tried automation without knowledgeable workers, and it doesn't work … We put a tremendous amount of automation and electronics into our Cadillac plant in Hamtramck. And we couldn't run it because our people didn't understand what we were asking them to do.[16]

The difficulty of FMS is that the flexibility of the physical assets is nested in the organizational capability of the firm to operate flexibly. Physical equipment promising flexibility can be easily bought on the market. The more important platform value is the development of the capability to know how to run a plant flexibly, and then to expand this organizing heuristic to other operations.[17]

Country platforms

In the home country, managers take for granted that when a new product is launched, the customer already knows the brand label, the distribution channels are in place, and the salesforce knows the product and buyer. The product manager evaluating a new proposal need not calculate the cost of establishing these invisible assets of goodwill and acquired know-how.

An iron law of competing internationally, however, is that the first investment overseas will lose money. An investment in a foreign market underscores dramatically the value of owning platforms for sequential product launches. There may be few corporate and business assets established in the country. Because of the SBU incentive system, the costs of launching a single product appears as exorbitantly too high.

This view is clearly myopic, for the first investment establishes a country platform for the future. By establishing distribution channels and learning how to do business in a country, the initial entry generates the capability to launch subsequent products from this platform. The investment as a stand alone project may look unattractive, but the platform value is especially large for the first entry.

The importance of this platform is reflected in the debate on whether the product should carry a corporate label or be uniquely advertised. The corporate label establishes a platform by advertising the firm; advertising the product will result in higher market penetration. The choice comes down to evaluating the option value in the corporate label against the foregone revenues by not advertising the product.

The bias in a myopic approach is frequently revealed in country risk analysis. When confronted with a choice between investing in a developing country with a volatile market and a developed country, a manager is often advised to slap down a risk premium on the developing country project. Yet, if the initial investment is largely important for establishing a platform, the higher variance of the developing country should actually be seen as attractive. The upside of a Mexican investment is much larger for many products than the most optimistic scenario of an investment in the U.S. or other developed countries.

There is reason to be cautious, however. As shown in figure 16.2, a platform investment is only valuable when acting today provides the capability to seize an opportunity in the future. Investing in the country carries no platform value if there is no advantage for early investment. For many firms already exporting to Europe, the 1992 policies of the European Community presented exactly this dilemma. With brand labels and distribution channels in place, the argument to invest before 1992 as a platform is *not* persuasive. Table 16.1 illustrates why this case is not a platform. For this analysis, the project with the plant in Europe against the export operation should be compared. We make the assumption that a new plant can be built in a year for a cost of 200. If a policy raising tariffs is imposed, the export operation pays a penalty of no sales until a European plant comes on stream. If the plant investment costs 200, the project with the new plant earns a net cash flow of −100 in the first year (investment costs plus the 100 from continued exports). The export project only builds the plant if barriers are imposed, and pays the investment costs of 200, with no export earnings for one year while the plant is being built. The cash flows for exporting should then be weighted by the probability of such a policy imposition.

This analysis is standard in any capital budgeting procedure; no platform value need be considered. As long as the option to invest in the future remained open, an early investment in a manufacturing plant generates little in the way of a platform; there is no time dependence. We could, of course, make the case that the plant builds goodwill with the Community which serves future product entries. But our point is that the case for such a platform has to be made and evaluated against the costs; it cannot be simply assumed and used to rationalize every investment.[18]

Short-run Accountability for Long-run Results

The last example of the burden on a SBU in making a first investment in a country points to the importance of a corporate vision. If a country is deemed as vital, the corporate office should be willing to underwrite part of the investment. The criticism of this kind of proposal is the charge of the loss of accountability (which is the mirror image of the problem of discretion noted in figure 16.2). There can be little doubt what the response from a room of SBU managers will be if corporate headquarters states that losses will be underwritten for investments into country X. The only problem will be sorting out which manager has the right to lose the money first.

A policy of funding platforms must resolves the problem of accountability. If the investment were to be in a financial stock option, prices of the security could be tracked even if a market for the option did not exist. Such markets do not exist by which to compare an investment in long-term capabilities. What, then, should be the criteria by which to monitor the platform value?

Most companies implicitly monitor this value. Figure 16.4, provides an example for evaluating a joint venture. The performance of the venture is measured along two lines. The first is the net cash flows (including dividends, transfer payments, and other fees) from assets currently in place. The second is a set of criteria for examining the progress of the venture along other lines. If the purpose is to learn new manufacturing techniques, the rate of what is to be learned over time should

Table 16.1 Cash flows of European plant versus export

	1990	1991	1992	1993	1994	1995
European plant	−100	100	100	100	100	100
Export						
If no barrier	100	100	100	100	100	100
If barrier	100	100	−200	100	100	100

Profits from venture as is:

- Fees
- Dividends
- Margins on sales to venture

Evaluation of platform:

- Brand label recognition
- Transfer of skills to other businesses
- Acquisition of contacts with new customers
- Improved relations with government regulatory bodies

Figure 16.4 Evaluation of a joint venture

be established and then performance measured against this benchmark. The extent to which brand labels are recognized or knowledge of government regulatory bodies is improved can also be measured and evaluated on a year-by-year basis against the goals established at the time of the venture formation. The hard part, however, is understanding that these investments are valuable only if discretion is exercised; so every evaluation must also have an understanding of the menu of opportunities that should have been exploited.

In some cases, the evaluation can be made more exacting by estimating the value of the option over time. Reasonable benchmarks have been suggested for the evaluation of the option value of oil drilling, flexible manufacturing, and other investments whose value depends upon a price of a commodity or instruments traded in markets. For example, the value of establishing two plants with excess capacity in two countries with the option to switch overtime between them is primarily a function of exchange rate (or relative price) movements. This type of option is amenable to formal evaluation.

Ultimately, accountability rests with managers, who must gather the appropriate information for measurement and must understand the sources of uncertainty for defining when discretion should be taken. It may be difficult to break away from using the standard financial criteria of hurdle rates. Neglecting other forms of measurement will cause the evaluation system to tend inevitably toward myopic measurements.

Market Structure and the Risk of Preemption

The emphasis upon organizational capabilities and platforms should not lead to an underestimation of the competitive environment. Since platform investments can dramatically alter the structure of a market, it is important to understand how strategy itself influences the evolution of the industry. Clearly, the decision to invest in a country will generate competitive responses, which then influence an array of strategic variables such as prices, retaliation, and increases in output. The most difficult aspect of the analysis of platforms is incorporating the actions and responses of competitors.

It is important to understand how these investments influence a firm's commitment to a market. Too much flexibility can send the wrong signal in industries where entry is imminent. The option to wait before launching a new product that cannibalizes existing sales is attractive for a leader, until someone else enters and exploits the opportunity.

Though these are difficult issues, a few heuristics can be given with confidence. A common piece of advice has been that it is better to wait than to commit too early to a technology when there is high uncertainty over what customers want. Yet, at the same time, early commitment to a technology is often the way in which uncertainty is resolved; by early commitment, a firm can influence the evolution of the industry to favor their platform. As a rule, early commitment in such industries will tend to dominate the advantages of waiting.

Of course, there are cases when early commitment is not advisable. A good example is the restriction on the sale of cellular phones and services by some governments. In Japan, one electronics company developed what its managers felt were advanced proprietary technologies. This investment raised the costs of development and, consequently, the price of the phone. Offering less expensive but still high-quality systems, Motorola and NTT won the two licenses granted by the ministry for telecommunications to serve a particular region in Japan.

If not for the government restrictions, the investment in new cellular technologies may have proved worthwhile. The high costs of the technologies would cause initial losses, but there were anticipated benefits. Learning how to apply, develop, and manufacture products using the technology is earned over time; customers may then identify the technology with the firm (e.g. Xerox or Velcro). But neither benefit can be gained without experience selling to a market; government regulation eradicated the value of this platform.

The Luxury of Losing Money

It is important for financial institutions and corporate management to underwrite losses in the short run if there are to be any long-term advantages. Of course, Keynes's dictum that "we are all dead in the long run" has a peculiar implication. Firms unable to finance these losses get locked in a vicious cycle, whereby concerns over surviving the threat of bankruptcy dominates the ability to invest in the long run. In the meantime, firms with sufficient foresight and resources are on a virtuous cycle of investments in capabilities which build the platforms for years to come. Not surprisingly, firms that begin their lives during difficult times have a hard time catching up; they never had the luxury of being able to invest for tomorrow.[19]

It has been a point of contention over the past few years that trends such as leveraged buyouts forebode a brighter future – the resulting debt burden forces management to bear down on the fundamentals of making money. However, the evidence shows that too severe pressure on cash flows drains money from R&D and other investments with long-term payoffs.[20] In industries with substantial growth opportunities, Keynes' dictum will be proven right just because the short-run question of survival dominates the necessity of foresight.

The United States and many other countries have now emerged from a decade of excess that centered on the short run. Many corporations are flatter and more focussed than ever. If they face a danger, it is the failure to develop heuristics to guide investments for future growth. The idea of a platform investment is directed at developing such heuristics to aid the understanding of how capabilities must be built in anticipation of the future. Flexibility is of no value in the absence of the

resources required for execution. Learning new capabilities is ultimately the most critical investment in opportunity for the long haul.

Notes

1   See Stewart Myers "Determinants of Corporate Borrowing," *Journal of Financial Economics*, **5** 147–75; see also
    S. Myers, "Finance Theory and Financial Strategy," In A. Hax (ed.) *Readings on Strategic Management*,
    Cambridge, MA: Ballinger, 1984. These ideas have been expanded by Carl Kester, "Today's Options for
    Tomorrow's Growth," *Harvard Business Review* (March/April 1984); William Hamilton and Graham
    Mitchell, "What Is Your R&D Worth," *The McKinsey Quarterly* (1990), pp. 150–60; and Tom Copeland and
    Jon Weiner, "Proactive Management of Uncertainty," *The McKinsey Quarterly* (1990), pp. 133–52; Leon
    Trigeorsis and Scott Mason,"Valuing Managerial Flexibility," *Midland Corporate Finance Journal* (1988), pp.
    14–21.
2   See Jay Barney, "Strategic Factor Markets: Expectations, Luck, and Business Strategy," *Management Science*, **32**
    (1986): 1231–41; Richard Rumelt, "Towards a Strategic Theory of the Firm," in Robert Boyden Lamb (ed.)
    Competitive Strategic Management, Englewood Cliffs, NJ: Prentice Hall, Inc., 1984; Sidney Winter, "Knowledge
    and Competence as Strategic Assets," in D. Teece (ed.) *The Competitive Challenge – Strategies for Industrial
    Innovation and Renewal*, Cambridge, MA: Ballinger, 1987; and David Teece, Gary Pisano, and Amy Shuen,
    "Resource-Based View of the Firm," mimeo, 1991.
3   There are more technical obstacles to the application of exact formulations, with a principal problem being the
    strong assumptions of "risk-neutral" valuations in the absence of arbitrage opportunities. Techniques, such as
    Monte Carlo simulations or decision trees, generally ignore entirely the option value, even they treat
    uncertainty explicitly.
4   Johnson and Kaplan (1987) *Relevance Lost: The Rise and Fall of Management Accounting*. Boston, MA: Harvard
    Business School Press.
5   For two explanations, see Michael Dertouzos, Richard Lester, and Robert Solow, *Made in America: Regaining the
    Productive Edge*, Cambridge, MA: MIT Press, 1989; and Michael Porter (ed.) *Investment Horizons in American
    Business*, Boston, MA: Harvard Business School Press.
6   Useem and Gottlieb estimate the share of institutions holding equity in the U.S. to have risen from 29 percent
    in 1980 to 46 percent in 1990. See Michael Useem and Martin Gottlieb, "Corporate Restructuring, Ownership-
    Disciplined Alignment, and the Reorganization of Management." *Human Resource Management*, **29** (1990);
    285–306. Unpublished data from the Tokyo Stock Exchange shows financial institutions holding 38.5 percent
    of Japanese equity in 1980 and 42.5 percent in 1988. For an overview, see Michael Porter, "Capital Disadvan-
    tage: America's Failing Capital Investment System," *Harvard Business Review* (September/October 1992), pp.
    65–82.
7   Stephen Prowse (1990) "Institutional Investment Patterns and Corporate Financial Behavior in the United
    States and Japan," *Journal of Financial Economics*, **27**, pp. 43–66; Michael Gerlach, "The Japanese Corporate
    Network: A Blockmodel Approach," *Administrative Science Quarterly*, **37** (1992), 105–139; and Erik Berglof and
    Enrico Perotti, "The Japanese Financial Keiretsu as a Collective Enforcement Mechanism," working paper 91–
    09, MIT Japan Program, 1991.
8   The data are summarized in Bruce Kogut, "Capital Structure and Financial Institutions in the Federal Republic
    of Germany," unpublished manuscript, 1982; primary data are drawn from Studienkommission, *Grundsatzfragen
    der Kreditwirtschaft*, Bericht der Studienkommission, Ministry of Finance, Bonn: Wilhelm Stollfuss Verlag,
    1979; reliance on short-term debt is described in Charles Calomiris, "Regulation, Industrial Structure, and
    Instability in U.S. Banking: An Historical Perspective," mimeo, Wharton School, University of Pennsylvania,
    1992.
9   Takeo Hoshi, Anil Kashyap, and David Schaftstein (1990) "Bank Monitoring and Investment: Evidence from

the Changing Structure of Japanese Corporate Banking Relationships," in R. Glenn Hubbard (ed.) *Information, Investment, and Capital Markets*, Chicago, IL: University of Chicago.

10 J. Bradford Long (1991) "Did J.P. Morgan's Men Add Value?" in Peter Temin (ed.) *Inside the Business Enterprise: Historical Perspectives on the Use of Information*, Chicago, IL: University of Chicago Press.

11 Michael Porter's *Competitive Strategy* (New York, NY: Free Press, 1980) represents the most well-known statement of this approach.

12 See Bruce Kogut and Udo Zander (1992) "Knowledge of the Firm, Combinative Capabilities, and the Replication of Technology," *Organization Science*, 3, 383–97. Carliss Baldwin and Kim Clark ["Capabilities and Capital Investment: New Perspectives on Capital Budgeting," working paper 92–004, 1991, Harvard Business School] develop in detail the link between options and capabilities.

13 Prahalad, C.K. and Hamel, G (1990) "The Core Competence of the Corporation," *Harvard Business Review* (May–June), pp. 79–91.

14 See the fascinating account by Paul Adler, "The Learning Bureaucracy: New United Motor Manufacturing," in B. Staw and L. Cummings (eds) *Research in Organizational Behavior*, Greenwich, CT: JAI Press.

15 See also, Bruce Kogut "Joint Ventures and the Option to Acquire and to Expand," *Management Science* (1991), pp. 19–33.

16 *Fortune*, 1992, p. 60; cited by Bernard Wolf and Steven Globerman, "Strategic Alliances in the Automotive Industry: Motives and Implications," mimeo, York University, 1992.

17 See also, Nalin Kulatilaka (1993) *The Value of Flexibility: The Case of a Dual-fuel Industrial Steam Boiler*, Financial Management Association, pp. 271–80.

18 See also, Bruce Kogut and Nalin Kulatilaka, "Operating Flexibility, Global Manufacturing, and the Option Value of a Multinational Network," *Management Science* (forthcoming).

19 See Glenn Carroll and Michael Hannan (1989) "Density Delay in the Evolution of Organizational Populations: A Model and Five Empirical Tests," *Administrative Science Quarterly*, 34 (3).

20 See Bronwyn Hall (1991) "Corporate Restructuring and Investment Horizons," Working Paper 3794, National Bureau of Economic Research.

17

Another Hidden Edge: Japanese Management Accounting

TOSHIRO HIROMOTO

HITOTSUBASHI UNIVERSITY

Much has been written about why Japanese manufacturers continue to outperform their U.S. competitors in cost, quality, and on-time delivery. Most experts point to practices like just-in-time production, total quality control, and the aggressive use of flexible manufacturing technologies. One area that has received less attention, but that I believe contributes mightily to Japanese competitiveness, is how many companies' management accounting systems reinforce a top-to-bottom commitment to process and product innovation.

I have studied management accounting systems at Japanese companies in several major industries including automobiles, computers, consumer electronics, and semiconductors. Although practices varied greatly, several related patterns did emerge. These patterns differentiate certain aspects of Japanese management accounting from established practices in the United States.

Like their U.S. counterparts, Japanese companies must value inventory for tax purposes and financial statements. But the Japanese don't let these accounting procedures determine how they measure and control organizational activities. Japanese companies tend to use their management control systems to support and reinforce their manufacturing strategies. A more direct link therefore exists between management accounting practices and corporate goals.

Japanese companies seem to use accounting systems more to motivate employees to act in accordance with long-term manufacturing strategies than to provide senior management with precise data on costs, variances, and profits. Accounting plays more of an "influencing" role than an "informing" role. For example, high-level Japanese managers seem to worry less about whether an overhead allocation systems reflects the precise demands each product makes on corporate resources than about how the system affects the cost-reduction priorities of middle managers and shop-floor workers. As a result, they sometimes use allocation techniques that executives in the United States might dismiss as simplistic or even misguided.

Accounting in Japan also reflects and reinforces an overriding commitment to market-driven management. When estimating costs on new products, for example, many companies make it a point not to rely completely on prevailing engineering standards. Instead, they establish target costs derived from estimates of a competitive market price. These target costs are usually well below currently achievable costs, which are based on standard technologies and processes. Managers then set benchmarks to measure incremental progress toward meeting the target cost objectives.

Several companies I studied also de-emphasize standard cost systems for monitoring factory performance. In general, Japanese management accounting does not stress optimizing within existing constraints. Rather, it encourages employees to make continual improvements by tightening those constraints.

The following cases highlight some of the differences between management accounting in Japan and the United States. My intention is to be suggestive, not definitive. Not all Japanese companies use the techniques I describe, and some U.S. companies have adopted approaches similar to what I have seen in Japan.

Allocating Overhead

American executives have been barraged with criticism about how long-accepted techniques for allocating manufacturing overhead can distort product costs and paint a flawed picture of the profitability of manufacturing operations. Accounting experts challenge direct labor hours as an overhead allocation base since direct labor represents only a small percentage of total costs in most manufacturing environments. They argue that a logical and causal relationship should exist between the overhead burden and the assignment of costs to individual products. They believe that an allocation system should capture as precisely as possible the reality of shop-floor costs.

Japanese companies are certainly aware of this perspective, but many of the companies I examined don't seem to share it. Consider the practices of the Hitachi division that operates the world's largest factory devoted exclusively to videocassette recorders. The Hitachi VCR plant is highly automated yet continues to use direct labor as the basis for allocating manufacturing overhead. Overhead allocation doesn't reflect the actual production process in the factory's automated environment. When I asked the accountants whether that policy might lead to bad decisions, they responded with an emphatic no. Hitachi, like many large Japanese manufacturers, is convinced that reducing direct labor is essential for ongoing cost improvement. The company is committed to aggressive automation to promote long-term competitiveness. Allocating overhead based on direct labor creates the desired strong proautomation incentives throughout the organization.

The perspective offered by Hitachi managers seems to be shared by their counterparts at many other companies. It is more important, they argue, to have an overhead allocation system (and other aspects of management accounting) that motivates employees to work in harmony with the company's long-term goals than to pinpoint production costs. Japanese managers want their accounting systems to help create a competitive future, not quantify the performance of their organizations at this moment.

Another Hitachi factory (this one in the refrigeration and air-conditioning equipment sector) employs an overhead allocation technique, based on the number of parts in product models, to influence its engineers' design decisions. Japanese companies have long known what more and more U.S. companies are now recognizing – that the number of parts in a product, especially custom parts, directly relates to the amount of overhead. Manufacturing costs increase with the complexity of the production process, as measured, for example, by the range of products built in a factory or the number of parts per product. In plants assembling diverse products, reducing the number of parts and promoting the use of standard parts across product lines can lower costs dramatically.

Using standard parts can also lower materials costs, insofar as it creates possibilities for more aggressive volume buying. Yet on a product-by-product basis, many cost systems fail to recognize these economies.

Consider a factory building several different products. The products all use one or both of two parts, A and B, which the factory buys in roughly equal amounts. Most of the products use both parts. The unit cost of part A is $7, of part B, $10. Part B has more capabilities than part A; in fact, B can replace A. If the factory doubles its purchases of part B, it qualifies for a discounted $8 unit price. For products that incorporate both parts, substituting B for A makes sense to qualify for the discount. (The total parts cost is $17 using A and B, $16 using Bs only.) Part B, in other words, should become a standard part for the factory. But departments building products that use only part A may be reluctant to accept the substitute part B because, even discounted, the cost of B exceeds that of A.

This factory needs an accounting system that motivates departments to look beyond their parochial interests for the sake of enterprise-level cost reduction. Hitachi has adopted such an approach by adding overhead surcharges to products that use non-standard parts. The more custom parts in a product, the higher the overhead charge.

Accounting for Market-driven Design

By the time a new product enters the manufacturing stage, opportunities to economize significantly are limited. As the Hitachi refrigerator example suggests, Japanese companies have long recognized that the design stage holds the greatest promise for supporting low-cost production. Many U.S. manufacturers, including Texas Instruments, Hewlett-Packard, and Ford, are also making competitive strides in this area. But certain Japanese companies have taken the process even further. They don't simply design products to make better use of technologies and work flows; they design and build products that will meet the price required for market success – whether or not that price is supported by current manufacturing practices. Their management accounting systems incorporate this commitment.

Daihatsu Motor Company, a medium-sized automobile producer that has yet to enter the U.S. market, provides a good example of market-driven accounting practices. It installed the *genka kikaku* product development system in its factories soon after affiliating with Toyota, which pioneered the approach. The *genka kikaku* process at Daihatsu usually lasts three years, at which time the new car goes into production. The process begins when the *shusa* (the product manager responsible for a new car from planning through sales) instructs the functional departments to submit the features and performance specifications that they believe the car should include. The *shusa* then makes recommendations to the senior managers, who issue a development order.

Next comes cost estimation. Management does not simply turn over the development order to the accountants and ask what it would cost to build the car based on existing engineering standards. Rather, Daihatsu establishes a target selling price based on what it believes the market will accept and specifies a target profit margin that reflects the company's strategic plans and financial projections. The difference between these two figures represents the "allowable cost" per car.

In practice, this target cost is far below what realistically can be attained. So each department calculates an "accumulated cost" based on current technologies and practices – that is, the standard cost achievable with no innovation. Finally, management establishes a target cost that represents a middle ground between these two estimates. This adjusted price-profit margin cost becomes the goal toward which everyone works.

At the design stage, engineers working on different parts of the car interact frequently with the various players (purchasing, shop-floor supervisors, parts suppliers) who will implement the final design. As the design process unfolds, the participants compare estimated costs with the target. The variances are fed back to the product developers, and the cycle repeats: design proposals, cost estimates, variance calculations, value engineering analysis to include desired features at the lowest possible cost, and redesign. The cycle ends with the approval of a final design that meets the target cost.

A similar dynamic operates at the production stage, where Daihatsu uses complementary approaches to manage costs: total plant cost management and *dai-atari kanri*, or perunit cost management.

Reports based on total plant cost management are prepared for senior executives and plant managers. The studies compare budgeted costs with actual costs for an entire factory. Reports generated by the *dai-atari kanri* system are intended for managers at specific workstations. Comparisons between budgeted and actual costs are made only for "variable" charges, which include some costs, like tools, that do not vary strictly with short-term output. Put simply, items subject to *dai-atari kanri* include all costs that can be reduced through workers' continual efforts and process improvement activities – that is, controllable costs.

In production, as in the design stage, Daihatsu does not take a static approach to cost management. During the first year of production for a new car, the budgeted cost reflects targets set during the *genka kikaku* process. This cost is a starting point, however, not an ultimate goal; over the course of the year, it is tightened monthly by a cost-reduction rate based on short-term profit objectives. In subsequent years, the actual cost of the previous period becomes the starting point for further tightening, thereby creating a cost-reduction dynamic for as long as the model remains in production.

Good-bye to Standard Costs

The market-driven philosophy at Daihatsu and other Japanese companies helps to explains why standard cost systems are not used as widely in Japan as they are in the United States. Standard costs reflect an engineering mind-set and technology-driven management. The goal is to minimize variances between budgeted and actual costs – to perform as closely as possible to best available practice. Market-driven management, on the other hand, emphasizes doing what it takes to achieve a desired performance level under market conditions. How efficiently a company *should* be able to build a product is less important to the Japanese than how efficiently it *must* be able to build it for maximum marketplace success.

Many Japanese companies that have used standard cost systems seem to be moving beyond them. NEC, the diversified electronics giant, designed and installed its standard cost system in the 1950s. The company still uses standard cost reports as a factory management tool and continues to train new employees in the system. But NEC recognizes that it has reached a strategic turning point and it is adjusting its management accounting policies accordingly.

NEC installed its standard cost system when it was supplying a stable product range (mostly telephones and exchangers) at stable prices to a large and stable customer, Nippon Telegraph & Telephone (NTT). Today NEC produces a vast array of products subject to rapid obsolescence and technological change. Its product line poses severe challenges to the standard cost system. The cost standards cannot be revised quickly enough for many products, so variance reports are increasingly open to question. (NEC revises its cost standards every 6 months, and even then only for a subset of products.) As a result, the company is relying more heavily on departmental budgets than product-by-product variances from standard costs. As with Daihatsu, targets are based on market demands and planned profit levels and are tightened over time.

The U.S. subsidiary of a major Japanese electronics company takes this budgeting approach even further. Its production and marketing departments operate as separate profit centers. These departments interact to establish internal transfer prices for products. The transfer price is a negotiated percentage of the market prices. Under this method, market prices critically influence departmental performance, since market prices are the basis for determining transfer prices. Both the production and marketing functions are encouraged to respond to market demand and competitive trends rather than focus solely on internal indicators.

The company recently extended this approach to its sales department, which is separate from marketing. Selling costs used to be allocated to individual products under a standard cost approach. Now the sales department operates as a profit center and negotiates commission levels with the marketing department. Through the cost system, these commissions are then assigned to products. Thus the marketing department can make product decisions without accepting selling expenses as given, which increases pressure on the sales force to operate as efficiently as possible.

Accounting and Strategy

The accounting practices I have described do not necessarily represent Japanese practices as a whole. They do, however, point to a central principle that seems to guide management accounting in Japan – that accounting policies should be subservient to corporate strategy, not independent of it. Japanese manufacturing strategy places high premiums on quality and timely delivery in addition to low-cost production. Thus companies make extensive use, certainly more than many of their U.S. competitors, of nonfinancial measures to evaluate factory performance. The reason is straightforward: if a management accounting system measures only costs, employees tend to focus on costs exclusively.

I have encountered many practices designed to capture the nonfinancial dimensions of factory performance. One Japanese automaker wanted to motivate its managers and employees to reduce throughout time in assembly operations. It recognized that direct labor hours measure costs, not the actual time required to build and ship a car. So for time-management purposes, the company has replaced direct labor hours with a variable called managed hours per unit. In addition to direct labor, this new measure incorporates the time required for nonproductive activities like equipment maintenance and product repairs.

In an effort to improve machine and equipment efficiency, many companies are emphasizing preventive and corrective maintenance over breakdown maintenance. (Corrective maintenance means redesigning equipment to reduce failures and facilitate routine maintenance.) This emphasis goes beyond exhorting shop-floor personnel to pay more attention to their machines. Companies regularly measure rates of unexpected equipment failures, ratios of preventive and corrective maintenance to total maintenance, and other variables that track machine performance. These results are widely distributed and evaluated during small group discussions in the factory.

For companies to maintain competitive advantage, employees must be continually innovative. This requires motivation. A product designer must be motivated to play a significant role in cost reduction. Shop-floor workers and supervisors must constantly strive to improve efficiency beyond what "best practice" currently dictates. The Japanese have demonstrated that management accounting can play a significant role in integrating the innovative efforts of employees with the company's long-term strategies and goals.

VI

IMPLEMENTING GLOBAL STRATEGY

The acid test of a well-managed company is being able to conceive, develop, and implement an effective global strategy. Because of its inherent difficulties, global strategy development presents one of the stiffest challenges for managers today. Companies that operate on a global scale today need to integrate their world-wide strategy in contrast to the earlier multinational or multidomestic approach. The earlier strategies would more truly be categorized as multidomestic strategies rather than as global strategies.

The implications of a distinction between multidomestic and global strategy are quite profound. In a multidomestic strategy, a firm manages its international activities like a portfolio. Its subsidiaries or other operations around the world each control all the important activities necessary to maximize their returns in their area of operation independent of the activities of other subsidiaries in the firm. The subsidiaries enjoy a large degree of autonomy and the firms' activities in each of the national markets in which it operates is determined by the competitive conditions in that national market. In contrast, a global strategy integrates the activities of a firm on a world-wide basis to capture the linkages among countries and to treat the entire world as a single borderless market. This requires more than the transferring of intangible assets between countries.

Chapter 18 explores ways in which U.S. companies can gain global competitiveness. The nation's global competitiveness hinges on the strengths of companies operating in and out the country. A policy premised on "progressive knowledge" is proposed to promote the market environment for design and manufacturing process research and training. The future of the U.S. depends on the ability of its firms to lead the world in their organizational learning capabilities.

Chapter 19 discusses fundamental differences in *modus operandi* between U.S. and Japanese companies that have been the primary source of strategy gaps widely debated over the years. The postwar "economic miracles" of the East and Southeast Asian countries have shifted the pendulum of international trade from cross-Atlantic to cross-Pacific in recent years. The nature of the cross-Pacific bilateral and multilateral trade and investment has been shaped mostly by companies from the United States and Japan, the two largest economies in the world. This chapter addresses how U.S. and Japanese companies have taken part in the growth of the cross-Pacific trade and how their strategy has affected their respective long-term competitiveness.

Chapter 20 focuses on the crux of the sources of global competitiveness and explores how R&D resources should be allocated and where they should be used. One aspect of R&D strategies that often goes unheeded is how implementation is related to the corporation's core competency – what it does best. Technological advances, R&D, and strategic visions must be developed in concert with the corporation's core competencies, affording it the opportunity to leverage past success into future opportunities.

18

How the United States Can Be Number One Again: Resurrecting the Industrial Policy Debate

PETER R. DICKSON

UNIVERSITY OF WISCONSIN

AND

MICHAEL R. CZINKOTA

GEORGETOWN UNIVERSITY

I would ask whether, upon the whole, you consider any danger likely to arise to our manufacture from competition, even if the French were supplied with machinery equally good and cheap as our own? – They will always be behind us until their general habits approximate to ours: and they must be behind us for many reasons that I have before given. Why must they be behind us? – One other reason is, that a cotton manufacturer who left Manchester seven years ago, would be driven out of the market by the men who are now living in it, provided his knowledge had not kept pace with those who have been during that time constantly profiting by the progressive improvements that have taken place in that period: this progressive knowledge and experience is our great power and advantage.

– Charles Babbage[1]

Charles Babbage, one of the first total quality management (TQM) experts of the Industrial Revolution said this in an 1830s report of a Committee of the British House of Commons "On the Export of Tools and Machinery." The answer to the competitive threat that American enterprise and the U.S. economy face today is the same: *the application of progressive knowledge and experience (i.e. managerial innovation) is our great power and advantage.*

Great Britain ignored this profound insight and did not invest in manufacturing and design research and education as heavily as its emerging economic rivals Germany and the United States. Great Britain squandered its lead in progressive knowledge and lost its greatness. By 1929, helped by Henry Ford's automobile design and manufacturing innovations, the U.S. economy generated 34.4 percent of the world's total production (Britain, debilitated by the first world war, was next with 10.4

"How the U.S. Can Be Number One Again: Resurrecting the Industrial Policy Debate," by Peter R. Dickson and Michael R. Czinkota, *Columbia Journal of World Business*, **31**, 3, Fall 1996: 76–87. Reprinted by permission of JAI Press Inc.

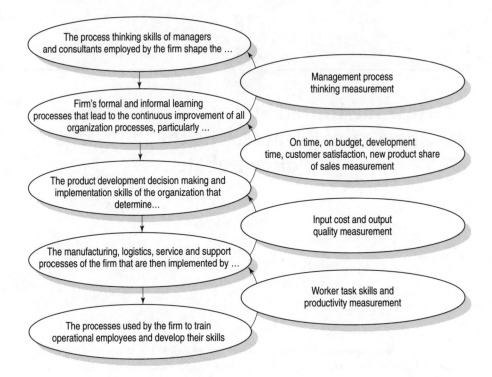

Figure 18.1 The hierarchy of process skills

percent).[2] At the end of WW II, the United States reached the zenith of its dominance. Since then, a significant amount of this lead in progressive knowledge and experience in manufacturing and product design has been lost.

The purpose of this paper is to discuss how the United States can reverse this trend, which is the most direct cause of the stagnation of the average American's standard of living over the last 20 years. We do so by examining the recommendations of Peter Drucker, who has been a leading thinker and writer on management theory and practice for four decades; Michael Porter, the Harvard industrial organization economist who has led the development of competitive strategy thinking over the last 10 years; and Robert Reich, the labor economist and President Clinton's high-profile Secretary of Labor.

We use the emergent process learning paradigm to evaluate the economic insights and policy recommendations of these high-visibility thinkers and to offer an alternative policy. The extraordinary success of the TQM and continuous-process improvement movements have swept away the old paradigms of economic growth, organization economics and management theory and replaced them with a single, parsimonious paradigm of process learning and process capital.[3]

The theory of process capital posits a hierarchy of process skills that are needed in the global labor market (see figure 18.1). The primary responsibility of senior management is to develop the organization's higher-order learning processes that build the process capital of the firm. Be it small or large, a family business or a multinational, a firm must apply these learning skills to constantly improve its product development processes, which will in turn shape its manufacturing or operations processes. Finally, production and service workers must be trained and retrained to be able to execute and improve the manufacturing and operations processes.

The learning processes of an organization create competitive advantage. They are a form of capital in that they generate future profit streams. Common to all firms' success and survival are the learning processes that a firm develops to continually improve its lower-order processes. The most important higher-order learning processes are the benchmarking processes that improve a firm's ability to quickly imitate the world's best and the systematic experimentation processes that a firm uses to introduce innovations into its processes. One such recommended experimentation process has been called "plan–do–assess–act" and has been widely applied to continuously improve manufacturing and distribution processes.[4] Other higher-order processes that are critical drivers of an organization's learning capabilities are the reward processes that a firm uses to reinforce learning and the feedback control processes that a firm uses to measure process input, output and flow characteristics, such as costs, time taken, quality and customer satisfaction (see figure 18.1). They are called higher-order processes because they influence the improvement of all of a firm's processes.

Where firms differ is in the owners' and managers' choice of lower-order processes that they attempt to develop into a distinctive competency.[5] Some choose to develop skills in applying particular technologies to manufacturing processes, as Intel did in the manufacture of computer chips. Others focus on distribution and communication technologies, such as the efforts of Federal Express in the areas of logistics and tracking. However, they all employ similar generic higher-order learning processes (e.g. benchmarking and activity-based cost control) to develop such distinctive process competencies.

The economic development of manufacturing firms in emerging economies can be conceptualized as progressing up the process skills hierarchy. For example, having mastered many manufacturing processes, Korean firms are now raising their product development processes to compete with the world's best. To stay ahead, American and Japanese firms are having to continuously improve all of their processes by becoming superior learning organizations led by superior process thinkers. They are getting help from consultants such as Shinijursu in Japan, which has became famous for its expertise in *kaizen* (continuous improvement learning) processes, and Andersen Consulting in the United States, which markets its benchmarking and other higher-order learning skills.

The process skills hierarchy crystallizes the challenges confronting American industrial policy. Over the last 50 years, the industrial policy of Japan, Korea, Taiwan, Malaysia and other high-growth Asian countries has been to shelter their infant industries behind some form of trade barriers, invest heavily in manufacturing process research and training institutes, subsidize R&D investment and help domestic firms license and learn the latest innovations in manufacturing processes and technologies. What America needs is a stay-ahead industrial policy that enables American firms to become learning organizations that improve their processes more efficiently, more effectively and faster than their foreign rivals. From this perspective, we evaluate the industrial policy prescriptions of three leading experts.

The Policy Prescriptions of Drucker, Porter and Reich

Peter Drucker, Michael Porter and Robert Reich have all recently published books on national competitiveness that contain their perspectives, theories and policy prescriptions. What distinguishes their thinking from others is that all of these books were bestsellers and, therefore, very likely to shape the agenda of any industrial policy reform. They also come from three distinctive intellectual traditions: Drucker from management, Porter from industrial organization economics and Reich from labor economics. Their common thread is that all three recognize that the key to competitive advantage is (progressive) knowledge. In this section we contrast and compare their views.

A MARXIAN MISTAKE

According to Peter Drucker's view of economic history, capitalist society was dominated by two social classes: the capitalist who owned the means of production and the workers who were variously alienated and exploited. The individual "capitalists" reached their zenith of influence in the late nineteenth century, and blue collar worker influence peaked about 1950, before the "management revolution" occurred. In Drucker's post-capitalist society:

> The basic economic resource – "the means of production" to use the economist's term – is no longer capital, nor natural resources (the economists' land), nor "labor." It is and will be knowledge ... value is now created by "productivity" and "innovation" both applications of knowledge at work.[6]

In fact, inventions in economic organization processes have been creating and recreating capitalist societies since their emergence in the seventeenth century. Consequently, the term post-capitalist is catchy, but misleading, because capitalist societies have never been dominated by the capitalist or the laborer but by the inventor and entrepreneur and their creative destruction.[7] The investor class and the working class benefited to varying degrees from such innovation/imitation, but Drucker, like Marx, is fundamentally wrong in believing that either one of these classes was ever, or will ever be, the dominant player. The real movers and shakers of the world economy are the manufacturing, design and organizational learning process innovators. It is they who change the economic processes. These economic processes in turn change the economic, social and political structure. Robert Reich calls for symbolic analysts who identify, analyze, solve or broker problems by manipulating symbols and asserts that, "In this new world economy, symbolic analysts hold a dominant position."[8] The implication is that routine production and service workers are more vulnerable to the export of jobs and capital to cheaper labor markets in developing countries.

From the process paradigm perspective, Peter Drucker is, however, correct in identifying that America's future will depend upon the ability of its economic enterprise to become knowledge-generating, learning and teaching organizations: "Every organization of today has to build into its very structure the management of change."[9] The implementation of such constant change processes described in figure 18.1 must become an organization core competence – requiring ever better organizational learning processes. This will require organizations staffed with well-trained engineers and technicians (symbolic analysts) with the capacity and the motivation to continuously learn how to improve manufacturing, design and learning processes through experimentation, innovation and imitation.

DETERMINANTS AND DRIVERS

In his book *The Competitive Advantage of Nations*, Michael Porter asserts that the task is to understand why a nation is a desirable home base to develop strategy, the core product and processes and the firm's proprietary skills.[10] Like Drucker, Porter recognizes that "firms gain and sustain competitive advantage in international competition through improvement, innovation and upgrading" (p. 70). He recognizes the importance of how a nation's firms mobilize the available resources and technologies (including procedures and routines used) and calls such resourcefulness "advanced factors" (p. 76).

The limitation of Porter's analysis is that, unlike Drucker and Reich, he does not make such process innovation/imitation skills the focus of his treatise. He calls for a theory of competitive disequilibrium to explain how a nation might foster the competitive thinking of its enterprises. But instead of developing such a theory of product and process innovation, Porter opts for the more traditional international trade paradigm by proposing that factors of production, home demand, supporting industries and the competitive structure of firms within the nation determine a nation's success in a particular industry. He forms these four determinants into a "diamond" that is used to analyze national competitiveness.

By contrast, Drucker and Reich propose that the underlying driver of this diamond is the competitive rationality and process thinking skills of the management of firms within a nation.[11] Rapid innovation and learning affect supply conditions, which in turn direct, shape and determine the demand conditions within the home nation (besides exogenous factors such as climate, geography and cultural influences on demand). Such organizational process thinking also creates the new economic processes that change the competitive and economic structure of the home industry. Furthermore, it creates the supporting supply industries and ultimately shapes the economic and social structure of the nation.

As an example, the development of new deep mining processes in the late 1700s in England required the pumping of massive volumes of water, which led to better pumps, better metal boring processes and better steam engines to drive the pumps. As a nation of fishermen, throughout the 1600s the Dutch further developed ship building skills, which led to rope making skills, sail making process skills and fine carpentry skills.[12] The processes that a nation's firms use in manufacturing, distribution, new product development and in learning how to improve all of the processes and routines used in the firm were the very essence of international competition and the economic prosperity of nations in the past and continue in their crucial role in today's world.[13]

OF CAUSE AND EFFECT

Both Porter and Drucker also seem to understate the role of the emerging third world economies as creative forces in the new world economic order. For example, Drucker posits that "The forces that are creating the post-capitalist society and post-capitalist polity originate in the developed world."[14] Many would argue that this premise is wrong, leading to overconfidence in our control over our comparative advantage and economic future.

The changing global political parameters have already, and will continue to, precipitate major shifts in geo-economics. A new world order is emerging as a result of the integration into the global economy of the newly capitalist nations and much of the developing world. With more than three billion inhabitants, many of them hungry for a better life, these new free market adherents are competing as never before in the global marketplace. For example, in just three years the developing world's exports have jumped by some three percentage points to a 20 percent share of global exports.[15]

The drive, intense ambitions and imitative skills of the workers and management in the newly "top-tier" economies, such as South Korea, Taiwan, Singapore, Hong Kong and Malaysia, and current third world countries, such as China, have already been shown to more than compensate for a historic lack of process innovation skill and capital. As these economies blossom, they have created tremendous competitive pressures on the old world advanced economies to accelerate their rate of process innovation. For example, European and Japanese multinationals are responding by putting increasing effort into process innovations.[16] Furthermore, the emergence of highly efficient global transportation and information highways is facilitating the possibility of a tremendous growth in production out-sourcing to suppliers in the emerging economies.[17] It is the very rapid development of developing economies that is forcing the industries and firms in developed economies to become even more innovative in their use of knowledge and technology.[18] Most of the innovations may be made in the developed world, but the competitive pressure to so innovate is coming from the developing world that is chasing the innovators down their process learning curves. The drivers of the global marketplace over the next 20 to 30 years will be the emerging massive skilled labor and consumer markets that stretch from Warsaw down to Delhi and across to Shanghai. How the developed countries co-develop with the vigorous new economies, their immense pools of human enterprise and imitative skills and their immense pent-up demand for consumer goods and services, is a fundamental issue.[19]

A LESSON IN TRANSACTION COSTS

Absent from any of these three eminent analysts' visions are further lessons that we can learn from economic history, particularly from the rise of the British global trading empire. The British economy was able to gain a lead over its European rival economies in the period from 1650 to 1900 because it had developed a more efficient transportation infrastructure and a minimum of feudal baronies or estates demanding throughway tolls. It also owned the largest international merchant fleet through its Rule Britannia navy policy. The British developed much better ships and much cheaper iron cannons. Through their access to low-cost American wood and iron resources, they were able to have as much as half of their merchant fleet built of American resources.[20] The British continued to build on their shipping advantage by achieving remarkable breakthroughs in streamshipping. So efficient was the British merchant steamship of the 1890s, with its triple-expansion engine and assembly line construction, that it could carry a ton of cargo per knot on "scarcely more than the energy released by the burning of a couple of sheets of writing paper."[21] The resulting lower transaction costs enabled greater general commerce, including a larger mass market and supply out-sourcing.[22]

In contrast, today, Eastern Europe and the former Soviet Union are faced with exceedingly high transaction costs. These countries are battling space constraints, poor supply lines, limited rolling stock and insufficient transportation systems. Producers know little about benchmarking, inventory carrying cost, store assortment efficiencies and replenishment techniques. The need to develop integrated supplier-distributor alliances and efficient communication systems, such as electronic data interchange, is poorly understood. As a result of all these distribution process inefficiencies, distribution costs alone are well above 30 percent GNP – compared to 11 percent for both the United States and Japan.[23] These logistic shortcomings are severe inhibitors to the participation of these countries in global commerce and the rebuilding of their economies.

On the other hand, we are frequently told that American business is poised to gain major comparative advantages through its innovative use of the new global information highways. What is not addressed is the sustainability of these transaction costs and control advantages. Britain was able to maintain its lead for more than two centuries. The advantage the United States has today in its use of the new global information highway will not be sustainable for long, as foreign competitors quickly imitate by using the same global information highways themselves. Indeed, it is possible that a major use of the information superhighway will be to make it much easier for foreign businesses to use the skills of American symbolic analysts to improve the design and control of their manufacturing and distribution processes. What Robert Reich fails to sufficiently recognize in his vision of a borderless global labor market is that the same competitive forces that lead American firms to export jobs to cheaper labor markets will cause foreign firms to import and imitate the symbolic analytic skills of the American labor market. Basically, what all three authorities fail to fully appreciate is the pent-up motivation and creative ability of foreign firms and labor markets to catch up with American know-how. At the root of their lack of analytical incisiveness is the fundamental process capital and economic development principle that imitative learning curves are steeper than innovative learning curves.

THE EXPERTS' POLICY PRESCRIPTIONS

The concrete policy proposals of Drucker, Porter and Reich also lack decisiveness. Peter Drucker's prescriptions fall into three types: implementation of *periodic* learning processes and rules, organization recommendations, and tax policy. Although the emphasis of his management prescriptions is on innovation and knowledge acquisition and use, Drucker's proposed macroeconomic policy only indirectly promotes the *continuous* learning and dissemination of manufacturing and design process knowledge and skills.

Michael Porter's prescriptions can be summarized as having a heavy emphasis on learning through education, improving communication between research and industry, creating a more supportive tax policy and improving government regulatory processes. They have considerable merit, but, from the process capital perspective, are not focused enough on the source of the country's future competitiveness and prosperity – which is the progressiveness of its design and manufacturing process innovation.

Robert Reich's policy prescriptions are perhaps the most disappointing, because they are the least consistent with his analysis. He proposes that the future of the U.S. economy depends on Americans teaching themselves revolutionary production and problem-solving processes, i.e. developing the higher-order process skills presented in figure 18.1. Yet when it comes to policy, he recommends increased funding of general literacy, incentives to increase investment in information systems and economic inducements to attract foreign demand for symbolic analysts. He has not explained how raising the general literacy is an efficient way of creating the relatively small cadre of several hundred thousand world-beating symbolic analysts that the American economy needs to sustain its competitiveness. Promoting the export of the latest progressive knowledge that increases the competitiveness of foreign labor defies understanding. Is the Secretary of Labor seriously suggesting that we encourage our future W. Edwards Demings to spend their careers helping to create the next offshore economic miracle? Charles Babbage's recommendation is emphatically clear. Export the products of the progressive knowledge, but not the progressive knowledge itself.

A Progressive Knowledge Development Policy

So how might the United States become number one again? The industrial development policy that we propose is based on an extension of an old metaphor. It is better to teach a man to fish than to give him a fish. Yet it is *even better* to teach him how to keep improving his fishing skills. It also recognizes the following reality, emphatically stated in a recent economic report on competitiveness:

> The primary responsibility for determining how America competes with other nations rests with the managers and owners of industry. They decide whether to implement new production strategies and training policies, to invest in new equipment, to launch research projects, or introduce new products. Their decisions, which cannot be dictated from Washington, will shape the competitiveness of industry – and, ultimately, the standard of living of American workers.[24]

Washington cannot dictate corporate policy, but it can influence and support research and training to help owners, managers and engineers learn to make ever better decisions about "whether to implement new production strategies and training policies, to invest in new equipment, to launch research projects, or introduce new products." If the primary responsibility rests with managers to make excellent decisions, then the primary responsibility of government should be to do everything it can to help firms help themselves improve the quality of their managerial decision making and develop the nation's "powers of production."[25]

The most effective way of increasing the global competitiveness of American firms is for American managers to improve their management of innovation in products and processes. The best way of improving such skills is for the federal and state governments to energize the market for production and management process skills in four ways:

1. Making the *market* for process skill learning more efficient through higher quality market information;
2. Encouraging a better supply of process management skills through very focused public-private sector education and research initiatives;
3. Encouraging more demand among firms for higher process skills through tax incentives; and
4. Encouraging innovations in learning and training by designing processes and technology to match the skills of workers, rather than vice versa.

It may not be too far-fetched to envision parallels to some of the guiding principles of the General Agreement on Tariffs and Trade. These are information availability and transparency, a reduction in access barriers and a focus on efficiency. What has served to trigger major growth for world trade should also be helpful in restoring domestic economic growth and world trade leadership.

GOVERNMENT AS A PROCESS EXPERTISE MARKET FACILITATOR

There are various roles that government can play to enhance the development, use and absorption of process management skills. One key step will be an effort to establish information availability and transparency. The government, through, for example, the Department of Commerce's Technology Administration, can act as a facilitator and broker in the market for process expertise by fostering the creation and marketing of a set of sector-related Process Skills Business Directories. Put most simply, a cornerstone of our proposed industrial policy should be the encouragement of business yellow pages that list process expertise. Existing directories that come closest to this concept are directories of industrial engineering consultants, reengineering consultants, TQM consultants and design consultants. However, their primary purpose is to provide out-sourced services for a specific project rather than organizational process training and process research. These directories would provide information on all of the consultants, training companies, design companies, engineering companies, research institutes and university scholars that carry out work on management process skills.[26] In keeping with state-of-the-art technology, such directories would be available on a website, with suppliers paying for space that presents their credentials, past and present clients and other information that would increase the quality and reduce the cost of a firm searching for assistance.

The design of such an innovative directory and the organization of the process skills offered in such directories will require in-depth feasibility studies involving government officials, industry executives, professional organizations and leading scholars. However, a crucial aspect of our proposal is that the venture should be undertaken by private enterprise that is willing and able to quickly develop, launch and continue to improve the information service. If executed well and distributed widely, such directories will help create a much more efficient, competitive and progressive *process expertise market* in the United States, which will raise the average process expertise of all American firms. This approach combines market forces and the government's information gathering and dissemination capabilities to encourage the development of quality suppliers of research and training in product design process innovation and manufacturing process innovation. Existing and potential suppliers are consulting companies, trade associations, manufacturing extension partnerships sponsored by the National Bureau of Standards and Technology, industry-sponsored research and training centers, colleges of engineering, colleges of business, colleges of arts and design schools.

The idea of creating a credible electronic database on sources of process expertise and making it readily available to small and large businesses is based on a simple economic principle. If one makes the transmission of process innovation knowledge more efficient, then the rate of learning of buyers and sellers will accelerate, and the market's efficiency will increase. The principle has been applied many times in economic history.

In antiquity, centers of process learning expertise evolved that reduced the cost of transmission of ideas and innovations across professions and trades. These centers were the genesis of our modern medical schools, schools of fine arts and universities. In modern times, perhaps the best example of the value of creating learning networks, where the cost of transmitting knowledge around the network became very low and the value of the knowledge very high, are the German engineering trade schools founded in the late nineteenth century. They tended to specialize in particular manufacturing processes and, through their network of alumni and sponsors, quickly transmitted a great deal of expertise about the latest process innovations across German industry. This largely explains the superior engineering quality of German products commonly observed. In post-war

Japan, "innovation communities" were created around government laboratories, the Ministry of International Trade and Industry (MITI) and physics societies,[27] leading to similar, rapid dissemination of new processes.

We recommend the imitation of this policy, the building of many more centers of excellence in specific technologies. But we also believe that the power of the Internet can be used to disseminate more accurate information at less cost about where to find expertise in particular industrial and management processes. Making the search for and access to communities of innovation much more open, available, less costly and more rewarding is applying a fundamental principle of information economics to industrial policy. If the benefits of searching are increased and the cost of searching reduced, then more searches will be undertaken, more buyers will enter the market, and the market will become more efficient and dynamic.

A second necessary step consists of increasing the supply of process expertise. One approach to such a goal would be an increase in research funds to undertake studies of the learning processes of firms. Applied and very focused field research, rather than fuzzily related laboratory experimental research, should be particularly encouraged. University research centers could be created to study the learning processes of particular industrial sectors. Decentralization into multiple research centers would foster research innovation and strengthen the ties between academia and business. Another approach would be for federal and state governments to work with trade associations and individual companies to invest in new institutes of technology dedicated to particular process technologies.[28] While the existing Manufacturing Extension Partnership of the Commerce Department is a useful beginning, universities and trade schools should be asked to bid for such institutes. The awarding of a new institute would be based on the willingness of the applicant to marshal its existing resources around the institute and evidence of its current innovations in engineering and management education that indicate it will be progressive enough to lead rather than follow in its research and training programs. Such institutes might learn from the successes and failures of existing institutes such as MIT, CalTech, Carnegie Mellon and the Georgia Institute of Technology. The activities of the many recently created Centers for International Business Education and Research (CIBER) may also provide useful benchmark comparisons.

A third step would consist of increasing the demand for process expertise. A strategically directed tax policy could encourage demand for the buying of higher-order process learning expertise. Such a policy could be helpful in that economic historians have noted that the market for learning new technological and management processes is not always efficient and has sometimes had to be encouraged in the past by exhibitions, prizes (e.g. the Baldrige Awards) and other means.[29] Peter Drucker has attributed such resistance to managerial ego:

> To abandon anything is always bitterly resisted. People in any organization, including bureaucrats and politicians, are always attached to the obsolete; the obsolescent; the things that should have worked but didn't; the things that once were productive and no longer are. They are most attached to what in an earlier book I called "investments in managerial ego."[30]

We are, however, least optimistic that such tax incentives will work because of the high probability that an initially enlightened tax policy providing incentives to learn to use plants and equipment more efficiently would soon be perverted to provide tax incentives for the purchase of new plants and equipment. It's not the machine, it's how you use the machine that is important!

A fourth very important step consists of addressing the learning process and its direction. Even though Ross Perot's predicted giant sucking sound of displaced workers has not materialized, the fact remains that unskilled and unmotivated workers are faced with growing employment difficulties. On a regional, national and even international basis, the opportunities for these workers are shrinking and their standard of living is in decline. If the fiber of society is not to be wrung dry by transfer payments or torn apart by ever rising inequity, individual learning will have to assume a major new role.

With regards to *learning processes* themselves, we need to consider applying process innovation to learning just as we advocate its application for all other economic activities. Terms like learning efficiency, effectiveness, retention and relevance must become part and parcel of any discussion on learning. The use of new technologies, self-paced and footloose instruction, person-specific content responsiveness, benchmarking, learning absorption resting, critical knowledge deficiency detection and specific learning recycling must become commonplace in the education industry.

At the same time, however, the direction of learning must be reexamined. Currently, learning approaches focus on increasing the skills and knowledge of individuals to bring them up to "standard" for participation in the economic process. Neglected is the reverse direction, namely the need to employ the skills of the symbolic analyst to bring the economic process closer to the skill levels of individuals. A few industries have had significant success with the latter approach. For example, in the computer field, the acceptance and effective use of personal computing devices is not mainly attributable to the increased programming skills of the population at large, but rather to the simplification of computer usage.

Learning must therefore consist of two components. For the individual, it needs to focus on an improvement in the acquisition of skills and knowledge. For process innovators, it must focus on reducing the complexity of processes and bringing them into closer harmony with the existing capabilities of large portions of the workforce. New decision and implementation processes must also be learned that bring together the craft skills on the shop floor and the engineering and design skills of management.[31]

Finally, all of these policies must be largely inward-looking. Absolute priorities must be given to increasing the progressive knowledge of America's high-growth entrepreneurial firms that have created the vast majority of new, higher-paying jobs in the American economy. The fundamental objective must be to help 10,000 gifted entrepreneurs create 10,000 gifted learning organizations. This may mean limiting access of foreign firms to government supported information services, favoring research and education institutions that work with high-growth American firms that are creating jobs and focusing on the domestic development of such process skills rather than on their export. Put most simply, we can no longer afford to keep giving away our most valuable progressive knowledge to the rest of the world. Educators and policy makers who object to such self-interested economic development policy are as misdirected as isolationist extremists in the other direction who would erect crude trade barriers around America to preserve its competitiveness and living standard.

Conclusion

The zeitgeist of the new millennium will be the spirit of free economic competition and co-evolution between nations. Nations peopled by highly educated, open-minded, driven entrepreneurs who create productive enterprises through constant innovation and fast imitation will flourish. Such nations must also be led by progressive politicians who understand that central to their economic policy is the fostering of progressive knowledge about design and manufacturing processes.

The flowering of the global economy in the last 10 years has been overshadowed by the totally unexpected implosion of the controlled economies of the Soviet Union and its satellites. The post-Cold War world is no longer a competition between two rival economic doctrines. Instead, it is a world of competition between 200 nations all racing to develop more efficient and effective systems of capitalism. How long will it take for the leadership of the United States to change its geopolitical diplomacy and trade policy to the new reality?

As the Washington establishment discusses national self-interest in the context of Bosnia and Haiti, Japan and China are locked in an extraordinary race for the economic leadership of Asia and perhaps the world. China counts on its immense size, its pent-up demand for free-market choice, its extraordinarily opportunistic entrepreneurs, its hard-working, adaptive, fast-learning, entrepreneurial, low-cost labor, its astonishing growth rate and perhaps the best global trading diaspora of any nation.[32] Japan relies on its superb skills in production and design process innovation, its nationalism, its ethic of group before self and its immense current wealth. China's growth will drive Japan to even higher levels of learning process skills, to stay ahead of the fast-imitating and innovating Chinese. The deeply appreciated historical competition between China and Japan (far more ancient and profound than the competition between Rome and Carthage, England and Spain, England and France or France and Germany) will ensure that the Japanese do not lack the will to rise to the challenge.

The fundamental issue and primary responsibility for the leadership of the United States is to ensure the country's continued superiority in this race for leadership in product and service research, development and design skills, and related manufacturing skills. All other government policies, be they law and order, health care, welfare, defense, environmental protection or global diplomatic philosophy, are secondary. They are secondary because they are derivative, depending on a healthy growing economy that is creating jobs and revenues to *enable* the achievement of such policies. Two hikers in the wilderness may not be able to outrun the charging bear, but it is better for one of them to outrun the other. Japan needs to outrun China, and we must outrun Japan.

Free trade offers new markets, which create growth in global consumption and production. Government collaboration with industry will reduce inefficient friction. But free trade and government collaboration alone will not ensure that the U.S. economy will grow. The future of the United States depends on the ability of its economic enterprises to lead the world in learning processes, research, development and design and manufacturing processes. At present, an absurdly small amount of attention is being paid to this reality.

Notes

1 Charles Babbage, *Economy of Machinery and Manufactures*, 2nd ed. (London, 1833), 368.

2 Paul Johnson, *Modern Times* (New York: Harper-Perennial, 1993), 228.

3 See William Lazonick, *Business Organization and the Myth of the Market Economy* (Cambridge University Press, 1991); Richard R. Nelson and Sidney G. Winter, *An Evolutionary Theory of Economic Change* (Cambridge, MA.: Harvard University Press, 1982); Peter Dickson, "Process Capital," Working paper, A.C. Nielsen Center for Marketing Research, The University of Wisconsin, Madison, 1996.

4 David A. Garvin, "Building a Learning Organization," *Harvard Business Review* (July–August 1993): 78–91; J.M. Juran, *Juran on Quality by Design: The New Steps for Planning Quality into Goods and Services* (New York: The Free Press, 1992); Andrea Gabot, *The Man Who Discovered Quality: How W. Edwards Deming Brought the Quality Revolution to America* (New York: Times Books, 1990).

5   Ronald H. Coase, "The Nature of the Firm," *Economica*, **4** (1937) 386–405; C.K. Prahalad and Gary Hamel, "The Core Competence of the Corporation," *Harvard Business Review*, **68** (May–June 1990), 79–91.

6   Peter Drucker, *Post-Capitalist Society* (New York: Harper Business, 1993), 8.

7   See William Lazonick, *Business Organization and the Myth of the Market Economy* (Cambridge University Press, 1991); Joseph A. Schumpeter, *The Theory of Economic Development* (Cambridge, MA: Harvard University Press, 1934); F. A. Hayek, *The Road to Serfdom* (The Chicago Press, 1944).

8   Robert Reich, *The Work of Nations* (New York: Alfred A. Knopf, 1991), 244.

9   Drucker, 59.

10 Michael Porter, *The Competitive Advantage of Nations* (New York: Free Press, 1990), 69.

11 Peter Reid Dickson, "Toward A General Theory of Competitive Rationality," *Journal of Marketing* (February 1992); *Marketing Management* (Fort Worth, TX: The Dryden Press, 1997), Chapter 1.

12 Joel Mokyr, *The Lever of Riches* (Oxford: Oxford University Press), 163.

13 Dickson, "Process Capital."

14 Drucker, *Post-Capitalist Society*, 14.

15 Christopher Farrell *et al.* "What's Wrong," *Business Week*, August 2, 1993.

16 Masaaki Kotabe, "Corporate Product Policy and Innovative Behavior of European and Japanese Multinationals: An Empirical Investigation," *Journal of Marketing*, **54** (April 1990), 19–33.

17 Interestingly, Drucker predicts a great increase in out-sourcing within the American economy (pp. 93–95) but is silent about out-sourcing across the global economy.

18 See Michael Czinkota and Masaaki Kotabe, "Product Development the Japanese Way," *The Journal of Business Strategy* (November–December 1990), 31–36. (See Chapter 12.)

19 In making this assertion we acknowledge that some concerns over third world growth are ill-founded; see Paul Krugman, "Does Third World Growth Hurt First World Prosperity," *Harvard Business Review* (July–August 1994), 113–121.

20 Peter J. Hugill, *World Trade Since 1431: Geography, Technology, and Capitalism* (Baltimore: The Johns Hopkins University Press, 1993), 20–28.

21 Robin Craig, *The Ship, vol. 10, The Revolution in Merchant Shipping 1850–1950* (London: National Maritime Museum, H.M.S.O.), 14, as quoted in Hugill, 30.

22 Robert Heilbroner, *The Making of Economic Society*, 9th edn (Englewood Cliffs, New Jersey: Prentice Hall, 1993).

23 Michael R. Czinkota, "Global Neighbors: Poor Relations," *Marketing Management*, **2** (4, 1994), 46–52. (See Chapter 3.)

24 Lee Smith, *Rebuilding Economic Strength* (Armonk, NY: M.E. Sharpe, 1993), 94.

25 See Frederich List, *The National System of Political Economy*, 1837. His belief that governments should actively promote the development of the productive capacity of a nation through direct investment and protectionism has been the guiding philosophy behind the tremendous success of a number of Asian economies.

26 One of the most useful ways of increasing the quality of health care processes and reducing the cost of health care processes would be to stimulate the free market in health care process expertise by promoting a special Health Care Processes Skills Directory.

27 N. Mohan Reddy, John D. Aram, and Leonard H. Lynn, "Institutional Domain of Technology Diffusion," *Journal of Product Innovation Management*, **8** (December 1991), 295–304.

28 Each of these institutes could offer its own specialized process research and training directory. It is instructive that the founding and funding of the new engineering schools in the 1890s have been credited with playing a major role in moving the United States to the preeminent global economic superpower that it undoubtedly still remains; see Lazoncik, p. 31. Perhaps a similarly enlightened industrial policy involving both public and private funding will emerge in the 1990s.

29 See Mokyr.

30 Drucker, 164.

31 Lazonick (37) identifies this combining of innovation and skills as a defining characteristic of Japan's collective capitalism.

32 See Andrew Tanzer, "The Bamboo Network," *Forbes*, July 18, 1994.

19

Global Sourcing Strategy in the Pacific: American and Japanese Multinational Companies

THE UNIVERSITY OF TEXAS AT AUSTIN

The postwar "economic miracles" of the East and Southeast Asian countries have shifted the pendulum of international trade from cross-Atlantic to cross-Pacific in recent years. The nature of the cross-Pacific bilateral and multilateral trade and investment has been shaped mostly by companies from the United States and Japan, the two largest economies in the world.

In 1970, North America's (the United States and Canada) trade with the European Community was almost twice as large as its trade with five leading Asian nations (Japan and the four Tigers of South Korea, Taiwan, Hong Kong and Singapore). While North America's trade with the European Community increased almost ninefold from $27.5 billion in 1970 to $242 billion in 1993, its trade with Japan surged 13-fold from $13 billion to $172 billion while its trade with the four Asian Tigers shot up almost 70 times from a meagre $1.8 billion to $125 billion during the same period. Today, as a result, North America's trade with these five Asian countries alone exceeds its trade with the European Community by upwards of 20 percent. Similarly, Japan's trade with the Asian Tigers experienced a 33-fold increase from $3.3 billion to $109 billion during the 1970–93 period. The recent trade statistics in the Pacific Rim are presented in figure 19.1.

Another significant characteristic of the cross-Pacific trade is that the U.S. trade positions with these Asian countries have largely deteriorated over the years, while Japan's trade with the United States and the Asian Tigers has been in surplus. Such an imbalance in cross-pacific trade has been a source of criticism against Japan's trade practices.

Unfortunately, trade statistics reveal little more than the amount of bilateral trade flows between countries. It is false to assume that trade is always a business transaction between independent buyers and sellers across national boundaries. It is equally false to assume that a country's trade deficit in a certain *industry* equates with a decline in the competitiveness of *companies* in that industry.

In this chapter, I shall examine how U.S. and Japanese companies have taken part in the growth of

"Global Sourcing Strategy in the Pacific: American and Japanese Multinational Companies," by Masaaki Kotabe. In Gavin Boyd (ed.) *Structural Competitiveness in the Pacific: Corporate and State Rivalries.* Copyright ©1996. Reprinted by permission of Edward Elgar Publishing Limited.

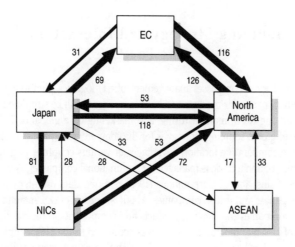

Notes:
North America: The United States, Canada.
EC: Britain, W. Germany, France, Italy, the Netherlands, Belgium, Luxembourg, Denmark, Ireland, Spain, Portugal, Greece.
NICs: S. Korea, Taiwan, Hong Kong, Singapore.
ASEAN: Indonesia, Malaysia, the Philippines, Thailand.
Source: United Nations trade statistics.

Figure 19.1 Pacific trade flows in global perspective, 1993 ($US billion)

the cross-Pacific trade and how their strategy has affected their respective long-term competitiveness. Initially, the primary objectives of many U.S. companies were to compete with Japanese companies that had built their strengths on cost competitiveness in the 1960s and 1970s. As Japanese firms gradually lost cost competitiveness as a result of the yen's appreciation in the 1980s, companies from other Asian countries began to strengthen their competitive edge in low-cost manufacturing *vis-à-vis* U.S. companies. Consequently, U.S. companies have had to emphasize cost efficiency in competing with Japanese and other Asian companies. To do so, U.S. companies have increased sourcing of components and finished products from the four Asian Tigers and other Southeast Asian countries, thereby contributing to the increased U.S. trade with the region. So have the Japanese companies.

However, there is a noticeable difference in sourcing objectives. Generally, U.S. companies have continually emphasized economic *efficiency* in pursuing cost competitiveness through global sourcing, while Japanese companies have focused more on competitiveness based on *effectiveness* in satisfying customers through quality, reliability and swift product development. The normative implications of this strategic difference between U.S. and Japanese companies are explored in conjunction with their sourcing strategies in the Pacific region.

Global Sourcing Strategy and International Trade in the Pacific

Global sourcing strategy encompasses management of: (1) logistics identifying which production units will serve which particular markets and how components will be supplied for production, and (2) the interfaces among R&D, manufacturing, and marketing on a global basis (Kotabe 1992). The ultimate objective of global sourcing strategy is for the company to exploit both its own competitive advantages and the comparative location advantages of various countries in global competition.

Today, much international trade is managed by multinational companies. A survey by the United Nations Centre on Transnational Corporations (1988) reported data on international trade directly managed by US, Japanese and British companies. About 30 percent of U.S. manufactured exports was attributed to U.S. companies transferring products and components to their affiliates overseas, and about 40 percent of U.S. manufactured imports was accounted for by U.S. companies sourcing from their foreign affiliates. For both Japan and Britain, such transactions were estimated to account for approximately 30 percent of their total trade flows (exports and imports combined), respectively. These intrafirm trade rations have been virtually unchanged in the past 20 years (Organization for Economic Cooperation and Development 1993).

An earlier study of 76 U.S. manufacturing multinational companies also revealed that U.S. companies' imports from their overseas affiliates and contractors comprised: finished goods 20–25 percent, components 65–70 percent, and raw materials 10 percent (Business International 1982). From the sourcing perspective, it appears that U.S. manufacturing companies were sourcing less expensive supplies of components and finished products for sale in the United States.

The "offshore" sourcing by U.S. companies for the U.S. market has been encouraged by U.S. tariff provisions for products imported under tariff items 9802.00.60 and 9802.00.80 of the U.S. Harmonized Tariff Schedule (until 1989 known as 806.30 and 807.00 of the Tariff Schedules of the United States). These tariff provisions permit duty-free reentry to the United States of US-made components sent abroad for further processing or assembly. U.S. companies have taken advantage of these favourable tariff provisions by using Asian countries and Mexico as production and assembly locations.

The countries in the European Union and Japan have similar, although somewhat more restrictive, tariff arrangements (Grunwald and Flamm 1985). The sourcing patterns of European and Japanese companies, moreover, have been significantly different from those of U.S. companies. Generally, European companies do relatively little foreign production for reimport to the home market, while Japanese companies establish transplants to manufacture components and products abroad, especially in Southeast Asia, primarily for export to countries other than Japan.

Evidence clearly suggests a much more complex pattern of trade and foreign production *managed* by multinational companies across national boundaries than is portrayed in international economics textbooks. The development of global sourcing and marketing strategies across different foreign markets has become a central issue for many multinational companies from North America and Japan. In the past, a polycentric approach by which to organize operations on a country-by-country basis was the primary *modus operandi* by many multinationals. But, today, there is a growing realization of the advantages to be acquired by coordinating and integrating operations across national boundaries (Porter 1986; Johansson and Yip 1994).

Trends in Global Sourcing Strategy

Over the last 20 years or so, gradual yet significant changes have taken place in global sourcing strategy. The cost-saving justification for international procurement in the 1960s and 1970s has been gradually supplanted by quality and reliability concerns in the 1980s and 1990s. However, most of the changes have been in the way business executives think of the scope of global sourcing for their companies and exploit various opportunities available from it as a source of competitive advantage (Swamidass 1993). Peter Drucker, a famed management guru and business historian, once said that sourcing and logistics would remain the darkest continent of business – the least exploited area of business for competitive advantage. Naturally, many companies, regardless of their nationality, that have a limited scope of global sourcing are at a disadvantage over those that exploit it to their fullest extent in a globally competitive marketplace.

DECLINE OF THE EXCHANGE RATE DETERMINISM
OF SOURCING

Since the early 1970s, exchange rates have fluctuated rather erratically. As many U.S. companies emphasized short-term financial performance, the appreciation of the U.S. dollar led them to de-emphasize manufacturing in the United States. As a result, manufacturing management gradually lost its influence within business organizations (Buffa 1984).

Production managers' decision-making authority was reduced such that R&D personnel prepared specifications with which production complied and marketing imposed its own delivery, inventory and quality conditions, but with little product quality and reliability considerations. In a sense, production managers gradually took on the role of outside suppliers within their own companies. The reduced influence of production managers led to a belief that manufacturing functions could be spun off easily to independent operators and subcontractors, depending upon the cost differential between in-house and contracted-out production.

Therefore, in order to lower production costs under competitive pressure, U.S. multinational companies turned increasingly to sourcing components and finished products from newly industrialized countries such as South Korea, Taiwan, Singapore, Hong Kong, Malaysia, Brazil and Mexico, among others. The appreciation of the dollar was reflected immediately in the surge of U.S. imports. Akio Morita, a co-founder of Sony, a highly innovative Japanese electronics company, chided such U.S. multinational companies as *hollow corporations* which simply put their well-known brand names on foreign-made products and sold them as if the products were their own. *Business Week* (1986) debated the "hollowing-out" of U.S. companies and criticized their "hollowing-out" strategy as "an economics of instant gratification, an abdication of responsibility to future (American) investors, workers, and consumers."

A counterargument widely held by U.S. companies, then, was that once the dollar depreciated, U.S. companies would increase domestic procurement because they would find it increasingly difficult to depend on foreign supplies at higher dollar prices. In this scenario, companies consider the exchange rate determining the extent to which they can engage in foreign sourcing. However, despite the depreciation of the dollar since the late 1980s. U.S. companies have continued or even increased their dependence on foreign supplies (*Business Week* 1992). The exchange rate determinism of sourcing was strictly based on cost considerations alone. Obviously, factors other than cost have kept many U.S. companies from reducing their dependence on foreign supplies of components and finished products.

NEW COMPETITIVE ENVIRONMENT CAUSED BY EXCESS
WORLD-WIDE CAPACITY

The world-wide growth in the number of manufacturers has added excess production capacity in most industries. As a result of the proliferation of manufacturers around the world, including Southeast Asia, in increasingly sophisticated, capital-intensive, manufactured products, there has been a tremendous downward pressure on prices of many components and products. Although the ability to deliver a high volume of products of satisfactory quality at a reasonable price was once the hallmark of many successful U.S. companies, the increasing number of global suppliers has made the delivery of volume in an acceptable time a less feasible competitive option.

Hence, there has been a strategic shift from *price* and *quantity* to *quality* and *reliability* of products as a determinant of competitive strength (Starr and Ullman 1988). Thus, according to a recent survey (Min and Galle 1991), better product and component quality, lower price, unavailability of items in the United States, and more advanced technology abroad are among the most important reasons for increased sourcing by U.S. companies from abroad.

When U.S. companies were actively procuring components and finished products from suppliers in Southeast Asia on a contractual basis (i.e. *contractual* sourcing or *out-sourcing*), Japanese companies were building transplants there for manufacturing their own components and finished products and/or transferring abroad their famed *keiretsu* relationships with suppliers for strategic as well as for cost saving purposes (i.e. *intrafirm* sourcing).[1] Cost reduction has been as important to Japanese as to U.S. companies, but for slightly different reasons. As Japanese companies have historically emphasized cost competitiveness early on in the product life cycle, securing inexpensive production locations primarily in Southeast Asia has been their *proactive strategy* (Kotler, Fahey and Jatusripitak 1985). Furthermore, exporting Japanese products made in Southeast Asian countries to the United States has been part of their strategy to diffuse U.S. protectionist sentiment. For many U.S. companies, it has generally been a *reactive* strategy, reacting to cost inflation as a result of the dollar appreciation since the mid-1970s (Birou and Fawcett 1993; Swamidass 1993).

Obviously, procuring necessary components and products from suppliers in Southeast Asia on a contractual basis has been *efficient* for U.S. companies for both macroeconomic and microeconomic reasons. First, at the macroeconomic level, offshore sourcing has promoted the division of labour and specialization across the Pacific. Second, from a microeconomic or corporate point of view, it has allowed U.S. companies to lower prices and, furthermore, reduce fixed cost from their manufacturing operations and thus lower break-even points for improved profitability.

While cost competitiveness remains important to Japanese companies, the appreciation of the yen over the years has forced them to shift from cost competitiveness to competitiveness based on their ability to satisfy customers through assurance of quality and reliability and swift product development. U.S. companies have then reacted again to the changing nature of Japanese competition.

The sudden and steep depreciation of the U.S. dollar *vis-à-vis* the Japanese yen in recent years has been helping U.S. companies gain market shares lost earlier to Japanese competition. However, neither U.S. gains in market shares nor Japanese losses of market shares should be construed as fundamental corporate weaknesses or strengths as often portrayed in recent publications (Norton 1994).

Exchange rate-determined cost competitiveness does not reflect the fundamental competitive strengths of a company. It could prove to be fleeting for U.S. companies if the dollar appreciates again as it did in the 1980s. The increased offshore sourcing of U.S. companies from independent foreign suppliers is not necessarily indicative of superior management of corporate and locational resources. A company's long-lasting competitive strengths hinge on its ability to exploit globalization potential (Johansson and Yip 1994) by managing and coordinating geographically separated R&D, manufacturing and marketing interfaces on a global basis (Porter 1986; Kotabe 1992).

Functional Interfaces in the Value Chain

The design of global sourcing strategy is based on interplay between a company's competitive advantages and the comparative advantages of various countries. The competitive advantage of a company influences the decision as to in *what* activities and technologies it should concentrate investment and managerial resources. The comparative advantages of various countries affect the company's decision on *where* to source and market, based on the lower cost of labor and other location factors.

Five continuous and interactive steps are involved in developing such a global sourcing strategy along the value chain (Robinson (ed.) 1987):

1. The separable links (R&D, manufacturing, and marketing) in the company's value chain are identified.
2. In the context of those links, the company's competitive advantages, considering both economies of scale and scope, are determined.
3. Transaction costs (e.g. cost of negotiation, cost of monitoring activities, and uncertainty resulting from contracts) between links in the value chain, internal and external, are assessed, and the lowest cost mode is selected.
4. The comparative advantages of countries (including the company's home country) relative to each

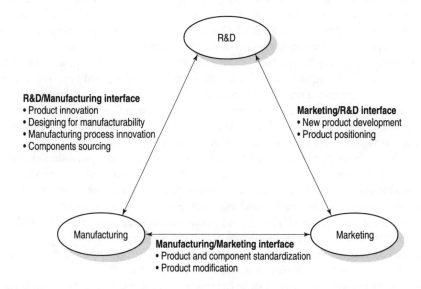

Figure 19.2 R&D, manufacturing and marketing interfaces.

link in the value chain and to the relevant transaction costs are determined.

5. Adequate flexibility in corporate decision making and organizational design is developed to permit the company to respond to changes in its competitive advantages and the comparative advantages of countries.

In this section, I focus on the three most important interrelated activities in the value chain: R&D (technology development, product design and engineering), manufacturing and marketing activities. Management of the interfaces, or linkages, between these value-adding activities is a crucial determinant of a company's competitive advantage. A basic framework of management of R&D, manufacturing and marketing interfaces is outlined in figure 19.2. These value-adding activities should be examined as holistically as possible in the context of their linkages.

R&D/MANUFACTURING INTERFACE

Technology is broadly defined as know-how comprising *product* technology (the set of ideas embodied in the product) and *process* technology (the set of ideas involved in manufacturing or the steps necessary to combine new materials to produce a finished product). Executives tend to focus solely on product-related technology as the driving force of a company's competitiveness. Product technology alone, however, may not provide a long-term competitive edge unless it is matched with sufficient manufacturing capabilities (Guile and Brooks (eds) 1987).

Before a short-term financial performance orientation became a major driving principle in U.S. firms during the 1970s, they had enjoyed effective R&D and manufacturing interfaces (Buffa 1984). CAT (computer-aided tomography) scan technology represents a classic example. EMI, a British company, developed and slowly began marketing CAT scanners in Britain in 1972 for which its inventors, Godfrey Houndsfield and Allan Cormack, won a Nobel Prize. This British company's CAT scanner represented state-of-the-art technology that was inherently difficult to manufacture. As a result, the company was not able to manufacture fast enough to meet an increased demand for CAT scanners in the United States, the largest market for this device. It was then General Electric, among others, which took advantage of the void in competition and swiftly captured the market with its own CAT scanners which were technologically inferior, but more easily manufacturable than the original British model.

Similar cases exist throughout history. The British discovered and developed penicillin, but it was, again, a small U.S. company, Pfizer, which improved on the fermentation (i.e. manufacturing) process and, as a result, became the world's foremost manufacturer of penicillin. The first jet engine was developed in Britain and Germany, but it was again U.S. companies, Boeing and Douglas, which improved on the technology and eventually dominated the jet aircraft market.

Beginning in the 1970s, however, many U.S. companies placed emphasis on product innovations (i.e. product proliferation and modifications) to improve financial performance. It is widely known that their growth and profits come largely from new products (Booz, Allen & Hamilton, Inc. 1982). Product proliferation and modifications made interchangeability of components across products increasingly difficult, thus compelling many U.S. companies to source various components and/or finished products for resale from specialized suppliers at home and abroad. Further, as U.S. technological leads over foreign competition evaporated, there were fewer products that U.S. companies could export simply because no one else had the technology to manufacture them (Thurow 1985).

Stressing the historical linkage of imitation and product innovations, it is contended that imitation (manufacturing process learning), followed by more innovative adaptation, leading to pioneering product design and innovation, forms the natural sequence of industrial development (Pavitt 1988; Starr and Ullman 1988). In other words, product innovation and manufacturing activities are intertwined, so that continual improvement in manufacturing processes can enable the company not only to maintain product innovation-based competitiveness, but also to improve its product innovative abilities in the long run (Brooks 1983; Hayes, Wheelwright and Clark 1988; Kotabe 1992).

These examples amply suggest that manufacturing processes should also be innovative. To facilitate the transferability of new product innovations to manufacturing, a team of product designers and engineers should strive to design components such that they are conducive to manufacturing without undue retooling and that components may be used interchangeably for different models. Low levels of retooling requirements and interchangeability of components are necessary conditions for efficient global sourcing strategy. If different equipment and components are used in various manufacturing plants, it is extremely difficult to establish a highly coordinated sourcing plan on a global basis.

MANUFACTURING/MARKETING INTERFACE

There is continual conflict between manufacturing and marketing divisions. It is to the manufacturing division's advantage if all the products and components are standardized to facilitate standardized, low-cost production. The marketing division, however, is more interested in satisfying the diverse needs of consumers, requiring broad product lines and frequent product modifications which add cost to manufacturing. How have successful companies coped with this conflict?

Recently, there has been an increasing interest in the strategic linkages between product policy and manufacturing long ignored in traditional considerations of global strategy development. With aggressive competition from Japanese multinational companies emphasizing product innovation and concomitant manufacturing, many companies have realized that product innovations alone cannot sustain their long-term competitive position without an effective policy linking product and manufacturing process innovations (Kotabe 1990).

Four different ways of developing a global product policy are generally considered effective to streamline manufacturing, while lowering component procurement and manufacturing costs, without sacrificing sourcing flexibility: 1) core components standardization, 2) product design family, 3) universal product with all features, and 4) universal product with different positioning.[2] These are recognized to be Japanese companies' competitive strengths that many U.S. companies failed to achieve (Takeuchi and Porter 1986).

Core components standardization

Successful global product policy mandates the development of universal products or products which require no more than cosmetic change for adaptation to differing local needs and use conditions. A few examples illustrate the point. Seiko, a Japanese watchmaker, offers a wide range of designs and models, but based only on a handful of different operating mechanisms. Similarly, the best-performing German machine toolmaking companies have a narrow range of products, use up to 50 percent fewer parts than their less successful rivals, and make continual, incremental product and design improvements, with new developments passed rapidly on to customers.

Another good example is Black & Decker. Confronted with rapidly rising wage costs in the United States and incessant foreign competition in the consumer power tool industry, Black & Decker, unlike many other U.S. companies, decided against increasing sourcing of components from independent suppliers abroad and instead redesigned the product line and developed a family look, simplified the product offerings, reduced manufacturing costs, automated manufacturing, standardized components, incorporated new materials and new product features, improved product performance and provided world-wide product specifications. Behind the company's successful transition was collaborative effort among design, engineering and manufacturing divisions. Not only did this program reduce production and marketing costs (increasing market share and profitability), but also it further improved the company's manufacturing and new product development capability (Lehnerd 1987).

Product design family

This is a variant of core component standardization. For companies marketing an extremely wide range of products, because of cultural differences in product-use patterns around the world, it is also possible to reap economies of scale. For example, Toyota offers several car models based on a similar family design, ranging from Lexus models to Toyota Avalons, Camrys and Corollas. Many of the Lexus features well received by customers have been adopted into the Toyota lines with just a few minor modifications (mostly downsizing). In the process, Toyota has been able to cut product development costs and meet the needs of different market segments. Similarly, Electrolux, a Swedish appliance manufacturer, has adopted the concept of "design families," offering different products under four different brand names, but using the same basic designs. A key to such product design standardization lies in standardization of components, including motors, pumps and compressors. Thus, White Consolidated in the United State and Zanussi in Italy, Electrolux's subsidiaries, have the main responsibility for components production within the group for world-wide application.

Universal product with all features

As noted above, competitive advantage can result from standardization of core components and/or product design families. One variant of components and product standardization is to develop a universal product with all the features demanded anywhere in the world. Japan's Canon has done so successfully with its AE-1 cameras and newer models. After extensive market analyses around the world, Canon identified a set of common features customers wanted in a camera, including good picture quality, ease of operation with automatic features, technical sophistication, professional looks and reasonable price. To develop such cameras, the company introduced a few breakthroughs in camera design and manufacturing, such as use of an electronic integrated circuitry brain to control camera operations, modularized production, and standardization and reduction of parts.

Universal product with different positioning

Alternatively, a universal product can be developed with different market segments in mind. Thus, a universal product may be positioned differently in different markets. This is where marketing promotion plays a major role to accomplish such a feat. Product and/or components standardization, however, does not necessarily imply either production standardization or a narrow product line. For example, Japanese automobile manufacturers have gradually stretched out their product line offerings, while marketing them with little adaptation in many parts of the world. This strategy requires manufacturing flexibility. The crux of global product or components standardization calls for proactive identification of homogeneous segments around the world, and is different from the concept of marketing abroad a product originally developed for the home market. A proactive approach to product policy has gained momentum in recent years as is made possible by intermarket segmentation (Levitt 1983). In addition to the clustering of countries and identification of homogeneous segments in different countries, targeting different segments in different countries with the same products is another way to maintain a product policy of standardization.

For example, Honda has marketed almost identical Accord cars around the world by positioning them differently from country to country. Accord has been promoted as a family sedan in Japan, a relatively inexpensive sports car in Germany, and a reliable commuter car in the United States. In recent years, however, Honda has begun developing some regional variations of the Accord for the United States, European and Japanese markets. None the less, Honda adheres to a policy of *core component standardization* such that at least 50 percent of the components, including the chassis and transmission, are shared across the variations of the Accord.

MARKETING/R&D INTERFACE

Both R&D and manufacturing activities are technically outside marketing managers' responsibility. However, marketing managers' knowledge of the consumers' needs is indispensable in product development. Without a good understanding of the consumers' needs, product designers and engineers are prone to impose their technical specifications on the product rather than fitting them to what consumers want. After all, consumers, not product designers or engineers, have the final say in deciding whether or not to buy the product.

Japanese companies, in particular, excel in management of the marketing/R&D interface (Czinkota and Kotabe 1990). Indeed, their source of competitive advantage often lies in marketing and R&D divisions' willingness to coordinate their respective activities concurrently. In a traditional product development, *either* a new product was developed and pushed down from the R&D division to the manufacturing and to the marketing division for sales, *or* a new product idea was pushed up from the marketing division to the R&D division for development. This top-down or bottom-up new product development takes too much time in an era of global competition in which a short product development cycle is crucial to meet constant competitive pressure from new products introduced by rival companies around the world.

R&D and marketing divisions of Japanese companies are always on the lookout for use of emerging technologies, initially in existing products, to satisfy customer needs better than those products and their competitiors'. This affords an opportunity to gain experience, increase the interchangeability of components, debug technological glitches, reduce costs, boost performance and adapt designs for world-wide customer use. As a result, they have been able to increase the speed of new product introductions, meet the competitive demands of a rapidly changing marketplace, and capture market share.

In other words, the marketplace becomes a virtual R&D laboratory for Japanese companies to gain production and marketing experience as well as to improve on product technology. This requires close contact with customers, whose inputs help Japanese companies improve upon their products on an ongoing basis. In the process, they introduce new products one after another. Year after year, Japanese companies unveil not-entirely-new products that keep getting better in design, more reliable and less expensive. For example, Philips marketed the first practical VCR in 1972, 3 years before Japanese competitors entered the market. However, Philips took 7 years to replace the first generation VCR with the all-new V2000, while the late-coming Japanese manufacturers launched an onslaught of no fewer than three generations of improved VCRs in this 5 year period.

Another recent example is the exploitation of the so-called "fuzzy" logic by Hitachi and others (Armstrong 1990). Ever since fuzzy logic was conceived in the mid-1960s by Lotfi A. Zadeh, a computer science professor at the University of California at Berkeley, only Japanese companies have examined its potential application in ordinary products. The fuzzy logic allows computers to deal with shades of gray or something vague between 0 and 1 – no small feat in a world of the binary computers that exist today. Today, Hitachi, Matsushita, Mitsubishi, Sony and Nissan Motors, among others, use fuzzy logic in their products. For example, Hitachi introduced a fuzzy train that automatically accelerates and brakes so smoothly that no one uses the hanging straps. Matsushita, maker of Panasonics, began marketing a fuzzy washing machine with only one start button that automatically judges the size and dirtiness of the load and decides the optimum cycle times, amount of detergent needed, and water level. Sony introduced a palm-size computer capable of recognizing written Japanese, with a fuzzy circuit to iron out the inconsistencies in different writing styles. Now fuzzy circuits are put into the autofocus mechanisms of video cameras to get constantly clear pictures. By the beginning of 1990, fuzzy chips were appearing at a fast pace in a wide range of consumer products.

The continual introduction of *newer* and *better designed* products also brings a greater likelihood of market success (Czinkota and Kotabe 1990). Ideal products often require a giant leap in technology and product development, and naturally are subject not only to much more difficulty in procuring/ manufacturing newly required components but also to a higher risk of consumer rejection. The Japanese incremental approach allows for continual improvement and a stream of new products, and permits quicker consumer adoption. Consumers are likely to accept improved products more quickly than very different products, since the former are more compatible with the existing patterns of product use and lifestyles.

Logistics of Sourcing Strategy

Sourcing strategy includes a number of basic choices companies make in deciding how to serve foreign markets. One choice relates to the use of imports, assembly or production within the country to serve a foreign market. Another decision involves the use of internal or external supplies of components or finished goods. Therefore, the term, "sourcing," is used to describe management by multinational companies of the flow of components and finished products in serving foreign markets.

In developing viable sourcing strategies on a global scale, companies must consider not only manufacturing costs, the costs of various resources, and exchange rate fluctuations, but also the availability of infrastructure (including transportation, communications and energy), industrial and cultural environments, the ease of working with foreign host governments, and so on. Managers also have to be aware that the complex nature of sourcing strategy on a global scale spawns many barriers to its successful execution. In particular, logistics, inventory management, distance, nationalism and lack of working knowledge about foreign business practices, among others, are major operational problems identified by both U.S. and foreign multinational companies engaging in international sourcing.

Studies have shown, however, that despite, or maybe, as a result of, those operational problems, *where* to source major components seems much less important than *how* to source them (see, for example, Kotabe 1992). Thus, when examining the relationship between sourcing and the competitiveness of multinational companies, it is crucial to distinguish between sourcing on a "contractual" basis and sourcing on an "intrafirm" basis, for these two types of sourcing will have different impacts on their long-run competitiveness.

PROS AND CONS OF PRODUCTION SHARING

One school of thought popularized in the 1980s argues that many successful companies have developed a dynamic organizational network through increased use of joint ventures, subcontracting and licensing across international borders (Miles and Snow 1986). This system is broadly referred to as a network of strategic alliances, or in a sourcing sense, it has been known as *production sharing* (Drucker 1979; Kim 1986).

As noted by Prahalad and Hamel (1990), companies have been strongly encouraged to develop world-class core competence in *some* areas of the value chain in the industry. There is an inherent difficulty in gaining a superb competitive advantage in every aspect of an industry. Production sharing thus allows each participant to develop its particular core competence, thereby maintaining a nimble competitive position in a very fluid competitive environment. Therefore, each network participant can be seen as complementing rather than competing with the others for common goals. Production sharing may even be formed by competing companies in the same industry to develop complementary capabilities (new technologies or skills).

The other school of thought argues, however, that while networking may facilitate cost reduction in the short run, there can be negative long-term consequences resulting from a company's dependence on independent suppliers and the difficulty of keeping abreast of constantly evolving design and engineering technologies without engaging in those developmental activities. In reality, while cost reduction remains important to any business, quality and reliability of components, among others, should be at least equally, or even more, important factors to be considered. Since it takes time to develop overseas suppliers for non-cost purposes, purchasing managers cannot easily drop a foreign supplier when exchange rate changes have an adverse effect on the cost of imported components and products. Moreover, U.S. domestic suppliers are known to increase prices to match rising import prices following the dollar depreciation. As a result, switching to a domestic supplier may not even ensure cost advantages.

DEPENDENCE

Hayes and Wheelwright (1984) used some anecdotal evidence to assess the importance of intrafirm sourcing of major components regardless of their procurement locations. In 1983, Japanese television manufacturers dominated several U.S. market segments even though many U.S. manufacturers enjoyed the same low labor cost advantages of "offshore" production or procurement of finished products from local suppliers in Asia. Also, German machine tool and automotive producers have secured a big portion of the U.S. market even though their labor rates have risen above those in the United States. Similarly, Swatch decided to make the whole watch in Switzerland despite its high costs, in order to keep control of crucial design and production and avoid giving away profit margins to subcontractors.

Further, Kim's (1986) study showed that Japanese companies, rather than U.S. companies, had been the major suppliers of complex components for the four Asian Tigers (i.e. Hong Kong, South Korea, Singapore and Taiwan). Japanese companies export to the United States through these countries by supplying them intermediate goods which are then assembled into finished products to be sold in the United States. It appears that U.S. companies' increased dependence on major components from independent foreign suppliers did not alleviate, but rather accelerated, their competitive decline in the 1970s and 1980s.

It is not until recently, however, that some researchers have paid attention to the corporate performance implications of intrafirm sourcing over out-sourcing transactions on a global basis. For example, the market performance implications of various sourcing strategies have been empirically explored by Kotabe (1992), Kotabe and Swan (1994), and Murray, Kotabe and Wildt (1995). *Findings are that the extent of intrafirm sourcing of major components, that is, the company's ability to procure major components from within its corporate system on a global basis, appears to be a crucial determinant of its market performance, while sourcing and production locations do not.* These findings apply to companies of any nationality. The difference is that many more Japanese companies have employed intrafirm-based global sourcing than U.S. companies. In other words, these empirical findings cast serious doubt on the alleged benefits (i.e. cost competitiveness and alleged nimbleness) of international sourcing, *unless* it is intrafirm.

SUSTAINABLE CORE COMPETENCE VS. TRANSITORY CORE COMPETENCE

If U.S. and Japanese companies had been pursuing their own respective core competences for competitive advantage, then they should have achieved similar levels of market performance. Obviously, it has not been the case in the past 30 or so years. I submit that there should be some specialization as a core competence that is inherently more sustainable than others.

I have argued elsewhere that product innovation alone can no longer provide adequate competitive edge and that strong manufacturing and marketing capabilities are of the utmost importance for companies to maintain long-term sustainable competitive position (Kotabe 1992, chapter 9). It is primarily because, in today's highly competitive market, legal means of protecting proprietary technology have become ineffective as new product innovations are easily reverse-engineered, improved upon, and invented around by competitors without violating patents and other proprietary protections. Levin *et al.* (1987) confirm empirically that the most effective ways of securing maximum returns from a new product innovation are through lead time and moving fast down the experience curve (i.e. quickly resorting to large-volume production). Production sharing facilitates technology diffusion through official and unofficial channels among competitors. Obviously, the value of owning technology has lessened drastically in recent years as the inventing company's temporary monopoly over its technology has become transitory.

History has shown repeatedly that many higher-cost producers will also begin to out-source finished products from the lower-cost producer on a contractual OEM (original equipment manufacture) basis. While out-sourcing may be an easy way out from a short-term perspective of cost efficiency, however, it tends to prevent out-sourcing companies from keeping abreast of emerging product and manufacturing technologies that might be employed for further product and design improvement. Hence it can cause a long-term decline in manufacturing competences and innovative ability.

Both U.S. and Japanese companies, respectively, have established different manufacturing and sourcing networks with Southeast Asian countries. However, one crucial difference lies in what their intended core competence should be. As implied in the *Business Week* (1986) accusation, U.S. companies gradually severed part of their value chain and, in search of cost competitiveness and nimbleness (i.e. cost efficiency), willingly increased their dependence on foreign suppliers for components and finished products that became ever more technologically sophisticated. On the other hand, Japanese companies kept their commitment to manufacturing capabilities (more specifically, quality and reliability of components and finished products) as their primary core competence and competitive weapon irrespective of their actual production location.

Such commitment requires close scrutiny of manufacturing activities in Southeast Asia. Whenever possible, Japanese companies own and directly manage manufacturing facilities with a large number of Japanese engineers and technical support staff expatriated from home. Unlike typical U.S. companies, Japanese companies tend to emphasize a dual role for the technical expatriates: it is not only to transfer expertise to the foreign plants but also to bring newly gained production expertise back to their parent companies in order to keep internalized the very part of the value chain that many U.S. companies were willing to let go. For Japanese companies, exchange rate fluctuations are viewed rather as a transitory problem – however serious – in developing an "internalized" global sourcing network with the belief that such a sourcing network could absorb the impact of exchange rate fluctuations through better cost containment and consistent supply of superior components within the system.

Apart from the benefit of cost reduction and nimbleness, sourcing from independent suppliers on a "contractual" basis, whether domestically or from abroad, appears to have other long-term consequences. First, a firm tends to assign part of the most important value-creating activites to, and also become dependent on, independent operators for assurance of components quality (Kumpe and Bolwijn 1988). Second, competition is promoted among independent suppliers to ensure continuing availability of materials and exploit full benefits of changing market conditions. But the suppliers are forced to operate in an uncertain business environment which inherently necessitates a shorter planning horizon. The uncertainty about the potential loss of orders to competitors often forces individual suppliers to make operating decisions that will likely increase their own long-term production and material costs (Hahn, Kim, and Kim 1986). In the process, it tends to adversely affect U.S. companies sourcing components and/or finished products from those suppliers.

Third and of utmost importance, the out-sourcing firms tend to lose sight of emerging technologies and expertise which could be incorporated into the development of new manufacturing processes as well as new products. The creation of new technology is a gradual and painstaking learning process of continual adjustment and refinement, as new productive methods are tested and adapted in the light of a company's accumulated experience. Thus, over-reliance on acquisition of technology (in the form of components and finished products) from others may not result in the same sustainable competitive advantages available through internal development (Hayes, Wheelwright, and Clark 1988; Cantwell 1989; Huber 1991).

Thus, continual sourcing from independent suppliers forebodes long-term loss of the ability to manufacture at competitive cost and, as a result, loss of long-term global competitiveness (Morgan and Morgan 1991). However, if technology and expertise developed by a multinational company are exploited within its multinational corporate system (i.e. by its foreign affiliates and by the parent company itself), the company can retain its technological base without undue dissemination as though it were a "public" good. The benefit of such internalization is great, particularly when technology is highly idiosyncratic or specific with limited alternative use, or when it is novel in the marketplace. Yet its true economic value to the firm tends to be undervalued in the marketplace because of uncertainty associated with the technology as perceived by potential buyers (Buckley and Casson 1976; Rugman 1982; Dunning 1988).

Management of the quality of major components is required to retain the goodwill and confidence of consumers in the quality and reliability of finished products (Casson 1982). As a result, "intrafirm" sourcing of major components and finished products between the parent company and its affiliates abroad and between its foreign affiliates themselves enables a company to retain a long-term competitive edge built on quality and reliability, among other things.

As a result, Hayes, Wheelwright, and Clark (1988) succinctly conclude that world-class manufacturers dislike being dependent on outside organizations for expertise

One can develop less of one's own new technology – new product ideas and new processing techniques – and borrow or buy it from the companies that do develop new technology . . . this kind of leverage may allow a company to augment its profitability in the near term, but it will eventually find itself at a disadvantage *vis-à-vis* those of its competitors who try to be leaders (p. 18).

Toyota's global operations illustrate one such world-class case. The Japanese carmaker is equipping its operations in the United States, Europe and Southeast Asia with integrated capabilities for creating and marketing automobiles. The company gives the managers at those operations ample authority to accommodate local circumstances and values without diluting the benefit of integrated global operations. Thus, in the United States, Calty Design Research, a Toyota subsidiary in California, designs the bodies and interiors of new Toyota models, including Previa and Lexus. Toyota has technical centers in the United States and in Brussels to adapt engine and vehicle specifications to local needs. Toyota operations that make automobiles in Southeast Asia supply each other with key components to foster increased economies of scale and standardization in those components – gasoline engines in Indonesia, steering components in Malaysia, transmissions in the Philippines and diesel engines in Thailand.

Strategic emphasis on intrafirm sourcing on a global basis has also helped Japanese companies become as skilled at swift product development and marketing around the world as originally intended by out-sourcing U.S. companies. By getting involved in design, key component development and production on their own, many Japanese companies have kept abreast of emerging technologies and innovations originating anywhere in the world for potential use and swift adoption in the future. In the process, Japanese companies have been able to manage the interfaces among R&D, manufacturing and marketing on a global basis better than U.S. companies.

Thus, the long-term competitive strengths of those Japanese companies lie in their broadly based in-house capabilities in the value chain. Their short-term weaknesses have also been evidenced of late, however. The Japanese integrated sourcing system requires a higher level of asset commitment than the U.S. companies, which rely more on out-sourcing. When exchange rates change drastically, out-sourcing U.S. companies can realign suppliers more quickly and economically than Japanese counterparts, while risking the loss of vital capabilities in the long run.

Conclusions

The scope of global sourcing has expanded over time. Multinational companies design their sourcing decision based on the interplay between their competitive advantages and the comparative advantages of various sourcing locations for long-term gains. A major theme of this chapter is that many U.S. companies have generally increased their dependence on independent contractual suppliers in Southeast Asia for components and finished products, whereas many Japanese companies have built their sourcing strategy by way of their transplants located in the region. The implications of efficiency vs. effectiveness issues of global sourcing in Southeast Asia have been explored.

Relatively speaking, U.S. companies have stressed cost efficiency, while Japanese companies have emphasized such non-cost factors as quality, reliability and product development cycle. Over time, U.S. companies seem to have compromised, while Japanese companies have improved, some crucial long-run capabilities in the value chain.

Whether or not to procure components or products from abroad was once determined strictly on price and was thus strongly influenced by the fluctuating exchange rate. Thus the appreciation of the dollar would prompt U.S. companies to increase offshore sourcing, while the depreciation of the dollar would encourage domestic sourcing. Indeed, from the mid-1970s to the late 1980s when the dollar was appreciating, many U.S. companies increased foreign procurement of components and finished products, particularly in Southeast Asian countries. Increased offshore sourcing helped U.S. companies maintain cost-efficient operations by limiting costs of components and finished products and lowering their break-even points in order to compete with low-cost Asian manufacturers.

However, since the dollar depreciation began in the late 1980s, the expected U.S. reversal of dependence on offshore sourcing has failed to materialize. Japanese companies have expanded their global sourcing strategy more methodically by building a larger network of transplants in various parts of Southeast Asia.

Today many companies consider not simply price but also quality, reliability and technology of components and products to be procured. Increased U.S. corporate reliance on Southeast Asia for components and finished products suggests some loss of ability to manage production of components of world-class quality and reliability and of capacity to reduce product development cycles in exchange for cost efficiency.

The management of trade and foreign production by multinational companies is very complex. In growing global competition, the sourcing of components and finished products around the world within multinational companies has increased. The development of global sourcing and marketing strategies across different foreign markets has become a central requirement. Traditionally, a polycentric approach to organizing operations on a country-by-country basis allowed each country manager to tailor marketing strategy to local peculiarities. Product adaptations and modifications were considered necessary to better cater to the different needs and wants of customers in various countries. Product adaptation, however, then tends to be reactive, rather than proactive. A high level of product adaptation may make it difficult for multinational companies to reap economies of scale in production and marketing and coordinate their networks of activities on a global scale.[3]

Global sourcing strategy requires close global coordination of R&D, manufacturing and marketing activities. With geographically separated R&D, manufacturing, and marketing activities, companies face difficult coordination problems as they strive to integrate their operations and adapt them to different legal, political and cultural environments. Further, the separation of manufacturing activities involves a risk that manufacturing in the value chain will gradually become neglected. Such a neglect can be costly because continued involvement in manufacturing leads to pioneering product design and innovation over time. An effective global sourcing strategy calls for continual efforts to streamline manufacturing without loss of marketing flexibility. This requires conscious efforts to develop core components in-house, or product design families, or universal products.

Finally, a caveat should be also noted. While a company's ability to develop core components and products and sell them in the world markets on its own is preferred, such a vast task should be examined in the light of rapid international changes in technology and customer needs. Those changes make the product life cycle extremely short, sometimes too short for many multinational companies to pursue product development, manufacturing, and marketing on a global basis without strategic alliance partners. The benefits of maintaining an independent proprietary position, while preferred in the long run, should always be weighed against the time cost of delayed market entry in the short run.

References

Armstrong, Larry (1990) "Why 'Fuzzy Logic' Beats Black-or-White Thinking," *Business Week,* **21** (May), 92–3.

Birou, Laura M. and Stanley E. Fawcett (1993) "International Purchasing: Benefits, Requirements, and Challenges," *International Journal of Purchasing and Materials Management,* **29** (Spring), 28–37.

Bolton, Michele K., Roger Malmrose and William G. Ouchi (1994), "The Organization of Innovation in the United States and Japan: Neoclassical and Relational Contracting," *Journal of Management Studies,* **31,** (September), 653–79.

Booz, Allen & Hamilton, Inc (1982) *New Products Management for the 1980s.* New York: Booz, Allen & Hamilton.

Brooks, Harvey (1983) "Japanese Technological Advances and Possible United States Responses Using Research Joint Ventures," presented at House Subcommittee on Investigations and Oversight and the Subcommittee on Science, Research, and Technology of the Committee on Science and Technology, 98th Congress, 1st session, 29–30 June.

Buckley, Peter J. and Mark Casson (1976) *The Future of the Multinational Enterprise,* London: Macmillan.

Buffa, Elwood S (1984) "Making American Manufacturing Competitive," *California Management Review,* **26** (Spring), 29–46.

Business International (1982) *The Effects of U.S. Corporate Foreign Investment 1970–1980.* New York: Business International Corporation, May.

Business Week (1986) "Special Report: The Hollow Corporation," 3 March, 56–9.

—— (1992), "Guess Who Isn't Buying American: For many U.S. Companies, Imported Goods are Cheaper and Better-Made," 2 November, 26–7.

Cantwell, John (1989) *Technological Innovation and Multinational Corporations.* Oxford: Basil Blackwell Ltd.

Casson, Mark C (1982) "Transaction Costs and the Theory of the Multinational Enterprise." In Alan M. Rugman (ed.) *New Theories of the Multinational Enterprise.* London: Croom Helm, 24–54.

Czinkota, Michael R. and Masaaki Kotabe (1990) "Product Development the Japanese Way," *Journal of Business Strategy,* **11** (November/December), 31–6. (See Chapter 12.)

Drucker, Peter F. (1979) "Production Sharing, Concepts and Definitions," *Journal of the Flagstaff Institute,* **3** (January), 2–9.

Dunning, John H. (1988) "The Eclectic Paradigm of International Production: A Restatement and Some Possible Extensions," *Journal of International Business Studies,* **19** (Spring), 1–31.

Economist (1995) "The Kindergarten That Will Change the World," **4** (March), 63–4.

Grunwald, Joseph and Kenneth Flamm (1985) *The Global Factory: Foreign Assembly in International Trade.* Washington, D.C.: The Brookings Institution.

Guile, Bruce R. and Harvey Brooks (eds) (1987) *Technology and Global Industry: Companies and Nations in the World Economy.* Washington, D.C.: National Academy Press.

Hahn, Chan K., Kyoo H. Kim and Jong S. Kim (1986) "Costs of Competition: Implications for Purchasing Strategy," *Journal of Purchasing and Materials Management,* **22** (Fall), 2–7.

Hayes, Robert H. and Steven C. Wheelwright (1984) *Restoring Our Competitive Edge: Competing through Manufacturing.* New York: John Wiley & Sons.

—— and Kim B. Clark (1988) *Dynamic Manufacturing: Creating the Learning Organization.* New York: The Free Press.

Huber, George P. (1991) "Organizational Learning: The Contributing Process and the Literatures," *Organizational Science,* **2** (1), 88–115.

Johansson, Johny K. and George S. Yip (1994) "Exploiting Globalization Potential: U.S. and Japanese Strategies," *Strategic Management Journal,* **15** (October), 579–601.

Kim, W. Chan (1986) "Global Production Sharing: An Empirical Investigation of the Pacific Electronics Industry," *Management International Review,* **26** (2), 62–70.

Kotabe, Masaaki (1990) "Corporate Product Policy and Innovative Behavior of European and Japanese Multinationals: An Empirical Investigation," *Journal of Marketing,* **54** (April), 19–33.

—— (1992) *Global Sourcing Strategy: R&D, Manufacturing, and Marketing Interfaces*. New York: Quorum Books.

Kotabe, Masaaki and K. Scott Swan (1994) "Offshore Sourcing: Reaction, Maturation, and Consolidation of U.S. Multinationals," *Journal of International Business Studies*, **25** (First Quarter), 115–40.

Kotler, Philip, Liam Fahey and Somkid Jatusripitak (1985) *The New Competition*. Englewood Cliffs, NJ: Prentice Hall.

Kumpe, Ted and Piet T. Bolwijn (1988) "Manufacturing: The New Case for Vertical Integration," *Harvard Business Review*, **66** (March–April), 75–81.

Lehnerd, Alvin P. (1987) "Revitalizing the Manufacture and Design of Mature Global Products." In Bruce R. Guile and Harvey Brooks (eds) *Technology and Global Industry: Companies and Nations in the World Economy*. Washington, D.C.: National Academy Press, 49–64.

Levin, Richard C., Alvin K. Klevorick, Richard R. Nelson, and Sidney G. Winter (1987) "Appropriating the Returns from Industrial Research and Development," *Brookings Papers on Economic Activity*, Issue 3, 783–831.

Levitt, Theodore (1983) "The Globalization of Markets," *Harvard Business Review*, **61** (May–June), 92–102.

Miles, Raymond E. and Charles C. Snow (1986) "Organizations: New Concepts for New Forms," *California Management Review*, **28** (Spring), 62–73.

Min, Hokey and William P. Galle (1991) "International Purchasing Strategies of Multinational U.S. Firms," *International Journal of Purchasing and Materials Management*, **27** (Summer), 9–19.

Morgan, James C. and J. Jeffrey Morgan (1991) *Cracking the Japanese Market: Strategies for Success in the New Global Economy*. New York: The Free Press.

Murray, Janet Y., Masaaki Kotabe, and Albert R. Wildt (1995) "Strategic and Financial Performance Implications of Global Sourcing Strategy: A Contingency Analysis," *Journal of International Business Studies*, **26** (First Quarter).

Nishiguchi, Toshihiro (1994) *Strategic Industrial Sourcing: The Japanese Advantage*. New York: Oxford University Press.

Norton, Rob (1994) "Strategies for the New Export Boom," *Fortune*, 22 August, 124–32.

Organization for Economic Cooperation and Development (1993) *Intra-Firm Trade*. Paris: OECD.

Pavitt, Keith (1988) "International Patterns of Technological Accumulation." In N. Hood and J.E. Vahne (eds) *Strategies in Global Competition*. London: Croom Helm.

Porter, Michael E. (1986) *Competition in Global Industries*. Cambridge, Mass.: Harvard Business School Press.

Prahalad, C.K. and Gary Hamel (1990) "The Core Competence of the Corporation," *Harvard Business Review*, **68**, (May–June), 79–91.

Robinson, Richard D. (ed.) (1987) *Direct Foreign Investment: Costs and Benefits*. New York: Praeger.

Rugman, Alan M. (1982) "Internalization and Non-Equity Forms of International Involvement." In Alan M. Rugman (ed.) *New Theories of the Multinational Enterprise*. London: Croom Helm.

Starr, Martin K. and John E. Ullman (1988) "The Myth of Industrial Supremacy." In Martin K. Starr (ed.) *Global Competitiveness*. New York: W.W. Norton & Co.

Swamidass, Paul M. (1993) "Import Sourcing Dynamics: An Integrative Perspective," *Journal of International Business Studies*, **24** (Fourth Quarter), 671–91.

Takeuchi, Hirotaka and Michael E. Porter (1986) "Three Roles of International Marketing in Global Strategy." In Michael E. Porter (ed.) *Competition in Global Industries*. Boston, Mass.: Harvard Business School Press, 111–46

Thurow, Lester C. (1985) *The Management Challenge*. Cambridge, Mass.: MIT Press.

United Nations Center on Transnational Corporations (1988) *Transnational Corporations in World Development: Trends and Perspectives*. New York: United Nations.

Notes

1 Technically speaking, suppliers in a Japanese vertical *keiretsu* are not necessarily owned in any significant way by a principal company. In most cases, a principal company owns no more than 10 percent of the stock

of its suppliers, and those suppliers also hold some of the principal company's shares. Such a mutual partial ownership is designed to enhance mutual trust and long-term commitment to each other. A transfer of executives, engineers and some R&D funding from the principal company to its *keiretsu* member suppliers in exchange for the suppliers' commitment to the principal company is so common that a *keiretsu* can be considered a highly integrated corporate system (thus, intrafirm sourcing) rather than a buyer–supplier relationship on a spot or contractual basis (e.g. Bolton, Malmrose, and Ouchi 1994; Nishiguchi 1994).

2 It has been argued that computer-aided designing and computer-aided manufacturing (CAD/CAM) technology makes mass manufacturing obsolete as it permits mass customization of products to different consumer taste around the world. While I do not deny either its theoretical possibility or its continued operational improvement over time, however, actually observed improvements in CAD/CAM technology have been far from sufficient to anticipate its widespread global applicability in the foreseeable future. For example, Toyota recently found that although the company's famed lean production system reduced the number of line workers at a factory, the number of maintenance personnel rose dramatically, therefore proving the promised economies to be false. As a result, Toyota is shifting away from automation towards a more human-based system (*The Economist* 1995).

3 In the 1960s and 1970s, many U.S. firms had their own manufacturing subsidiaries in Southeast Asian countries. However, when U.S. parent companies increased procurement of components from abroad for production in the United States in the mid-1970s, many of those subsidiaries were either not used strategically for integrated global manufacturing purposes or sold away to local interests. Selling of U.S. assets in Southeast Asia was partly due to the local government's 'fade-out' policy, mostly in the 1960s, to gradually increase local participation in US-owned businesses, and also partly due to U.S. firms' desire to reduce fixed costs in order to lower break-even point.

20

Third Generation R&D: The Key to Leveraging Core Competencies

MARK KESLER, DIANA KOLSTAD, AND W.E. CLARKE

ARTHUR D. LITTLE, INC.

While business leaders have always faced complex challenges, the challenges of today appear more daunting than ever before. Major advances in all technologies, particularly communications, have resulted in an accelerating rate of change in the world.[1]

Technologies diffuse throughout industry faster than ever before, making it harder to sustain technological leadership. Product life cycles are compressing, the product creation process is shorter than ever before, and the consumer now expects that new products will be available nearly every time he or she shops. Thus, although human capabilities are essentially the same as in the past, the events that managers must deal with are changing more rapidly than ever before – an intimidating prospect! Given these realities, managers ask:

- How can we continually adapt to constant and ever-increasing change, while at the same time keeping the company true to its identity?
- How can we achieve and maintain leadership in the face of shortening product life cycles?
- How do we develop a long-term vision for our business that will guide us and establish the strategies that will lead to long-term success?

Researchers Gary Hamel and C.K. Prahalad have made a contribution to helping managers with these challenges by articulating the concept of "core competencies."[2] Essentially, core competencies define the identity of the organization; "who we are" and "what we are good at." In sum, core competencies:

- provide access to a wide range of markets (through sometimes diverse products),
- form the basis for new businesses (successful new businesses are based on core competencies)
- make contributions to the key bases of competition in the marketplace
- should be difficult to imitate because they embody harmonizations of technologies and other important skills.

"Third Generation R&D," by Mark Kesler, Diana Kolstad, and W.E. Clarke, *The Columbia Journal of World Business*, Fall 1993, pp. 34–44. Reprinted by permission of Jai Press Inc.

To put it simply, a successful business integrates "what we are good at" with the needs of the marketplace, and in doing so establishes core competencies and a corporate identity. As Hamel and Prahalad point out, successful corporations recognize, articulate, and manage their core competencies to establish long-range strategies for their current businesses and to provide platforms for future businesses. To put it differently, corporations succeed when they develop businesses that are aligned with their core competencies and corporate identities. Dozens of examples bear witness to companies who ignored this fact: Exxon's purchase of Reliance Electric, Mobil's experience with Montgomery Ward, Sears' recently discontinued efforts to enter the Finance and Insurance businesses, AT&T's poorly executed venture into personal computers in the 1980s and Shell Oil's aborted efforts to develop a pharmaceutical business through investments in genetic engineering technology are a few examples. The lessons from these missteps are clear: In a world that is changing rapidly, businesses should be at least consistent with, if not based on, the collective learning in the organization and the corporate identity.

Once the concept of core competencies is clear, the issue then involves determining how to align the company with them. The Hamel-Prahalad model provides a basis for understanding core competencies, but only hints at specific, pragmatic methods to build, identify and exploit them. Moreover, their model of core competencies, core products and end products is too static, given the constant rate of change technology imposes.

We believe that core competencies must be strategically managed in light of our changing environment. It is necessary to identify and develop core competency strategies based on a technology management model and to use technology to adapt to the rapid changes that technology itself causes. Indeed, as technology is one of the reasons for rapid change and dislocations in society, technology also provides hope for understanding and orienting the company to face these challenges.

Technology is the Basis for Strategic Vision and Intent

We believe that long-range strategies, or strategic visions, should be formed from an integration of an understanding of the marketplace (the customer and the competitors), the company and the future (as shown in figure 20.1). That is, strategic visions must address the current and future needs of the customer and the responses of competitors, while at the same time being consistent with the capabilities and culture of the organization. The future holds many changes: technological, social, political and economic. To continue to be successful in an unknown future the corporation must constantly manage its capabilities and reorient itself as the world changes.

Technology is fundamental to the three elements of strategic visioning: It provides the essence for developing sustainable competitive advantages in the marketplace, it provides insights into the products and processes of the future, and it forms the basis for many of the company's core capabilities (and hence, competencies).

Technology provides sustainable competitive advantage by embodying key product attributes which meet the current or unrealized needs of customers, e.g. product cost, quality, performance. Technology is the basis for the key attributes of most products. This can be illustrated through an examination of almost any product familiar to our daily lives: for example, plastics.

Plastic materials have been incorporated into thousands of products that in total use billions of pounds each year. Plastics have achieved this level of acceptance because they offer improved

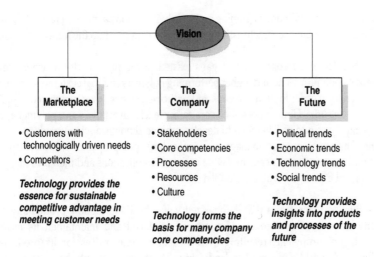

Figure 20.1

properties or attributes compared with the materials they replace, such as wood, steel and paper; plastics cost less, they are lighter, more processable, more durable, cleaner, more aesthetic (for most applications), etc. These properties have been attained through the application of polymer sciences and technologies. And, as time goes on, the upper and lower boundaries of these product attributes can be increased only through further efforts. A plastics company can achieve sustainable competitive advantages only by continually offering products with better properties or attributes than its competition, at ever lower cost. To do this requires a complete understanding of the technological basis of the products.

Technology also provides insights into the products and processes of the future that will meet unrealized customer needs. If technologies form the basis for product attributes, then changes in technologies will directly affect the attributes of future products. If one can forecast changes in technologies, then one can also forecast the changes in important commercial products based on these technologies. Forecasting these changes, therefore, is critical to provide long-term direction and guidance for future product planning and strategic visions.

If technologies form the basis of a company's current and future products and processes, then, almost by default, technology must form the basis for many of the core capabilities of the successful company.

Companies that understand the technological basis of their products and their capabilities can leverage this understanding to form the basis for successful strategic business visions. For example, Himont, a world-wide leader in the production of polypropylene resins, has illustrated the use of these concepts in achieving competitive advantages in its main polypropylene business. Polypropylene is a high-volume standard thermoplastic found in common consumer items such as food packaging, children's toys. At the raw material level, before being turned into a product, most grades of polypropylene were not differential based on product performance, and therefore they competed on price. Most competitors in the polypropylene market resigned themselves to commodity-based strategies in which the participants are forced to take high risks for relatively low returns; high profitability was obtained only through economies of scale (requiring huge capital spending) and aggressive cost control. Himont, beginning in the early 1980s, took a different tack. They recognized key market and technology characteristics which would continue into the future:

- *Marketplace*: Himont recognized that gaps existed in the price/performance curve between commodity polypropylene and higher performing polymers and that customers would welcome new materials in order to fill those gaps and reduce expensive "overengineered" applications.
- *Company capabilities*: Himont possessed core competencies in catalysis and polymer applications technology that could be leveraged to develop advanced polypropylene products.
- *Future*: Himont's technology managers recognized that polypropylene was a versatile material that could meet customer needs in a wide variety of applications and therefore they continued development efforts when others stopped.

These insights led to strategies that emphasized value, breaking the low profitability curse of a commodity-based strategy. Indeed, Himont has enhanced and maintained its technological leadership in polypropylene, resulting in consistently higher prices for its products, higher profitability and world-wide market leadership. These achievements have been based on a comprehensive understanding of the product technology and leveraging of the company's technology-based competencies, implemented through effective linkages of business and technology strategies.

An understanding of one's core competencies can also help companies identify businesses which do not leverage the core capabilities of the organization and therefore are not a good fit with the company. For example, in 1989, Union Carbide used this type of analysis to decide the future of its polysilicon business, which produced and sold polysilicon for use in semiconductor chips. Union Carbide had entered the business in the 1970s based on market projections of high growth and profitability. As time went on, however, the expected revenues and profits had not materialized. UCC re-evaluated the market, but also assessed the fit of the polysilicon business with UCC's strategies, visions, technical capabilities and corporate culture (its core competencies, or corporate identity). UCC found that the business did not achieve expectations primarily because of the mismatches between the business's key success factors and UCC's core competencies. Since the marketplace was relatively new to Union Carbide and had little synergy with other UCC businesses, the company had a poor understanding of the customers' needs. Essentially, the technologies needed to serve this marketplace were foreign to Union Carbide's core technology competencies. Business strategy and technology strategy were disconnected – a situation that hindered success. The polysilicon market, however, still appeared attractive, and Union Carbide decided to sell the business to an organization whose core compentencies were better aligned with the needs of the market.

The Third Generation R&D Management Model

Third Generation R&D as defined by Roussel, Erickson, and Saad can be used to build, identify and exploit technology core competencies. Third Generation R&D is a strategic approach that integrates business strategies and technology strategies as a seamless whole (we call this a holistic approach). Third Generation R&D is a way of managing research and development strategically and its techniques help companies identify and manage technology core competencies. Its value

1940	1950	1960	1970	1980	1990	Future

Business environment	• Post WW2, many growth businesses • R&D provides inventions, which business managers produce and market	• Era of conglomerates and financial engineering • R&D supports individual businesses in corporation	• Focus on core capabilities, rational expansions/growth • Increased rate of change due to rapid communication channels • Agile and flexible corporations
Research and development approach	**First Generation R&D** • The strategy of hope • R&D decides future activities • No explicit link to business strategy • Line item in budget • Fatalistic	**Second Generation R&D** • Rational approach on a project-by-project basis • Mutual commitment to goals • Consideration of strategy • Control systems • No integration corporate-wide	**Third Generation R&D** • Rational, holistic strategic approach guided by general managers who together establish and continually reorient the business vision and its portfolio of technologies

Figure 20.2

can be illustrated by contrasting it with first and second generation R&D (as shown in figure 20.2).[3]

First Generation R&D is consistent with an era of slower changes and less mature businesses as seen prior to the 1960s. Business managers employed the "strategy of hope," which often worked because significant discoveries were abundant. New products were developed by R&D, then "thrown over the fence" to business personnel, who manufactured and sold those products. Few checks existed to ensure that the resulting programs benefitted or even related to the organization's competencies. Businesses viewed the R&D function mystically and left it alone to "create."

Second Generation R&D is consistent with the era of conglomerates and financial engineering in the 1960s, 1970s and 1980s. In those years R&D was considered an asset whose funding was based on rules of thumb such as percentage of sales. R&D managers then allocated these funds on a project-by-project basis, often disconnected from the overall strategies of the business. While this approach provided checks and balances on R&D, it suffered from several things:

- the lack of long-term strategic goals
- little leveraging across projects or across businesses
- allocation of resources disconnected from the strategic plans of the business.

The Third Generation R&D approach is now necessary in order to keep pace with and capitalize on the increasing rate of change. Only agile and flexible corporations with a clear sense of their required technology competencies will stay ahead and grow. The company must focus on doing things that leverage their core competencies, instead of learning as they go along. Companies must take a holistic approach to business and technology strategy and develop them hand in hand, so that business strategy is directly linked to technology core competencies (and vice versa). No longer can an organization tolerate small pockets of activities or projects that aren't recognized across the organization as contributing to the technology strategy.

Instead of managing R&D on a project-by-project basis, Third Generation R&D companies

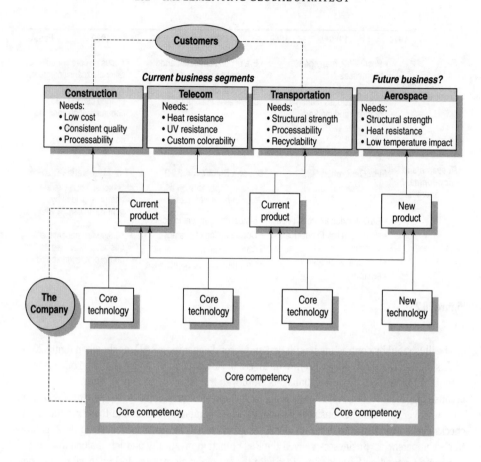

Figure 20.3 Core competencies underlie the products that meet customer needs

manage portfolios of projects that have strategic importance to individual businesses and to the corporation as a whole. Business managers and R&D managers work jointly to explicitly assess the core competencies of the organization and plan its technology needs.

Third Generation R&D Principles and Techniques and the Core Competence, Technology-based Organization

We believe that for a company to succeed in its corporate vision, it must recognize and harness the proper core technology competencies to gain long-term competitive advantage and sustained growth. This requires:

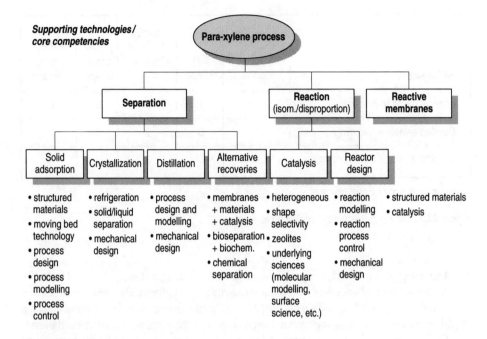

Figure 20.4 Technology unbundling

- identifying and leveraging technology core competencies
- continually linking business strategies with the core competencies
- actively managing core competencies for the future.

IDENTIFYING CORE COMPETENCIES

Third Generation R&D companies use a variety of techniques to help them identify core competencies. They recognize that core technologies exist at the interface between the marketplace and the core competencies of the company (as illustrated in figure 20.3). Technology core competencies are the bundles of technologies that underlie current products which meet various customer needs. As the figure shows, a core technology alone is not sufficient to define a core competency. Rather, bundles of core technologies must generate a product attribute which meets the needs of the customer. Some core technologies may also provide the basis for future products (and core competencies) which meet unrealized customer needs and thus provide opportunities for growth.

An important tool for identifying and screening core technologies is a "strategic technology architecture" (STA). The architecture is basically a matrix that matches commercial products or R&D projects with the technologies that comprise them. This technique helps to identify several technologies that are critical to the company's most important products or processes. This can be used as the first screen for identifying technology-based core competencies. The construction of a technology architecture comprises two steps:

R&D strategy	Heterogeneous catalysis	Solid adsorption	Reactive membrane development/ design	Fischer- tropsch synthesis	Reaction modelling design
Improve p-xylene process	1	1	2	0	2
Develop selective reforming	1	0	2	0	1
Develop methane-based aromatics	1	0	2		1

1 = primary; 2 = Secondary; 0 = Not important)

Figure 20.5 Strategic technology architecture

1. "Technology unbundling." Any product or process can be thought of as a "bundle" of technologies that support, or underlie it; e.g., a home cassette player utilizes technologies in electronics (amplification, recording, noise reduction) and mechanical devices (switches, controls and tape drive mechanisms). Technology unbundling is an exercise that maps out and describes the levels of technology that underlie products and processes. Each major classification or level can be further unbundled into underlying components, continuing through successive levels down to the basic sciences. However, the tool is best utilized when the unbundling proceeds down only a few levels – enough to adequately define classes of technologies rather than the basic sciences. Figure 20.4 illustrates the unbundling of a chemical process to produce para-xylene, a raw material for the production of polyester. It is important to note that the unbundling should include all current and future technologies (within reason) that comprise a product, so as to be able to identify technology gaps. As more and more of the products are unbundled, gaps common to them may be identified, highlighting a technology weakness that may have to be corrected.

2. "Generating the Strategic Technology Architecture." After unbundling many of the company's products and processes, the lists of technologies generated can be plotted against the products and processes to create a matrix such as that shown in figure 20.5. These matrices can help to quickly screen the dozens of technologies that are or could be practiced by a company, to identify those that have the most impact on the company's current and potential future product lines.

The technology unbundling and development of STAs can help to identify gaps across products and processes. It can also help to identify key points of leverage or common technologies practiced in different areas of the corporation. This can be particularly helpful to large companies that have several research centers; often, these firms will find that groups in the various centers will be conducting R&D in areas that have large overlap. If this is the case, efficiency and effectiveness might be increased by leveraging the most critical resources. As an example, figure 20.5 illustrates a situation we encountered in which a client was conducting three separate R&D projects (improve p-xylene process, develop selective reforming and develop methane-based aromatics) in three centers located in different parts of the United States. One of the primary technologies required for success in the programs involved certain aspects of heterogeneous catalysis. Much of this research was being duplicated in each of the three centers. The use of STA helped to identify this, which resulted in a management push for greater technology transfer and cooperation between the R&D centers, which in turn resulted in improved efficiency. We suggest that the strategic management of core competencies should include the development and maintenance of charts comprising the important STAs of the company.

After generating the STA, further characterization of technologies allows the company to focus more closely on the core technologies which can provide sustainable advantage. Technology characteristics such as contribution to the company's vision, the company's ability to control the technology, and the technology's competitive impact help to identify the true "core" technologies and, therefore, technology core competencies. Ultimately, it is the network of these core technologies which create uniquely defined technology core competencies for the organization.

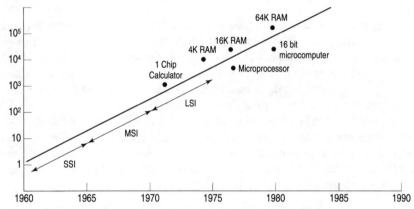

Technology Roadmap Matrix summarizes technological requirements for future products.
This example is for broadcast automotive FM receiver.

Tuning	Push button	Push button-synthesizers		Touch pad-synthesizers		Voice activated
Selectivity	Ceramic resonators	SAWs		Digital signal processors		
Subcarrier function	Stereo		Paging	Data		Maps
IC technology	Linear	5µ CMOS	3µ CMOS		1µ CMOS	
Display	LEDs	Liquid crystal		Fluorescence		
Vehicular LAN				Single wire	Glass fiber	
Digital Modulation						500 kHz Bandwidth
Products	**Receiver 1** *Stereo*	**Receiver 2** *Push* *Scan* *Seek*	**Receiver 3** *Push* *Personal paging*	**Next generation** *Push* *Stock market* *Road information* *Remote amplifiers* *Remote controls*	**Future generation** *A new service* *Super hi-fi* *Local maps*	

Figure 20.6 A technology forecast and roadmap matrix for computers

MANAGING TECHNOLOGY CORE COMPETENCIES

Once core technologies have been identified, the organization must work to maintain leadership by actively managing the competitive position of their core technologies. Typically, a company's competitive position is managed through the organization's R&D programs. As such, the development, selection, and management of R&D programs is critical to managing core technology leadership. Third Generation R&D companies use various techniques to manage their R&D portfolios to do just that. Strategic characterizations of projects such as time to commercialization, technology maturity, competitive intensity, and technical and commercial risk help companies prioritize projects and analyze their activities in terms of short-and long-term rewards. Like any investment portfolio, the R&D portfolio needs to be balanced according to risk/reward and across core technologies. In light of limited resources, the third generation R&D portfolio techniques also help companies make assessments of trade-offs for funding one project vs. another, or one portfolio vs. another.

Managing technology core competencies also requires a future-oriented perspective, and the ability to forecast changes in technologies to anticipate the application of developing technologies in the marketplace. Several tools are helpful for this forecasting. One approach, introduced by Motorola in the 1980s, is called a "product/technology roadmap," which provides a comprehensive description of the technologies that provide the basis for their product line, over time (10 years or so).[4] The roadmaps contain many elements: two of the most important are the technology forecast and the technology roadmap matrix, which are illustrated in figure 20.6. Taken together, these charts provide management with an excellent view of product direction and technology timing. This type of analysis helps companies predict the rate of change in technology in the future and therefore prepare for those developments. In this way, the company is able to manage its critical technology "assets" (core competencies).

Conclusions

The companies that will succeed in today's global competition will develop clearly understood business visions which are intimately linked with core technology strategies. In order to achieve this, these companies will take a holistic approach to their business and its technological basis and will therefore integrate the efforts of business and technology/R&D managers to form a cohesive identity and strategy.

Technology is fundamental to the three elements of strategic visioning: It provides the essence for developing sustainable competitive advantages in the marketplace, it provides insights into the products and processes of the future and it forms the basis for many of the company's core capabilities (and hence, competencies).

We believe that for a company to succeed in its corporate vision, it must recognize and harness the proper core technology competencies to gain long-term competitive advantage and sustained growth. This requires:

- identifying and leveraging technology core competencies
- continually linking business strategies with core competencies
- actively managing core competencies for the future.

Third generation R&D companies use various tools and techniques to achieve these objectives, including R&D portfolio management, technology forecasting, technology unbundling and strategic technology architecture.

Vision development and core competencies management must be ongoing business processes. To succeed in the marketplace of today and in the future, firms must be agile enough to continually reorient them-selves to changes, while maintaining leadership in their core technologies. Less agile and committed competitors will be unable to capitalize on and create innovation and will inevitably lose their way.

Notes

1 James Burke, *Connections* (Boston: Little, Brown: 1978).
2 C.K. Prahalad and Gary Hamel, "The Core Competence of the Corporation," *Harvard Business Review* (May–June 1990), 79–91.
3 Phillip A. Roussel, Kamal N. Saad, and Tamara J. Erickson, *Third Generation R&D: Managing the Link to Corporate Strategy* (Boston: Harvard Business School Press, 1991).
4 Charles H. Wilyard and Cheryl W. McClees, "Motorola's Technology Roadmap Process," *Research and Technology Management* (September–October 1990).

VII

EMERGING ISSUES

The only constant feature of international business is ever-changing trends. Environmental changes call for different strategy and different orientation, literally, on a global scale. As one globe-trotting executive put it, "If you don't do it, then somebody else will . . . at your cost." Particularly in the past several years, many political and economic events have happened that affect the nature of global competition. The demise of the Soviet Union, the establishment of the European Union and the North American Free Trade Area, deregulation and privatization of state-owned industries around the world have also changed the market environments around the world. Furthermore, the emerging markets of Eastern Europe and the rapidly growing markets of the Southeast Asia also add promises to international businesses. Unfortunately, the fast pace of economic development also causes additional undue strain on environments.

In this section, we will highlight three fundamental changes that are reshaping the nature of global competition into the twenty-first century. Chapter 21 provides the reality check for globalization movement. While it sounds antithetical, people around the world have also begun to assert their regional identity as they are being swamped with similar information, similar products, similar political systems, and so on. Indeed, the vast majority of international business managers view the advantages of globalization as being much more thoretical than real, particularly in view of these countering forces. This chapter argues that management of the regionalization process is often as important as design of the strategy. Flexibility is critical for both parents and subsidiaries as they negotiate roles and tasks in the restructuring of operations.

Chapters 22 and 23 address environmental concerns. Chapter 22 cautions that, notwithstanding the recent proliferation of literature on the benefits of green management, many managers continue to see environmentally sound strategies as detrimental to the principal goals of profitability, maintaining markets, controlling costs, and efficient production. Such conclusions about the environmental drag on business are based on mistaken assumptions about the incentives business encounter. Stricter government regulation of the environment in developed nations changes the equation. This chapter explores many opportunities for managers to profit from environmentally sound strategies that are independent of public pressures.

Chapter 23 addresses the ultimate concern of the human races – sustainable growth. Sustainable growth is an achievable goal but it would require a greatly increased use of energy, especially of fossil fuels. There is a basic conflict between those who advocate sustainable growth and those who wish to restrict the use of energy. In particular, it is difficult to see how one can avoid increasing the concentration of atmospheric greenhouse gases significantly if one wants to raise the living standard of the developing world. Possible solutions to this dilemma are discussed.

21

Globalization versus Regionalization: Which Way for the Multinational?

ALLEN J. MORRISON

THUNDERBIRD, THE AMERICAN GRADUATE SCHOOL OF INTERNATIONAL MANAGEMENT

DAVID A. RICKS

THUNDERBIRD, THE AMERICAN GRADUATE SCHOOL OF INTERNATIONAL MANAGEMENT

AND

KENDALL ROTH

UNIVERSITY OF SOUTH CAROLINA

Increasingly, managers are confronted by calls for dramatic change in the way their businesses should compete internationally. Nowhere is this more apparent than in so-called "global" industries, where managers have been urged to introduce offshore manufacturing, cut costs through world-wide economies of scale, standardize products internationally, and subsidize national market-share battles through international cash flows or other support activities. These actions form the basis of "global strategies" that have been suggested as the emerging pattern of international competition.

Two fundamental assumptions drive this thinking. The first is that a sizable number of competitors are indeed using global strategies to compete; the second is that performance can be improved by pursuing global strategies, particularly in an industry that has global structural characteristics. For managers in global industries the message has been, "Either quickly adopt a global strategy or see your competitiveness diminish."

In fact, some observers have gone so far as to suggest that the imperatives to globalize are so great and the benefits so pronounced that globalization is fast becoming the strategic norm rather than the exception. Although such comments are directed toward managers in the front-line global industries (for example, semiconductors, aircraft parts, pharmaceuticals, and heavy machinery), they are also being heard by senior managers in numerous other industries that are beginning to face greater and greater levels of international competition.

Research Assistance

Three years ago, we started a major research project to examine these assumptions with the objective of giving managers some assistance as they face the turbulent 1990s. Our study involved an extensive examination of the organizational strategy and design of 115 medium and large multinational corporations and 103 affiliated subsidiaries located in the United States, Canada, the U.K., France, Germany, and Japan. The study methodology is more fully described below.

STUDY METHODOLOGY

In this two-phase research project, the first phase involved classifying the international and competitive strategies of U.S.-based corporations (head-office divisions or stand-alone, single-industry corporations) in global industries.

The global industries were identified through a three-stage process described in Allen J. Morrison's *Competition in Global Industries: How U.S. Businesses Compete* (Quorum Books, 1990). The stages included: (1) a review of the literature that has previously identified global industries; (2) a verification of the existence of at least one global competitor in the industry; and (3) an examination of the industry's trade ratio.

The data for the first phase of this research were collected through a combination of questionnaire surveys, secondary data analysis, and in-depth interviews. The survey consisted of a rather detailed instrument containing questions focused on competitive positioning, investment, political and integration activities, and assessments of environmental imperatives and performance.

The data from the questionnaires were analyzed by using a variety of univariate and multivariate procedures. These were complemented by the use of extensive secondary data involving randomly selected businesses in the sample. Post-tests involving in-depth interviews with top executives from nine different corporations in seven of the eleven S.I.C. code industries were also conducted at head offices throughout the United States.

For the second phase of the study, the strategies of affiliated subsidiaries were studied with the objective of better understanding their changing role in the implementation of global and regional strategies. In this phase, 103 responses to a questionnaire were received. Interviews were conducted with senior managers in 31 of the responding subsidiaries.

RESULTS

The results presented here, which focus on the way international companies are currently responding to global competitive dynamics, suggest that managers should view with skepticism much of the current discussion on the topic. We suggest that, instead of developing global organizational responses to international competition, managers should reassess their strategies with the objective of strengthening regional competitiveness. Such a response, however, requires considerable organizational change. Our analysis highlights the critical tasks that parent corporations and their subsidiaries must undertake to facilitate this change.

Ongoing Challenges: Environmental Volatility

With few exceptions, there was widespread concurrence among the study's participants that environmental change had accelerated during the last half of the 1980s. To many managers, fundamental international changes – economic, political, technological, and social – were occurring in an independent manner, seemingly independent of each other. As a result, managers were often perplexed in their attempts to sort out opportunities from threats in the competitive environment. Corporate managers in particular faced myriad perspectives generated by far-flung operations in which managers must deal with their own unique challenges.

Managers have historically coped with uncertainty and complexity by constructing mental frameworks for interpreting phenomena. For U.S. managers, conventional wisdom held that the U.S. market was of paramount importance and that business practices successful at home would be successful overseas. Using this reasoning, many companies entered foreign markets either by exporting or by establishing overseas subsidiaries as "miniature replicas" of the U.S. parent. A miniature replica, which is a scaled-down version of the parent, basically produces the same products as those produced by the parent but in lower volumes for the smaller "domestic" market. Consider the following examples.

In home appliances, General Electric established its Camco subsidiary in Canada in 1976 by merging the appliance divisions of GSW and GE Canada and subsequently acquiring Westinghouse's Canadian major appliance operations. Protected by Canadian tariff barriers averaging 12 percent and aided by considerable corporate resources, Camco established production facilities for refrigerators, ranges, dishwashers, stoves, and washers and dryers to serve Canadian demand. Although the scale of these facilities did not render them internationally cost-efficient, Camco has gone on to become Canada's largest major appliance manufacturer.

In healthcare products, the Kendall Healthcare Products Company established a German subsidiary to manufacture and market a wide line of products developed in the United States. A broad range of the parent's urological products, critical-care products, and vascular-care products are locally manufactured for German consumption. Localized manufacturing has historically made sense, given that product standards have varied considerably from country to country and that the German healthcare system has been a major customer of the firm's products.

In consumer electronics, Matsushita Electric Industrial Company paid $108 million in 1974 for an ailing Motorola television manufacturing facility in Illinois. Under the Quasar Electronics name, Matsushita channelled funds and designs to the upgraded, miniature replica of the parent with the objective of producing television sets in the United States that were similar in quality and price to those developed in Japan.

The management of international operations through either exports or miniature replicas was relatively easy for the parent. Minimal strategic input from local managers was required beyond the local market, thus reassuring head-office managers and encouraging their continued preoccupation with home-country competition. However, this arrangement often resulted in limited communication between parent and subsidiary and certainly restricted corporate advancement opportunities for the overseas managers. The end result in many companies was a perpetuation of the norm that international operations should be treated as appendages to home-country operations.

Unravelling Home-Country Orientation: The Rise of Global Mania

When this home-country orientation began to unravel in the late 1970s, the greatest effect was felt by U.S. managers. As U.S. economic dominance declined, many American managers began to realize that international markets were critically important and that, if they were to compete effectively, new international strategies would be required. This ushered in a new era of what we refer to as "global mania."

An interest in global management began to pick up in the early 1980s and was accelerated, in part, by the declining competitiveness of the United States *vis-à-vis* Japan. Within the emerging mind-set, managers began to perceive the world differently. Home-country competitive pressures, for example, were put in the context of broader international pressures.

Managers began to see a link between what happened at home and what happened overseas. As an indicator of the globalization of competition, experts pointed to a real shrinkage in differences from country to country – a shrinkage brought on by rising monetary interdependence, transportation and communication efficiencies, various GATT (General Agreement on Tariffs and Trade) rulings, and so on.

By the mid-1980s, numerous academic articles were lauding the merits of pursuing global strategies. Key – and often strategic – industries were identified as having global structural characteristics. These characteristics included low tariff and non-tariff barriers to trade, high factor-cost differentials (i.e. in land, labor, and capital costs) between host countries, the possibility of achieving major economies of scale through world-wide production runs, and standardized product demand. Businesses were urged to respond by integrating operations around the world and by developing highly standardized products and marketing approaches.

To support these recommendations, observers noted that such companies as Caterpillar Inc., L.M. Ericsson, and Honda Motor Co., Ltd. had been highly rewarded for pursuing global integration strategies. Other observers pointed to the increasingly "stateless" world of manufacturing, in which dozens of the world's largest corporations generated more than half their sales outside their home country. Examples included ICI, which generated 78 percent of it sales outside the U.K.; Sony Corp., which produced 66 percent of total sales from outside Japan; and IBM, which received almost 63 percent of sales from activities not based in the United States.

The notion of a global strategy has had considerable appeal for corporate managers, largely because such strategies are best managed through tight central control. These strategies, like miniature replica strategies, let corporate managers ultimately determine what is produced and where it is produced. In other words, the center would continue to dominate the periphery. The global "solution" was also a concrete step – and concrete steps were called for in an era of cutthroat international competition.

However, despite the advice calling for pursuit of global strategies, our research failed to uncover widespread support for such an organizational response. The managers in our study generally did not see the world as an undifferentiated global marketplace. Interestingly, competitors in the U.S. regarded the U.S. as *preeminently* important in matters of investment, product development, position, and so on. A similar though somewhat less pronounced pattern was observed for British, German, French, Canadian, and Japanese firms with respect to their home markets.

Thus, though managers sensed that markets were becoming more competitive internationally, their loyalties remained primarily home-based. Even though they recognized that considerable international opportunities were slipping away, the vast majority of managers did not consider globalization the preferred approach for pursuing them. These managers simply viewed the advantages of globalization as being much more theoretical than real, particularly in view of some common problems that included the following:

Industry standards remain diverse. In spite of talk about the convergence of standards – in the European television industry, for example – there are currently seven different technical standards governing such matters as voltage and broadcasting frequencies. To meet this diverse set of standards, Toshiba Corporation in 1981 acquired the assets of a local British consumer electronics firm and began manufacturing television sets for the European market. From a centralized plant in Plymouth, the company now produces 110 models of television sets from 14" to 28" in size, "custom" manufactured for local country needs within Europe.

Customers continue to demand locally differentiated products. In many industries in Europe, North America, and Japan, subsidiaries continue to focus on reformulations, blending, and packaging activities. In the pharmaceutical industry, for example, differences in standards, tastes, and perceived needs remain a major obstacle to globalization. Prescription dosages for many products can vary up to 100 percent between Europe and Japan. Medical training and healthcare delivery systems, which vary considerably from country to country, significantly influence the types of prescriptions written and the delivery of both ethical and over-the-counter drugs. In response, Parke-Davis in France and both American Cyanamid Co. and Pfizer Inc. in Germany continue to focus much of their efforts on reformulating dosages and repackaging them.

Being an insider remains critically important. In theory, one advantage of a global strategy is that world-scale production maximizes production efficiencies and underwrites heavy product-development expenses. The result is supposed to be a standardized, low-cost product that, when combined with local marketing input, produces a competitive advantage for the global competitor. In reality, however, such advantages have taken on mythical proportions.

The example of Inmos provides a case in point. Formed in 1978, the semiconductor manufacturer based in Bristol, U.K. is now a subsidiary of S.G.S.-Thomson Microelectronics, Inc. Inmos produces a variety of fast static RAMs, high-performance microprocessors (transputers), and graphics components for the world-wide market. Inmos's products are intended for global customers, and some 90 percent of its revenues are generated outside the U.K.

However, it has observed a definite bias in the industry in favor of hardware developed in Silicon Valley. Moreover, it has found that Japanese and, particularly, U.S. customers are often skeptical of European products – and that such skepticism is more psychological than based on rational assessments of the technology and costs involved. As a result, Inmos has joined with a host of other European and Japanese semiconductor producers to consider manufacturing locally in the United States. Being perceived as an insider is still a critical concern for many firms.

Global organizations are difficult to manage. To effectively implement a global strategy, managers must find ways to coordinate far-flung operations. To do this, they must denationalize operations and replace home-country loyalties with a system of common corporate values and loyalties. This is particularly challenging because globalization by definition involves exposure to and linkages with broadly divergent national cultures. Globalization is also based on huge world-scale plants in which acculturation and communication become real challenges. Production economies also reach upper limits with size – limits that of course often restrict the benefits of globalization.

Many companies face clear, often insurmountable operational obstacles to globalization. At Cyanamid's German subsidiary, for example, a critical shortage of labor makes it nearly impossible to run a plant 24 hours a day. Furthermore, the labor laws that forbid many women in Germany from working at night compound the staffing problem. Language is another simple, though very real, obstacle to globalization.

In Germany, Cyanamid has determined that implementing a global strategy, which would require the insertion of technical product information into packages, would mean the proliferation of centralized packaging. To speed the packaging function and to give medical practitioners in the field timely back-up support, the company estimates that it would need staff members with technical fluency in approximately 12 to 15 languages at global headquarters.

They argue further that German law outlaws global market-share battles in which profits are artificially generated in one market to support operations in another. Clearly, the promises of globalization must be viewed in the context of very real organizational obstacles and costs to be overcome.

Globalization often circumvents subsidiary competencies. Many global strategies are based on rationalizing operations so that subsidiaries contribute a portion of a finished product's value-added content. Subsidiaries, which in the past functioned as miniature replicas, face a role change that often involves a reduction in their strategic autonomy.

A case in point is Alkaril Chemicals, Ltd. of Canada, which was recently acquired by Rhone-Poulenc. Alkaril had considerable skills in developing low-volume, specialty chemicals. For surfactants in particular, the company had developed a noteworthy reputation for customized product formulation and flexible production. With the acquisition, Alkaril has been left wondering what role it will play in Rhone-Poulenc's broader strategy, which emphasizes rationalized production and greater economies of scale.

Although subsidiaries have typically responded promptly to corporate initiatives, globalization is being resisted by many subsidiary managers who fear the loss of autonomy and personal contribution that comes with globalization. Unless they handle this situation delicately, corporations risk losing many of the top managers who ran miniature replica subsidiaries. Another very real risk is that subsidiary managers may take initiatives that restrict the parent from making future moves to rationalize operations.

The Regional Alternative

The move toward the globalization of competition was paralleled in the latter half of the 1980s by a dramatic upsurge in regional competitive pressures. Although regional pressures come from a variety of sources, the most important developments are in the formalization of trading blocks. In North America, the Free Trade Agreement between Canada and the United States is having a far-reaching impact on the business environment. This Agreement, which was signed on January 2,

1988, promised to remove all tariffs for a wide variety of industries by 1988. Although trade barriers will remain in place in the areas of agriculture, culture, and maritime-related industries, virtually every other industry faces liberalized trade.

Within the European Union, 1992 was a pivotal year in eliminating trade barriers among the member-nations. The goal of Europe 1992, as specified first in the 1985 White Paper and reaffirmed in the 1987 Single European Act, is to sweep away the non-tariff barriers that restrict the flow of goods, services, and capital throughout the trading block. Three categories of barriers are to be either eliminated or reduced: fiscal, physical, and technical barriers.

In 1989, 21 of the 22 richest industrialized nations in the world – the exception being Japan – belonged to regional trading groups. Japan, as the dominant economic power of the Pacific Rim, has long attempted to strengthen its position in the region. The countries of the Pacific Rim now have the fastest-growing economies in the world, caused in part by the huge influx of Japanese investment.

Many Japanese companies, aided by the strong yen, have transferred whole manufacturing bases to such countries as Thailand and Singapore. Production in these newly industrialized economies is now increasingly being referred to as "JapaNIEs" manufacturing. Japanese economic aid to the region has shown similar growth; in 1989 it was almost 14 times greater than that supplied by the United States.

With all this investment, trade has skyrocketed. Trade within Pacific Asia is now growing at an annual rate of 30 percent and promises to surpass Pacific Asia–North American levels of $250 billion by 1991. Fearful of being left out of the development of the region, Australia and Thailand have proposed the establishment of formal Asian–Pacific consultative bodies with many similarities to the Canada–U.S. Free Trade Agreement and the Europe 1992 phenomenon.

The rise of regional trading blocks has led many companies to reassess the anticipated rise of globalization. Some are taking their cues from governments that established free-trade associations at least in part to encourage and control the economic adjustments that ultimately result in improved global competitiveness. Increasingly, regionalization is being viewed by managers as a stepping-stone to more effective global competition. This view is ably summarized by Wisse Dekker, chairman of the Supervisory Board of N. V. Philips, in an interview with Nan Stone that was reported in the *Harvard Business Review* (May–June, 1989, pp. 90–95):

> [We] need a single European market with common technical standards. Without it, we cannot achieve the optimum scale and the lower unit costs we need to be competitive worldwide.

This reasoning was shared by many managers in our study – namely, that regional strategies are increasingly providing the primary determinant of competitive advantage. In fact, according to the majority of companies surveyed, the evolution to true global competition is currently on hold. Instead of globalization managers are finding that regional competitive pressures are taking on an ever-greater importance by introducing a set of distinct opportunities and threats.

Regional Competition

A consequence of regionalization pressures, our research found, is that home-oriented parents and subsidiaries – whether in Europe, North America, or Japan – were pressured to become more regionally focused or face a competitive disadvantage, even in so-called global industries. Similarly, companies that had attempted to pursue global strategies were coming under intense pressure to scale back their efforts to meet regional competitive conditions.

Under a regional strategy, companies extend home-country loyalities to the entire region. Local markets are intentionally linked within the region where competitive strategies are formulated. It is within the region that top managers determine investment locations, product mix, competitive positioning, and performance appraisals. Managers are given the opportunity to solve regional challenges regionally.

The importance of responding to the upsurge in regional pressures was not going unnoticed in the companies we studied – witness the following examples:

Thomson Consumer Electronics, Inc. has been trying for several years to regionalize its strategy for its television sets. To do so it has established four Thomson factories in Europe: EWD in Germany, Seipel in France, Cedosa in Spain, and Ferguson in the U.K. Each of these factories assembles specific types of television sets for the European market. EWD, for example, has a European mandate to produce high-feature, large television sets; Cedosa of Spain focuses on low-cost, small-screen sets. The marketing and distribution of the sets is handled by a separate Thomson division that has a similar regional mandate.

In North America, Thomson manufactures television sets under the RCA and GE nameplates. In spite of sourcing some common low-cost components from the Far East, the North American and European operations are run separately. Thomson has established a network of regional suppliers and subassemblers – largely in Mexico – to maintain the regional integrity of North American operations.

Warner Lambert Co. has had operations in Europe since the 1920s through its Parke-Davis subsidiary. The company currently has manufacturing facilities in the U.K., France, Italy, Spain, Germany, Belgium, and Ireland. Historically, these plants have focused on blending and packaging to meet local needs.

In 1987, discussions were begun under the direction of the parent to dramatically restructure operations to maximize regional responsiveness. After three years of often heated discussions, a plan was adopted to cut the number of manufacturing units to less than half of 1990 levels and to specialize in each unit. Instead of producing a large number of products for each local market, each plant would produce fewer products for the entire European market.

To the majority of the companies studied, regionalization represented a compromise between the traditional strategies adopted by miniature replica subsidiaries and the global strategies currently being advocated. Regional production facilities have often proved to be as scale-efficient as global facilities while being more forgiving of the need to tailor key product features for local markets. Regional plants also avoid many of the very real staffing, communication, and motivational problems of huge global facilities.

By shifting operations and decision making to the region, the company is also better able to maintain an insider advantage. Many of the Japanese regional investments in the automobile and consumer electronics industries have, for example, been based on the objective of developing insider market advantages. Finally, regionalization allows corporations to more effectively leverage subsidiary competencies by encouraging affiliate involvement in activities that extend beyond local markets.

The regionalization of competition is occurring irrespective of the often very real opportunities to globalize certain aspects of company operations. Indeed, many of the companies studied were sourcing raw materials and commodity components across regions; others were sharing R&D between laboratories across regions. What regionalization does suggest is that even companies in so-called global industries should move to exploit strengths and determine competitive strategies separately on a region-by-region basis. To do so may require some macro, transregional facilitation, but strategic decision making should not unilaterally emanate from world headquarters.

New Organizational Challenges

The move toward regional competition brings with it significant changes in the tasks and responsibilities of both home-country and subsidiary managers. For many companies, the organizational obstacles are extensive, suggesting a bumpy road to change.

The challenge is all the more daunting in view of the sheer magnitude of overseas investment and the weak understanding of many company managers of the opportunities and threats at hand. In 1987, for example, the value of goods and services produced by American firms in the European Union exceeded $235 billion, a figure four times the value of U.S. exports to the region. The gap continues to widen, and similar trends have been observed in North America and Japan.

For the parent, often far removed from distant markets and operations, several tasks and responsibilities become critical. That is, the parent needs to:

Stay abreast of local market conditions. In many instances, subsidiary managers felt that the parent dangerously misunderstood local or regional market conditions. Adjectives such as "naive" or "simplistic" were commonly used by subsidiary managers in describing their parents' understanding of local or regional conditions. A frequently stated belief was that the parent typically overestimates the similarities between markets and consequently pushes too hard and too fast for global consolidation. Subsidiaries often act in conjunction with one another to convince the parent to proceed more cautiously.

Stay abreast of subsidiary strengths and weaknesses. Many of the subsidiary managers who participated in this study commented that the parent often has only superficial understanding of the strengths and weaknesses of their operations. Though it was not unusual for a parent to know the product/market mix and sales levels of a subsidiary, it was far less common for the parent to understand the subsidiary's competitiveness on a product-by-product basis. Parents too often assumed that the subsidiary was uncompetitive outside local markets – even though, in many cases, the subsidiary could have competed on equal ground with the parent in terms of product development and cost competitiveness.

Prepare to shift autonomy to regional managers. For many a corporate parent, regionalization involves a greater leap of faith than it does for a subsidary; after all, the parent is removed from decision making, while the subsidiary remains a central participant in the process. Our research found that the adjustment to regional decision making was easiest for European managers and most difficult for Japanese managers. The Japanese difficulties stemmed from two sources: a fairly thin cadre of Japanese managers with international training and experience, and a legacy of tight top-to-bottom control that seriously frustrated non-Japanese managers.

In one instance, the general manager of European operations for one of Japan's largest consumer electronics companies commented that he constantly felt like an outsider in the corporation. As a non-Japanese, he felt that his opportunities for further advancement were nil and that his contributions to corporate thinking were largely ignored. Unless this kind of situation changes, Japanese ability to respond to mounting regional pressures will be severely hampered.

North American corporate managers also face serious challenges. One assessment of corporate preparedness for Europe 1992 ranked Canadian managers at 39 and U.S. managers at 38 out of a possible maximum score of 100. Not surprisingly, European managers fared significantly better. American corporate managers have also been criticized for their lack of preparedness in penetrating the Japanese market and the Pacific Asian market.

For the subsidiary, a different set of tasks is important. Subsidiaries need to:

Prepare to take strategic initiatives. Our research found that subsidiaries can and often do influence their future roles under regionalization. Take the example of Motorola Canada. Like managers at other subsidiaries, managers at Motorola Canada were somewhat apprehensive about the risks associated with the expected rationalization of operations that would come under the Canada–U.S. Free Trade Agreement. Although the subsidiary is U.S.-owned, it employs about 2,500 people – virtually all of whom are Canadians. These people feared that, under free trade, many of their jobs would become redundant.

In an effort to maintain some control over developments, managers began as far back as the late 1970s to take several important initiatives. First, they beefed up their R&D group; then they began looking for new products that would complement existing offerings while providing export potential independent of the parent. What resulted was a series of products – including land-mobile radios and systems, modems, and data multiplexers – for which the subsidiary was given product mandates. Such mandates have given the subsidiary considerable influence in corporate decision making while providing the parent with new sales and manufacturing resources.

In the case of Motorola, the Canadian subsidiary was granted product mandates that allowed it access to the parent's world-wide distribution system. However, in the drive toward globalization, only a tiny fraction of the subsidiary's export sales went outside the region. To have attempted to develop, manufacture, and market universal products to worldwide customers would probably have overwhelmed the subsidiary at a time when it was struggling to gain credibility in the eyes of its parent. The more realistic initiative taken was to move regionally before pursuing a global presence.

Exploit existing competencies/build new strengths. Subsidiary managers need to look for opportunities to position themselves as "natural leaders" in selected products within the region. This implies a gradual build-up of competencies through small studies, pilot production in existing facilities, and so on. With expertise comes the influence that determines the subsidiary's position within the region.

The case of Cyanamid Canada is illustrative in this regard. Since 1907, Cyanamid has had Canadian operations that have benefited from high Canadian tariffs. In the early 1980s, however, the parent undertook a number of initiatives to strengthen itself as a company involved in biotechnology and specialty chemicals. What followed was a series of divestitures that caused the subsidiary to lose more than half its employees. With the movement toward free trade, concern mounted in the subsidiary that operations would be cut further as the parent rationalized operations on a regional basis.

In spite of these troubling conditions, however, subsidiary managers clearly believed that much could be done to reverse the situation. The feeling was that the subsidiary's competitive advantage lay in producing smaller-run products that required high levels of technological input.

Consequently, beginning in 1988, Cyanamid Canada began focusing efforts on reaching out to new technologies in highly specialized fields where it could best exploit its unique strengths; this resulted in two recent acquisitions of Canadian biotechnology companies. Both acquisitions provided the subsidiary with considerable control over operations and an opportunity to strengthen its competencies in ways that will ensure its position in the ongoing restructuring of the parent's operations.

Manage structural mechanisms more effectively. Although there was a strong awareness of changing parent and subsidiary roles in all the companies we studied, many subsidiary managers were concerned about how to proceed with the necessary changes. At some subsidiaries, a damaging "us versus them" attitude had emerged. In these subsidiaries, managers often attempted to quietly sabotage change, frequently by entrenching the subsidiary through long-term supply or service contracts. These elaborate measures often severely tied the parents' hands and proved costly to both parent and subsidiary. In many of these organizations, morale was low and prospects for the future bleak.

Instead of avoiding inevitable integration, successful subsidiaries moved to preempt change through the artful use of a variety of structural mechanisms. These integrative mechanisms included a variety of such tools as personal contact between managers and the use of committees, task forces, and boards of directors. Knowing how and when to use appropriate structural mechanisms can maximize subsidiary influence while facilitating integration at multiple levels in the organization.

Structural mechanisms play a vital role because the move to a regional organization is a time-consuming and strenuous process. It was not uncommon for negotiations concerning a move toward regionalization to take three years or more; in many of the companies studied, negotiations that began in the mid-1980s were still ongoing 5 years later. Negotiations typically involved regular meetings of subsidiary managers and corporate executives and often served as the springboard for establishing more formal, regional decision-making bodies.

Conclusions: Capability and Flexibility Are the Keys

Few companies remain untouched by the complex environmental changes sweeping the world. In responding to these changes, however, managers have been urged to abandon the dated "miniature replica" approaches in favor of full-fledged global strategies. Although a global strategy promises in theory to be highly efficient, we found in this study that globalization is no panacea. In fact, global imperatives are being eclipsed by an upsurge in regional pressures. Companies are finding that the implementation of global strategies is often prohibitively costly in terms of morale, internal opposition, and lost opportunities to exploit key subsidiary strengths. As a consequence, both parents and subsidiaries are finding that regional strategies represent a safer, more manageable option.

In the course of our study, we also found that management of the regionalization process is often as important as design of the strategy. Flexibility is critical for both parents and subsidiaries as they negotiate roles and tasks in the restructuring of operations.

Here, however, managers are finding that flexibility is only as good as the competencies within the organization. As competitive pressures heat up, organizations that effectively nurture and exploit distinctive competencies stand the greatest chance of success. We suggest that regionalization provides a controlled approach to change and that it builds upon the distinctive competencies of the entire organization while responding to the legitimate pressures for greater integration.

Selected Bibliography

For a more complete discussion of the "miniature replica" model of subsidiary strategy, see Rod White and Thomas Poynter's "Strategies for Foreign-Owned Subsidiaries in Canada" (*Business Quarterly*, Summer 1984) and Harold Crookell's "Specialization and International Competitiveness" (*Business Quarterly*), Fall 1984).

To review some current discussions on the need to become global competitors, see Barrie James's "Reducing the Risks of Globalization" (*Long-Range Planning*), 23, 1990, p. 80). "The Stateless Corporation" (*Business Week*, May 14, 1990), and "How to go Global – and Why" (*Fortune*, August 28, 1989).

Several articles treat this topic more systematically and comprehensively. One of the first discussions of a global strategic option was outlined by C.K. Prahalad in "The Strategic Process in a Multinational Corporation," (Boston: unpublished doctoral dissertation, Harvard Graduate School of Business Administration, 1976) and later adapted by Yves Doz in "Strategic Management in Multinational Companies" (*Sloan Management Review*, Winter 1980, pp. 27–46) and by Thomas Hout, Michael Porter, and Eileen Rudden in their "How Global Companies Win Out," (*Harvard Business Review*, September–October 1982, pp. 98–108). Treatments of a more rigorous nature may be found in Sumantra Ghoshal's "Global Strategy: An Organizing Framework" (*Strategic Management Journal*, 8 (5), 1987, pp. 425–40), Bruce Kogut's "Designing Global Strategies: Comparative and Competitive Value-Added Chains" (*Sloan Management Review*, Summer 1985, pp. 15–28. 1985), and "A Note on Global Strategies" (*Strategic Management Journal*, 10, (4, 1989, pp. 383–389).

The trend toward scaling back global strategies to a more regional focus is corroborated by a recent Conference Board study, "Building Global Teamwork for Growth and Survival" (Research Bulletin No. 228, 1989, p. 13), which found that companies are shifting up to regional strategies as a logical outgrowth of EC developments on their country-by-country businesses. Global companies were in turn shifting down to regional strategies after finding their "global businesses too cumbersome or insensitive to specific market needs."

22

It Pays to Be Green: The Managerial Incentive Structure and Environmentally Sound Strategies

GIULIO M. GALLAROTTI

WESLEYAN UNIVERSITY

The Traditional View: Pollution Pays, Pollution Prevention Doesn't

Despite the visibility of a growing environmental wave that has been changing the fundamental structure of the business climate in developed nations over the past two decades, many managers still cling to the view that pollution pays, pollution prevention doesn't.[1] Pursuing environmentally sound strategies continues to be seen by a large cross section of managers as detrimental to the principal managerial goals of profitability, maintaining markets, controlling costs and efficient production. Such conclusions about an environmental drag on business are based on three fundamental beliefs.[2] First, the benefits of being *green* or environmentally sound practices cannot be fully appropriated by companies that follow such strategies (e.g. local residents will not pay companies for limiting water and air pollution). Second, the costs associated with environmentally sound strategies are significant. Much is supposedly sacrificed in terms of: (1) the diversion of investment and scarce resources (both economic and human) from productive areas to unproductive areas (i.e. designing, operating and maintaining pollution control equipment); (2) the standard costs and delays associated with the introduction of new products; and (3) the disruption caused by plans for constructing new production facilities and entering new markets.[3] Finally, there is limited liability in the market for pollution. In other words, companies do not bear the full costs of their environmental degradation, and because of these free uses of the environment, note Anderson and Leal (1991, 14), companies " 'overuse' the air or water as garbage dumps."

This traditional view has come under close scrutiny in the past two decades, especially in developed countries. With greater governmental regulation, many of the public-goods problems in

The author gratefully acknowledges the comments of Dennis Collins, Richard Grossman, David Titus, Gary Yohe and an anonymous reviewer.

"It Pays to Be Green: The Managerial Incentive Structure and Environmentally Sound Strategies," by Giulio M. Gallarotti, *The Columbia Journal of World Business*, Winter 1995, pp. 38–57. Reprinted by permission of Jai Press Inc.

the market for environmentalism have abated. Companies have found themselves bearing greater costs for their environmental degradation (through fines, taxes, and litigation) and have enjoyed greater benefits as a result of green practices (through subsidies, marketable pollution permits and fewer bureaucratic "hassles" from public authorities).[4] Corporate responses to the environment, however, continue to be perceived by many as adversarial. The view is still quite common that companies are coerced into adopting principles of green management rather than doing so voluntarily; that is, in the absence of regulation, managers would have little incentive to make their companies environmentally sound. But even the image of green managers as reluctant environmentalists underestimates the benefits of following environmentally sound strategies. Even without public coercion, the growing environmental consciousness in the developed world has opened up a plethora of opportunities to companies that are becoming greener.[5] Even without the public vigilantes, the trend toward being environmentally sound is becoming more compelling to managers.

The idea that green management can indeed be profitable is not new. As far back as 1966, Dow Chemical chairman Carl Gerstacker laid out the fundamental compatibility between profitability and the environment. Dow went on to institute an environmental strategy in the early 1970s geared toward "waste elimination, improved productivity and sustainable growth."[6] In 1975 3M launched the now celebrated Pollution Prevention Pays (3P) program, which was oriented around cost reduction through pollution prevention. In fact, the underlying philosophy of the program was that pollution represented "an inefficient use of resources." Operationally, 3P moved toward limiting the generation of waste and reusing residual materials through raw material substitution, end-product substitution, process modification, equipment redesign, recovery, good housekeeping, inventory control, segregation and direct recycling.[7]

Notwithstanding these early manifestations of the profitability of green management, it is only recently (1990s) that a proliferation of literature emphasizing the entrepreneurial opportunities embodied in environmentally sound strategies has occurred. The most celebrated statements of such opportunities have come from Vice President Al Gore (1993) and Michael Porter (1990, 1991), who suggest that companies increase their international and national competitiveness by moving toward greener production methods and products. But to go beyond the now familiar arguments of Porter and Gore, the opportunities are far more diverse and complex than a matter of simple efficiency gains and new markets and processes.

Together with the pressure from public authorities (regulation), these opportunities create a managerial incentive structure that pervades all dimensions of corporate operations. Costs can be reduced through low-bulk production and packaging, limiting the use of energy and raw materials, recycling and reusing energy and materials, substituting non-hazardous materials for hazardous ones, maximizing containment and improving quality control and byproduct use.

A proenvironment strategy also enhances managerial and organizational skills by placing a premium on thinking and operating in teams and networks, thinking in global and long-run terms and becoming familiar with all operations of a company as well as with an entire industry.

Markets can be better penetrated, maintained and even dominated as a result of environmental product differentiation and competition. Vertical links in the chains of production and distribution create greater pressures to produce green products as companies demand greener inputs and retailers respond to growing consumer demand for green goods. Moreover, green complementarities in production are increasingly squeezing nongreen complements out of the market. Environmentalism has also opened up numerous opportunities for cooperation among companies in product development, competition and production.

Managers are also faced with a variety of financial incentives to go green. A company's environmental record bears strongly on the desirability of its stock, its access to credit and, ultimately, the discretion with which it manages its own finances. Finally, the increasing exposure to litigation that has resulted from the pace of environmental legislation and enforcement has pressured companies to better manage environmental risk.

Given the pervasiveness of these environmental incentives, it is increasingly apparent that green management is consistent with good business. This article provides an analysis of this managerial incentive structure. The factors composing the structure can be organized under six categories: 1) efficiency (the supply side); 2) gaining and maintaining market shares (the demand side); 3) interdependencies in production and distribution; 4) rent seeking; 5) finance; and 6) risk management.

The Managerial Incentive Structure and Environmentally Sound Strategies

THE SUPPLY SIDE: EFFICIENCY AND OPTIMAL MANAGEMENT

Although corporate culture has come to look at the EPA's exhortations to clean up as clouded by a dogmatism not sympathetic toward business, it has become more apparent that the EPA's contention about the compatibility of environmentalism and profitability is in fact especially visible on the supply side.[8] A number of companies have recently undertaken broad environmental initiatives under the recognition that indeed "there is money to be made from saving the planet."[9] These companies, some of which have been traditionally vilified by environmentalists, have introduced pervasive environmental programs oriented to a large extent around cost-efficient reorganization of production and distribution: 3M's "Pollution Prevention Pays" (3P), Chevron's "Save Money and Reduce Toxics" (SMART), Texaco's "Wipe Out Waste" (WOW) and Dow's "Waste Reduction Always Pays" (WRAP).[10] The advantages of these high-profile initiatives have not escaped other companies, many of which have adopted a more selective implementation of cost-effective environmental strategies. The specific strategies highlighted in all these initiatives have been the reduction of bulk in products and packaging, reduction in energy use, recycling and reuse of materials and energy, reduction in the use of raw materials, substituting non-hazardous materials for hazardous ones, increased quality control, byproduct use and the maximization of containment.

The diversification toward lower bulk is perfectly in keeping with a normal evolution toward more cost-efficient production and distribution. Aside from reducing post-consumption waste (a serious environmental problem), scale reduction in production and distribution carries a variety of cost advantages.[11] Lighter products (e.g. concentrated liquids, more absorbent diapers) and packaging (e.g. shrink-wrapped plastic instead of corrugated cardboard) minimize the raw material and energy input to satisfy any given consumption preference.[12] The smaller scale in products and packaging further reduces transport, waste disposal and storage costs.[13] And, of course, inventories can be more effectively managed and manipulated to meet unanticipated shifts in demand: greater storage capacity means that any exogenous shifts in demand can be met out of existing stocks without having to start new production runs.[14]

Reducing energy use, which at present is primarily dependent on the burning of fossil fuels, has been a managerial priority since as far back as 1973 and the first oil crisis. The current green emphasis on energy conservation fits well into this priority. On a global scale, per capita demand for commercial energy was the same in 1987 as it was in 1977, even though real income had risen 12 percent in that period.[15] Since as much as 70 percent to 90 percent of carbon dioxide emissions are generated by fossil-fuel use, energy conservation can be an important check against global warming.[16] The green emphasis has been instrumental in making energy conservation pervasive across corporate operations, even in the office. Croxton Collaborative, for example, a green architectural company, saves energy through the use of highly efficient fixtures and compact fluorescent bulbs.[17]

Initiatives to recycle and reuse energy and material bear directly on the environment through the reduction of waste. Reducing waste has been an ongoing priority among companies, primarily as a means of cost control. Stricter regulations on waste management have significantly raised the operating costs of landfills, and these costs have been passed on to businesses. In the United States, dumping hazardous wastes in landfills rose from $80 a ton in 1980 to $255 a ton in 1990. In Europe, the cost of dumping asbestos rose tenfold across that same period.[18]

Production strategies oriented around "industrial ecology" ("closing the loop" or "cradle to grave") have not only reduced wastes and the use of raw materials, but have also led to alternative production possibilities that allow companies to turn what was formerly waste into marketable inputs.[19] The desirability of these residual and recycled inputs has grown as environmental regulators have placed greater emphasis on reused and recycled materials.[20] For example, a Finnish process for sulfur dioxide elimination from the production of copper creates various residuals that can be sold as inputs. An extension of this process in the Philippines integrates the production of sulfuric acid with the creation of phosphate fertilizer via the extraction of phosphate rock. The calcium sulfate residues are then eliminated through the production of gypsum, which can be used as material for building roads. Hence, what was once a process that produced one useful product (copper) and one harmful waste product (sulfur dioxide) now produces four useful products and very little waste. Alden Rubber saves $150,000 a year from converting toluene vapors (captured by enclosing their machines) into liquid form and then reusing it.[21] Similarly, organic waste from the agribusiness and food industries has found increasing use as a substitute in the fermentation processes that produce amino acids, ethanol, vitamins and penicillin. Along with the cost-saving benefits of reconsumption, these residual goods offer opportunities for diversification in production that fit well into the growing market for waste exchange.[22] Along with using residual products, those firms that were formerly the worst pollution offenders have established special divisions that market environmental know-how and technology.[23] Projections show that this will continue to be a strong growth industry in the future.[24]

Furthermore, reuse in energy and products and a more parsimonious use of raw materials eliminate or reduce several uncertainties regarding supply. Changes in the availability of virgin-material inputs and energy-producing resources (e.g. the supply of water) will have less of an impact on production. Reusable products reduce inventories and allow managers to more accurately accommodate demand.[25] The diversification of production toward environmental products (especially recycled or residual materials) also introduces a counter-cyclical hedge. Sales in secondary markets for raw materials should increase when general business conditions are poor because companies may be less able to afford virgin materials as inputs.

The substitution of nonhazardous materials for hazardous ones has provided another means by which companies can use lower-cost materials in the production process. One way companies have dealt with the problem of solvents has been to substitute water-based processes for more expensive solvent-based processes in cleaning and painting. Polaroid and Volvo have been especially noted for the reversion of their production strategies away from organic solvents.[26] Similarly, the reversion from CFC to non-CFC use has generated some significant cost reductions for companies that have shifted from aerosol spray cans to mechanical pump dispensers (the latter being much cheaper to produce).[27]

With respect to environmentalism and efficiency, the environmental problems experienced by companies are in fact often the results of poor operation and organization. Much of the environmental degradation perpetrated by businesses is the result of inefficient use of raw materials, leakages and substandard production (e.g. rejected products having to be dumped).[28] This is consistent with the view that a shift toward environmentalism will actually increase a company's competitiveness.[29] Inattention to containment has always been both a source of pollution and inefficiency. In the vinyl chloride industry, for example, companies producing the chemical found that greater containment both reduced worker exposure to hazardous emissions and increased output significantly. Elsewhere, in 1980 the Conoco coal company introduced a spray device that limited the emission of coal dust into the atmosphere during transportation. Estimates show that this saved the company about 80 tons per trainload.[30] Corporate studies invariably find that the avenues to better performance are coterminous with these avenues to reduced waste, reduced leakages and the elimination of inefficiencies in general.[31]

A pro-environment strategy can in many ways also enhance management and organizational skills. Dealing with the complexity of environmentally sound production, distribution and waste management requires state-of-the-art management techniques. Such demands certainly put an emphasis on thinking and operating in networks and teams (which include shareholders and board members) rather than in isolated and hierarchical modes (the former being a source of great success in Japanese industry), something that is being done more often in American industry for reasons other than the environment. Environmental complexity essentially encourages a "governed corporation": a corporation that minimizes organizational failure by better integrating a broad range of players in the decision-making process.[32] In short, the environmentally sound company will be a better managed company because it encourages managers to deal more effectively with local communities as well as think and operate in teams and networks, forces managers to consider the preferences of a variety of stakeholders, puts a premium on limiting risk and long-term thinking, encourages performance at maximum efficiency (i.e. maximizing the quantity of usable product from the very earliest to the latest stages of production) and enhances a company's capacity to acquire the best candidates in the labor market.[33]

At the international level, management can be standardized if multinationals establish uniform environmental strategies across their global operations, which in turn encourages economies of scale in the application of managerial skills (i.e. less need for excess management with regionally specific skills). It is not uncommon for multinationals to impose the highest-common-denominator-environmental standards (i.e. produce for the very greenest markets) so as to maximize access to all regional markets. This encourages the greenest standardization in international production and distribution strategies.[34]

Although companies bear considerable short-term burdens in the expenditures necessitated by environmentally sound production, it is incorrect (as traditional thinking on the issue does) to compare such a strategy to one in which these pollution control costs are avoided altogether. Growing regulation of the environment will likely force such costs upon companies in any case. Initiating such a strategy beforehand (i.e. preempting the law) carries several advantages. First, it is generally more costly to have to deal with pollution post-hoc ("end-of-pipe" environmentalism) than to prevent it.[35] (In some cases, depending on the industry, the cost of post-hoc treatment is virtually prohibitive.)[36] Diceon Electronics, for example, experienced a significant net reduction in operating costs because the introduction of a new, less toxic chemical in the production process reduced water treatment costs by more than two-thirds.[37] The American auto industry has also enjoyed similar reductions in costs after substituting water for solvents, the latter requiring very expensive pollution treatment technology. Depending on the industry, investments in pollution control technology can be recouped within a fairly short time as a result of cost reductions.[38] Furthermore, companies often avoid bearing the full costs of developing and introducing environmental technologies. It has been common, especially in the oil and chemical industries, for companies to codevelop technology and coimplement environmental strategies. This introduces greater economies of scale and cost-sharing in the control of pollution.[39]

Second, voluntarily initiating an environmental strategy allows managers to carry out such a strategy in their own way, rather than having the implementation of such a strategy be dictated by public authorities who are neither knowledgeable about nor sympathetic toward the company in question. A public statement by Monsanto is representative; it underscores the desirability of dealing with environmental imperatives "our way" by "applying technologies and making changes that arrive at desired ends – ways that make sense for us – rather than reacting to prescriptive regulations that can result in inefficiencies and unnecessarily burdensome costs."[40] Voluntary initiation of an environmental strategy allows greater discretion over its implementation. This allows managers to better control costs and more advantageously manage the financing of implementation.[41] For example, leveraging capital expenditures for implementation can be done when interest rates are low. Furthermore, managers may opt for pervasive implementation in one shot so as to take advantage of economies of scale. One-shot implementation would also minimize the time period of disruption in operations during transition. Greater discretion also maximizes the number of alternative strategies that managers can apply. Finally, a voluntary strategy will be more organizationally compatible than an imposed strategy that necessitates more external supervision and accountability.[42]

THE DEMAND SIDE: GAINING AND MAINTAINING MARKET SHARES

Demand-side considerations bearing on corporate environmentalism gravitate around the need to protect established markets and opportunities to penetrate new markets. Maintaining and penetrating markets in a period of environmental awareness necessitates sensitivity to the propensity toward "green consumption." Market studies overwhelmingly show that consumer preferences have shifted toward environmentally sound products (and concomitantly away from environmentally unsound products), and that this shift is neither ephemeral nor faddish.[43] Peattie and Ratnayaka (1992, 104–5) in fact stress that marketing executives are overwhelmingly of the opinion that companies must reorient their production methods for the long run toward what will be a permanent proenvironmental consumption style in developed countries.[44] This structural shift in consumption patterns generates both an active and a reactive dimension to business's response to the environmental challenge. The active side is caught up in penetrating new green markets, while the reactive side has to do with maintaining markets for existing products.

On the active side new green markets have proliferated. Managers have responded very strongly to the opportunities for creating new markets. It is on the active side that most of the advantages accrue to "early movers."[45] Unlike a decade or so ago, the market for green products is no longer very small and the marketing no longer extremely specialized.[46] Indeed, the market has become quite large and the products quite general in their functions and appeal. The most overt manifestation of this phenomenon has been in green retailing. Large stores like Wal-Mart (which has pursued a green labeling program) and the Canadian chain Loblaws (which has introduced special sections of environmentally sound products called Nature's Choice) are the most visible embodiment of this trend.[47]

On the reactive side, not jumping onto the environmental bandwagon can produce substantial penalties for laggard companies. Market surveys invariably show that consumers react negatively to poor environmental performance. Hence a relative decline in environmental performance translates into a loss of market shares.[48] In one poll of 23,000 American adults conducted by Simmons Market Research Bureau, 60 percent showed a disposition toward boycotting the products of polluting industries.[49] The impetus to maintain relative environmental performance *vis-à-vis* competitors is all the more enhanced by the significant rise in environmental scrutiny on the part of individual consumers and public and private agencies.[50]

Possibilities for evading this scrutiny have increasingly diminished through stricter environmental disclosure rules, such as Title III of the 1986 Superfund Amendments and Reauthorization Act (which requests full disclosure of polluting emissions) and independent eco-labeling by public and private organizations.[51] It is, therefore, of little surprise that well-publicized environmental initiatives by one company generate large-scale responses from their competitors. When Monsanto announced its 90-percent program, for example, IBM, Merck, Union Carbide, GE and DuPont followed closely behind and announced similar initiatives.[52] Interestingly, with respect to the impact of environmental performance on consumer perceptions of companies, poor performance often hurts the industry as much as individual companies. As Smart (1992, 164) notes, "an industry's reputation tracks that of its least admired member."

Maintaining market shares through environmentalism also takes into account the ever-changing legal structure that affects business in both the short and long runs. Making environmentally sound products not only keeps companies competitive *vis-à-vis* other companies, but also ensures that their products are acceptable to public authorities.[53] Deficiencies in either area can seriously affect a company's viability. Maintaining acceptable products keeps producers one step ahead of ever-increasing environmental regulation. Companies that produced and marketed low-bulk and recyclable products in Germany in the 1980s, for example, actually welcomed the imposition of stricter limits on the generation of household waste.[54]

Lagging too far behind the course of regulation while competitors do not can affect the competitiveness of an entire product line.[55] This is especially true for companies that complete internationally. Producing for the most regulated national markets maximizes international competitiveness. Hewlett-Packard, for example, set its world-wide business machine packaging to conform to German laws, which are the strictest environmentally, so as to ensure access to all markets. Where companies are following the toughest standards, there is an incentive for entire industries' environmental performances to gravitate toward this highest common-environmental denominator.[56] Anticipation can also prevent environmental accidents whose publicity could seriously affect popular perceptions of companies and their products.[57]

Both the active and reactive processes of environmentalism compose a form of nonprice competition on the part of companies.[58] By marketing their products in this respect, firms are conforming to broad shifts in consumer preferences over the non-price aspects of the products they consume.[59] Many marketing specialists, in fact, see the recent wave of green marketing as the equivalent of the quality movement in the 1980s.[60] Certainly, with respect to the environmental aspects of products, market studies have conclusively shown that consumers are indifferent to price differentials within certain ranges. Consumers will pay more for environmentally safe products.[61] Companies may also find that a proenvironment image translates into greater sales across product lines.[62] After Monsanto announced its 90-percent program, for example, its market studies showed that the positive public opinion about Monsanto spilled over into some of its non-chemical product lines.[63]

INTERDEPENDENCIES IN PRODUCTION AND DISTRIBUTION

Environmental market pressures represent forces that encourage the replacement of environmentally unsound products with environmentally sound ones through both direct and indirect processes. The direct pressures (discussed in the above section) cause green products to crowd nongreen products out of markets because companies are responding to competitive forces that are increasingly oriented toward environmental consumerism. Companies also face more indirect pressures that produce a similar bias in favor of green products. These indirect forces are tied up in the interdependencies in production and distribution that are manifest in the relations that businesses carry on with each other.

Companies face pressures to be environmentally sound through vertical links in the chains of production and distribution, as well as links created by complementarities in production. Since companies purchase their inputs from other companies, any environmental priorities in the former will also tend to impact the latter. In Germany, manufacturers of drink products have put great pressure on their bottlers to provide drinks in receptacles that can be easily recycled or reused. Similarly, Hoechst Celanese scrambled to develop bottle recycling technology so it could remain Coca-Cola's main supplier.[64] In the United States, suppliers of containers that hold liquid products have faced greater pressure to increase the recycled content of those containers. S.C. Johnson Wax, for example, has demanded that all its suppliers participate in an environmental program called "Partners Working for a Better World."[65] These initiatives have been a response to stricter laws about recycling as well as a result of a desire to conform all stages of production to green consumerism.[66] Green consumerism also was a principal force behind the recent push on the part of leading tuna canners to demand that their suppliers catch tuna only in ways that are dolphin-safe.[67]

In a survey of attitudes on the part of companies toward their suppliers conducted by 3M, the most important concern that emerged (mentioned by 20 percent of the respondents) was about the environmental soundness of the goods they purchased from these suppliers.[68] The incentive to pressure suppliers at lower levels of value added is raised all the more because it represents a subtle (and politically viable) way of shifting the cost of environmental cleansing down along the vertical chain of production. Environmental costs at each higher step in the chain of production are reduced to the extent that greater environmentalism is practiced at previous stages. The costs of dumping toxic wastes, for example, are reduced when companies purchase inputs that contain fewer hazardous materials. Similarly, other prevention and post-hoc treatment costs (e.g. containment, emissions treatment) are also reduced when final products make use of inputs that went through environmentally sound early stages of production.

Extending the life cycle of the product to distribution, we see a similar process of environmental pressure through interdependence. Given retailers' sensitivity to environmental consumption patterns, the companies supplying these retailers have felt increasing pressure to conform final products to greener tastes.[69] The recent trend in large-scale retailing (from food to general merchandise) has been to stock greener products.[70] The demands for such environmental performance from suppliers often extends through the entire chain of production. For example, Marks and Spencer, a large British retailer, has insisted that its suppliers of beef graze cattle on non-deforested pasture. They, in fact, have sent representatives to Brazil to scrutinize these grazing practices. Similarly, McDonald's has been carefully monitoring grazing practices by its suppliers.[71] Provigo, a grocery chain based in Quebec, and Tangelmann, a British home improvement chain, have demanded that their suppliers ship goods in packaging that is CFC-safe and chlorine-free.[72] In Germany, retailers reluctantly stock products without the green dot – an eco-label guaranteeing that the product's packaging will be recycled.[73]

Beyond the distribution stage, post-consumption practices can also create environmental pressures that reverberate across the chain of production. More stringent laws limiting the amount of household waste have pressured companies to produce lower-bulk products. In Germany, for example, limitations on the number of household waste cans encouraged Procter & Gamble to introduce its Lenor concentrated fabric softener in a refillable pouch.[74]

Finally, interdependent pressures for environmentalism show up in complementarities in production. The demand for some products will often be linked to the demand for other products. Such products are referred to as complements. For example, as the demand for automobiles rises, so too will the demand for gasoline; gasoline and automobiles are complements. Similarly, the demand for lamps and light bulbs are linked in complementary fashion. The existence of green products essentially encourages green complements. As the demand for green complements increases, nongreen complements will be crowded out of the market. More products that traditionally made use of CFCs, for example, are now being reoriented to use CFC substitutes. The pressures toward environmentalism here are circular, since the greater production of one increases the demand for the other.[75] Hence, products that use CFC substitutes will crowd CFC-using products out of the market as CFC substitutes crowd CFCs out of their respective markets. In this case, even if manufacturers of CFCs and CFC-using products found the costs of environmentalism onerous, they would still be forced to conform because the availability of their non-green complementary products would diminish.[76]

RENT SEEKING: GAINING MARKET POWER THROUGH ENVIRONMENTALISM

Environmentalism also offers companies various opportunities for imposing and extending their domination over markets. These opportunities are synonymous with possibilities for monopolization and/or cooperation (i.e. oligopoly) in markets for specific products. This, in turn, creates opportunities for companies to gain greater profits through the manipulation of supply (i.e. rent seeking). Environmentally sound products face demand conditions that are already very well suited to rent seeking *vis-à-vis* environmentally unsound products since, as noted above, the former face a more inelastic demand compared to the latter (i.e. consumers will tolerate higher prices for environmentally sound products). This means that environmentally sound products have an advantage over environmentally unsound products such that the former will have greater appeal to consumers at prices that are above the competitive level.[77]

The opportunities for rent seeking are stimulated by factors in both the private and public sectors: green consumption in the private sector and the growing environmental regulation from the public sector. In responding to the growing wave of environmental consumption, companies have found that introducing greener characteristics in their products has served to differentiate their products from others, environmentally sound and not. Such differentiation serves to create

292 • EMERGING ISSUES

opportunities to control markets through two avenues. First, it makes the demand for the environmentally sound product more price inelastic; second, it can make entry into the industry more costly.[78] Both elements allow greater possibilities for rents, since companies can raise prices without sacrificing sales.

This accounts for what has amounted to a race to open environmental niches across selected product lines, from atmosphere-friendly products to biodegradable garbage bags and diapers.[79] Being first in a niche carries special advantages with respect to opportunities for dominating markets. A company can earn exclusive rents while others are trying to catch up. But even after others have entered the market, having been the first in a product line generates a competitive advantage over time through such things as consumer loyalty, visibility, and perceptions of quality.

Aside from shifts in consumer preferences, niches can also be created by environmental regulations. Companies can dominate such niches by keeping up with or anticipating changing environmental laws.[80] For companies competing on the international level, this means monitoring the evolution of regulation across many countries. DuPont, for example, has sought to strengthen its position in Europe by developing a capacity to recycle plastic from municipal waste in response to expectations of tougher European recycling cycling laws.[81]

Business frequently joins environmentalist groups to form strong alliances in favor of tougher environmental regulation when such laws grant existing companies in selected product lines the means of keeping competitors from entering their markets.[82] Environmentalists received enormous support from CFC-producing companies in bringing pressure to bear upon the U.S. government to sign both the Vienna (1985) and Montreal (1987) multilateral agreements to place limits on the production of CFCs. Aside from a concern with their image (CFC producers in the United States were few and hence quite visible), they found that limits could freeze production at levels that excluded new competitors, thus allowing them to continue their domination of the CFC market.[83] Furthermore, producers found that the market for CFC substitutes offered even more favorable conditions than the market for CFCs. Substitutes were more costly to produce, which meant greater barriers to entry for potential competitors (start-up costs were raised by expenditures on R&D), and the profit margins on substitues were greater than those on CFCs. Hence, for these producers, stricter limits on CFC use meant both greater rents in the present market for CFCs by keeping competitors out by law, and rents in the market for substitutes through the natural barriers to entry that existed there.[84] Producers of roll-on deodorants also found the ban on CFCs a convenient means of eliminating some competitors (i.e. deodorants in aerosol spray cans).[85] Similarly, the glass industry has been trying to limit the competition from plastics manufacturers by supporting higher levels of mandatory use of recycled materials; the glass industry has traditionally employed more recycled materials in their products than have plastics manufacturers.[86]

At the international level, multinational companies competing in less developed countries may prefer stricter rather than looser environmental regulation in host nations because they tend to have greener products than domestic producers, thus giving themselves the means to gain an advantage over these companies.[87] Conversely, in nations that have fairly green companies, domestic business groups have supported stricter environmental standards as a means of excluding international competition. For example, U.S. companies have been able to limit imports of tuna through lobbying for laws that restrict tuna that is not dolphin-safe. Similarly, U.S. farmers have argued for restrictions on foreign imports of agricultural goods based on looser standards in pesticide use overseas. These are just two of a plethora of environmental criteria used to restrict foreign competition. The use of such criteria to limit trade has grown to a level that has produced minor crises for the General Agreement on Tariffs and Trade (GATT) and the World Trade Organization.[88]

Finally, the environmental revolution has opened up numerous opportunities that have facilitated cooperation among companies, thus enhancing the possibilities for oligopolizing markets. The closer intercompany cooperation toward environmental production methods and products, much of which is strongly encouraged by public authorities, has made it easier for groups of large companies to dominate markets in existing and new goods. The incentive to cooperate is raised all the more by the fact that (as noted) the environmental image of an entire industry usually reflects the performance of its least successful (i.e. dirtiest) member, thus forcing all companies to monitor the developments among their competitors and discourage any laggards. In the quest to solve the ozone depletion problem, for example, the Program for Alternative Fluorocarbon Toxicity Testing (initiated by the Montreal Protocol) has collectivized and centralized the research on CFC substitutes, which essentially opens up opportunities to reduce the competition in the market for substitutes by encouraging coordination in product development and marketing. This reduces the risk of drastic changes in market shares among existing companies when producers make a transition away from CFCs.[89] Elsewhere, the Industry Cooperative for Ozone Layer Protection (ICOLP) has moved the international electronics industry toward greater cooperation through information exchange on CFC substitutes.[90] In the U.S. chemical industry, the Responsible Care initiative of the 1980s forged greater links among existing companies in managing their transition to environmentally sound production, thus enhancing the ability of these companies to control competition among themselves when introducing new products and production methods.[91]

The opportunities to impose greater control over markets is not in fact only restricted to companies' traditional product lines. Companies find that the environmental revolution in business has opened up possibilities to enter into other markets in advantageous positions. In fact, while antitrust laws often make collusion in established markets difficult, they are far more tolerant of cooperation in new environmental product lines. For example, the links among large chemical companies have been strengthened through the National Polystyrene Recycling Company. This is a joint venture among leading chemical companies to recycle polystyrene into non-food packaging. Furthermore, sharing information, even on peripheral operations, allows greater coordination of production and marketing strategies in main product lines as well.[92]

FINANCIAL INCENTIVES

Companies have found that the penalties for poor environmental performance also extend into a variety of areas that compose the financial health of the company. For one thing, firms face adverse consequences with respect to the value and attractiveness of their equity. Investors, both large and small, have increasingly become sensitized to the environmental makeup of their portfolios. This is part of a greater sensitivity to the "ethical content" of portfolios among present-day investors. Just as carrying on operations in pariah countries like South Africa has had an adverse impact on the value and demand for a company's stock, so too can investor perceptions of a company's social impact – environmental performance being central to such perceptions – sway decisions about the content of portfolios. This growing trend toward ethical screening on the part of investors has made the desirability of equity contingent on a much more complex set of performance criteria than just simply the size of returns or dividends.[93] In fact, the use of special consultants or in-house staff to screen the environmental performance of targets for investment has become a fairly commonplace characteristic of large-scale institutional investing in developed countries.[94] Indicative of this trend toward environmental investment has been the recent growth of green funds, mutual funds comprising the stocks of companies carefully screened and designated as carrying on their operations in an environmentally friendly way.

Given the adverse consequences of poor environmental performance on the equity of companies, it is no surprise that much of the impetus to move toward environmentally sound practices with which companies are faced comes from shareholders.[95] The environmentally curious and demanding shareholder confronts managers with even greater incentives to carefully audit all environmental impacts of the company. With the increase in environmental scrutiny, environmental performance is increasingly transparent. In the United States, for example, SEC rules dictate that companies must state potential environmental liabilities in annual reports.[96]

Investors' concern for environmental performance reflects much more than just a social concern. In a fundamental respect, it is a highly rational reaction to the link between environmental performance and profitability (for all the reasons pointed out in this paper), a link that ultimately has an impact on the returns on their investments. Hence, even purely unethical investors would find green companies a desirable target. As Jean Morissette, vice president of Montreal's Desjardins Trust, notes, "A company that effectively manages the environment is usually well managed overall and will provide superior returns in the long run."[97] The fact that environmentally sound companies are perceived as well managed, and that their production strategies keep them in tune with trends in environmental regulation and consumer choice, make them a natural target for investors looking for safe/long-run portfolio positions (i.e. fairly low-risk assets).[98]

This means that investors would, in fact, tolerate lower returns from their green funds in the short run. But the performance of green equities has not disappointed even in this respect. It is not uncommon for green funds to outperform their respective markets. Peter Kinder of SIF tracked the performance of 400 green stocks and found that group doing better than S&P's 500 index over the period 1984 to 1989.[99] In some cases, fund managers have attempted to take advantage of the environmental revolution in business by going ultragreen – investing in companies that stand to profit from the trend toward greener production (e.g. waste services, pollution prevention technology and companies providing alternative energy sources). This new growth industry has even attracted aggressive investors (i.e. those more swayed by short-run returns) as a result of the enormous rise in the demand for such services.[100]

Environmental performance also affects the company itself as an investor. Access to commercial credit has increasingly become linked to companies' environmental records. Large banks are showing a greater environmental component in their lending strategies. According to a statement by Bank of America regarding its commercial credit policy, officers will "increasingly weigh the degree of environmental responsibility displayed by potential borrowers and their affiliates."[101] In some cases, commercial lending is exclusively earmarked for green companies. In Germany, for example, the Okobank of Frankfurt was founded for the sole purpose of funding environmentally sound business projects.[102] As in the case of investment in equities, this is far from a purely ethical phenomenon. To the extent that creditors acknowledge the link between environmental performance and overall performance (i.e. profitability, market share, etc.), they will be biased in favor of environmentally sound borrowers since these appear to be lower credit risks.[103]

Finally, environmental performance affects the company's own internal investment decisions as well as the discretion with which finances can be managed. Companies that face greater potential environmental liabilities may find that the freedom to manage their finances is more restricted than that of environmentally sound companies. They face a greater need to tie up funds to cover such things as legal claims and expenses involved in cleaning up after environmental accidents. Such things invariably create cash flow problems that adversely affect short-run financial management.[104]

Decisions over changes in internal organization may be affected as well. An environmentally insensitive company may, for example, find it difficult to invest in expanding its number of plants. Aside from the fact that, as noted, commercial credit will be more difficult to obtain, resistance from local communities would make such expansions difficult to initiate and costly to manage.[105]

RISK MANAGEMENT

The last set of incentives that encourage companies to become more environmentally sound are related to the management of risk. Companies are increasingly finding that insensitivity to the environmental consequences of their operations generates increasing risks in a variety of areas.[106] The growing potential for environmental litigation against companies has greatly increased the risk facing companies that are not environmentally sound. According to Hunt and Auster (1990, 7), "the costs can be devastating" for companies that fail to manage such risks. Over the past decade, prosecution of companies on the grounds of environmental transgressions has increased dramatically.[107]

There are various factors explaining the greater incidence of such litigation. First, environmental laws (especially in the developed world) have expanded the range of actions designated as environmental crimes. Second, because of the pace of environmental legislation and competing jurisdictions (i.e. local versus federal statutes), it is difficult for companies to keep up with legal changes, thus making themselves more vulnerable to litigation.[108] Third, environmental prosecutors gain greater popularity at the local level by bringing such suits. Finally, courts have increasingly accepted the view of extended liability for environmental crimes. One attorney (James Rogers of Skadden, Arps, Slate, Meagher and Flom) goes so far as to state that the "possibility of criminal liability for environmental violations may well be a greater threat to corporate governance than a possible hostile...takeover."[109]

In the United States, the trail of Superfund legislation has exhibited an especially draconian system of legal liability involving environmental transgressions. Retroactive and socialized offense provisions greatly extend liability on environmental crimes. Past owners, for example, are held liable for any harm caused by wastes (without statutes of limitation), even well after waste sites have been abandoned; in fact, they are liable for such harmful effects even if they obeyed all federal regulations in force at the time they were disposing of the wastes. Furthermore, not just proprietors are liable for environmental crimes. All parties involved in the disposal of the wastes are also liable, from the providers of waste disposal services to any banks that financed such operations. Parties that have contaminated even in small amounts can be liable for all of the clean-up.

Moreover, a company need not technically be proven guilty of perpetrating a specific environmental crime in order to be held accountable for damages. Under the socialized offense provision, a person need not have to identify the specific company responsible for an environmental transgression that harmed him or her. He or she need only prove that the toxic wastes that were dumped by a specific company or companies had the potential to cause the harm in order to be entitled to compensation. Also, under citizen-suit provisions in U.S. law, any citizen (whether he or she is the harmed party or not) can bring a suit against violators of environmental laws.[110] Provisions of the Clean Air Act have followed along in stride by raising intentional (i.e. "knowing") environmental violations to a felony.[111] Given this uncompromising direction in environmental law, companies face pronounced incentives to purge their operations and products of any potential environmental hazards.

The risks do not simply emanate from potential settlements that have to be paid to plaintiffs. There are a variety of risks relevant to the ongoing management of the company. Firms perceived as environmentally hazardous may be forced to relocate or experience project delays because of hostile local groups.[112] Relocation risks are especially great where start-up costs are large, capital expenditures are site-specific (e.g. large buildings, immovable capital stock) and there is acute dependence on local resources. Under such circumstances, relocation may threaten the very viability of the business. No less threatening might be the possibility that some environmentally unsound operations become prohibitively expensive, if not impossible.[113]

As noted above, more immediate operating risks, such as supply uncertainties, can also be dealt with more satisfactorily.[114] Reducing bulk in final products, economizing on energy use, as well as recycling and reusing inputs can make a company less dependent on raw materials and hence less vulnerable to any interruptions in supply.[115] Furthermore, dealing with state and local authorities will be a more secure and predictable process for green as opposed to non-green companies. Such things as permits and operating licenses will be renewed with minimal trouble and scrutiny for the former, but the non-green companies will not likely enjoy similar treatment.[116] In many cases, green companies also minimize the risk of adverse regulation by behaving in environmentally sound ways. Officials will allow greater operating discretion to such companies than to non-green companies.[117]

Finally, managing any given level of risk emanating from poor environmental performance is becoming increasingly difficult for all companies, but especially for non-green companies.[118] Insurance against environmental accidents is increasingly more expensive and difficult to obtain.[119] Companies are finding that underwriters are more frequently linking the size of premiums and access to insurance to the companies' environmental records.[120] Under such conditions, companies will find themselves increasingly faced with unacceptable exposure to risk if they resist environmental standards in their operations.

Conclusions: Adapting to the New Business Ecosystem

Companies, like organisms, face a constant need to adapt according to fundamental changes in the ecosystems they inhabit. Just as physical ecosystems select the best adapted organisms for survival and the least adapted for extinction, the "business ecosystem" confronts managers with pressures to conform to structural shifts in the business climate in order to survive and thrive.[121] Like the challenges of the quality movement and globalization, the current environmental revolution presents companies with a new adaptation imperative. As Moore (1993, 86) notes, "Executives whose horizons are bounded by traditional industry perspectives will find themselves missing the real challenges and opportunities that face their companies." At the broadest strategic level, this requires managers to "regard the environmental imperative as an integral part of their business goals."[122] Those that do not will find the business climate in the twenty-first century far less hospitable than those that do.

For the adaptive manager seeking to address the demands of the green revolution, green management must be pervasive; environmental imperatives and opportunities cover all dimensions of corporate operations. The reasons for going green show up everywhere in the management of the corporation. With respect to the managerial goal of efficiency, pollution prevention provides a variety of opportunities to limit costs and maximize the quantity of production for any given input.

Pollution prevention reduces the need for raw materials and energy. Low-bulk production and packaging not only reduce the need for raw materials and energy, but also reduce waste disposal and transport costs. Smaller product scale further reduces storage costs and allows superior inventory management. Some of the inputs that were traditionally purchased can be substituted through recovery, recycling and reuse. To the extent that recovery leads to new marketable substitutes for virgin material, a company may find new opportunities to diversify production toward the growing market in waste exchange. Production output can be enhanced through greater quality control and containment in productive processes. And while pollution-prevention technology and services come at a price, the manager may find a number of opportunities to share the costs (in cooperation) with other companies or with public agencies. Furthermore, a voluntary environmental strategy promises to be more cost-effective and managerially compatible than one that is forced upon a company.

In the competition for markets, managers will be forced to keep up with the present structural shift in consumption preferences toward green products. Production and marketing must be configured to the growing wave of green consumption. This will not only allow managers to maintain present markets; green innovations and product differentiation may lead to the all-important attainment of new markets (i.e. new green product niches). It is an important signpost of the pervasiveness of the environmental revolution's impact on business that a product's appeal is tied to the overall environmental record of its producer. Hence, it will take more than green marketing and the production of specific goods to maintain markets. Managers are marketing more than a product, they are marketing a company. Moreover, given the growth of environmental regulation, managers will be as concerned with keeping their products acceptable to public authorities as they are with green consumer appeal. Staying one step ahead of evolving green legislation may even lead to opportunities to dominate markets when laws change, a nice complement to the opportunities of dominating new niches through product differentiation.

Managers will also have to adapt to green pressures that present themselves in vertical relations with suppliers and distributors, as well as in complementarities in production. Managers of companies producing intermediate goods will have to be prepared to accommodate environmental pressures on their clients by producing greener inputs. For producers of final goods, the pressures will be predominantly a function of the growing wave of green retailing. In the production of complementary goods, managers must keep up with and even anticipate environmental nuances in their principal complements. In these markets, a changing law or new retailing strategy may make an entire product line obsolete.

With respect to intraindustry relations, managers can benefit from the new and more robust opportunities for cooperation that the environmental challenge has created. Not only have public authorities encouraged cooperation among companies for the purpose of reducing pollution; the trend in antitrust law designates proenvironment co-operation as a safe haven for collusion. But even more than responding to loopholes in regulation, managers are encouraged to take an industry-wide perspective, given that the reputation of any industry will reflect the performance of its least successful (i.e. least green-conscious) member.

With respect to the financial health of a company, managers will have to continue to adapt to the exigencies of social investment. Sensitivity to the changing priorities among shareholders dictates a movement toward greener strategies. Financial management itself is greatly improved through environmentally sound strategies. It is increasingly the case that green companies are being deemed more creditworthy. Furthermore, managers will enjoy far greater discretion in managing finances.

Managers will also be increasingly forced to adapt to the rapid pace of environmental legislation

298 • EMERGING ISSUES

and enforcement. No well-managed company will be without a comprehensive environmental risk program. In fact, such a program must now occupy the very highest priority in any general managerial strategy. Not keeping up with the wave of green law will expose laggards to devastating consequences, something no responsible manager should tolerate.

In conclusion, the implications of the pervasiveness of green incentives for present-day and future managers suggest that at the most general level of management style, it has become clear that the green manager will embody the central characteristics of the best manager – one who strives for efficiency (maximizes output per unit of input, minimizes costs, minimizes waste), minimizes risk, protects old markets, penetrates new markets, is sensitive to the priorities of shareholders, emphasizes teamwork, thinks globally and in long-range terms, carefully tracks developments in his or her industry as a whole and knows the operations of his or her company inside and out.[123]

References

Anderson, Terry L and Donald R. Leal (1991) *Free Market Environmentalism*. San Francisco: Pacific Research Institute for Public Policy.

Barbera, Anthony J. and Virginia D. McConnell (1990) "The Impact of Environmental Regulation on Industry Productivity: Direct and Indirect Effects," *Journal of Environmental Economics and Management*, **18** (January), 50–65.

Beaumont, John R. (1992) "Managing the Environment: Business Opportunity and Responsibility," *Futures*, (April), 187–205.

Biddle, David (1993) "Recycling for Profit: The New Green Business Frontier," *Harvard Business Review*, **71** (November-December), 145–56.

Cairncross, Frances (1992) *Costing the Earth*. Cambridge, MA: Harvard Business School Press.

Castleman, Barry I. (1987) "Workplace Health Standards and Multinational Corporations in Developing Countries." In *Multinational Corporations, Environment, and the Third World Business Matters*, ed. Charles S. Pearson. Durham, NC: Duke University Press, 149–74.

"The Challenge of Going Green," *Harvard Business Review*, **72** (July–August 1994), 37–50.

Chisholm, Patricia (1988) "Greening the Profits," *Macleans*, **101** (November 7), 40–1.

"Costing the Earth," *Economist*, September 2, 1989, 1–18.

di Benedetto, C. Anthony and Rajan Chandran (1995) "Behaviors of Environmentally Concerned Firms: An Agenda for Effective Strategic Development." In *Environmental Marketing: Strategies, Practice, Theory, and Research*, eds. Michael J. Polonsky and Alma T. Mintu-Wimsatt. New York: Haworth Press, 269–91.

"Eco-Babble," *Economist*, September 21, 1991, 84–5.

Ekelund, Robert B., J, and David S. Saurman (1988) *Advertising and the Market Process*. San Francisco: Pacific Research Institute for Public Policy.

"Empires of the Chainsaws," *Economist*, August 10, 1991, 36–7.

Epstein, Marc (1991) "What Shareholders Really Want," *New York Times*, April 28.

Epstein, Marc and Moses Pava (1992) "Corporations and the Environment: Shareholders Demand Accountability," *USA Today*, **121** (November), 32–3.

Epstein, Robin (1994) "Ranking the Heavy Emitters," *The Nation*, December 5, 688–94.

Fischetti, Mark (1992) "Green Entrepreneurs," *Technology Review*, **95** (April), 38–43.

Flavin, Christopher and John Young (1994) "Shaping the Next Industrial Revolution," *USA Today*, **122** (March), 78–81.

"Free Trade's Green Hurdle," *Economist*, June 15, 1991, 61-2.

Frosch, Robert A. (1994) "Industrial Ecology: Minimizing the Impact of Industrial Waste," *Physics Today*, **47** (November), 63–8.

Fuller, Donald A. and Jeff Allen (1995) "A Typology of Reverse Channel Systems for Post-Consumer Recyclables." In *Environmental Marketing: Strategies, Practice, Theory, and Research*, eds. Michael J. Polonsky and Alma, T. Mintu-Wimsatt. New York: Haworth Press, 241–66.

Gore, Al (1993) *Earth in the Balance: Ecology and the Human Spirit*. New York: Penguin.

"Greenbacks," *Economist*, August 3, 1991, 73–4.

Greeno, J. Ladd and S. Noble Robinson (1992) "Rethinking Corporate Environmental Management," *Columbia Journal of World Business*, **27** (Fall and Winter), 222–32.

Greve, Michael S. (1992) "Private Enforcement, Private Rewards: How Environmental Citizen Suits Became an Entitlement Program." In *Environmental Politics: Public Costs, Private Rewards*, eds. Michael S. Greve and Fred L. Smith, Jr. New York: Praeger, 105–28.

Griffith, James J. and Charles R. Knoeber (1986) "Why Do Corporations Contribute to Nature Conservancy," *Public Choice*, **49**, 69–77.

Haltiwanger, John and Michael Waldman (1985) "Rational Expectations and the Limits of Rationality: An Analysis of Heterogeneity," *American Economic Review*, **75** (June), 326–40.

"Hole-Stoppers," *Economist*, March 7, 1992, 76.

"How to Throw Things Away," *Economist*, April 13, 1991, 17–22.

Hunt, Christopher B and Ellen R. Auster (1990) "Proactive Environmental Management: Avoiding the Toxic Trap," *Sloan Management Review*, **7** (Winter), 7–18.

Hutchinson, Colin (1992) "Corporate Strategy and the Environment," *Long Range Planning*, **25** (August), 9–21.

Kangun, Norman, Les Carlson, and Stephen J. Grove (1991) "Environmental Advertising Claims: A Preliminary Investigation," *Journal of Public Policy and Marketing*, **10** (Fall), 47–58.

Koelble, Thomas (1989) "Luxembourg: The 'Greng Alternative'." In *New Politics in Western Europe: The Rise and Success of Green Parties and Alternative Lists*, ed. Ferdinand Muller-Rommel. Boulder, CO: Westview Press, 131–8.

Kotter, John P. (1995) "Leading Change: Why Transformation Efforts Fail," *Harvard Business Review*, **73** (March-April), 59-67.

Landy, Marc K. and Mary Hague (1992) "The Coalition for Waste: Private Interests and Superfund." In *Environmental Politics: Public Costs, Private Rewards*, eds. Michael S. Greve and Fred L. Smith, Jr. New York: Praeger, 67–88.

Lepkowski, Wil (1987) "The Disaster at Bhopal – Chemical Safety in the Third World." In *Multinational Corporations, Environment, and the Third World Business Matters*, ed. Charles S. Pearson. Durham, NC: Duke University Press, 25–54.

Litvan, Laura M. (1993) "Turning Trash into Profit," *Nation's Business*, **81** (December), 49-53.

—— (1994a) "Environmental Expertise," *Nation's Business*, **82** (May), 45–7.

—— (1994b) "The Growing Ranks of Enviro-Cops," *Nation's Business*, **82** (June), 29–32.

—— (1994c) "Voluntary Efforts to Cut Pollution," *Nation's Business*, **82** (September), 62–4.

—— (1995) "Going 'Green' in the '90s," *Nation's Business*, **83** (February), 30–2.

Lozada, Hector R. and Alma T. Mintu-Wimsatt (1995) "Green-Based Innovation: Sustainable Development in Product Management." In *Environmental Marketing: Strategies, Practice, Theory, and Research*, eds. Michael J. Polonsky and Alma T. Mintu-Wimsatt. New York: Haworth Press, 179–96.

McInnis, Daniel F. (1992) "Ozone Layers and Oligopoly Profits." In *Environmental Politics: Public Costs, Private Rewards*, eds. Michael S. Greve and Fred L. Smith, Jr. New York: Praeger, 129–54.

McKee, Bradford (1991) "The Best Defense Against Pollution," *Nation's Business*, **79** (November), 53–5.

McMurdy, Deirdre (1991) "Green is the Color of Money," *Maclean's*, **104** (December), 49–50

Menagh, Melanie (1991) "The Business of Going Green," *Omni*, **13** (June), 42–8.

Moore, James F. (1993) "Predators and Prey: A New Ecology of Competition," *Harvard Business Review*, **71** (May-June), 75–86.

Nulty, Peter (1990) "Recycling Becomes a Big Business," *Fortune*, **122** (August 13), 81–6.

Ottman, Jacquelyn A. (1993) *Green Marketing*. Lincolnwood, IL: NTC Business Books.

Pearson, Charles S. (1987) "Environmental Standards, Industrial Relocation, and Pollution Havens." In *Multinational Corporations, Environment, and the Third World Business Matters*, ed. Charles S. Pearson. Durham. NC: Duke University Press, 113–28.

Peattie, Ken and Moira Ratnayaka (1992) "Responding to the Green Movement," *Industrial Marketing Management*, **21**, 103–10.

Polonsky, Michael J. and Alma T. Mintu-Wimsatt (eds.) (1995) *Environmental Marketing: Strategies, Practice, Theory, and Research*, New York: Haworth Press.

Porter, Michael E. (1990) *The Competitive Advantage of Nations*. New York: Free Press.

—— (1991) "America's Green Strategy," *Scientfic American*, **264** (April), 168.

Pound, John (1995) "The Promise of the Governed Corporation," *Harvard Business Review*, **73** (March-April), 89–98.

"A Quick Fix on Ozone," *Economist*, November 28, 1992, 50.

Regan, Mary Beth (1993) "Uncle Sam Goes on an Eco-Trip, " *Business Week*, June 28, p. 76.

Royston, Michael G. (1979) *Pollution Prevention Pays*. Oxford: Pergamon Press,

—— (1985) "Local and Multinational Corporations: Reapprasing Environmental Management," *Environment*, **27** (January-February), 12-43.

Ruttenberg, Ruth (1984) "The Gold in Rules," In *Business and the Environment: Toward Common Ground*, ed. Kent Gilbreath. Washington: The Conservation Foundation, 68–75.

Sandler, Todd (1992) *Collective Action: Theory and Applications*. Ann Arbor: University of Michigan Press.

Scarlett, Lynn (1992) "It's All in the Packaging," *Reason*, **24** (August–September), 54–5.

Schmalensee, Richard (1972) *"The Economics of Advertising*. Amsterdam: North-Holland.

Schmidheiny, Stephan (1992) "The Business Logic of Sustainable Development," *Columbia Journal of World Business*, **27** (Fall & Winter), 18–24.

"Sharing," *Economist*, May 30, 1992, 3–24.

Sheets, Kenneth R. (1990) "Business's Green Revolution," *Fortune*, **108** (February 19), 45–8.

Simon, Françoise L. (1992) "Marketing Green Products in the Triad," *Columbia Journal of World Business*, **27** (Fall and Winter), 268–85.

Smart, Bruce (ed.) (1992) *Beyond Compliance A New Industry View of the Environment*. Washington, D.C.: World Resources Institute.

Stix, Gary (1993) "Turning Green," *Scientific American*, **269** (November), 104.

Strong, Maurice (1990) "Strategies for Change, Reasons for Hope," *EPA Journal*, **16** (July–August), 61–3.

Suris, Oscar (1994) "States' Petition on Emissions Moves Forwards," *New York Times*, September 14, A4.

Walley, Noah and Bradley Whitehead (1994) "It's Not Easy Being Green," *Harvard Business Review*, **72** (May–June), 46–52.

Washington and Lee Law Review (1992) (special issue on environmental quality and free trade) **49** (Fall).

White, Robert M. and Deanna J. White (1992) "Industry's Duty of Care," *Technology Review*, **95** (October), 5.

Zeithaml, Carl P. and Valerie A. Zeithaml (1984) "Environmental Management: Revising the Marketing Perspective," *Journal of Marketing*, **48** (Spring), 46–53.

Notes

1   The most celebrated recent statement of the view can be found in Walley and Whitehead (1994). Robert Stavins goes so far as to state that this view still represents the "conventional wisdom." For responses from both the academic and business communities to Walley and Whitehead's arguments, see "The Challenge of Going Green" (1994). For Stavins's statement, see "The Challenge of Going Green" (1994), 38.

2   The logic here asserts that where problems of public goods exist, markets will fail to produce outcomes that are socially efficient (in this case, more pollution than is socially optimal). On public-goods theory, see Sandler, 1992.

3 Peattie and Ratnayaka (1992, 108) succinctly summarize the traditional logic: "Going green can be costly, and the benefits are often long term and not guaranteed." Even advocates of environmental managerial strategies like Porter (1991, 168) concede that "increased short-term costs and the need to redesign products and processes are unsettling at the least." For Walley and Whitehead (1994) the environment–profitability nexus is rarely "win-win" (i.e. you can have both situations), but more often presents managers with a potentially dangerous trade-off. See also Royston (1985, 14).

4 For Hunt and Auster (1990), the growing green wave in legislation has made a comprehensive management of environmental risk in the corporation an absolute necessity.

5 Maurice Strong (1990, 62) refers to this new set of opportunities as the "eco-industrial revolution."

6 See Smart (1992, 90–1).

7 Cairncross (1992, 258, 260) and Smart (1992, 11–7).

8 Menagh (1991, 48). Similarly, insofar as European green parties have been probusiness, like Dei Greng Alternativ in Luxembourg, they have argued that companies increase their competitiveness through proenvironment strategies. See Koelble (1989, 135).

9 Menagh (1991, 42).

10 The first of these programs, 3M's 3P, which started in 1975, is estimated to have saved the company more than $482 million in its first 15 years of operation. AT&T, UNOCAL and Xerox have also introduced fairly high-profile environmental programs. See Smart (1992, 12, 90) and Cairncross (1992, 260).

11 It has been estimated that in the United States 12 percent of waste is made up of corrugated cardboard, traditionally the most common material used for transporting products. See Cairncross (1992, 272).

12 Estimates on the cost-effectiveness of lighter packaging suggests an average reduction in packaging bulk by a factor of four and an average reduction in energy use by a factor of two. See Cairncross (1992, 272–3).

13 Simon (1992, 280).

14 Smart (1992, 13).

15 Cairncross (1992, 182).

16 "Costing the Earth" (1989, 13).

17 Estimates suggest that a company can save $21.50 per socket per year by using compact fluorescent bulbs instead of regular bulbs. See Menagh (1991, 44–8) and Litvan (1993, 49–50).

18 Nulty (1990, 82), Smart (1992, 91–2) and Cairncross (1992, 220–1).

19 Frosch (1994, 64) describes the managerial mandate of industrial ecology as considering "the entire material and energy stream, from the input and manufacturing through the life of the product and its eventual reuse or disposal." The mandate has even begun to be embodied in law as recent Japanese and German legislation encourages product design that results in a more environmentally sound product life cycle. See also White and White (1992, 5).

20 The emergence of intermediaries that put buyers in contact with sellers, such as the Waste Exchange, attests to the growth of the market for recycled and residual material over the past two decades. See Royston (1979, 110).

21 Litvan (1994c, 63).

22 On waste exchange, the market in residual materials, see Litvan (1993); Fuller and Allen (1995).

23 Royston (1979, 53, 68, 74, 94, 99); Cairncross (1992, 262–3); Ruttenberg (1984, 71–2): Smart (1992, 35).

24 Environmental Business International Inc. estimates that the market in environmental goods and services will grow to $426 billion by 1997 (up from $295 billion in 1992). See Litvan (1994a); Hutchinson (1992, 10).

25 Reuse essentially eliminates a link in the chain of production. Hence, shifts in demand can be accommodated more easily since the chain of production that needs to be manipulated is effectively smaller.

26 Cairncross (1992, 262).

27 McInnis (1992, 136).

28 Nowhere is this more evident than in the lumber industry. The tendency toward deforestation is reduced to the extent that wood-product manufacturers can make greater use of the wood on a log. See "Empires of the Chainsaws" (1991).

29 Porter (1990 and 1991).

30 Ruttenberg (1984, 69–71).

31 Royston (1979, 51, 81); Barbera and McConnell (1990); Litvan (1994c); Cairncross (1992, 260).

32 Hunt and Auster (1990, 14). On the governed corporation, see Pound (1995).

33 Studies on priorities among candidates for white collar employment in the United States suggest that companies' environmental records are central concerns for young Americans entering the labor force. Surveys done within companies on the environmental sensitivity of current employees are also consistent with these findings. In fact, companies that have been prompted to undertake more environmental strategies have found much of the pressure emanating from stakeholders (employees and shareholders). See Menagh (1991, 48); Schmidheiny (1992, 22); Smart (1992, 94; 104); "Costing the Earth" (1989, 16).

34 In a survey of multinationals with operations in West Germany, 90 percent stated that they use the same environmental standards in their subsidiaries in less developed nations that they use in Germany. See Pearson (1987, 116, 123).

35 The costs of both post-hoc and preventive environmentalism are often canceled out by more productive technologies and/or inputs. Substitutes for CFCs, are generally more expensive than CFCs, but many are so much more productive than CFCs that far less of them are required. See "Hole-Stoppers" (1992); Flavin and Young (1994, 80).

36 The U.S.'s Electric Power Research Institute estimated that pollution treatment equipment (scrubbers, cooling towers, electrostatic precipitators) in coal-fired power plants would add 45 percent to the plants' capital costs and 30 percent to their operating costs. On a more general level, however, empirical studies have shown that pollution control (both post-hoc and prevention) does not normally take up a large proportion of a company's costs. See Pearson (1987, 124).

37 McKee, (1991, 53).

38 Royston (1979, 88–94).

39 In many cases, companies in the United States also share the costs of such programs with governmental agencies. The EPA and National Science Foundation have recently funded a number of programs to develop substitutes for toxic substances and encourage green production processes in the chemical industry. The EPA also announced (January 1994) a $36-million grant to fund U.S. commercial development of new technologies to clean up and monitor pollution. See Litvan (1994a); Stix (1993); Royston (1979. 11).

40 Document reprinted in Smart (1992, 124). The EPA, in fact, provides technical guidance to businesses through numerous programs that encourage voluntary pollution prevention. See Litvan (1994c).

41 Monsanto, for example, achieved a longer period to comply with clean-air standards by instituting its 90-percent programs: the 1990 Clean Air Act amendements gave a 6-year extension to companies that voluntarily reduced their harmful air emissions by 90 percent. See Smart (1992, 124).

42 It is indicative of the preferability of voluntary strategies that in an analysis of more than 700 environmental initiatives undertaken at DuPont, the voluntary initiatives were on average three times more cost-effective than those responding to government regulation. See "The Challenge of Going Green" (1994, 46).

43 Litvan (1995); Polonsky and Mintu-Wimsatt (1995); Ottman (1993); Kangun et al. (1991, 48); Greeno and Robinson (1992, 225); Peattie and Ratnayaka (1992, 104–5); Chisholm (1992); Fischetti (1992, 41–2); Simon (1992, 282).

44 In a survey of 52 top American marketers. 80 percent stated that American businesses will have to drastically change their practices in response to the new environmentalism among consumers. Furthermore, 90 percent believed that environmentalism represents a permanent concern as opposed to a fad. See Peattie and Ratnayaka (1992, 104–5); Schmidheiny (1992, 22).

45 "The Challenges of Going Green" (1994, 42).

46 In fact, marketing green products is increasingly incorporating traditional elements of price and quality competition. See Litvan (1995).

47 With respect to performance, Wal-Mart reported that their green labeling program contributed to a 25 percent increase in sales in 1989. See Lozada and Mintu-Wimsatt (1995, 187).

48 Guarding market shares should also take into account large institutional consumption as more businesses are moving toward green inputs. Even the federal government, under a Clinton initiative, has committed to greener consumption. For example, all new federally purchased computers must satisfy the EPA's Energy Star

Standards. See Regan (1993); Litvan (1993, 50).

49 Simon (1992, 273). In general, consumers buy from producers they trust. A 1992 Roper poll found that 34 percent of the public retrains from buying from certain manufacturers. See Ottman (1993, 36).

50 The enhanced scrutiny has caused managers to concentrate on the entire product and production process in order to appeal to environmentally sensitive consumption. Being CFC-free, for example, will not be enough if the product or the production method harms the environment in other ways. See "Costing the Earth" (1989, 16).

That the environmental impact of products is closely monitored and publicized destroys the validity of arguments attributing a high level of market failure (because of public-goods problems) to environmental degradation by business. Although the assignment of property rights is such that a company will not have to bear *de jure* many of the costs it imposes on society through pollution (e.g., they cannot be assessed fines for destroying the ozone layer or warming the planet), the fact that independent scrutiny can publicize such degradation in a way that will hurt sales means that in fact the companies are punished for their transgressions. The incentives toward environmentalism are raised all the more by the fact that business, according to popular polling, bears most of the blame for environmental problems. See Smart (1992, 152).

51 Independent eco-labeling (e.g., the Blue Angel in Germany, the Eco-mark in Japan, Environmental Choice in Canada and the Green Cross and the Green Seal in the United States) and the publication of lists tracking environmental performance (e.g. "biggest polluter" lists) have made it difficult for companies to escape public scrutiny of the environmental impact of their products and operations. In fact, companies greatly desire favourable eco-labeling given its impact on consumer choice. The greater scrutiny has also reduced the possibilities for fraudulent green marketing. With the greater attention paid to "green washing" (false environmental claims), companies have been increasingly forced to practice what they preach. See di Benedetto and Chandran (1995, 282); Regan (1993); "Eco-Babble" (1991); Epstein (1994); Simon (1992, 271); Kangun et al. (1991, 49).

52 The recent scrambles to perfect the biodegradable disposable diaper and garbage bag are indicative of the intensity of environmental competition in selected product lines. See di Benedetto and Chandran (1995, 276); Smart (1992, 28, 124).

53 Scarlett (1992, 55).

54 "Costing the Earth" (1989, 17).

55 The Canadian utilities industry appears to be a case of post-hoc adjustment to changing laws. However, since this was a situation of quasimonopoly, differential performances did not seriously affect market shares. See Smart (1992, 91–4).

56 Simon (1992, 270). Operating at the highest common-environmental denominator is all the more important since, aside from the European Union, industrial nations are yet to initiate harmonization of eco-labeling. See Beaumont (1992, 199).

57 Invariably, for large companies, environmental accidents or disasters are followed by well-publicized environmental initiatives aimed at retrieving lost public confidence. See Smart (1992, 247).

58 The non-price competition emanates form the fact that markets in these products are characterized by monopolistic competition where divergences in prices can persist because products are not homogeneous but somewhat diversified.

59 Green marketing can also serve a proactive purpose (i.e. reshape the business climate itself) by reorienting consumption in an environmental direction. On proactive marketing, see Zeithaml and Zeithaml (1984); di Benedetto and Chandran (1995). On green marketing, see especially Polonsky and Mintu-Wimsatt (1995); Ottman (1993).

60 Simon (1992, 269, 282); Sheets (1990, 45). A 1989 MORI poll showed that environmental concern had stimulated the biggest shift in consumer behavior since the increase in the price of oil during the shock of 1973. A survey by the Opinion Research Corporation in 1990 found that consumers rated a company's environmental performance about as highly as the reputational elements, such as dependability and honesty. See Greeno and Robinson (1992, 225); Peattie and Ratnayaka (1992, 103).

61 Chisholm (1992); Fischetti (1992, 41–2); Beaumont (1992, 1997); and Kangun et al. (1991, 47–8). Ottman (1993,

43–4) notes that for green products offering health benefits (e.g. natural foods), people will pay premiums in excess of 15 percent.

62 An image of environmental concern enhances a company's reputation. Enhanced reputation, emanating from whatever reason, serves to stimulate a positive consumer response toward all productive activities undertaken by a particular company. See Griffith and Knoeber (1986, 70–1); Cairncross (1992, 194–5). See Schmalensee (1972) for a general discussion of reputational effects on sales.

63 Smart (1992, 124).

64 Biddle (1993, 154).

65 Smart (1992, 170).

66 "How to Throw Things Away" (1991). As noted above, environmental transgressions in any stage of production, given the close monitoring of environmental effects, can affect the marketability of the entire and product.

67 Cairncross (1992, 195).

68 The second greatest concern was over whether they were getting the best value for their money. See Cairncross (1992, 289).

69 di Benedetto and Chandran (1995, 282); Chisholm (1992); "How to Throw Things Away" (1991); Beaumont (1992). Even the largest companies find it difficult to resist the pressure. Procter & Gamble's phosphate-free detergent, in fact, came along in a period when Canada's Loblaws was trying to persuade it to introduce such a product. See Cairncross (1992, 194–5).

70 Increasingly, the large-scale marketing of green products is done through the use of special green sections. See Chisholm (1992).

71 Beaumont (1992, 197); Cairncross (1992, 195).

72 Chisholm (1992); Cairncross (1992, 195).

73 Biddle (1993, 148).

74 Smart (1992, 91–2).

75 Economists refer to this as a synergistic market process, whereby crowding reinforces itself across complementary products. For example, as one type of computer software comes to dominate a market, the appropriate hardware in which it is used also comes to dominate its own market. As each further crowds competing products out of its respective market, it reinforces the crowding effects of its complements. See Haltiwanger and Waldman (1985).

76 "Hole-Stoppers" (1992).

77 Of course, in the absence of such things as legal barriers to entry (e.g. patents) or very successful collusion, the domination of markets will invariably be a short-run phenomenon because other producers will enter the market with environmentally sound products of their own.

78 Barriers can be created through product loyalty and increasing start-up costs. On the effects of product differentiation on market structure, see Ekelund and Saurman (1988, 21–40).

79 The recent races to perfect the fully biodegradable diaper and garbage bag have been the most visible attempts at pioneering new environmental niches and thereby dominating the product lines. See di Benedetto and Chandran (1995, 276); Smart (1992, 37–40).

80 The early mover advantage makes staying ahead of the law all the more desirable if the legal trend is toward stricter environmental regulation (which is certainly the case in developed nations). As the law changes, it is the early movers that are in position to dominate markets while laggard companies try to catch up. See Ekelund and Saurman (1988, 41).

81 "Costing the Earth" (1989, 17).

82 The traditional view that posits business as invariably against tougher environmental laws assumes markets are fairly competitive. If, however, companies can establish monopoly or oligopoly positions through tougher laws, they will favor stricter regulation of the environment.

83 Producers of CFCs enjoyed windfall profits as well because the agreements caused the price of CFCs to increase 30 to 60 percent in the United States and 15 percent in Europe.

84 Also, existing producers of CFCs already had a head start in researching and developing substitutes. See

McInnis (1992, 144–9); "Sharing" (1992, 18); "A Quick Fix on Ozone" (1992).

85 McInnis (1992, 137).

86 Within the glass industry, an interesting attempt at rent seeking has come from Brandt Manufacturing Systems's (a glass-coating business) support for a ban on colored glass (the environmental rationale being that clear glass is easier to recycle). If such a law were passed, bottlers seeking colored receptacles would have to rely exclusively on the services of glass-coating companies such as Brandt. See Scarlett (1992, 55).

87 This contradicts the "safe haven" argument that suggests that MNCs seek out host countries with the least demanding environmental laws. See Pearson (1987, 120).

88 "Free Trade's Green Hurdle" (1991).

89 McInnis (1992, 148–9).

90 Smart (1992, 74–7).

91 Smart (1992, 70–2).

92 Cairncross (1992, 274).

93 In 1990, for example, the Coalition for Environmentally Responsible Economics (a group of institutional investors that controlled $150 billion in pension funds and other assets) declared that it would divest from companies that refused to adhere to the Valdez principles governing environmentally dangerous practices. See Flavin and Young (1994, 81); Sheets (1990, 48); and Cairncross (1992, 204–5).

94 Many of Ethic Scan Canada's (an environmental tracking company) clients, for example, are large mutual fund managers. See "Greenbacks" (1991) and McMurdy (1991, 49–50).

95 See, for example, Smart (1992, 49). In a survey of U.S. stockholders, the two areas that were most underscored in terms of where the shareholders would like to see improvements were, first, cleaning up plants and reducing pollution and, second, producing safer products. In fact, survey results also show a disposition toward sacrificing dividends in favor of a better environmental record. See Epstein (1991) and Epstein and Pava (1992).

96 Sheets (1990, 48).

97 Quoted in McMurdy (1991, 49).

98 It is common, for example, for the bond ratings of companies that are repeatedly sued for environmental transgressions to decline. See Castleman (1987, 159) and Menagh (1991, 44).

99 Cairncross (1992, 206); McMurdy (1991, 49–50). It is no surprise, therefore, that companies with poor environmental records find it increasingly harder to issue new stock. See Flavin and Young (1994, 81).

100 Menagh (1991, 42); Cairncross (1992, 205); and "Greenbacks" (1991).

101 Reprinted in Smart (1992, 173–4). See also Schmidheiny (1992, 22).

102 Cairncross (1992, 206).

103 One relevant concern connected with the risks of lending to environmentally insensitive companies in the United States involves banks' apprehension about the extension of environmental liability under the Superfund laws. Banks that foreclose on commercial loans can in some cases be held legally responsible for environmental transgressions emanating from their new properties, even if the crimes originally resulted from actions of the former owners. There have, in fact, been several instances in which banks have been forced to pay for the cleaning up of foreclosed properties. See Sheets (1990, 48).

104 Chevron, for example, set aside $325 million from fourth-quarter profits in 1990 to cover any clean-up operations necessitated by serious oil spills. See Sheets (1990, 46).

105 AlliedSignal's problems with acquiring a new manufacturing site in Morris township, New Jersey, provides an interesting case in point. See Smart (1992, 204–5).

106 It is unfortunately all too common for companies to take account of these risks only after major accidents. For example, the CEO of Xerox, David Kearns, empowered Xerox's Corporate Environmental and Health Division to eliminate "all potential environmental hazards in the company, anywhere in the world" following Bhopal. See Smart (1992, 105). On managing environmental risk, see Hunt and Auster (1990).

107 From 1989 to 1994 the number of EPA police agents has tripled, and of the environmental cases (630 adjudicated from May 1988 to May 1993), 91 percent ended in conviction. See Litvan (1994b). The risk is as great from litigation from within the firm as it is from outside parties; the incidence of suits from workers

charging environmental harm has also grown significantly in recent years. See Castleman (1987, 159).

108 Hunt and Auster (1990, 8). Even if companies try to track legal changes carefully, there can still remain significant uncertainty about compliance. For example, the EPA recently approved auto-emission controls for 12 Northeastern states that are stricter than federal controls. Companies linking compliance to federal standards would be deficient with respect to the new state limits. See Suris (1994).

109 Rogers is quoted in Smart (1992, 218).

110 Hunt and Auster (1990); Greve (1992, 105–10); Sheets (1990, 46); and Landy and Hague (1992, 69).

111 McKee (1991, 53).

112 It was estimated that delays on the construction of the Alaskan pipeline caused by opposition groups resulted in $700 million in extra construction costs. See Royston (1979, 59–63).

113 One such risk comprises the large potential difficulties involved in disposing of waste in areas where the number of waste sites is shrinking. Trends in the regulations governing waste sites in the United States suggest significant risks in this area in the near future. The EPA has estimated that about 80 percent of the present landfills in the United States will be closed within a decade, and stricter local laws about waste sites make new landfills increasingly difficult to open. See Cairncross (1992, 217).

114 Producing marketable inputs through industrial ecology can also benefit a company in the form of diversification, hence reducing vulnerability to adverse outcomes in any given product line. On diversification as a proactive strategy, see Zeithaml and Zeithaml (1984).

115 The Robbins Company, a plating company in Massachusetts, experienced ongoing difficulties in securing a dependable supply of water from municipal utilities. Reducing water use by 97.5 percent as a result of an initiative to eliminate polluting discharge effectively eliminated this problem in operations. See McKee (1991, 56); Greeno and Robinson (1992, 226). An interesting twist on this theme concerns pharmaceutical companies (which are dependent on the maintenance of genetic diversity in plant life) that contribute to Nature Conservancy, whose actions, in turn, are directed toward preserving biological diversity. See Griffith and Knoeber (1986, 70).

116 Royston (1979, 51).

117 Smart (1992, 71); Griffith and Knoeber (1986).

118 The environmental initiatives of Dow (in the 1970s) and Chevron (in the 1980s), for example, were strongly founded on a desire to limit their liability by more carefully managing wastes. See Smart (1992, 90–1, 103–4).

119 Castleman (1987, 159–160); "Costing the Earth" (1989, 17). Lepkowski (1987, 241) notes how companies operating in less developed countries found it extremely difficult to obtain disaster insurance after Bhopal.

120 Schmidheiny (1992, 22).

121 On business as an ecosystem, see Moore (1993).

122 White and Richards (1992, 5).

123 Specific recommendations for operationalizing an environmental program go beyond the scope of this article, but two good articles that make such recommendations are Hunt and Auster (1990) and di Benedetto and Chandran (1995). See also Kotter (1995) on what pitfalls must be avoided in making organizational transformations in general.

23

Sustainable Development versus Global Environment: Resolving the Conflict

S. FRED SINGER

UNIVERSITY OF VIRGINIA

A key purpose of the Rio de Janeiro UN Conference on Environment and Development (UNCED) was the drive for "sustainable development" (SD), especially by the developing nations of the South. Everyone agrees that SD is a desirable goal but opinions vary on what it means and on how to reach it.

In this chapter, I discuss a preferred definition of SD and examine the conditions under which it might be obtained. I conclude that it is an achievable goal but that it would require a greatly increased use of energy, especially of fossil fuels. If my argument is correct, then there is a basic conflict – not resolved at UNCED – between those who advocate SD and those who wish to restrict the use of energy. In particular, I do not seen how one can avoid increasing the concentration of atmospheric greenhouse gases significantly if one wants to raise the living standard of the developing world.

There may be a solution to this dilemma. The conventional greenhouse theory greatly overestimates the climate warming caused by increases in greenhouse gases like carbon dioxide (CO_2). If, therefore, the standard of living of the poor in the world can be raised rapidly, then the demographic transition to lower birth rates can be accomplished, perhaps before any measurable changes occur in the global climate.

Accomplishing this goal requires a transfer of technology and a transfer of political know-how, rather than just a transfer of resources. A program that simply shifts money from the developed countries to the developing countries – from the North to the South – may not do much more than expand and enrich indigenous bureaucracies; these, in turn, would expand statism and central economic planning, stifle free enterprise and threaten individual liberties, the essential ingredients for true economic development.

"Sustainable Development vs. Global Environment: Resolving the Conflict." by S. Fred Singer, *The Columbia Journal of World Business*, Fall and Winter 1992, pp. 154–162. Reprinted by permission of Jai Press Inc.

What is Sustainable Development? The Utopian View

Sustainable development (SD) is a concept that has gained currency in the past few years, since the publication by the United Nations of the Brundtland Report. But SD means different things to different people. Its critics portray it as a permanent financial aid program, funnelling resources without end and without noticeable impact from the industrialized countries of the North to the developing countries of the South. It is often equated with the New International Economic Order (NIEO), frequently described as a program to transfer money from the poor in the rich countries to the rich in the poor countries – an inverse "Robin Hood effect."

This characterization of SD may be unfair – certainly not what is intended by its advocates. Most of them appear to have a somewhat utopian view of a stabilized or even decreasing global population living a good life without using an appreciable amount of natural resources – clearly a make-believe picture of the real world. Under this romantic calculus, most resources are strictly limited and would therefore be depleted within a finite length of time. For followers of the Reverend Thomas Malthus, therefore, SD means using only renewable resources.

This quixotic viewpoint is not just confined to utopian dreamers but has penetrated into the minds of many of the world's statesmen, who are generally thought of as "hardheaded." But listen to the leader of a certain politically correct European nation, speaking at the conclusion of UNCED in June 1992:

> Many of the leading figures of the world have come together here as a sign of their strong commitment to this conference and its great objective. Millions of people around the globe are following the events here with close attention, aware that this conference in many respects is going to influence their lives, to meet their concerns.

After this preamble, one would expect to hear some new ideas, some new approaches, to SD. Instead we are treated to a rehash of a 1972 Club of Rome report, which by now has been thoroughly discredited. It predicted a Malthusian future for the world, with the world "running out" of most metals, fuels becoming scarce before the end of the century, and the disappearance of a substantial fraction of mankind due to pollution and starvation.

> In 1972, shortly before the Stockholm Conference of the United Nations was to convene, the American scientist Dennis Meadows published his report about the "Limits of Growth" (sic). When questioned again recently, Dennis Meadows conceded that mankind – in spite of some unfavorable, even damaging preconditions – would have a good chance to deal with these problems. He bases this assumption on the fact that environmental consciousness, the general awareness for environmental protection, has developed rapidly during those last 20 years. Therein he finds – and I would agree with him – the one and only base for continued progress.

It is not explained just how "awareness" is supposed to overcome the dire catastrophes that are supposed to follow from economic growth. In any case, the facts suggest quite the contrary: a general improvement in the well-being of the world's population since 1972, while the global consumption of energy and other resources grew rapidly. The speaker conveniently ignores this inconsistency as he recites the facts:

There are also other signs of hope and progress: infant mortality is declining, human life expectancy is on the rise, access to education is growing, and global food production increases faster than population growth. Nevertheless, in absolute numbers there are more people in the world going hungry than never before and their number is still growing, as is the number of those without safe homes, fuel or safe water. The gap between rich and poor is widening, not shrinking. It is imperative that this trend will be reversed. For one fact has become obvious: it is impossible to separate economic development from global environment issues. Poverty is cause as well as effect of global environmental problems.

So even the good news must be blamed on environmental problems. To the environmental utopian every silver cloud has a black, polluted lining that requires governmental action.

> This is our chance to reverse the trend. We have to take this chance in the conviction that protection of the environment, economic development, and economic prosperity are not mutually exclusive or contradictory, but are indeed two sides of one and the same coin.

Again, the facts are otherwise. Protection of the environment has come as a *consequence* of economic development in the Western world; only after the basic necessities were taken care of, only after people could afford it, did they invest in pollution control. In that sense, economic development and pollution control are compatible. (Here we are talking about local environmental problems and local pollution control. As we point out later, global environmental problems, such as the hypothesized global warming from increasing greenhouse gases, pose a very different issue.) But in order to improve the well-being of the world population, large amounts of energy are necessary, with an inevitable increase in greenhouse gases. This dilemma does not seem to bother our politician friend, who rambles on with grand words about nebulous concepts:

> I am convinced that in order to be successful, structural changes in the economic, the social, and the ecological systems of the industrialized states will be inevitable. I am convinced, and there are already many who share this conviction, that we have to look for a new definition of wealth, a definition that no longer adheres to the maxim of unlimited economic growth, but of sustained economic development. If we are serious about the principle of sustained economic development, then we have to accept the need for change in many areas, such as energy consumption, traffic, agriculture, industry, as well as in many of the bad habits of a consumer society.
>
> Sustainable development is indivisible. It is a process based on partnership and sharing, in which we are all students and teachers at the same time. If taken seriously it offers the opportunity for a joint learning process of global dimension, a learning process in which there can be no place for mutual reproach or accusation, and which takes into account that we are faced with interlocking problems. There is not an environmental crisis, a development crisis, and energy crisis. They are all one.

We interrupt our European statesman here for a view from the developing world, that of Mr. Kamal Nath, Indian's minister for environment. As quoted in the *Indian Express* of February 23, 1992, Indian's position at UNCED is that:

> Developed countries are mainly responsible for global environmental degradation and they must take the necessary corrective steps by modifying consumption patterns and lifestyles; developing countries can participate in global action, but not at the cost of their development efforts ... On climate change and greenhouse gases, India's stand is that global warming is not caused by emissions

of the gases *per se* but by excessive emissions. The responsibility for cutting back on the emissions rests on countries whose per capita consumption is high. India's stand is that *emissions in developed countries be reduced to tally with the per capita emission levels of developing countries* (emphasis added).

In other words, Mr. Nath would like to stop economic growth and reduce our living standards to a Third-World level, all for the sake of ecology – or, more precisely, for the sake of an unsubstantiated theory of climate warming.

The key, of course, is the way in which these politicians discuss the matter of increased energy needs – or, as it is usually referred to, the "energy problem." Returning to our European statesman:

> Certainly, a solution to the energy problem is one of the central questions in this regard and one that equally concerns the industrialized as well as the developing world. The energy systems presently in use, characterized as they are by the heavy reliance on fossil energy sources and in large parts also by the dependence on nuclear energy, in all probability cannot be maintained in the long term. In our view, especially the use of nuclear energy stands as symbol for risky and potentially very expensive technologies which are not in line with the principles and priorities of sustainable development. We are convinced that we have to find new energy policies which aim at minimizing the demand for energy and at the increased use of renewable sources of energy. As mentioned, we are convinced that the use of nuclear energy is not a viable option in the fight against the greenhouse effect and the related threat to the world climate. [My country] thus supports the introduction of a CO_2 tax on fossil sources of energy as well as on nuclear energy. This would present a first step in the right direction.

With one stroke, the "greenies" have "solved" the energy problem and added a new and lucrative method of taxation. They have eliminated nuclear energy, a truly non-polluting energy source, essentially inexhaustible, and becoming safer and less costly all the time. On the other side, they have throttled the use of fossil fuels by imposing a carbon tax. The fact that such a policy condemns most of the world's population to a life of continued poverty and misery is, of course, not spelled out – lest its immorality become self-evident. Instead, the developing countries of the South are thrown a few scraps:

> Today, the devastation of the tropical rain forests in the southern hemisphere demands our immediate attention . . . I am glad to announce that [my country] has earmarked an additional amount of [20 million dollars] for bilateral projects geared towards the protection of the tropical rain forests and towards the support of its inhabitants. I am aware that in view of the size of the problem this is only a small amount. We hope however that our projects, that will be formulated in close coordination with the indigenous population, can serve as models for possible solutions on a larger scale.

It's no wonder, then, that the policies of the North are regarded with deep suspicion by the developing countries, and as a new form of imperialism based on ecology, aptly labeled "eco-imperialism." For example, the *Times of India* of January 3, 1992, decries attempts by the North to ignore its "historic liability" by using an overall greenhouse gas index that includes all gases, not just CO_2, instead of treating each gas separately. The article objects to the fact that India and China, along with other predominantly agrarian societies, would be treated as big polluters because of methane produced by rice paddies and cattle raising. However, "Indian researchers are convinced that methane estimates have been highly exaggerated."

An article in *The Pioneer* of December 20, 1991, entitled "India and the Earth Summit: What's at

Stake in Rio," finally strips away the phoney ecological excuses. The author argues with refreshing candor that India must ensure that the issue of poverty and environmental degradation (presumably local water and air pollution) leads the agenda at UNCED rather than ozone layer depletion, climate change, and conservation of biodiversity that the industrialized countries are aiming for.

On the other hand, more cynical citizens of the Third World see the global warming threat as a way of improving their own standard of living by joining an expanded bureaucracy, preferably under the United Nations. Judging by past experience from foreign aid programs, Third-World "kleptocrats" who control the flow of development funds would use the drive for SD as a means for personal enrichment.

The Path Taken by Developed Nations: More Energy Use

A remarkable feature of the past century is the fact that for the first time in human history large population groups have reached a high standard of living. Only some 200 years ago, Western Europe was at the level of many of the developing nations in terms of life expectancy and living standard. It is generally agreed that the driving force for the improvement has been the development of technology and the concomitant increase in the use of energy. According to Chauncey Starr, former director of the Electric Power Research Institute, the per-capita rate of energy use in the United States is about 12 kilowatts, more than 10 times that of a typical LDC.

A major achievement of technology has been the development of natural resources, essential for economic growth and increased standard of living. Individual resources may become depleted but substitutes have always become available. Firewood was replaced by coal; whale oil was replaced by kerosene; as the grade of copper ore diminished new extraction and processing technology has kept the price from rising. As Alvin Weinberg, former director of the Oak Ridge National Laboratory, has pointed out in *Is There an Optimum Level of Population?*, we can always create the resource or its equivalent from lower-grade ores provided we have sufficiently low-priced energy.[1] And University of Maryland economist Julian Simon has demonstrated, in *Resourceful Earth* and other publications, that the real price of every commodity has been falling, measured in terms of the average wage.[2] These seminal publications totally destroy the Malthusian mirage.

With respect to energy, it is certainly true that the lowest-cost deposits of oil will eventually be depleted, but medium- and high-cost deposits will still be available throughout the world. Even as these are exploited and fossil fuels become more costly, nuclear energy in various forms will be able to take their place. The dependence of the world on Middle East oil may only be a temporary event in human history. If need be, liquid fuels, such as hydrogen, can be manufactured using nuclear energy, although currently at great cost. Again, as highest-grade uranium ores become depleted, lower-grade ores will still be available and widely distributed geographically. They can be economically exploited whenever suitable technology is employed.

One of the interesting political consequences that can be predicted with some degree of assurance is an increasing degree of autarky and *less interdependence*, as each nation finds that it has adequate low-grade resources. Even sea water and common rocks, like granite, may eventually become economic sources for energy and materials. This view runs counter to the common wisdom that views the world as becoming increasingly interdependent for natural resources.

Irrespective of how it is produced, energy is the vital ingredient for development. While energy efficiency and energy conservation are most desirable whenever they make economic sense, it is simply not possible to bring the LDCs up to the level of the developed countries without massive use of energy. Just consider the energy needs for building infrastructure, like roads, airports and power plants; for building factories and capital equipment; and for building the billions of refrigerators, cars, etc., for a world consisting of several billion households.

Those who put exclusive faith in energy conservation and the renewable energy have simply not thought through the details of the problem. Consider, for example, the issue of enforced conservation, or "overconservation." Building super-efficient appliances or automobiles is more costly – otherwise they would have been built and sold by now. Unless the investment can be recovered within a few years, it is not economic. Since a larger construction cost generally translates into the use of more energy, this means also that not only money but energy is wasted by overconservation – just as it is by too little conservation.

The same argument holds true for solar energy – at the present stage of technological development. Since the cost of solar energy is currently much higher than the cost of competing sources, this means that energy is wasted in constructing large-scale solar energy facilities.

Forecasts for energy use by responsible analysts show an increase by a factor of five for a doubled population by the middle of the next century. In other words, eradicating poverty and improving the living standards of the world population to at least a fraction of that of Western nations means increasing the world rate of energy use by a factor of 10. As technology stands now, most of this increase will have to come from fossil fuels. Inevitably, therefore, carbon dioxide released to the atmosphere will increase. With this in mind, let us now address the misguided policies to reduce these emissions.

The Wrong Path: Carbon Taxes and Entitlements

In the drive to reduce emissions of carbon dioxide, carbon taxes have become a favorite too. Economists generally agree that such taxes produce a more efficient solution, and therefore a somewhat lower cost, than direct controls by rationing or other administrative methods of command and and control. But this efficiency argument does not justify a need to reduce emissions and energy use.

Others favor carbon taxes because they produce a large revenue stream. For example, an increase of one penny in the U.S. gasoline tax increases revenues by $1 billion a year. In 1990 the Congressional Budget Office collated different economic studies that calculate tax levels required for a 20 percent reduction of carbon dioxide; they lead to a tripling of coal prices and a doubling of the cost of gasoline and electric power. Clearly, huge tax revenues are produced; but even if the situation is made revenue-neutral by reducing other taxes, the resultant distortion of the economy leads to losses of the order of 2 percent of GNP, some $100 billion per year.

Some further observations are appropriate:

- Stabilizing carbon dioxide *emissions* at the 1990 level – the general goal announced by European nations – will *not* stabilize atmospheric *concentration*; it merely reduces its rate of growth slightly. According to the UN scientific reports on climate change, stabilization requires that CO_2 emissions be reduced world-wide by 60 percent to 80 percent. No one has yet dared to estimate the economic cost of such drastic measures – never mind the political cost.

Contrast these numbers with European union plans to increase fuel prices by $3 a barrel, rising to $10 by 2000. That's only $0.08 to $0.25 a gallon, compared to the current European pump price of around $3 – and hardly likely to be effective in enforcing energy conservation. The EU Commission may simply be exploiting the greenhouse scare for raising tax revenues!

- But the greatest problem for any carbon tax proposal is how to divide up an agreed-to global emission level into national quotas. Relating them to 1990 emissions (which are roughly equivalent to National (GDPs) is clearly unfair to developing countries and won't fly. It would not permit their development and would keep them forever poor. Third-World nations would rightly consider any quota that's locked into 1990 emissions as a form of "eco-imperialism."

On the other hand, applying emission limits only to the major industrial countries – comprising less than 20 percent of the current world population – means that their emissions would soon become insignificant compared to those of the rapidly growing developing nations.

An often-mentioned compromise – a uniform per-capita quota – would be unworkable for the same reason. In addition, it provides the wrong incentives. If carbon tax revenues from rich countries are used to buy emission permits from poor countries, what's to stop rapacious rulers from keeping their subjects poor and encouraging rapid population growth to maximize this income transfer?

Economic Development versus the Global Environment

Are economic development and global environment compatible? If we believe in the global warming forecasts presented at UNCED and in the material that forms the scientific basis of the Global Climate Treaty, then the outlook is very dim. There would appear to be a fundamental conflict between environment and development, one that cannot be easily reconciled. We are not speaking here about local environmental problems, but rather the global effects that are ascribed to an increasing level of carbon dioxide in the atmosphere.

This basic dilemma was glossed over at the Rio Conference but it cannot be evaded. There are a number of ways of addressing the issue, but only one of them is morally acceptable.

- One can buy off Third-World politicians and bureaucrats with money, perks and jobs, and thereby finesse the problems of the vast masses of humanity in the LDCs. Only token amounts of monies would be needed, devoted mainly to setting up international organizations and bureaucracies, and paying for their upkeep. Of course, this only postpones the problem to a later date when populations are larger and solutions more difficult.
- Another possibility would be a really massive transfer of funds, using, for example, the proposed carbon tax as a revenue-raising device. Many see the world's salvation in such an automatic entitlement program; but they have not learned from experience. It is likely that, absent democratic processes, kleptocrats would be willing to sell out their countrymen for personal gain. Such transfers also tend to build up indigenous bureaucracies, which then strengthen their hold on the national economies, institute central planning or worse, and thereby prevent the development of a system of free enterprise that could truly produce the desired economic growth.
- Others put their faith entirely in the transfer of technology – which is of course less costly than the

transfer of resources and money. But technology alone cannot do the job. The receiving country has to be in a position to make use of the technology. In other words, there has to be a political system that provides incentives to the citizens to absorb the technology and adapt it to the building of business enterprises that create jobs and growth.

• Technology and the right political system – these are indeed the necessary and perhaps even sufficient ingredients. The recipe is proven and the pattern established: A nation, reasonably democratic and reasonably free-enterprise oriented, attracts investments by multinational corporations that supply capital and technology and create jobs and prosperity.

But how much time is left? Will it be possible to raise standards of living and achieve a demographic transition to lower population growth before global climate changes produce – as some fear – catastrophic results? Fortunately, the answer could be yes. As we shall see, the scientific evidence does not support global climate catastrophes; there may not even be detectable climate consequences within the next decades.

The Shaky Scientific Base for Greenhouse Warming

It's been 100 years now since Swedish chemist Svante Arrhenius calculated that increasing the carbon dioxide content of the atmosphere should enhance the natural greenhouse effect and lead to a modest climate warming. The "Arrhenius effect" has been rediscovered by the media and by politicians in the last ten years and has led to a superheated level of international activity. It has provided the main scientific rationale for UNCED, the Rio de Janeiro Earth Summit. Yet the scientific base has become less certain as research results have accumulated.

An international group of scientists, the Intergovernmental Panel on Climate Change, produced an elaborate report in 1990 and a supplement in 1992. These two documents stress the scientific uncertainties and conclude that there is as yet no firm observational evidence in the climate record for the Arrhenius effect, in spite of the fact that the content of carbon dioxide has risen by 25 percent over its pre-industrial value – and by 50 percent if the increase in other greenhouse gases (methane, nitrous oxide, CFCs) is added in.

The documents also discuss the shortcomings of current computer models that are used to predict future climate in the presence of increased greenhouse gases. But current computer models do not as yet adequately describe many natural physical processes, such as cloud formation, water vapor distribution, and ocean circulation, that determine the outcome of the calculations. Furthermore, the models do not include as yet human influences such as modification of the land surface, air pollution from industrial operations and biomass burning, and the atmospheric effects of growing high-altitude aircraft traffic. A majority of scientists, therefore, believe that these theoretical models have not been validated by data and thus cannot be relied on for policy conclusions.

These shortcomings notwithstanding, the IPCC documents have been widely interpreted as supporting a substantial Arrhenius effect. The reason for this is the publication of an IPCC Policymakers Summary which predicts a "best value" temperature increase of 0.3°C per decade and asserts that the observed climate record is "broadly consistent" with this result from the computer models.

In spite of the fact that there is no evidence in support of these claims of the Summary, and in spite of the fact that about half of the IPCC scientists responding to a survey, plus a good many others, consider the Summary to be misleading, it has been widely accepted by politicians and even described as a "scientific consensus." Nothing could be further from the truth.

Some Concluding Thoughts

It is curious that the Rio Earth Summit should try to link the concepts of environment and development without paying attention to the obvious conflict between the two. Nor did UNCED address the issue of population growth, which is fundamental to both topics. For if the UNCED goal is truly sustainable development for poorer countries, then one has to address all of the factors that further such development – including also setting up polities in the LDCs that permit and encourage free enterprise, removing any barriers to free trade put up by developed nations, and facilitating all means of technology transfer. In principle, use of modern methods of productive agriculture, and efficient transportation, manufacture, and energy generation should enable the LDCs to leap forward much faster than was possible by the industrialized countries – within decades rather than centuries – and with much less impact on the environment. The standard of living, and all the good things that go with it, should advance rapidly; birthrates should drop and the demographic transition should be reached quickly.

I may be accused here of undue optimism – or maybe just of believing in the wisdom of human beings, no matter where they are, to learn how to better their lives and those of their families when given the chance. The same cannot be said of international organizations and most statesmen, even those freely elected in democratic countries; they seem not to have grasped this opportunity for a change for the better.

Notes

1 S. Fred Singer, ed., *Is There An Optimum Level of Population?* (New York: McGraw-Hill, 1971).
2 Julian L. Simon and Herman Kahn, eds., *The Resourceful Earth* (Oxford: Basil Blackwell, 1984).

Index

Note: 'n.' after a page reference indicates the number of a note on that page.